PEDAGOGUES AND PROTESTERS

Pedagogues and Protesters

The Harvard College Student Diary of Stephen Peabody, 1767–1768

Edited by

CONRAD EDICK WRIGHT

University of Massachusetts Press
Amherst and Boston

in association with
Massachusetts Historical Society
Boston

Printed in the United States of America

ISBN 978-1-62534-256-0 (paper); 255-3 (cloth)

Designed by Jack Harrison
Set in Adobe Caslon Pro with Monotype Bell display
Printed and bound by The Maple-Vail Book Manufacturing Group

Cover design by Jack Harrison
Cover art: Pierre Eugène Du Simitière, *View of Harvard College* (1767–68).
Watercolor on paper, 5.15 x 2.11 inches on a leaf 9.14 x 15 inches.
Courtesy The Library Company of Philadelphia.

Library of Congress Cataloging-in-Publication Data
Names: Peabody, Stephen, 1741-1819, author. | Wright, Conrad Edick, editor.
Title: Pedagogues and protesters : the Harvard College student diary of
Stephen Peabody, 1767-1768 / edited by Conrad Edick Wright.
Description: Amherst : University of Massachusetts Press in association with
Massachusetts Historical Society, [2016] |
Includes bibliographical references and index.
Identifiers: LCCN 2016041707| ISBN 9781625342560 (pbk. : alk. paper) |
ISBN 9781625342553 (hardcover : alk. paper)
Subjects: LCSH: Harvard College (1636-1780)—Student strike, 1768. |
Peabody, Stephen, 1741-1819—Diaries.
Classification: LCC LD2152 .P38 2017 | DDC 378.744/409033—dc23
LC record available at https://lccn.loc.gov/2016041707

British Library Cataloguing-in-Publication Data
A catalog record for this book is available from the British Library.

For Abby and Betsy
The Students in My Life

Contents

Illustrations and Tables

Illustrations

Tables

Introduction

We know less than we think we do about the colleges of colonial North America. The nine schools that have survived to the present day, institutions that educated more than five thousand young men before the American Revolution, among them hundreds of provincial and revolutionary leaders, have become major universities, including some of the most distinguished and visible in the world. They seem so familiar to us that we may only realize the limitations of our accounts of their early years when these shortcomings are called to our attention. Harvard, William and Mary, Yale, Princeton, the University of Pennsylvania, Columbia, Brown, Dartmouth, and Rutgers—each school has an origins story passed down from one generation of alumni to the next. Harvard points to John Harvard's bequest of four hundred books, the University of Pennsylvania to Benjamin Franklin's role in its establishment, Dartmouth to Moor's Charity School and its mission to educate Christianized Native Americans for the Congregationalist ministry.[1] Although the details vary from college to college, these stories share a common focus on the activities of institutional leaders, often charismatic men, including founders, presidents, benefactors, professors, and trustees.

For the most part, the accounts of professional scholars concentrate no less on the schools' leaders. Biographies of Thomas Clap and Ezra Stiles of Yale and Samuel Johnson of Columbia, for example, spotlight the administrations of these presidents.[2] Institutional histories, often written to celebrate anniversaries, recite critical decisions, the ones that resulted in thriving colleges.[3] Specialized studies of such subjects as curricula, finances, and student discipline outline the mechanics of operating a school, always from the vantage point of its leaders.[4] There are, to be sure, occasional biographies of alumni that sketch their subjects' college lives, each usually devoting all or part of an early chapter of a much longer study to its protagonist's undergraduate years. However, even the best of these studies—and there are quite useful ones on men such as Fisher Ames, Rufus King, and Noah Webster—tend to look briefly for the roots of an extraordinary life in a generally unremarkable college career.[5]

There is a cost to recounting the histories of colonial North America's colleges from the top down. It creates the unspoken assumption that no one else really mattered, that the history of a school is little more than the sum of the accomplishments of the most prominent people within its orbit. From such an elevated perch the activities of all the others—tutors, minor administrators, craftsmen, cooks, cleaning ladies, and most of all students—are often blurry or even invisible. Tell the story of a colonial college from the perspective of its leaders and it becomes an institutional biography that highlights only a handful of characters. Think of a college as a living organism, however, a society composed of many scores of people—of dozens upon dozens of students as well as manual workers, faculty members, and administrators—and the account turns into something more complicated, subtle, and even surprising.

Stephen Peabody's undergraduate diary for 1767–68 offers an alternate entryway into the history of an early American college. This journal, which is, according to Harvard historian and archivist Clifford K. Shipton, "the most revealing document relating to colonial education which has come down to us," depicts with unparalleled detail and insight the daily life of the school, especially its students.[6] It introduces us to the members of the college community, their interactions, their religious beliefs, their leisure activities, what they read both for class and for personal enrichment, and the crises of their day. In it the college becomes a community of the boys and men (and a very few women) who filled its every station, an organism held together by the social gravity of interpersonal relationships—and sometimes torn apart by the nuclear repulsion of mistrust, animosity, and infighting. The account of a student strike beginning in March 1768, the most substantial such action at any American college during the colonial period, reveals just how badly the Harvard community could disintegrate under certain circumstances.

What is more, through Peabody's eyes we also see how the school and members of the Harvard College community related to the wider New England society of the late 1760s. Family members both close and distant, hometown neighbors as well as acquaintances in Cambridge and Boston, region-wide participants in Stephen's hoped-for professional community—all these men, women, and children find their way into Peabody's pages. The result is a journal that provides insight not only into the life of the diarist and his small ring of intimates, but more broadly into how New Englanders related to one another and even into how their society operated on the eve of the American Revolution.

Who was Stephen Peabody? Born at the northern tip of Boxford, Massachusetts, at a beautiful spot along the Andover town line more than twenty miles north of Cambridge on November 11, 1741, he was the fourth son of John and Sarah (Head) Peabody, the ninth of their ten children. His oldest sibling, a daughter their parents named Sarah after her mother, was almost nineteen when Stephen was born; he was only three years old at the time of Sarah's first marriage. Stephen was, in turn, nearly five years older than his sister Rebecca, his parents' youngest child, born in September 1746.[7]

The Peabodys were farmers, and for most of Stephen's youth there was every reason to expect that he would end up working the land. Boxford was the ancestral home of the Peabody family, at least in New England. Here John Peabody grew up, the sixth of eight children, and here he settled after his marriage in 1721 to Sarah Head of Newbury. Stephen's older brothers and sisters were all Boxford born, but in 1746 John successfully petitioned to move the town line, annexing his property to Andover's North Parish.[8] A large family meant that while Stephen was growing up, his daily life overflowed with relatives—parents, sisters, brothers, nieces, nephews, aunts, uncles, cousins. In addition to Peabodys, through marriage his paternal relatives included Symondses, Fosters, Kimballs, Stevenses, Peterses, Coburns, and Woods, most of whom lived in Boxford, Andover, or other nearby communities and dozens of whom appear at least fleetingly in his diary for 1767–68.[9]

Stephen worked the family farm with his father until his early twenties, but at some point he recognized a late calling to the Congregationalist ministry. The Peabodys were strong Calvinists, and Stephen's spiritual commitment was no doubt sincere. His decision was no mere pursuit of the social standing that resulted from entry into a respected profession but an honest product of heartfelt faith. Earnest belief was not enough in and of itself, however, to admit him to the pulpit. New England Congregationalists expected their clergy to have a liberal education. Because

Peabody committed himself to a learned profession when he was at least half a dozen years older than most other would-be clergymen, he had catching up to do—and he had to prepare himself quickly. In order to qualify for admission to Harvard, the nearest college to Andover, Stephen needed to master enough Greek and Latin to pass the school's oral and written entrance examinations. Most New England Congregationalists in the 1760s who aimed for college started to meet these requirements as young teenagers by studying ancient languages with their parish ministers, but in 1763, just as Peabody was about to prepare for the test, an alternative path presented itself about a dozen miles to the east. Some residents of Byfield, a parish that straddled the boundary between the Massachusetts towns of Rowley and Newbury, Stephen's mother's girlhood home, drew on a bequest to establish Dummer Academy (later Governor's Academy) to ready young men for college. Peabody entered the school as one of its first students in 1763 or 1764 and learned enough in subsequent months to win acceptance to the Harvard class of 1769, with which he matriculated in August 1765, one of nine Dummer boys in an entering cohort of forty-three.[10]

In many respects Peabody was an unexceptional collegian. Consider his social standing, for instance: New Englanders in the 1760s thought of humankind hierarchically, a segment of the Great Chain of Being that ordered all creatures great and small, from God and the angels down through innumerable links to the most insignificant insect. Until 1771, each year when a new class entered Harvard the faculty created a rank list of its members. On this social ladder neither personal achievement nor age nor even the alphabet played a role. The ABCs became the organizing principle for class lists at Harvard in the early 1770s, but in 1765 the college still followed its traditional practice of arranging its freshmen according to family merit by assessing the civic standing of each student's lineage. As undergraduates in recitations, chapel, and public exhibition, and thereafter whenever the members of a class formed a procession as alumni, the first in line were the sons of leading provincial officeholders and college graduates, a small minority of each class, followed in the descending order of honor that the faculty had decreed during their first year by the ambitious offspring of artisans and yeomen (see tables 1, 2). In March 1766, when the faculty "placed" the class of 1769, at its head came James Winthrop, whose father, John (Harvard A.B. 1732), was the college's Hollis Professor of Mathematics and Natural Philosophy. The Winthrops were descendants of John Winthrop, in 1630 the first governor of the Massachusetts Bay Colony, and ever since they had been numbered among the provincial leaders. James remained first until April 1768, when Peter Oliver, originally a member of the preceding class, returned to Cambridge after a year's suspension for gross misconduct and assumed the place of honor, causing everyone else to step down a rung. The son of Lieutenant Governor Andrew Oliver (A.B. 1724), Peter qualified to lead the class of 1769 based on family distinction, notwithstanding his own record of poor behavior. Whatever Peabody's other merits and shortcomings might have been, placed on Harvard's scale as the son of a farmer at matriculation he ranked thirty-sixth.[11]

There was, however, one way in which Stephen stood first in his class: he was its oldest member. Twenty-three years eight months at admission, he was two and a half years older than his next most senior classmate, William Bowers of Billerica. The youngest boy, Winthrop, was only thirteen years four months at admission. The mean age at matriculation

Table 1. Fathers' Occupations

Job	*1767*	*1768*	*1769*	*1770*	*1771*	*1767–71*
Minister	3	7	3	7	7	27
Merchant/Manufacturer	2	4	2	2	11	21
Artisan	4	2	2	4	3	15
Doctor	3	3	3	1	1	11
Farmer	2	1	2	1	4	10
Lawyer/Judge	1	4	1	1	0	7
Tavern/Innkeeper	0	0	2	0	4	6
College Official	1	1	1	1	1	5
Government Official	1	0	0	1	1	3
Sea Captain/Mariner	1	0	1	1	0	3
Teacher	1	1	0	0	0	2
Shopkeeper	0	0	0	0	1	1
Unknown/Deceased	23	19	26	24	26	118
Total	**42**	**42**	**43**	**43**	**59**	**229**

Sources: *Sibley's Harvard Graduates,* vols. 16–18.

Table 2. Fathers' College Connections

Class	*Connections*	*Percentage*
1767 (n = 42)	6 Harvard graduates	14.3
1768 (n = 42)	12 Harvard graduates 1 Yale graduate	31.0
1769 (n = 43)	6 Harvard graduates 1 Yale graduate	16.3
1770 (n = 43)	11 Harvard graduates 2 Yale graduates	30.2
1771 (n = 59)	14 Harvard graduates 1 college carpenter	25.4
Total (n = 229)	**54**	**23.6**

Sources: *Sibley's Harvard Graduates,* vols. 16–18.

of Harvard undergraduates in the late 1760s was between sixteen and seventeen, but calculating the average obscures substantial variation (see table 3). One undergraduate in 1767–68 had been as young as eleven and a half when he entered the school; the oldest, army veteran Jonathan French (A.B. 1771), two years behind Stephen, was all of twenty-seven and a half at admission. The age of undergraduates made at least one difference in Harvard's affairs because the administration and faculty typically turned to the older students to model maturity.[12]

Table 3. Age at Admission in Years

Class	*Average*	*Oldest*	*Youngest*
1767 (n = 42)	16.9	21.6	12.8
1768 (n = 42)	16.9	24.8	12.9
1769 (n = 43)	16.4	22.7	13.3
1770 (n = 43)	16.2	22.5	11.5
1771 (n = 59)	16.9	27.5	12.5
Total (n = 229)	**16.7**	**27.5**	**11.5**

Sources: *Sibley's Harvard Graduates,* 16:440–41; 17:2–3, 114–15, 332–33, 466–67. Arithmetic errors in the Birthday and Age columns of the 1771 class list both in Faculty Records 3:86–87, Harvard University Archives, and in *Sibley's Harvard Graduates,* 17:466–67, have been corrected through comparison with the entries, 17:468–679.

Such faculty confidence worked in Peabody's case through the winter of his junior year. He was not given to the mischievous or rebellious behavior, the pranks and drunken adventures that landed too many of his classmates in trouble. Until the early spring of 1768 Stephen's college record was unblemished, although in 1766 his participation in a protest against rancid butter in the college Commons revealed him to be willing to stand up to authority if he thought the circumstances demanded it. In fact, a close reading of his diary reveals that he sometimes quietly informed on misbehavior to the faculty if he disapproved of an activity. He even expressed satisfaction on December 16, 1767, that the other undergraduates could not figure out that he had tattled on some students who had misbehaved in chapel. Stephen's classmates looked up to him and recognized his standing in their own estimation by their possibly ironic nickname for him, Pater Omnium, Father of All.[13]

Through February 1768 Harvard's faculty considered Pater Omnium their intermediary in dealings with his younger, more irresponsible classmates. Much like the captain of a modern-day football team who represents the players to the coach and the coach to the players, Stephen became a channel for communication. On August 12, 1767, the faculty selected him as a student monitor, an unpopular job that entailed taking attendance at required events such as weekly church services and daily chapel exercises, revealing their belief that he would help to maintain the good order of the college.

Harvard College, founded in 1636, was approaching its 132nd year in May 1767 when Stephen's diary opens.[14] On May 24, the journal's first day, the end of Peabody's sophomore year was in sight. Each year Harvard's academic calendar began around the middle of August, and classes except for the seniors, whose coursework ended in the early spring, continued with multiple vacations until the end of the following June. A couple of weeks later, on the third Wednesday of July, the annual commencement ceremonies brought one school year to a close and set the stage for the one to come.

Harvard was established by the Puritan founders of the Massachusetts Bay Colony as a bastion of Calvinist orthodoxy. First and foremost, the college's organizers believed, Harvard's function was to supply the colony with an educated and orthodox clergy. Over time, however, the colony's religious consensus, never unchallenged, began to fray, and at important junctures the college leaned liberal to the anger of Calvinist traditionalists. In 1701 in New Haven, the founding of the Collegiate School, soon to be renamed Yale College, was orthodoxy's response to what the traditionalists believed to be Harvard's heterodoxy. Then in the early 1740s, when the British evangelist George Whitefield visited Cambridge, a serious clash with the faculty grew out of his judgment that the school had strayed from the true faith.[15] When Stephen Peabody matriculated in August 1765, Harvard's religious spectrum was still broad enough for a Calvinist such as himself to find a place, but he was undoubtedly well to its orthodox end, considerably more conservative in his views than either the faculty or the center of gravity of the student body.

In its theological leanings, Harvard in 1767 reflected a transformation well underway along New England's Atlantic Coast, where Arminianism, the doctrine that a sinner could actively prepare him- or herself to receive God's salvation, was overtaking the Calvinist, predestinarian teaching that men and women had no role at all in determining their eternal fates.[16] Harvard's increasingly liberal tilt was related to the fact that almost all the students came from the Arminian movement's geographic stronghold in eastern Massachusetts and southeastern New Hampshire near the coast. Of the rest, all but two (one each from Jamaica and North Carolina) were from elsewhere in New England (see table 4).[17]

Although small by later standards, by every contemporary measure Harvard in the late 1760s was a considerable place, the oldest, largest,

Table 4. Residence at Admission

Place	*1767*	*1768*	*1769*	*1770*	*1771*	*1767–71*
Massachusetts (not including Maine)	36	38	42	37	55	208
New Hampshire	5	2	1	1	0	9
Connecticut	0	0	0	4	1	5
Maine	0	1	0	1	2	4
Jamaica	1	0	0	0	0	1
North Carolina	0	1	0	0	0	1
Rhode Island	0	0	0	0	1	1
Total	**42**	**42**	**43**	**43**	**59**	**229**

Sources: *Sibley's Harvard Graduates,* 16:440–41; 17:2–3, 114–15, 332–33, 466–67.

Pierre Eugène Du Simitière, *View of Harvard College* (1767–1768). Watercolor on paper, 5.15 x 2.11 inches on a leaf 9.14 x 15 inches. The Library Company of Philadelphia. L-R: Holden Chapel, Hollis Hall, Harvard Hall, Stoughton Hall, Massachusetts Hall. Stoughton Hall was razed in 1781. The other buildings are still standing.

wealthiest, and most impressive college in the American colonies. At the same time it was insular, a school at which every faculty member and senior administrator was an alumnus. In May 1767, there were 9 faculty members (Yale had 4), 171 undergraduates (compared to approximately 125 at Yale), close to 1,100 living alumni (Yale had around 800), and 5 major buildings (Yale had 3). From the president at the top to the professors, tutors and librarian, ordered ranks of undergraduates, and employees, the college formed a social pyramid much like society at large, at least in the minds of those who were affiliated with it.

At the pinnacle was President Edward Holyoke (A.B. 1705). He had begun his career in 1716 as the minister of the Second Church in Marblehead, but twenty years later in 1736, the college Corporation, one of its two governing bodies (the other was the Board of Overseers), chose him to lead the school. He continued in that role for more than three decades, from 1737 until his death at age seventy-nine on June 1, 1769. A reformer who ended corporal punishment at Harvard, promoted instruction in the natural sciences, and supported the theological liberalization that saw Harvard evolve over time from orthodox Calvinism toward Unitarianism,

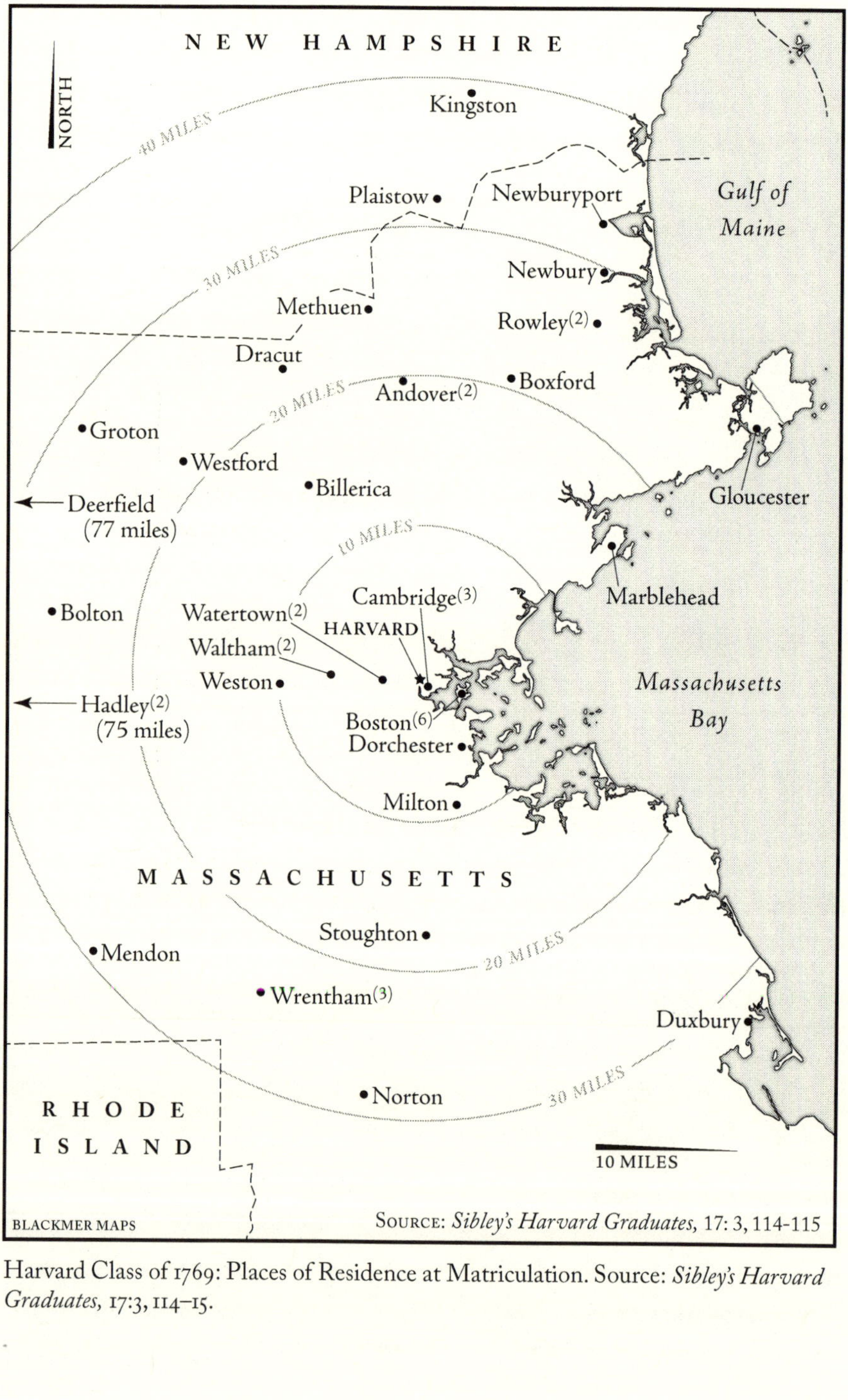

Harvard Class of 1769: Places of Residence at Matriculation. Source: *Sibley's Harvard Graduates,* 17:3, 114–15.

he was nevertheless roundly disliked by many of the students, who nicknamed him "Guts" in recognition of his ample girth. By the 1760s he affected an imperious, off-putting manner that many of the students found intimidating.[18]

Professors John Winthrop, Edward Wigglesworth (A.B. 1749), and Stephen Sewall (A.B. 1761) lectured on mathematics and science, theology, and Semitic languages respectively in this era. Each delivered two series of classes every year, introductory public talks that the undergraduates attended at the start of their academic careers, and advanced private lectures for which the upper classmen paid a supplementary fee. Although the college imposed no formal research demands on these senior members of the faculty, all of them were scholars of some accomplishment. Winthrop, elected a fellow of the Royal Society in 1766, was together with Benjamin Franklin probably the most distinguished American natural scientist of his generation. He conducted research in physics and astronomy, including leading an important expedition to Newfoundland in 1761 to observe the transit of Venus. Wigglesworth was the son of Edward Wigglesworth, Sr. (A.B. 1710), his predecessor in the Hollis professorship of theology. The younger Wigglesworth took an analytical approach to the study of his field, a methodology that alienated many of the undergraduates, especially orthodox Calvinists such as Peabody, who felt he should concentrate uncritically instead on promoting what they considered to be the great truths of reformed Christianity. Wigglesworth's most important scholarship was not in theology but demography, a study of American population growth. And Sewall, the Hancock Professor of Hebrew and Other Oriental Languages, was already probably the most respected American Hebraist of his day though still a young man of thirty-three in May 1767. He wrote among other works the text that his students used for his course, *An Hebrew Grammar Collected Chiefly from Those of Mr. Israel Lyons and the Rev. Richard Grey* (1763).[19]

In the days before academic tenure, the professors did not have the formal job security that later generations of faculty members have come to expect. They were subject to termination for misconduct, and in 1785 Harvard dismissed Sewall for chronic alcoholism.[20] Under normal circumstances, however, the professors could expect to remain in their chairs for decades, the permanent core of the college community, until overcome by death or infirmity. All three men lived with their families in Cambridge within a short walk of Harvard Yard.

The tutors, on three-year renewable appointments, ordinarily expected teaching at Harvard to constitute a stage in a career that would ultimately take them elsewhere. At any one time in the 1760s there were four tutors, whose primary role was to drill the students in the college's core subjects: Latin, Greek, natural philosophy (mathematics and science), and moral philosophy (including logic and metaphysics). Other subjects of secondary importance such as rhetoric and literature were also their responsibility. The wonderfully named Belcher Hancock (A.B. 1727) left his post in the course of 1767. The other tutors were Thomas Danforth (A.B. 1762), Joseph Willard (A.B. 1765), Stephen Scales (A.B. 1763), and Andrew Eliot (A.B. 1762), Hancock's replacement beginning that August.[21] Except for Hancock they were all young men themselves, only a few years older than the students they led in daily recitations while preparing themselves for the Congregationalist ministry. Until 1767, each tutor had taught one of the college's four classes all the subjects in the curriculum. During the year Stephen Peabody's diary covers, these instructors were finding their way as Harvard redefined their roles from generalists to subject specialists. Bachelors all, the tutors forfeited their offices if they married. They lived side by side with the undergraduates in Harvard's three dormitories—Hollis, Massachusetts, and Stoughton Halls—and were the immediate proctors of the students' behavior, an obligation that overwhelmed them in March 1768. The librarian, who ranked with the tutors, was responsible for a collection in Harvard Hall that comprised only between four and five thousand volumes but was nevertheless the largest at an American college. Andrew Eliot was the librarian as Peabody's diary opens, but upon his appointment as a tutor in Hancock's position, the faculty replaced him with Jonathan Moore (A.B. 1761).[22]

Together, the president, professors, tutors, and librarian constituted the college's faculty. At formal meetings every few days—more often if necessary—they enforced the college laws, excused absences, assigned minor paying jobs such as waiting on tables and winding the college clock to students in need of financial aid, and generally saw to the school's good order.[23] Harvard also employed Jonathan Hastings (A.B. 1730), the college steward, or business manager; his wife, Elizabeth, who ran the Commons, or dining hall; Nathaniel Ward (A.B. 1765), the butler, who was responsible for a small shop filled with the sundries the students might require such as pens, paper, and ribbons; a couple of cleaning ladies, referred to as sweepers, who kept the dormitories presentable; and an uncounted and effectively invisible number of cooks. Carpenters, glaziers, blacksmiths, and masons were plentiful in Cambridge, and each spring the college designated in advance those it favored in case a short-term need for their services arose.[24]

The school was in Cambridge but only uneasily a part of it. Except for the president, professors, and steward, after all, the college consisted of transients who would move away soon enough. Aside from the handful of local boys who entered the school each year, the students and tutors were only passing through town.

The two separate communities approached each other the most closely on Sundays. The Congregationalist members of the college worshiped each Sabbath with their neighbors at the First Church in Cambridge,

Pitman Model of Harvard as It Was in 1775. Photograph [1947]. Harvard University Archives. In the foreground is a corner of Cambridge Common. To the right of the college (center) is what is now Harvard Square, including the meetinghouse (steeple) and the courthouse (cupola). Boston is in the background.

where Nathaniel Appleton (A.B. 1712), its minister since 1717, was an institution in his own right, having just passed half a century in its pulpit at the opening of Peabody's journal. More practical than dogmatic in his theology, Appleton preached a faith that listeners across both the community's and the college's broad doctrinal spectrum could accept. Since 1717 he had been a power within the college as a member of the governing Corporation, also known as the President and Fellows of Harvard College. During the rest of the week, however, the town-gown relationship tended to be more transactional than intimate or enduring. Need a coat or a chair made or to rent a horse and rig? Then look for it in town. Fancy a drink? The Blue Anchor Tavern was close by. Want to dine in style with a leading citizen of Massachusetts? With luck an invitation might be forthcoming. Maybe the host would be William Brattle, a Cambridge native and 1722 graduate of the college who was also a member of the provincial Governor's Council as well as a brigadier in the Massachusetts militia. For the most part, though, in the late 1760s, Cambridge was a town of artisans, shopkeepers, and farmers, not college men who had gone on to provincial prominence, and typical Cantabrigians rarely found their way into the pages of Stephen Peabody's diary except when he went shopping. There was a low wall around Harvard Yard, too short to keep anyone either in or out, but it was high enough to distinguish the college from the surrounding community.[25]

Boys and young men attended Harvard for a variety of reasons. There were aspiring ministers, such as Peabody, who required a liberal education as a steppingstone to their chosen professions; 60 of the 229 members of the five classes that were in residence during some portion of Peabody's diary (1767–71) became ministers, or 26.2 percent. Most New England lawyers also attended college, although a bachelor's degree was nowhere mandatory and they all had to serve an apprenticeship with a member of the bar; of the boys and men of these classes, 36 (15.7%) were admitted to the bar. Apprenticeship was likewise the most common avenue into medicine. Many physicians did without college, but others undertook a liberal education first, including 42 members (18.3%) of the classes of 1767 through 1771 (see table 5).[26]

College was at best of marginal professional relevance for Harvard's other undergraduates, about two-fifths of the student body. Future merchants, farmers, and even grammar school teachers had no need for the

Table 5. Students' Primary Occupations

Job	*1767*	*1768*	*1769*	*1770*	*1771*	*1767–71*
Minister	12	10	14	14	10	60
Doctor	6	10	5	7	14	42
Lawyer/Judge	5	7	11	7	6	36
Merchant/Manufacturer	7	6	3	5	13	34
Teacher	6	1	2	2	5	16
Government Official	2	3	0	3	3	11
Farmer	1	2	2	2	0	7
Shopkeeper	0	0	2	2	0	4
Sea Captain/Mariner	1	0	0	1	1	3
College Official	0	0	1	0	1	2
Tavern/Innkeeper	0	0	1	0	1	2
Gentleman	0	0	0	0	1	1
Soldier	1	0	0	0	0	1
Unknown/Deceased	1	3	2	0	4	10
Total	**42**	**42**	**43**	**43**	**59**	**229**

Sources: *Sibley's Harvard Graduates,* vols. 16–18.

stamp of approval that a bachelor's degree conferred. Instead, college opened different avenues for them.

Other reasons besides career objectives for attending college included self-improvement and a related goal, an aspiration for community recognition as a refined and estimable citizen. Higher education often marked college men as potential community leaders. In the public eye, Harvard and the colonies' other colleges set graduates apart from their neighbors as especially intelligent, informed, and honorable men. Such were the sort to whom New Englanders typically turned to fill town offices including selectmen, provincial posts such as representatives to the General Court, and ecclesiastical positions like church deacons. A smattering of the dead languages, some limited facility at cyphering, and a modest acquaintance with philosophy, theology, and literature were enough to distinguish college men from their less-polished contemporaries. Outside of the formal curriculum some students even arranged for private French lessons and dancing classes (which often included instruction in etiquette) in the interest of additional refinement.[27]

If Stephen Peabody's diary is to be believed, of all the reasons modern commentators have sometimes recognized for attending college, the least persuasive must have been a passion for knowledge. Survey Peabody's 366 daily journal entries (1768 was a leap year) and you will find many signs of study but no evidence at all of an appetite for knowledge or satisfaction from learning, or even a thirst for academic honors, to say nothing of indications that through intellectual challenge his classes might actually have been a pleasure. On the contrary, schoolwork was a chore that interfered with other priorities. There were no grades, and in the classroom all the faculty could reasonably expect was an honest effort. For some of Peabody's classmates, having a good time headed their to-do lists. And even for Stephen, serious and intent as he was on preparing for the pulpit, there were other, better ways to pass the time than in classes or doing homework.

Over the course of the year from May 24, 1767, to May 23, 1768, Stephen Peabody spent all or part of 233 days in Cambridge. When classes were in session, every day but Sunday began with morning prayers, followed by a combination of the professors' lectures, recitations with the tutors, and studying. Breakfast and dinner at midday took place in the college Commons in Harvard Hall, where Elizabeth Hastings and her cooks served up unpalatable fare. For the evening meal Stephen returned to the Commons for something light to eat, perhaps a roll or a meat pie, which he ordinarily took back to his room, Hollis 19. On Sundays, most of the undergraduates attended Nathaniel Appleton's morning and afternoon services at the First Church, which occupied a meetinghouse adjacent to the Yard; a small band of churchmen received special permission to go a couple of hundred yards further to Christ Church, the local Anglican outpost. Pious students such as Peabody often passed the rest of the Lord's Day in religious meetings as well as in reading sermons, tracts, and other devotional writings.

Such a schedule made it perfectly possible to occupy most or all of each day with the academic and religious exercises that President Holyoke and his faculty prescribed as the heart of a Harvard education. In the fall of 1767, one overwhelmed freshman wrote his father, "The last time I wrote you I was in such a fear that I could hardly hold my pen, and now my studies are so severe I am obliged to write by candle light. We read Latin, Greek, Hebrew, Geography and Logic and are driven so close that we

Williams Jenks, *View from Hollis Window* [1796–1797]. Watercolor on paper, 6.12 x 5 inches. Harvard University Archives. Peabody occupied Hollis Hall 19 in 1767–1768. Hamilton Vaughan Bail concluded that this view to the northwest through a northern window is from what was then room 25. *Views of Harvard: A Pictorial Record to 1860* (Cambridge, Mass.: Harvard University Press, 1949), 101.

have as little comfort as a man who would run the gauntlet."[28] Over the course of four years in Cambridge each undergraduate might master, or at least sample, Latin, Greek, Hebrew, arithmetic as far as fractions and ratios, basic physics and astronomy, logic, the elements of moral philosophy, the fundamentals of reformed theology, oratory, writing, geography, and belles lettres. If students happened to fall short of proficiency, that was by their own choice.

And it was a choice most of them made. Too much attention to the students' formal schedule and classroom obligations provides a misleading picture of how most of them actually spent their days and what was important to them. Peabody's schoolboy Latin, crude phrases of which litter many journal entries, provides a better measure of his own level of achievement. In the late 1760s, the undergraduates constituted approximately 90 percent of the college community. Peabody's diary reveals the college's vital student life, a maze of friendships and antipathies, of organized meetings and informal interactions that injected Harvard with most of its energy.

Since Stephen Peabody's diary provides the best available entrée into the Harvard community in the late 1760s, a close look at his day—how he spent it and with whom—repays the effort. Without an acceptable excuse there was no easy way around certain obligations, including morning prayers, daily recitations and lectures, and Sunday services; as long as Stephen was in town he hardly ever missed them. Then it was important to study enough to avoid faculty harassment. There were other ways to pass the time, though, and Peabody was only too happy to succumb to them. A multiday wrestling competition between the freshmen and the sophomores beginning on August 20, 1767, engaged him and other observers. There was nutting, which Stephen and some friends did on October 3, a day when the trees were full of chestnuts. Singing was a popular pastime, and Peabody reported informal harmonizing, usually with other undergraduates, at least sixty times. There were evenings with schoolmates—often for pleasure but every Saturday for prayer and discussion of matters of faith at the weekly meeting of some of the college's more pious undergraduates. There were recreational excursions, including a day-long outing Stephen took with a friend on May 25, the second day of the journal, which steered him along a great loop from Charlestown to Boston, Brookline, Watertown, and then back to Cambridge. And there were errands to run, sometimes a few paces outside Harvard Yard in what is now Harvard Square, or more appealingly in Boston, where an outing might include attending a minister's weekday lecture, viewing the muster of a militia company, dropping off a short article for publication in one of the town's weeklies, or dining with acquaintances as well as visiting the metropolis's shops.

Most of all, there was reading. With a substantial provincial library at Peabody's fingertips it would be a waste not to read, and he did so avidly. Whether or not Stephen wrote in his diary about his curricular reading, apparently a subject of precious little consequence to him, his reading during his free time almost always merited a mention. In the course of the year Peabody's diary covers he reported reading seventy-two titles; many of these were short pamphlets but one, Samuel Richardson's epistolary novel *Clarissa Harlowe*, is well over one thousand pages long in

Paul Revere, *A View of Part of the Town of Boston in New-England and Brittish Ships of War Landing their Troops! 1768* [1770]. Massachusetts Historical Society facsimile of hand-colored engraving, 13.125 x 19 inches. Revere's depiction of the arrival of British troops is a reminder that Peabody wrote his diary at a time of rising imperial tensions.

modern editions. Some of these works were course reading, including Xenophon's *Cyropædia*, a biography of King Cyrus of Persia that the students grudgingly read passages from in Greek, and John Ward's *The Young Mathematician's Guide*, an arithmetic textbook. None of these required readings was absorbing, however, and Stephen never turned to them when he had leisure time. He kept up with current events by reading newspapers such as the *Boston Chronicle* and the *Boston News-Letter*, and for pleasure he consumed such works as Joseph Addison's and Richard Steele's *The Spectator*, a classic English collection of short pieces from the early eighteenth century that every educated man felt he needed to know, and William Smith's *History of the Province of New-York*, one of the first secular historical works on an American subject. There was often an element of self-improvement in Peabody's choices of leisure reading. Even *Clarissa Harlowe*, one of the first novels in the English language, revealed in him an element of grit and determination. Peabody began to read the book on August 31, 1767, and finally completed it five months later on January 29, 1768. Over this period he chipped away at it on at least thirty-five occasions.

Such titles were rarely Stephen's first choice when he had an opportunity to choose his own reading, however. Harvard provided a liberal rather than a vocational education, but Peabody could improve the time and his own professional preparation if he regularly read various kinds of religious works. Theological tomes such as Joseph Mede's *Clavis apocalyptica*, an explanation of millennial clues in scripture, helped clergymen actual and aspiring to decipher some of the Bible's most opaque passages. Devotional works such as Benjamin Jenks's *Meditations with Short Prayers Annexed* fostered piety. The *Koran* exposed him to an important world religion, if only to prepare him to counter what he considered its untruths. And works such as *Sermons on the Most Important and Useful Subjects* by Samuel Davies and *The Eloquence of the Pulpit* by James Fordyce provided practical examples of successful preaching. Controversy found its way into Peabody's religious reading beginning on September 13, 1767, when a dispute in Newburyport produced charges and counter-charges in a series of tracts. Even closer to Stephen, a dispute arose at Harvard in the summer of 1767 when James Dana preached two sermons of which the college's more orthodox students disapproved, then published them, explaining that he was doing so to satisfy the demand of his audience.[29] Newspaper correspondence ensued as the college Calvinists, led by Peabody, placed a disparaging letter in a Boston journal; Dana's supporters defended him; and the orthodox critics got in the last, generally unpersuasive word.

All told, of the seventy-two works Peabody reported reading in his diary, fully fifty-six were on religious themes. If a Harvard education did not provide an aspiring minister with seminary training, he could at least take advantage of his free time to create and work through his own list of useful professional readings.

Stephen could have spent a hermit's life of reading and prayer if that had been his wont, but in the eighteenth century no less than in the twenty-first, for most students college was at least as much a social as an educational experience. For that matter, a life of solitary contemplation and prayer had no place in the culture of colonial New England. Peabody's regular practice of reporting how he had passed the day is its most revealing when he mentions his interactions with intimates, acquaintances, and other contemporaries. In recording his daily doings with friends, classmates, and others, he also traced the relationships, the social networks, of his life in 1767–68.

In the course of writing his diary for this period, Stephen Peabody mentioned hundreds of contemporaries. A full, reliable tally is impossible because more than a few of his references are cryptic, often only a last name that could mean any of several known possibilities. And no doubt he did not mention every encounter each day, although he appears to have recorded those that seemed the most important to him. These limitations acknowledged, it is still apparent that a remarkable number of contemporaries, 650 more or less, found their way into Peabody's journal. Some of these were his intimates but others were no more than passing acquaintances or even in a few cases people he knew only by reputation.

To understand Peabody's social interactions it is important to make two separate assessments—of type and of context. Think of modern everyday life. Sometimes we talk with friends, perhaps over a sandwich at lunch or a cocktail at a party. We share a trip with a family member or have a meeting with a teacher or a student. We also sit next to a stranger on a subway, see someone we barely know at a distance, or go to a concert and listen to a performer we only know by name and reputation. Stephen's diary reports on five types of interactions in five distinct contexts. Of the various types of interactions, the first are mere mentions, sometimes to comment on having seen someone or heard something about the person.

The second are transactions—that is, commercial exchanges. Third, he sometimes recounted brief meetings, no more than passing interactions with acquaintances, either intimates or relative strangers. Fourth, there were large groups such as classes and religious services. And finally there were occasions when he actively socialized with close friends or relatives. These last exchanges were almost always intentional and sustained.

Five social networks, or contexts, also emerge in Peabody's journal, three fragmentarily, one in some detail, and one in high definition. There are suggestive bits and pieces in the record he kept of his interactions with acquaintances from Cambridge and Boston; with friends and neighbors from Andover, Boxford, and nearby towns; and with members of the clergy, his intended professional community. More important and more satisfying are his accounts of his interactions with his relatives. His daily doings with the members of the Harvard College community are the clearest of all. Within the first three networks Peabody reported on those he knew or with whom he dealt. By defining the limited universes of family members and Harvardians, within the last two networks it is also possible to figure out something equally important—everyone with whom he did not mention interacting often or at all.

The transactional nature of Stephen's dealings with the townsmen and -women of Cambridge and Boston made his record of this group among the most incomplete of his accounts of social networks. There are a few hints of more social relationships, including one with a Mr. Gridley, a member of a prominent Boston family with whom he dined on four occasions and had tea on a fifth. This connection, however, although one that Peabody sustained, was so intermittent, the references to it so cryptic, that it has not been possible using available clues even to determine Gridley's first name from among a number of possibilities. Otherwise, of the 1,600 or so residents of Cambridge and approximately 15,500 residents of Boston, only a handful appear by name in Stephen's journal.[30] What most of those he named had in common was the commercial nature of their mutual relationship. There were Henry Prentice, a Cambridge cask maker who occasionally rented him a horse; printers John and Thomas Fleet, who charged him to place a piece in their newspaper, the *Boston Evening-Post;* and "one Cook a young Woman" of Cambridge, who agreed to sew a greatcoat for Stephen in the late fall as winter threatened.[31] In fact, Peabody's pursuit of this overcoat is instructive because it reveals how complicated in the days before ready-to-wear clothing such a purchase could be, involving multiple commercial transactions. Before he even agreed with Miss Cook to make the garment he had to find a satisfactory piece of kersey and have the material prepared in several steps for sewing. Then there were multiple fittings. The process temporarily became even more complicated when he lost some of the pieces taking them from the tailor who cut them out to the seamstress for sewing.

Anna Warland, who was about the same age as the students, was an unusual case, a rare resident of Cambridge who also partied on October 7 in a dormitory room with some of the undergraduates. A daughter of Owen Warland, a Cambridge tailor, she was also a sister of Owen, Jr., who was a year behind Stephen at Harvard. But for her brother, who must have introduced her to his friends, it seems unlikely that she would have been included in any of the students' get-togethers.

The small number of Stephen's references to acquaintances in Boston, and particularly in Cambridge, reveals the social distance between Harvard's undergraduates and members of the surrounding community. When classes were in session the undergraduates amounted to about one-tenth of the people in Cambridge, but there were enough students to confine their socializing to the members of their transient community, rarely feeling a need to reach outside their own sphere for companionship. A small minority of the students, including Jacob Jewett, Peabody's roommate as the diary opens, went on to board with Harvard-approved families in the community instead of in the dormitories and must have developed a circle of acquaintances outside the college. Peabody, however, comfortably settled in college housing, apparently made only a few efforts to mix with the locals.

When Stephen was in Andover it was a different story. In the community where he had grown up there was never a sharp divide between the friends with whom he socialized and the neighbors with whom he conducted business. His accounts of days in his hometown are, in fact, filled with reports of visits made and guests received, almost to the point that it becomes unclear when anyone worked. Even trips to conduct business became games of hopscotch as he skipped from one acquaintance along his route to the next. Consider Samuel Johnson, an Andover farmer and shoemaker, as an example of a neighbor who was both Peabody's friend and his commercial supplier. Over the course of Stephen's diary he mentioned Johnson twenty-five times. There were social evenings, visits to order footwear, and combinations of the two. Dr. John Kittredge of

Andover similarly engaged in a business transaction with Peabody when the undergraduate needed medicine to cure the "itch" (that is, scabies) but socialized with him on other occasions.

Perhaps the most remarkable aspect of Stephen's social network in Andover was its geographical extent. Scholars have sometimes been tempted to think of colonial New England communities in isolation from their neighbors, as if moats surrounded Sudbury, Dedham, Plymouth, and even Andover.[32] In contrast, Stephen's diary offers interesting evidence of the distance that such relationships could cover. Across northeastern Massachusetts alone, he had non-college friends and acquaintances not only in Andover and Boxford but also in Bradford, Dracut, Haverhill, Methuen, Newbury, Newburyport, Rowley, and Woburn. In the course of the diary year they visited back and forth, and some friends from home even dropped in on him in Cambridge when their business took them to Boston. These communities cover an extended swath of northeastern Massachusetts and stretch from Dracut to Newbury, a distance as the crow flies of about twenty-four miles, or about thirty-five miles by road with Andover roughly in the middle. On the eve of the American Revolution these towns had a total population of approximately twenty thousand, only a small fraction of whom Peabody mentioned, but the geographical span of these friendships was surprising.[33] Indeed, on June 24 and October 30, 1767, he also mentioned acquaintances from as far away as Pigwocket (now Fryeburg), Maine, almost one hundred miles northwest of his home, a town where Andover residents had played a major role in settlement in the early 1760s.

Stephen's nascent professional network was also noteworthy for its geographical extent. One might speculate that an aspiring clergyman would attempt to develop friendships with the ministers in and around Andover and Boxford, seeing them as future colleagues, but that does not appear to have been the case with Peabody. The evidence of his diary is that two ministers occupied most of his attention, and one of them he strongly disliked. Nathaniel Appleton, as the longtime minister of the First Church in Cambridge, the preacher of most of the sermons Peabody heard during the course of the year his diary covers, was the most visible clergyman in the journal. Appleton was certainly more moderate theologically that Stephen, not the unyielding Calvinist that the diarist was, but Peabody did not make an issue of the minister's doctrines, and he respected the older man both for his professional standing and his judgment. This was not the situation with William Symmes (A.B. 1750), the pastor of Peabody's own church in the North Parish of Andover. Symmes was a theological liberal whose beliefs were so disturbing to Peabody that until late in the year his diary records he avoided the Arminian's preaching at almost all costs.[34] The relationship between the two men was so strained that in the spring of 1768, when Stephen found himself caught up in Harvard's student strike, he concluded on April 19 that Symmes was "no Friend to me."

Aside from Appleton and Symmes, Stephen mentioned local ministers only occasionally. Christopher Sargeant (A.B. 1725) of Methuen and Moses Parsons (A.B. 1736) of Newbury both had sons at Harvard, probably the reason Peabody interacted with these ministers from time to time. One clergyman he did not encounter in person during the course of the year was John Tucker (A.B. 1741), also of Newbury, but the Calvinist Peabody avidly followed a nasty pamphlet war between the liberal Tucker and orthodox members of his congregation. Samuel Williams (A.B. 1761) of Haverhill's First Church, later Harvard's Hollis Professor of Natural Philosophy, came closest among the local clergy to being Stephen's intimate and adviser. They took tea together occasionally, and they shared an appreciation for the published sermons of the Presbyterian preacher and educator Samuel Davies.

A 5-day, 125-mile tour of northeastern Massachusetts, eastern New Hampshire, and southeastern Maine that Stephen took from July 21–25, 1767, during the vacation after commencement best reveals his efforts to develop a network of professional connections. The trip was his longest of the year; travel was slow but safe in midcentury New England. Apparently interested in assessing the prospects for settling here, he passed from one community leader to the next, meeting both clergymen and laymen. Stephen found the expedition encouraging: "I am realy anamer'd with the eastern Country," he wrote on July 24, "& like things vastly better than what I expected to have done."

Throughout Stephen's diary he mentioned men much more often than women; it is striking that based on his record women seem to have played only a minor role in his daily life. Of the people he recognized who were identifiable by gender there were more than 550 men and boys and fewer than 100 women and girls. Such a gender division was inevitable in certain contexts; none of eighteenth-century New England's ministers and college students was female. Much more surprising is the gender distribution within his accounts of his own family (see appendix 1). This pattern probably had three reasons: the disrupted nature of his mother's nuclear family, the fact that when he did chores at home he did them with the other men of the family, and a bias in the kinds of interactions and activities he valued enough to report.

As a newlywed in 1721, Sarah Head Peabody moved several towns west from Newbury to Boxford, where she became a part of her husband's family. After Stephen's birth in 1741, his father's nearby relations played a much more significant role in his life day to day than his mother's, who were about fifteen miles away by road. Moreover, Sarah's family was not the large and complicated clan that the Peabodys were. She was her parents' only child. Her father disappeared from Newbury's vital records after her birth—he probably died, but there is no entry on his passing—and in 1710 Joanna Head took as her second husband Joseph Pike, Jr., of Newbury. Between 1711 and 1714, Joanna and Joseph had three daughters, half-sisters of Sarah, who retained her birthfather's surname.[35]

By the spring of 1767, Stephen's Head and Pike relatives played only a minor role in his life. Over the course of the year his diary covers he mentioned only one certain member of this side of his family, "Uncle Sawyer," Elisha Sawyer, the husband of Sarah's half-sister Rebecca.[36]

It was the Peabody side of Stephen's family that engaged his attention. Both grandparents and three of his father's seven siblings had died by 1767, but his uncle Richard lived in Pomfret, Connecticut, and aunts Mary Symonds (of Boxford), Hannah Foster (of Boxford), and Abial Kimball (of Bradford) were alive and lived close at hand.[37]

Although Mary, Hannah, and Abial were Stephen's blood relatives, it was the male family members who found their way into his diary. Of his aunts, only Abial, who visited his parents with her husband, Joseph, overnight on June 16, received any mention at all, and even then only as half of a couple. On the other hand, Joseph Kimball appeared four times without Abial and Jonathan Foster on seven occasions without Hannah; Mary Symonds's husband, Joseph, had died in 1759. By the same token nephews and male cousins appeared much more often than nieces and female cousins. On September 23, 1767, while at college, Stephen even met and mentioned Amasa Keyes, a son of his cousin Abigail Peabody Keyes, who visited in Cambridge while traveling on business in Boston from Pomfret, Connecticut, about seventy miles away.

Within Stephen's nuclear family, his father played a much more apparent role than his mother, and his brothers a more regular one than his sisters, even though Mary and Rebecca Peabody were living at home

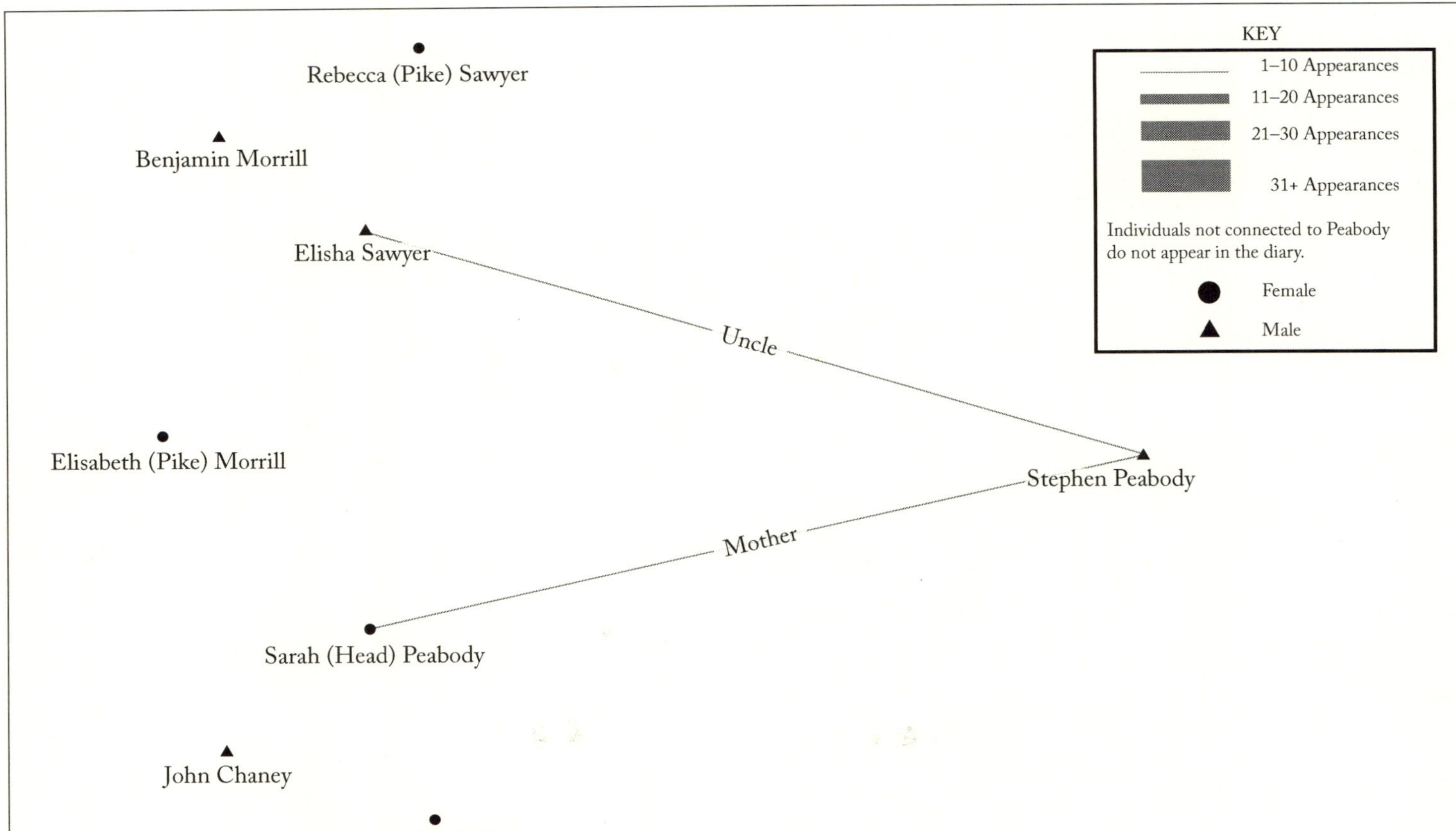

Peabody's Connections: Maternal Line

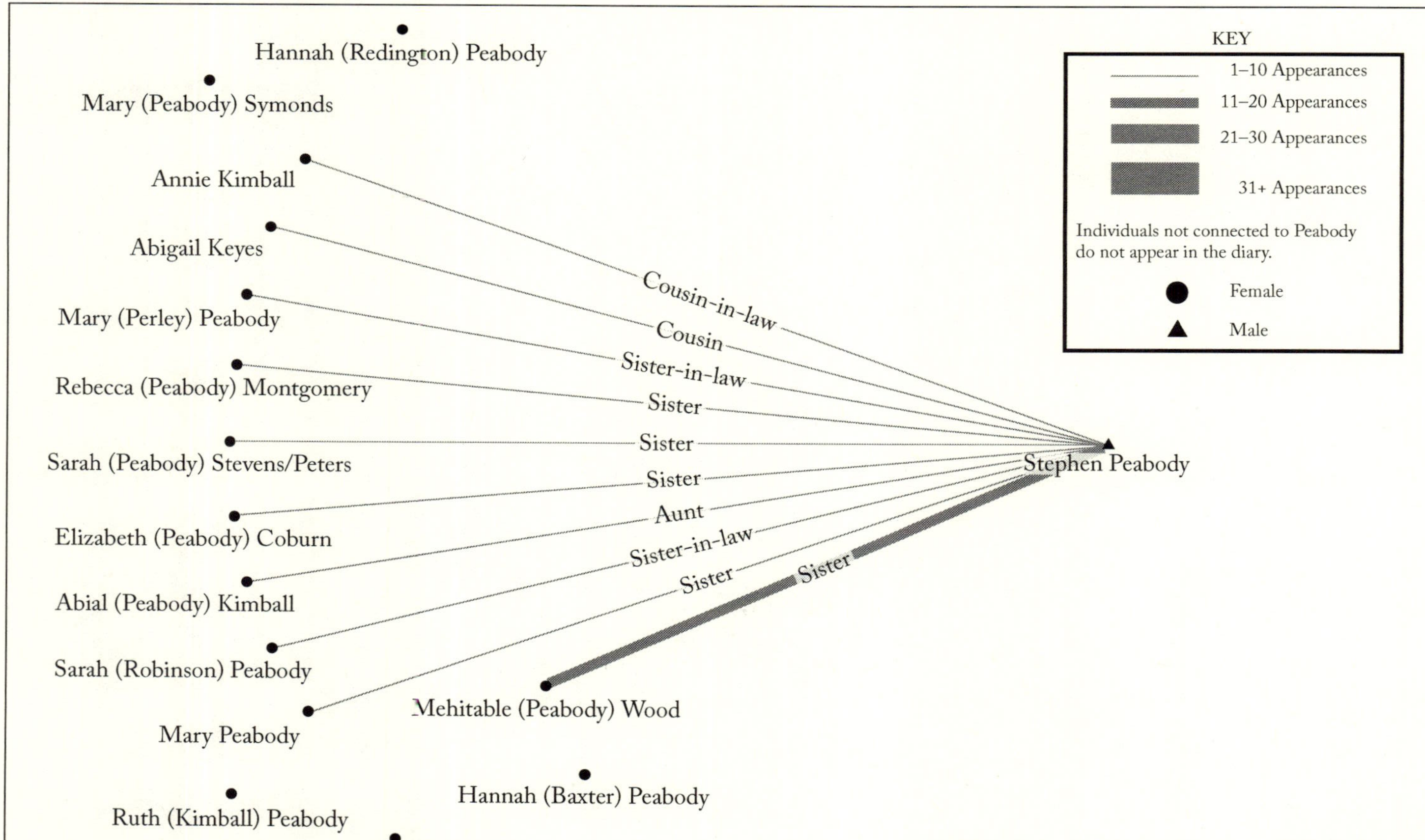

Peabody's Connections: Paternal Line (Females)

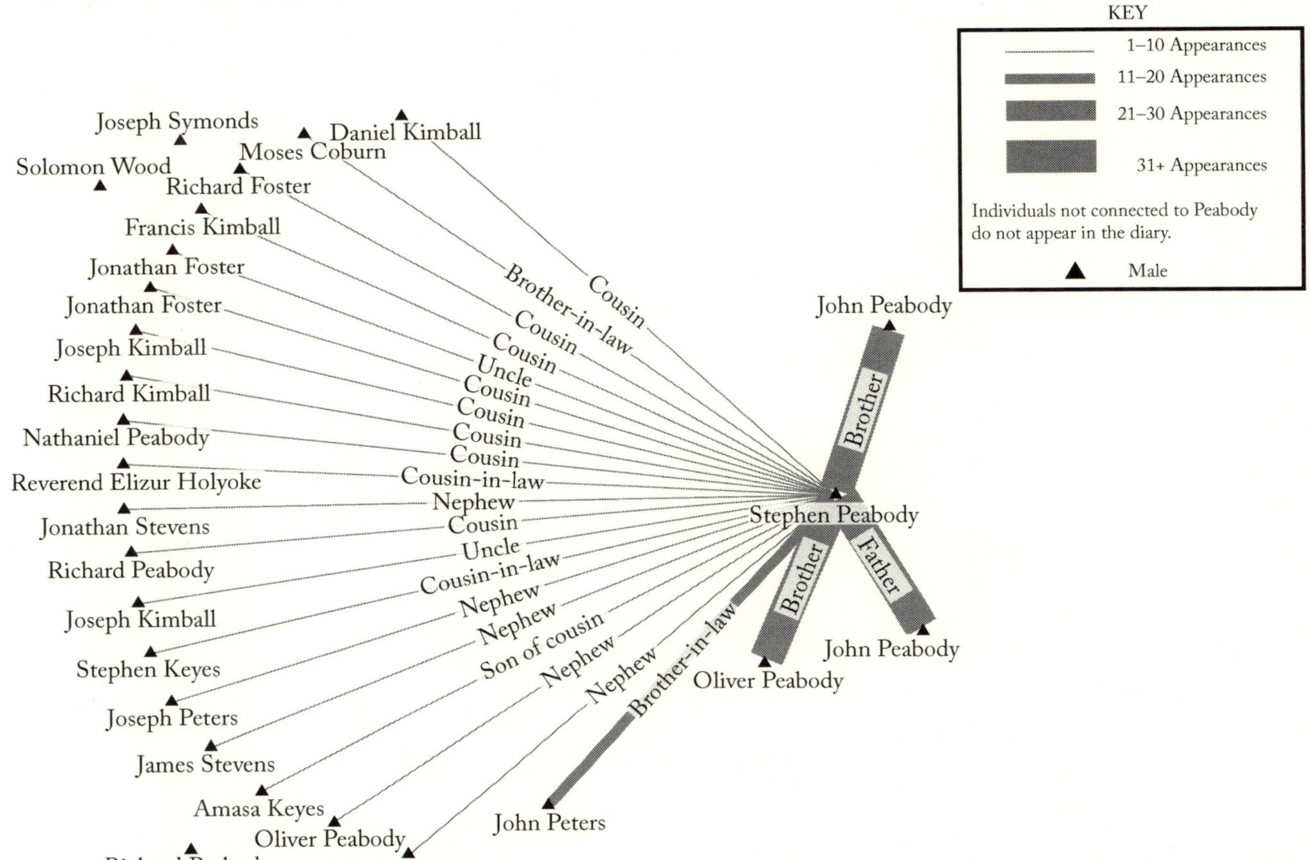

Peabody's Connections: Paternal Line (Males)

with their parents and were thus present whenever Stephen returned to Andover. Men's chores were often the occasion when Stephen mentioned his brothers and father; none of the help he sometimes provided his family when at home saw him working with any of the household's women, although occasionally he provided a sister with a ride when she went for a visit. John Peabody appears forty times in the diary, Sarah only three. Brothers Oliver and John show up thirty-three and fifty-five times respectively; of sisters Sarah Stevens Peters (of Andover), Mehitable Wood (of Boxford), Elizabeth Coburn (of Dracut), Mary (or Polly), and Rebecca, Stephen mentioned only Mehitable (eighteen times) in more than seven entries. The female members of the Peabody family, almost unseen, hardly ever did anything that Stephen thought to mention.

Harvard College was so much a male preserve in the 1760s that there were hardly ever any opportunities for Peabody to write in his journal about women at school. Instead, his account of Harvard life is valuable for its description of a more complicated undergraduate society than writers then or since have depicted (see appendix 2).

At any one time in the late 1760s, Harvard counted an undergraduate enrollment of between 170 and 190 students. A student body that size was small enough for the undergraduates to recognize each other—to have a vague idea of who all the others were—but too large for anyone to know everyone else well. The evidence of Stephen's diary is that Harvard College was a society made up of smaller circles, each consisting of boys and men who shared interests and common bonds. There is nothing surprising in the assertion that a student body the size of Harvard's consisted of smaller affinity groups whose members felt especially close to one another. The nature of these groups, however, to the extent that we can determine it, provides new insights into the life of the school.

For someone who arrived at Harvard without an established network of friends and acquaintances already there, making new contacts was the only alternative to loneliness. Peabody already knew many of his schoolmates when he arrived in Cambridge, however, and apparently he found this network so satisfactory that he made little effort to expand it. Almost all of his Harvard intimates were either from Andover, Boxford, and the surrounding towns or were fellow Dummer schoolmates or both. A weekly "private meeting" of the Association for the Suppression of Vice, which gathered each Saturday evening when school was in session for prayer and edifying discussion, may have been Stephen's only sustained opportunity for intimate conversations with a broader range of undergraduates. In addition to Peabody, the organization's seventeen other charter members at its founding six weeks before the opening of the diary included members from both south and west of Boston as well as northeastern Massachusetts and as far away as North Carolina, but aside from friends from home or Dummer Academy who also belonged to the group, Stephen hardly socialized with any of them outside of these meetings.[38]

It is not a surprise that Peabody tended to associate with students he already knew when he arrived at Harvard—in this era most students roomed with neighbors from home, friends with whom they had prepared for college, or relatives—but it was not the only possible pattern.[39] The college could have served as a melting pot where undergraduates from across New England and even farther away met, studied together, socialized, and formed friendships. If it did in other cases, it certainly did not in Stephen's.

An analysis of his diary reveals that between May 24, 1767, and May 23, 1768, he mentioned approximately 139 of the 228 members of the five classes (excluding himself) that were in residence for at least a portion of this period. The class of 1767, which graduated in July 1767, and the class of 1771, which matriculated the next month, were in Cambridge for only a part of this time. Either two years ahead or two years behind the class of 1769, their members were more shadowy figures than those of Stephen's own class and the ones immediately adjacent. Only twelve of the forty-two members of the class of 1767 are mentioned in the journal and twenty-nine of fifty-nine boys and men in the class of 1771. Stephen's roommate, or "chum," between August 1767 and April 1768 was a freshman, Samuel Phillips of Andover, a fact that almost certainly increased Peabody's contact with the members of that class and inflated their presence in his diary. Peabody paid more attention to the members of the classes of 1768 and 1770, and especially to his own classmates in the class of 1769. He referred to twenty-seven of forty-two members of the class of 1768, thirty-four of forty-three in the class of 1770, and all but five of his forty-two 1769 classmates (see appendix 2).

In effect, Stephen brought his friends with him when he entered Harvard. Within the five classes that were in residence at some point during the period of his journal, with only one major exception his intimates were from Andover, Boxford, and surrounding communities and most of them were also Dummer alumni. From the two classes ahead of Peabody the

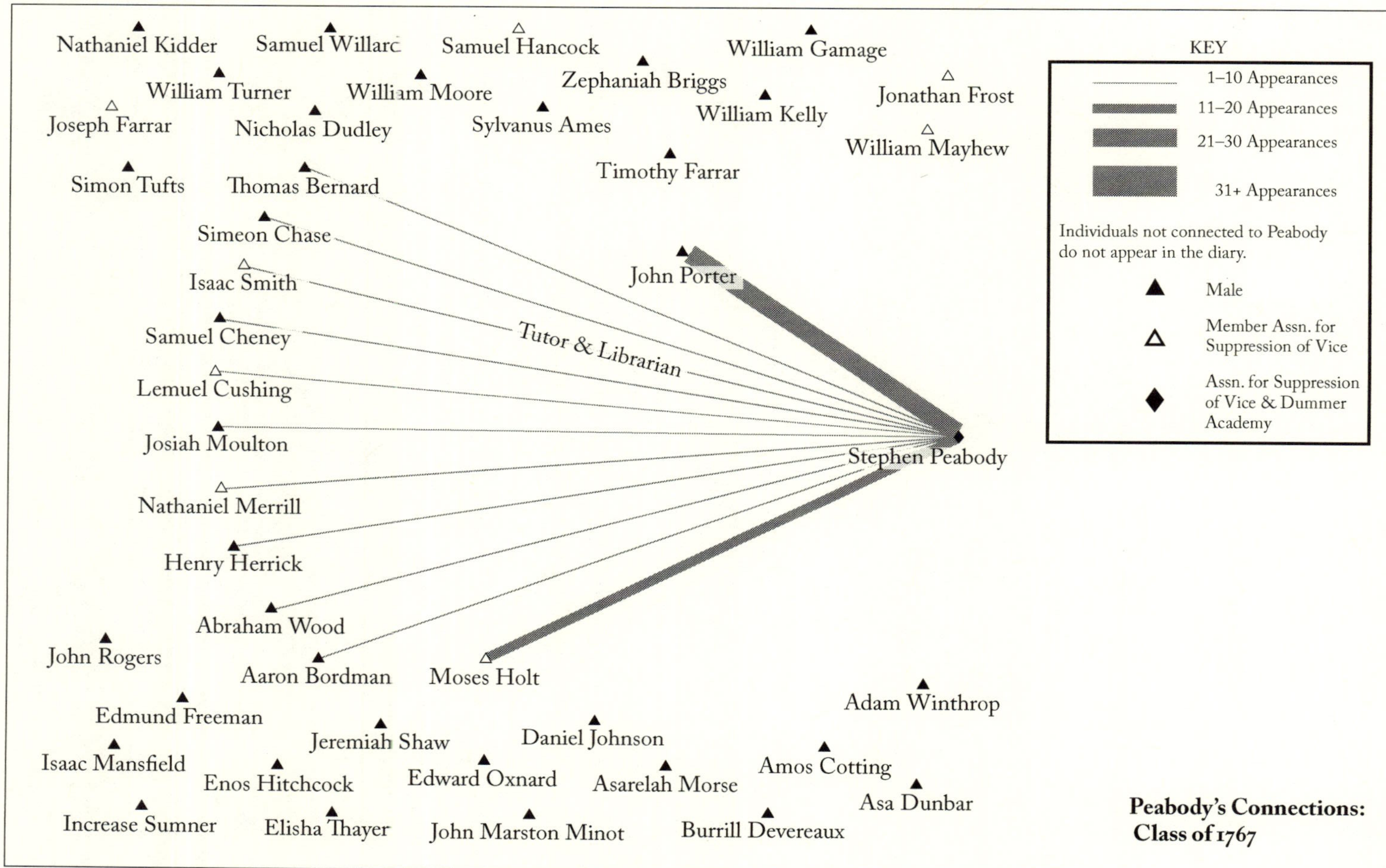

Peabody's Connections: Class of 1767

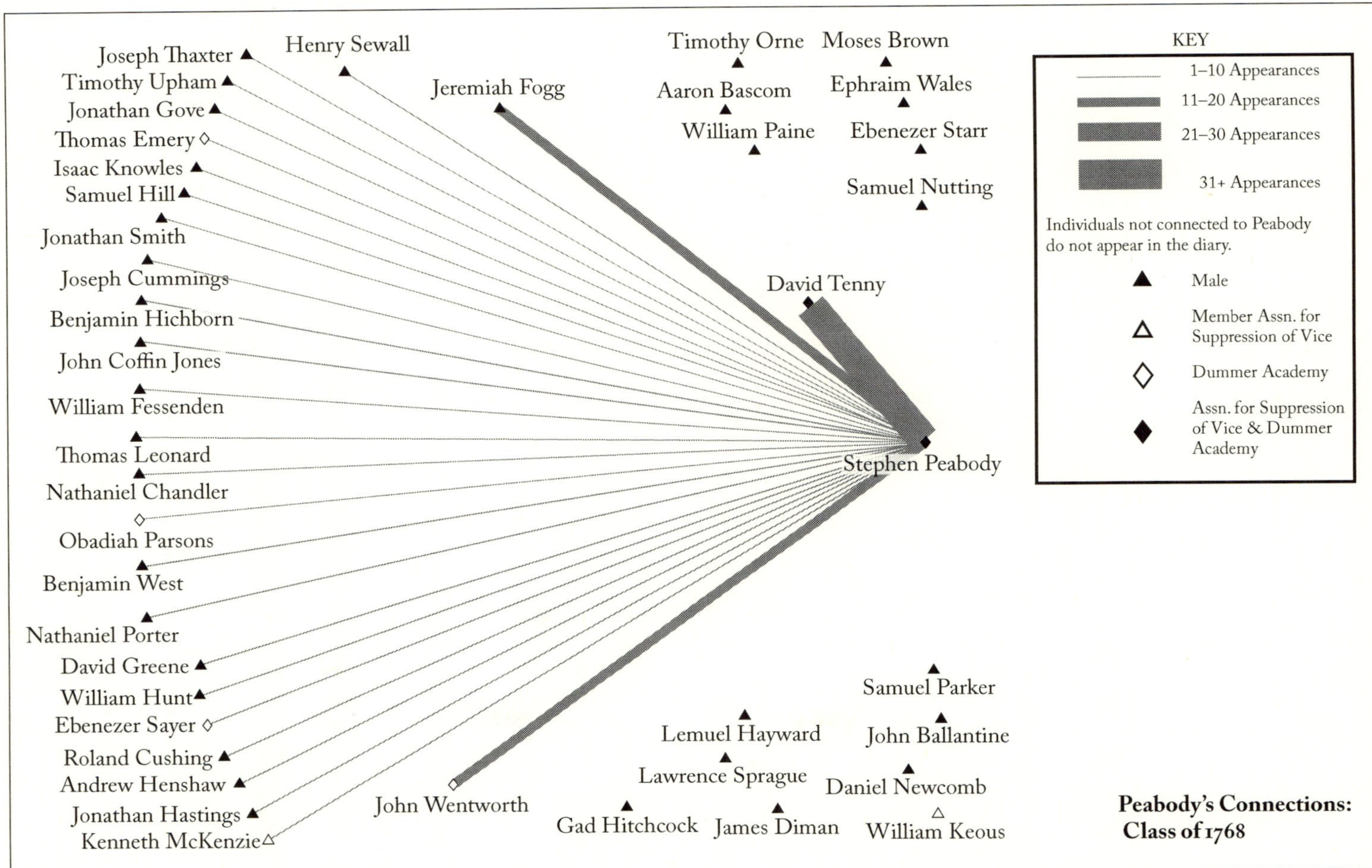

Peabody's Connections: Class of 1768

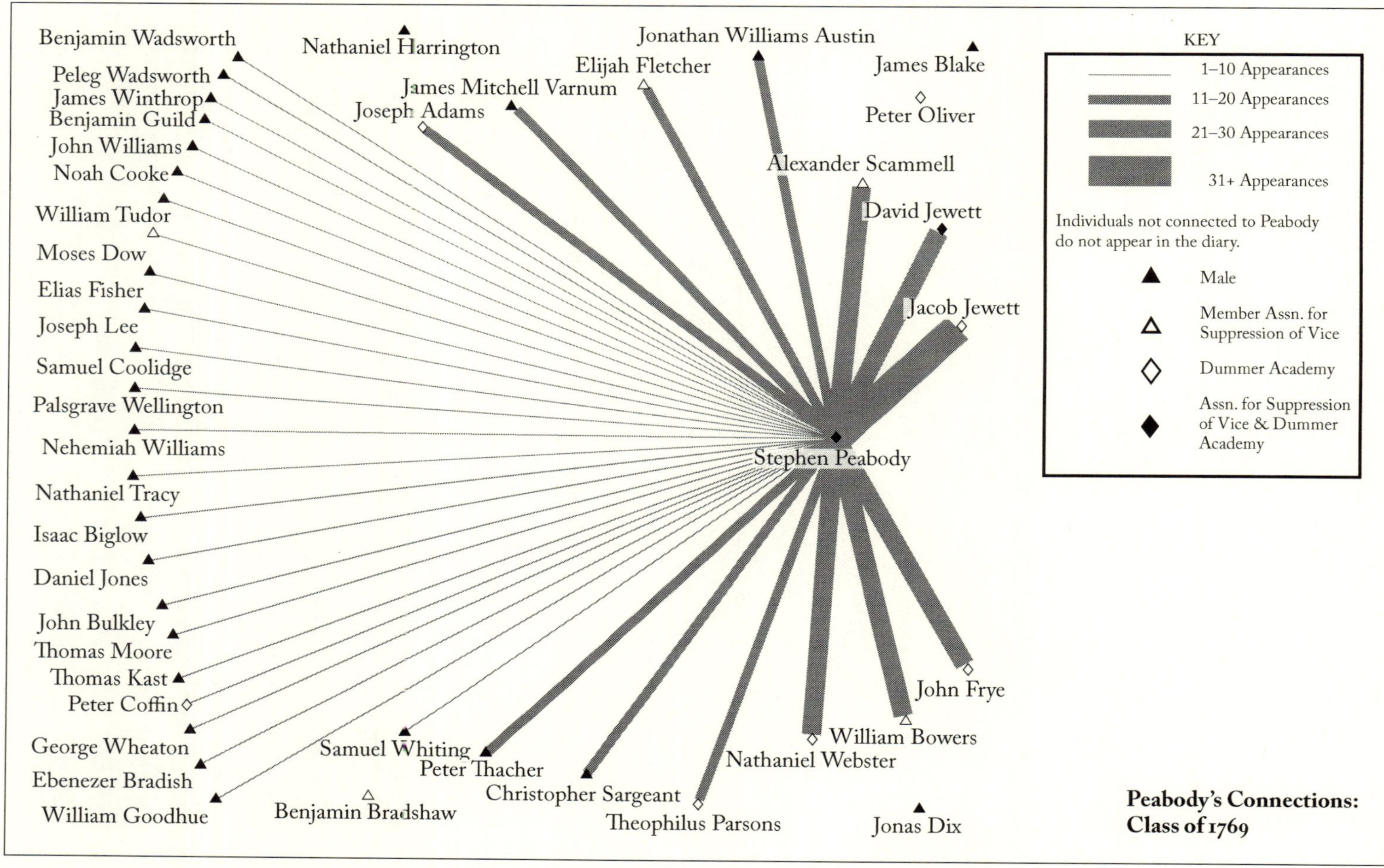

Peabody's Connections: Class of 1769

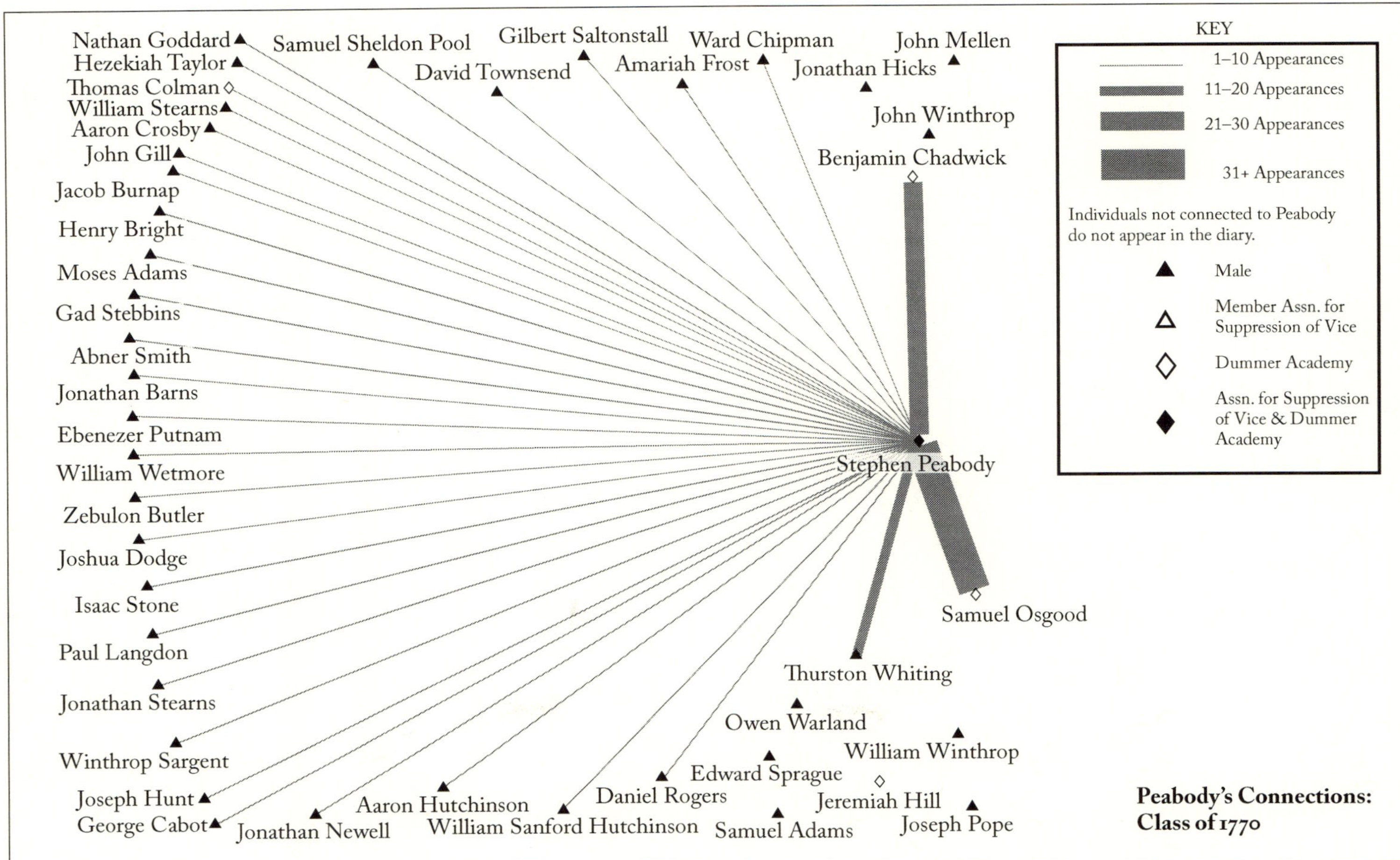

Peabody's Connections: Class of 1770

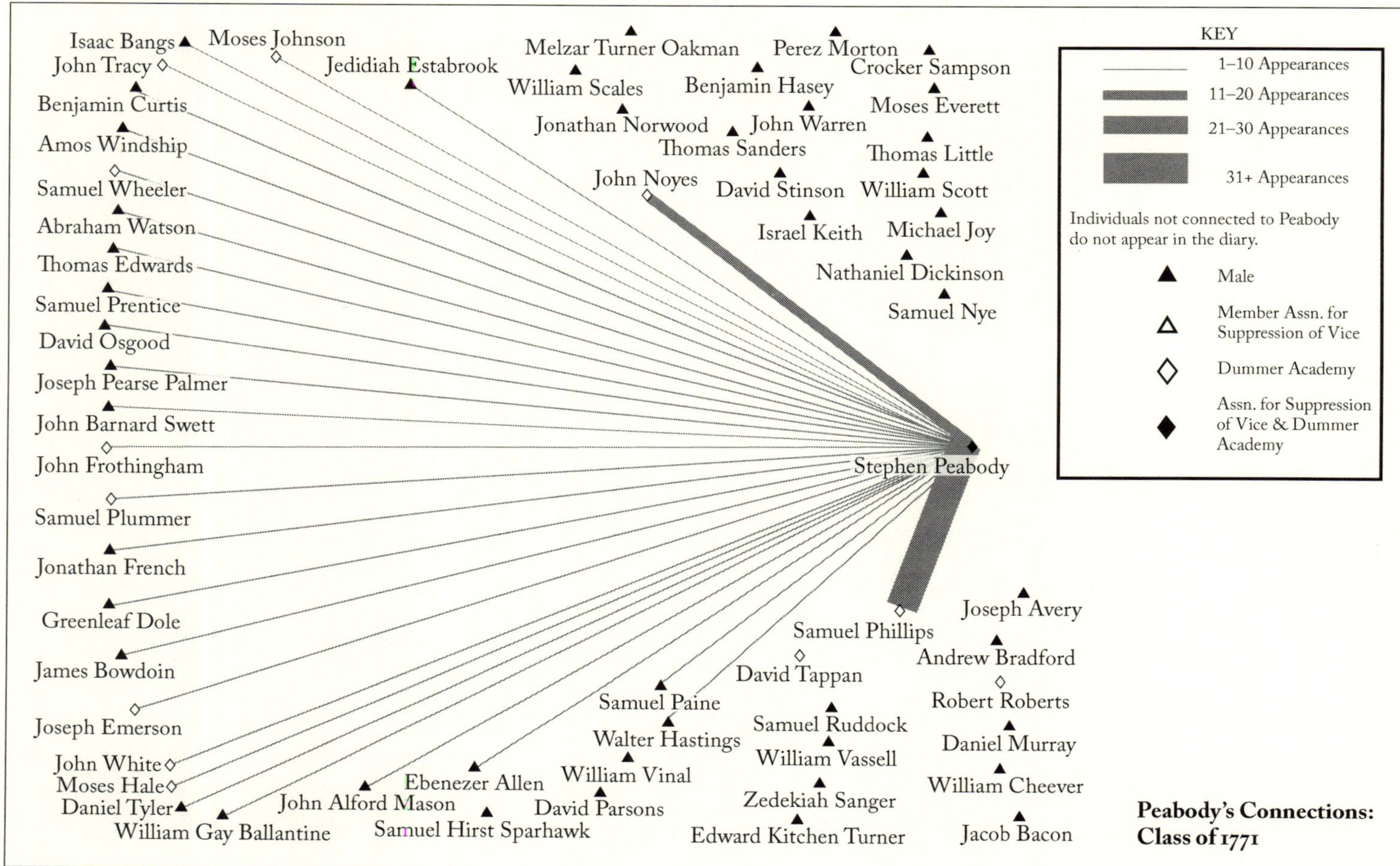

Peabody's Connections: Class of 1771

only two men he mentioned more than twenty times, John Porter (A.B. 1767) of Boxford and David Tenny (A.B. 1768) of Rowley, were both from Stephen's part of Massachusetts. Porter prepared for Harvard before the opening of Dummer Academy and Tenny was one of the school's first graduates. Benjamin Chadwick of Boxford and Samuel Osgood of Andover were both members of the class of 1770 and Dummer alumni. In the class of 1771, John Noyes of Newbury and Phillips had also prepared at Dummer. Within Stephen's own class, there were six members who appeared in the diary more than twenty times—William Bowers of Billerica, John Frye of Andover, David Jewett of Boxford, Jacob Jewett of Rowley, Alexander Scammell of Mendon, and Nathaniel Webster of Kingston, New Hampshire. Of this group, only Bowers and Scammell did not prepare for Harvard at Dummer, and only Scammell lived more than a day's ride from Peabody's home in Andover. Although it was not true that all those who attended Dummer and all at Harvard from the vicinity of Andover were intimates of Peabody, it was the case that of Peabody's close friends only Scammell was neither from Dummer nor from the neighborhood of Andover.

A look at Peabody's most intimate friends, the five schoolmates with whom he associated almost constantly, reinforces the conclusion that he brought his friends with him to Harvard. This circle consisted of David Tenny, first roommate Jacob Jewett, Benjamin Chadwick, Samuel Osgood, and second roommate Samuel Phillips. All five were Dummer graduates, and they all came from Andover, Boxford, or Rowley. These were the schoolmates who touched his heart. After Jewett moved out of Harvard housing to live with a Cambridge family Peabody took to calling him his "quondam," that is, his "ex." And Phillips triggered a burst of emotion on February 11, 1768, with a small gift, a black silk handkerchief: "My Heart glow'd with a kind of pleasing Gratitude to him for his unparalel'd Bounty & Generosity to me, which lays me under the strictest Obligations to him in every Respect wherein it is in my Power to serve him." Peabody recognized schoolmates whom he met at Harvard, he associated with some of them, and occasionally he even socialized with them. Aside from Scammell, however, none of these outsiders made it within his sphere of trusted friends.

Thus it was a tangled maze of student circles and cliques that came together briefly then unraveled in late March and early April of Stephen's junior year in the most sustained and disruptive student action at any American college during the colonial era. Under most circumstances the students did not form a single cohesive group but a stew of separate and distinct clusters of friends. Now, however, schoolmates who ordinarily had relatively little to do with one another briefly recognized a common interest in their opposition to what they considered faculty despotism before dissolving their united front when the consequences of their action became apparent. For Peabody and others, the weeks and months after March 22, 1768, were a stressful test, and their futures hung in the balance.

Strains between students and faculty had been apparent for most of the academic year when the tutors' promulgation of a new college rule on March 22 caused an immediate and intense flare-up. From time to time throughout the fall and winter the tutors had grown annoyed by student impudence, misconduct, and failure to prepare for recitations. These tensions reached an early flash point on December 24, 1767, when the faculty "rusticated" John Frye, an Andover native and Dummer graduate, for profanity and misconduct. President Edward Holyoke announced the decision and pronounced the sentence in the college chapel in the presence of the entire student body. Rusticated students, presumably properly chastened, had to take a year off from college, usually living with a pious and reliable country minister while they thought about what they had done wrong, but Frye did not take his punishment seriously: "As soon as the Sentence came out, he pronounc'd Amen with an audable Voice & put on his Hat & left the Chappel. The Amen was an imitation of Wigglesworth & it made a good deal of laugh in the Chappel." In fact, Stephen, who had little patience for misbehavior, believed that, Andover and Dummer boy or not, Frye's punishment was warranted; as a member of the Association for the Suppression of Vice this was just the kind of misconduct Peabody quietly reported to the college authorities himself. When it came to a controversy involving one of the professors, however, Stephen and the faculty were on opposing sides.

The problem was Professor Edward Wigglesworth, or at least that is what Peabody believed. The theology lectures, as far as Stephen was concerned, were worse than a waste of time because every minute spent listening to Wigglesworth drone on was forever lost to the cause of true religion. Stephen had more self-confidence than was either healthy or deserved, and he quickly arrived at the conclusion that the professor had to go, a position that his intimates shared. Peabody first expressed his

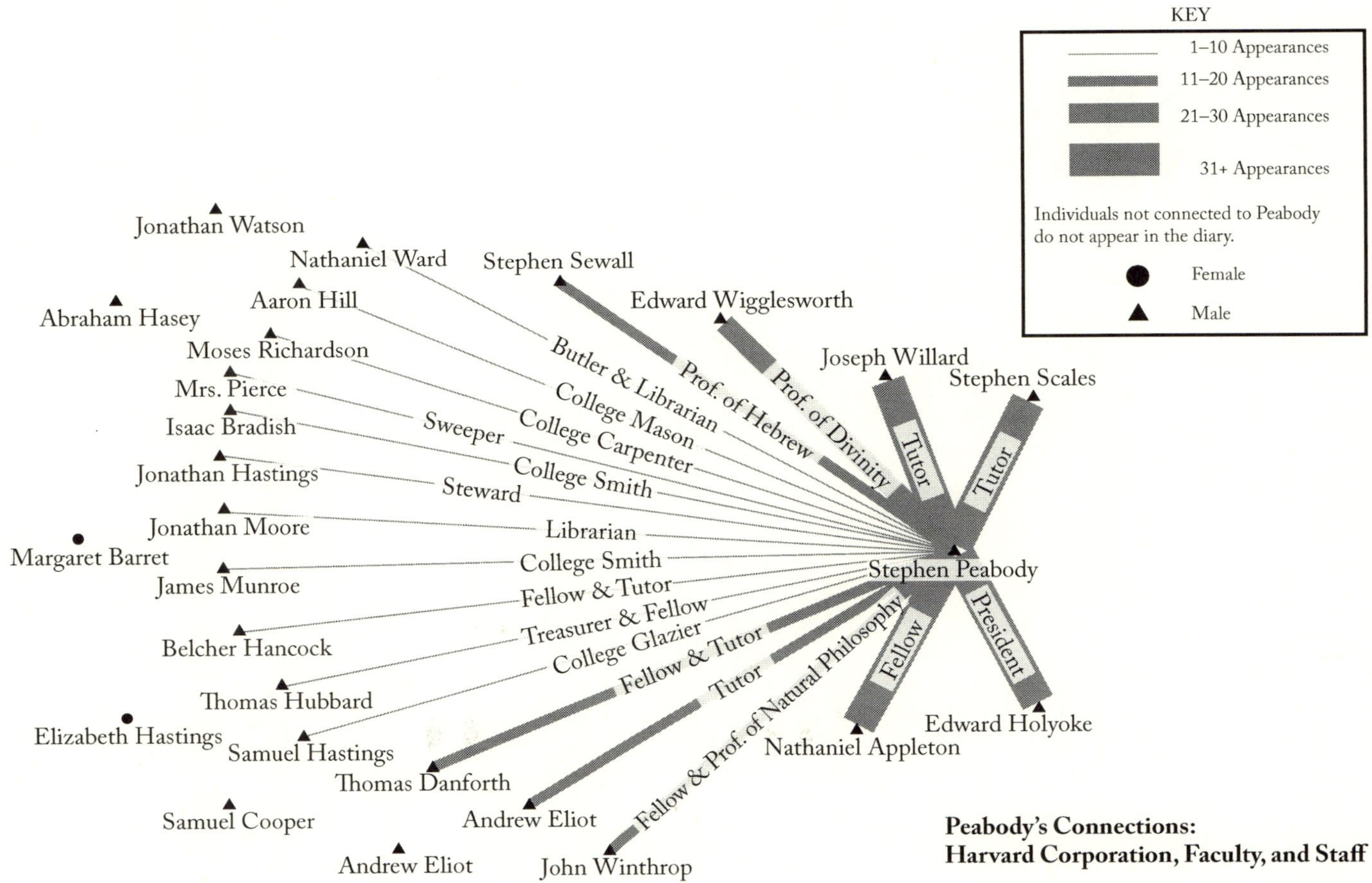

Peabody's Connections: Harvard Corporation, Faculty, and Staff

dissatisfaction after a theology private lecture on November 10, which he dismissed as "nihil ad Rem," or not to the point. By February 27, 1768, as dissatisfaction festered, Stephen and his friends "had some Talk of the Difficulties we labour under by having Wigglesworth set over us here & talk of trying to get him turn'd out by a Petition to the Overseers, which when I came to my Chamber I began to write." It was unrealistic of the undergraduates to think that they had the collective power to force Wigglesworth's dismissal, but they pressed their position by disrupting the Hollis Professor's lectures, as Peabody mentioned on March 2, 9, and 15. On March 2, they even took their case to Nathaniel Appleton, whose sorrow at the difficulties the students mistook for support for their efforts to rid themselves of their lecturer. Wigglesworth was "A Stupid Vilian," wasn't he, for forcing the undergraduates to put up with such classes?[40]

In the context of such tensions, of the rigid assertion of faculty prerogative versus student insubordination and plotting, of undergraduate outrage at faculty efforts to impose discipline in cases of misconduct, the confrontation came to a head on March 22 over an issue outsiders had difficulty taking seriously. The tutors announced a new college regulation that affected all the undergraduates except the seniors, whose classes were almost at an end. At recitations, the college custom had been for students to respond "nolo," that is, I don't want to, if they were unprepared to answer a question when called upon. The new rule required students who were not ready to recite to tell the tutor before the start of the class. If the faculty considered the new regulation a necessary crackdown, the students believed it to be an intolerable oppression. This infringement of tradition caused an immediate uproar; according to Stephen, it was "so rediculous that it is really sickish, & is resented highly." That evening at a secret class meeting, which Peabody moderated, the juniors "agreed to take no Notice" of the new regulation and to offer their excuses as before.

Over the next two weeks, the situation only grew worse. The undergraduates continued to resist the faculty's attempts to impose its will; brickbats flew through the tutors' windows, leading to the suspension of four students, and the tutors found their chamber doors smeared with manure. At one point a minor chimney fire of unknown origin broke out in Massachusetts Hall. At another a rumor circulated that tutor Joseph Willard had imprisoned one of the smallest students for most of a day in order to force him to inform on the leaders of the conspiracy. The approach one evening of a sheriff's posse consisting of men from the Cambridge community raised the unfounded rumor that the authorities were about to arrest a student. Only a handful of undergraduates declined to participate in the action. Peter Thacher of Boston, for one, a member of Stephen's class and a cordial friend, "betook [himself] to Boston," recognizing that he would become entangled in the dispute if he remained in Cambridge (see appendix 3).

The undergraduates were never more unified than on April 4, when about one hundred freshmen, sophomores, and juniors—all but roughly forty members of the three lowest classes—left college and went home. They had agreed to resign their connection with the school to pressure the administration to yield to their demands. The next day, in sympathy with the underclassmen, the seniors petitioned to be allowed to transfer to Yale. President Holyoke deferred action on this request, however, and it soon became apparent that many of those who had left Cambridge had not, in fact, formally withdrawn from school. Before long, many of them began to drift back, in some cases after having been actively recruited by the faculty. As the college resumed some semblance of its normal routine, Stephen and a handful of other hardliners found themselves on the outside looking in.

To follow Stephen over the course of his diary's final seven weeks is to join him briefly at a high point on April 4, when he and the strike's other leaders believed they were in control of the situation as the school's "Sons of Liberty" acted to defend student rights, then along a rapid descent as it became clear that the undergraduates' unified front had disintegrated.[41] When the strikers' rank and file returned to Cambridge, the administration dismissed some of them from the student jobs that provided them with financial aid. It also shuffled dormitory assignments as a way to break up the small social circles that had coalesced to produce the students' unified action. And it began to interrogate the students, building dossiers from the resulting depositions against those it perceived to be the ringleaders. Stephen was one of the principal targets.

In all, the faculty collected sixty-two depositions. Of these, two in the university archives' file on the disorder of 1768 are unattributed. Three students each made two statements, so the ascribed declarations of fifty-seven undergraduates are on the record: twenty-two freshmen, fifteen sophomores, eighteen juniors, and two seniors. The testimony is in most cases of witnesses actively and unabashedly attempting to curry favor with their interrogators in order to secure readmission to Harvard, so the depositions in no sense constitute impartial accounts of the strike.[42] In the hands of the college authorities, however, who were determined to make examples of the students they considered the worst troublemakers, the results of their questioning amounted to a damning bill of indictment against four juniors: Jonathan Williams Austin, Stephen Peabody, William Tudor, and James Mitchell Varnum.

Thirty-two of the depositions incorporated greater or lesser accusations against Stephen, including one of the unattributed statements and testimony in both of the declarations of two of the three students who spoke with the authorities more than once. Thus we can identify twenty-nine schoolmates, about one-sixth of the student body, who spoke against Peabody in these irregular proceedings, some at length and damagingly, others only in passing. The resulting evidence against Peabody, which someone summarized for the college records, accused him of stirring up resentments against the faculty and the new regulation, forcefully persuading other students to resign their college rooms, blocking the doorway to the chapel, threatening wavering undergraduates, suborning perjury, and even, according to Samuel Phillips, talking of "bringing down a Mob from Andover to College."[43] Similar summaries compiled the major accusations against Austin, Tudor, and Varnum.

There was nothing inadvertent or haphazard about the evidence the faculty compiled. Although the administration did not interrogate all of Peabody's intimates, it knew the undergraduates' relationships well enough to be able to identify many of his closest friends, including "quondam" Jacob Jewett, "chum" Samuel Phillips, and fellow associator against vice Alexander Scammell. Moreover, the questioning seems to have been quite leading; at any event, many of the same accusations appeared multiple times. Worried about their own standing within the college, many of the witnesses apparently offered little resistance to the damning implications of the faculty's interrogation. Peabody, for one, was shocked by some of the charges against him, including his supposed threat to bring down a mob. "It is remarkable [the] stories they have got against me," he confided to his journal, "but I cant hear as they have asserted that I wa[s] at the Bottom of all the Mischief."[44]

Stephen had hardly been an innocent bystander, but as his schoolmates scrambled to save themselves, he along with Austin, Tudor, and Varnum had now become convenient scapegoats. It was at least curious that none of the other three supposed agitators had been especially close to Peabody in the period from May 24, 1767, to March 21, 1768.[45] He had socialized with Austin from time to time, although the Bostonian and Boston Latin School graduate was not within his inner circle. As for Tudor and Varnum, both seem to have been casual acquaintances until the students exploded in discontent. Peabody had even had a confrontation with Varnum on January 5 over the diarist's monitor's report. How did this circle of four passing acquaintances so quickly entrust their futures to one another? This is not a question the faculty attempted to address, nor is it easy to answer long after the event. If Peabody and the others were in fact scapegoats, the faculty may have assumed their efforts were more coordinated than they really were.

The outcome was inevitable. The agitators would be rusticated. It was not certain that they would ever be restored, but if they were, the best they could hope for was readmission in April 1769 to the class of 1770. This was a sobering prospect, especially for Stephen, who was already among the oldest of the undergraduates and whose aspirations for the ministry depended on his successful completion of a liberal education.

Within days of going home, Peabody and the other students began to look for ways to apologize for what they gradually recognized as rashness on their part and to restore their status at Harvard. Stephen's first reaction to his circumstance was to defend what he had done and try to persuade family, friends, and acquaintances that any fault lay with the faculty. He was unfortunately overconfident in his dealings with others, and at least initially it does not seem to have occurred to him that anyone with common sense might question the justice of the students' actions. Several days of carrying his story to potential allies, however, along with reports both that many schoolmates had returned to college and that the authorities were threatening never to readmit him convinced him of the precariousness of his situation. One ominous report indicated that some of the faculty believed that in view of Stephen's "New Light," or evangelical, theology they were well rid of him.[46] Perhaps as Harvard became increasingly liberal religiously there was no longer any room for this traditional Calvinist's self-righteousness. Varnum, for his part, concluded that Harvard would never allow him back, so he transferred to Rhode Island College, now Brown University. That Baptist school, founded in 1764, had yet to graduate its first class and was willing to compromise its standards to fill out its student body.[47] James Manning, the school's president, happened to be on a tour nearby in Haverhill in mid-May, and on May 13

Peabody briefly explored transferring too, but he never seriously pursued the possibility.[48]

Over the course of his diary's final seven weeks, Peabody conducted several circuits of northeastern Massachusetts, broken up by a couple of visits to Cambridge to assess the strength of the opposition to his possible return. Somehow there had to be a way to pull the right strings. Reverend Elizur Holyoke (A.B. 1750), the minister of Boxford's East Parish, was a nephew of President Holyoke. He was willing to play the role of intermediary, although if his efforts bore any fruit, they flowered after the end of the journal. Samuel Moody, Stephen's mentor at Dummer Academy, was livid with his former student at first, but he gradually softened as the weeks passed. John Phillips, Esq., a Boston merchant and Samuel Phillips's influential uncle, was also willing to see what he could do. In a society in which face-to-face personal contacts were the best way to advance a cause, Peabody tested his connections, his social networks, to find what would work.[49]

At the same time Stephen was trying to further his cause, Austin and Tudor were on a similar mission. Sons of prominent Bostonians, both were better placed than Peabody to succeed because they could turn to affluent family friends who were longtime supporters of the college. John Hancock (A.B. 1754), writing on behalf of "poor young Austin," questioned Harvard's "very severe Censure" and predicted "that unless Redress'd it will be a Disadvantage to the College." Specifics of how redemption was secured remain hazy, but in early July, the Board of Overseers forcefully enjoined the Corporation to rescind its sentences provided each student offer a humble apology. As historian Samuel Eliot Morison concluded, the Corporation "readmitted the ringleaders on the ground that suitable penance had been performed, and many 'friends and benefactors' of the College had 'condescended to intercede in their behalf.'"[50] The final vote took place on July 5 over the outraged opposition of President Holyoke, who was indignant at being undermined by the two governing boards. The Corporation, which included Professor Winthrop and Tutor Danforth as well as Holyoke, ordinarily acted by consensus, not by assembling a majority, but on this occasion the "Presdt. Enter'd his protest against the . . . vote." Perhaps this experience was on his mind the next year when on his deathbed he declared, "if any man wishes to be humbled and mortified, let him become President of Harvard College."[51]

In at least one respect, Holyoke's lament encapsulated everyone's feelings in the aftermath of the strike. If the members of the faculty and Stephen Peabody shared anything it was an acute sense of disappointment and betrayal. In their comments about the storm the faculty revealed that it had never been blind to "New Light" Peabody's shortcomings—his priggishness, overabundant self-assurance, and religious rigidity—but until March 22 they had taken advantage of his willingness to serve as an informer in the service of controlling the more unruly of the undergraduates. Imagine their frustration at finding Peabody among the leaders of the opposition. And what of Stephen? If he believed that his age, maturity, and inside information entitled him to special considerations from the faculty, think of his anger at the administration's clumsy imposition of a regulation that he considered an affront to his standing within the college. By exercising their power over the students, especially the way they did, the tutors underscored the undergraduates' subordination. This meant that in the tutors' eyes, Stephen was no better than anyone else.

When the class of 1769 graduated in Cambridge the next year on July 19, Stephen Peabody was one of thirty-nine recipients of the first degree in arts. He had spent an uneventful senior year, almost certainly being wary of doing anything to draw attention to himself. Three years later he was one of thirty-three members of the class who returned to Harvard to qualify for the A.M. He had spent the interim in Andover teaching school and reading for the ministry. The local association of Congregationalist ministers had approved him to preach as a ministerial candidate on May 14, 1771; the following February 26, 1772, he received a call from the new church in Atkinson, New Hampshire, just across the provincial border, about a dozen miles due north of Andover.[52]

Stephen served the congregation in Atkinson for the next forty-seven years. Even the American Revolution drew him away from home for only five months' service as the chaplain for a New Hampshire regiment at the siege of Boston. He married twice. On January 19, 1773, he took Polly Haseltine of Bradford as his first wife. Peabody did not mention her by name in his diary but he might have been referring to her cryptically in Latin on several occasions when he used a term that can be translated as "girlfriend." They had two children, a son born not quite nine months later on October 6, 1773, and a daughter born on January 15, 1775. After Polly died on September 19, 1793, he married Elizabeth (Smith) Shaw on December 8, 1795. Betsy Shaw's first husband had been the late John Shaw

(A.B. 1772) of Haverhill, the Massachusetts town across the state line from Atkinson. She was the younger sister of Abigail Adams, so the marriage made Stephen the brother-in-law of the first vice president, and soon the second president, of the United States.[53]

No such honors or celebrity came to Peabody. His Harvard classmates included one of the most prominent jurists of their generation, Theophilus Parsons, who became the chief justice of the Massachusetts Supreme Judicial Court as well as an influential Federalist politician. Friend and classmate Peter Thacher served as the minister of the Brattle Street Church, one of Boston's most visible congregations. Classmate Alexander Scammell received a different kind of recognition on October 6, 1781, when as a colonel with the American forces at Yorktown he was one of the last Americans to die of wounds received during the culminating battle of the American Revolution.[54]

Stephen's second chum, Samuel Phillips, who served as the lieutenant governor of the commonwealth of Massachusetts in early 1802 but died a month after his inauguration, had two other claims to fame. The first came during the course of the year this journal covers, when his father protested Samuel's class rank, believing that a mistake in the college's calculations cost his son eight places in the class order. The resulting dispute was the proximate cause of the school's decision, beginning with the class of 1773, to use the alphabet for class lists. Samuel's second claim to fame, the more important one, was his founding of Phillips Academy in Andover in 1778.[55]

While Stephen's schoolmates were making names for themselves, he was ministering to his congregation, farming to make ends meet, and founding a school of his own. Atkinson Academy never achieved the renown of Phillips Academy Andover, although it eventually became the town's public elementary school, but it was the occasion of the fullest and kindest recollection of Peabody.[56]

Samuel Gilman, whose own most enduring accomplishment was composing the lyrics to "Fair Harvard," which he wrote for the college's bicentennial celebration in 1836, was a young boy in 1798 when his mother placed him with Peabody. Her husband had died, and she had no money, but Peabody took the boy in, saying, "Madam, leave your little boy with us. He shall be one of our family, and enter the academy. If Providence blesses your efforts to secure for yourself a livelihood, well and good; you may remunerate us in the usual way. But if you are doomed to struggle

John Johnston, *Stephen Peabody (1741–1819)* (1809). Oil on canvas, 29.25 x 24.5 inches. Courtesy American Antiquarian Society. Peabody commissioned this painting and one of his second wife, Betsy, at the insistence of stepson William Smith Shaw and brother-in-law John Adams.

with adversity, be not anxious about your son; here you may be sure that he shall have a home and an education." Gilman, who went on to graduate from Harvard and become the minister of the Unitarian church in Charleston, South Carolina, recalled his benefactor as large, commanding, and "the soul of good nature." Six feet tall and portly, Peabody was swarthy with bushy hair. Profane language still made him recoil, and he continued to be very musical. In addition to playing the violin, he had a voice that "was of vast compass, and exquisitely flexible." He used it wherever he went, during church services "rolling out a mellow and deep-toned bass, or warbling with his treble or counter over the whole concert, like an animated mocking-bird." He would also "sing on his rides about the town, or when traveling in his chaise, alone or accompanied, by night or by day."[57]

This musical and benevolent clergyman lost his wife Betsy on April 9, 1815. After four lonely and difficult years he followed her to the grave on May 23, 1819.[58]

Manuscript and Methods

Stephen Peabody made his own diary by folding large pieces of paper and trimming the edges to form fourteen signatures, which someone sewed to hold the sheets together. The process resulted in pages of irregular size but approximately 4" wide by 6½" high. For the most part, the manuscript, which is owned by the Massachusetts Historical Society in Boston, is in very good condition, although damage from flaking along the fore edge has cost a few words, particularly in the first and last signatures. Peabody's hand is almost always legible; except for words lost to flaking only a few have proved impossible to read.

There is an entry for each day from May 24, 1767, to May 23, 1768, but Peabody did not always end his day by recording one. Internal evidence makes it clear that sometimes at the same sitting he caught up with entries for several days. Keeping a journal became a habit for him. Although the present diary is the oldest of his journals to have survived, in several places he offers strong hints that this was not his first journal. Nor was it his last. The American Antiquarian Society holds his manuscript diaries from 1777 through 1814 as well as a portrait of him dated circa 1809. If he ever offered a reason for keeping a diary, it has not yet turned up.

The basis of this edition of Peabody's diary is a modernized transcription of the text. In the interests of readability, the editor has silently imposed capital letters at the beginnings of many sentences as well as terminal periods. Where gaps or dashes within a line of text seem to indicate the start of a new topic the editor has begun a new paragraph. Peabody constructed his manuscript as a single series of 366 daily entries, but to make the diary more navigable and usable the editor has divided them by months and placed the date, which begins each entry, on its own line. Throughout, superscripts have also been systematically brought down to the line. Brackets indicate illegibility or damage to the manuscript. If no conjectural reading seems possible, the brackets enclose three ellipsis points: [. . .]. Confident conjectural readings appear [like so]. Highly speculative readings add a question mark [like so?].

Commentary takes two forms. Most daily entries end in an explanatory paragraph. It begins by addressing any especially significant issues the entry raises. Then it turns to identifying people, places, and things, usually in the order they appear in Peabody's text, but only at the first mention. Because the diary reveals Peabody's social networks, special effort has gone into identifying as many of the people he mentions as possible. When someone has not been identified, the reason usually is that a cryptic reference could equally mean two or more individuals. The use of ALL CAPS keys the comment to the diary entry.

Numbered notes following explanatory paragraphs serve four purposes:

1. Indicating after brackets whether either a tear or illegibility has made what Peabody wrote impossible to determine. These notes also estimate how much text has been compromised.
2. Translating Latin (or in one case Greek). When Peabody used the same word or phrase more than once (i.e., "in mane"), it has been translated only the first time.
3. Providing a scriptural text or citation when the selection itself is a commentary on contemporary events. All texts are from the King James Version of the Bible.
4. Defining a local idiom.

Notes

1. Samuel Eliot Morison, *Three Centuries of Harvard* (Cambridge, Mass.: Harvard University Press, 1936), 7–9; Thomas Harrison Montgomery, *A History of the University of Pennsylvania* (Philadelphia: G. W. Jacobs, 1900), 11–40, 73–83; James Dow McCallum, *Eleazar Wheelock, Founder of Dartmouth College* (Hanover, N.H.: Dartmouth College Publications, 1939).

2. Louis Leonard Tucker, *Puritan Protagonist: President Thomas Clap of Yale College* (Chapel Hill: University of North Carolina Press, 1962); Edmund S. Morgan, *The Gentle Puritan: A Life of Ezra Stiles, 1727–1795* (Chapel Hill: University of North Carolina Press, 1962); Joseph Ellis, *The New England Mind in Transition: Samuel Johnson of Connecticut, 1696–1772* (New Haven, Conn.: Yale University Press, 1973).

3. Morison, *Three Centuries of Harvard*; Susan H. Godson et al., *The College of William and Mary: A History* (Williamsburg, Va.: King and Queen Press, 1993); Brooks Mather Kelley, *Yale: A History* (New Haven, Conn.: Yale University Press, 1974); Richard Warch, *The School of the Prophets: Yale College, 1701–1740* (New Haven, Conn.: Yale University Press, 1973); Thomas Jefferson Wertenbaker, *Princeton, 1746–1896* (Princeton, N.J.: Princeton University Press, 1946); Mark A. Noll, *Princeton and the Republic, 1768–1822: The Search for a Christian Enlightenment in the Era of Samuel Stanhope Smith* (Princeton, N.J.: Princeton University Press, 1989); Edward Potts Cheyney, *History of the University of Pennsylvania, 1740–1940* (Philadelphia: University of Pennsylvania Press, 1940); David Churchill Humphrey, *From King's College to Columbia, 1746–1800* (New York: Columbia University Press, 1976); Robert A. McCaughey, *Stand Columbia: A History of Columbia University in the City of New York, 1754–2004* (New York: Columbia University Press, 2004); Ted Widmer, *Brown: The History of an Idea* (New York: Thames and Hudson, 2015); Leon Burr Richardson, *History of Dartmouth College* (Hanover, N.H.: Dartmouth College Publications, 1932); Richard P. McCormick, *Rutgers: A Bicentennial History* (New Brunswick, N.J.: Rutgers University Press, 1966).

4. See, for example, Frederick Rudolph, *Curriculum: A History of the American Undergraduate Course of Study since 1636* (San Francisco: Jossey-Bass, 1977), 25–53; Norman Fiering, *Moral Philosophy at Seventeenth-Century Harvard* (Chapel Hill: University of North Carolina Press, 1981); Thomas Jay Siegel, "Governance and Curriculum at Harvard College in the 18th Century" (Ph.D. thesis, Harvard University, 1990); Margery Somers Foster, *"Out of Smalle Beginnings . . .": An Economic History of Harvard College in the Puritan Period* (Cambridge, Mass.: Harvard University Press, 1962); and Seymour E. Harris, *Economics of Harvard* (New York: McGraw-Hill, 1970). For works that do consider student life, see, for example, Sheldon S. Cohen, "The Turkish Tyranny," *New England Quarterly* 47 (1974): 569–83; Conrad Edick Wright, *Revolutionary Generation: Harvard Men and the Consequences of Independence* (Amherst: University of Massachusetts Press, 2005), 30–58; Helen Lefkowitz Horowitz, *Campus Life: Undergraduate Cultures from the End of the Eighteenth Century to the Present* (New York: Knopf, 1987); J. Lloyd Winstead, *When Colleges Sang: The Story of Singing in American College Life* (Tuscaloosa: University of Alabama Press, 2013), 1–50; and Roger L. Geiger, *The History of American Higher Education: Learning and Culture from the Founding to World War II* (Princeton, N.J.: Princeton University Press, 2015), 76–87.

5. Winfred E. A. Bernhard, *Fisher Ames, Federalist and Statesman, 1758–1808* (Chapel Hill: University of North Carolina Press, 1965), 20–29; Robert Ernst, *Rufus King, Federalist* (Chapel Hill: University of North Carolina Press, 1968), 14–20; Joshua Kendall, *The Forgotten Founding Father: Noah Webster's Obsession and the Creation of American Culture* (New York: G. P. Putnam's Sons, 2010), 23–35.

6. John Langdon Sibley et al., *Biographical Sketches of Graduates of Harvard University* [hereafter *Sibley's Harvard Graduates*] (Cambridge, Mass., and Boston, 1873–), 17:207n. Other colonial college diaries are not as revealing as Peabody's, but a number are worth reading. For Harvard, see Samuel Chandler, 1775 Diary and Account Book (photostat), Harvard University Archives, Cambridge, Mass. (excerpts published as S. E. Mulliken, ed., "Harvard on the Eve of the Revolution," *Harvard Graduates' Magazine* 10 (1902): 375–81, 529–35); L. H. Butterfield et al., eds., *The Earliest Diary of John Adams* (Cambridge, Mass.: Harvard University Press, 1966), 43–64; Maurice W. Armstrong, ed., "Diary of Caleb Gannett for the Year 1776," *William and Mary Quarterly*, 3rd ser., 3 (1946): 117–22; George S. Wright, ed., "Diary of Paul Litchfield," *Proceedings of the Massachusetts Historical Society* 9 (1881–82): 376–79; and Frederick Cheever Shattuck, ed., "William Cheever's

Diary, 1775–1776," *Proceedings of the Massachusetts Historical Society* 60 (1926–27): 91–97. For the early republic, see also David Grayson Allen et al., eds., *Diary of John Quincy Adams* (Cambridge, Mass.: Harvard University Press, 1981–), 2:1–266, and Ernest John Knapton, ed., "The Harvard Diary of Pitt Clarke, 1786–1791," *Publications of the Colonial Society of Massachusetts* 59 (1982): 231–361. For Rhode Island College (Brown), see Solomon Drowne, Journal, 1771–73, Drowne Family Papers, 1728–1936, Brown University Archives, Providence, R.I. A brief but interesting account of Princeton shortly before the Revolution appears in John Rogers Williams, ed., *Philip Vickers Fithian, Journal and Letters 1767–1774, Student at Princeton College, 1770–72, Tutor at Nomini Hall in Virginia, 1773–74* (Princeton, N.J.: Princeton University Library, 1900), 1–43; on the college routine, see esp. his letter to his father, Joseph Fithian, Nov. 30, 1770, pp. 6–10.

7. Selim Hobart Peabody, comp., and Charles Henry Pope, ed., *Peabody [Paybody, Pabody, Pabodie] Genealogy* [hereafter *Peabody Genealogy*] (Boston: Charles H. Pope, 1909), 25; Sarah Loring Bailey, *Historical Sketches of Andover* (Boston, 1880), 160.

8. Bailey, *Historical Sketches of Andover*, 160n.

9. *Peabody Genealogy*, 20, 25.

10. *Sibley's Harvard Graduates*, 17:207; John W. Ragle, *Governor Dummer Academy History* (South Byfield, Mass.: Governor Dummer Academy, 1963), 3–27; *Catalogue of the Officers and Students of Dummer Academy* (Salem, Mass., 1844), 18.

11. Clifford K. Shipton, "Ye Mystery of Ye Ages Solved; or, How Placing Worked at Colonial Harvard and Yale," *Harvard Alumni Bulletin*, Dec. 11, 1954, 256–59, 262–63; *Sibley's Harvard Graduates*, 17:114–15.

12. *Sibley's Harvard Graduates*, 16:440–41; 17:2–3, 114–15, 332–33, 466–67.

13. On the bad butter protest, see William C. Lane, "The Rebellion of 1766 in Harvard College," *Publications of the Colonial Society of Massachusetts* 10 (1908): 33–59, and *Sibley's Harvard Graduates*, 17:207.

14. This section draws its account of Harvard throughout from Wright, *Revolutionary Generation*, 30–58.

15. Conrad Wright, *The Beginnings of Unitarianism in America* (Boston: Beacon Press, 1955), 40–41, 57, 64, 136–37; Edwin Scott Gaustad, *The Great Awakening in New England* (New York: Harper, 1957), 32.

16. Wright, *Beginnings of Unitarianism*.

17. *Sibley's Harvard Graduates*, 16:439–552; 17:passim.

18. *Sibley's Harvard Graduates*, 5:265–78.

19. *Sibley's Harvard Graduates*, 9:240–64, 12:507–17, 15:107–14; Siegel, "Governance and Curriculum," 260–61.

20. *Sibley's Harvard Graduates*, 15:112–13.

21. *Sibley's Harvard Graduates*, 8:137–40; 15:217–20, 224–29, 492–93; 16:253–65.

22. *Sibley's Harvard Graduates*, 15:80–82.

23. On June 5, 1767, the faculty voted to meet every Tuesday and Friday at noon. Faculty Records, 3:46, Harvard University Archives.

24. *Sibley's Harvard Graduates*, 8:720–23, 16:250–51; Corporation Records, 2:277, 295, Harvard University Archives.

25. *Sibley's Harvard Graduates*, 5:599–609; 7:10–23. On the relationship between Harvard and Cambridge, see John D. Burton, "Puritan Town and Gown: Harvard College and Cambridge, Massachusetts, 1636–1800" (Ph.D. diss., College of William and Mary, 1996).

26. See appendix 2.

27. Wright, *Revolutionary Generation*, 42.

28. Israel Keith to Zephaniah Keith, Sept. 11, 1767, Keith Papers, Massachusetts Historical Society, Boston.

29. July 5, 1767.

30. Evarts B. Greene and Virginia D. Harrington, *American Population before the Federal Census of 1790* (New York: Columbia University Press, 1932), 22, 24.

31. November 21, 23, 26, 1767.

32. See, for instance, Sumner Chilton Powell, *Puritan Village: The Formation of a New England Town* (Garden City, N.Y.: Anchor Books, 1965); Kenneth A. Lockridge, *A New England Town: The First Hundred Years: Dedham, Massachusetts, 1636–1736* (New York: Norton, 1970); John Demos, *A Little Commonwealth: Family Life in Plymouth Colony* (New York: Oxford University Press, 1970); and Philip J. Greven, *Four Generations: Population, Land, and Family in Colonial Andover, Massachusetts* (Ithaca, N.Y.: Cornell University Press, 1970).

33. Greene and Harrington, *American Population*, 23–33.

34. Before the student strike, Peabody did attend the North Parish when Symmes was preaching on June 14 and September 13, 1767.

35. *Vital Records of Newbury, Massachusetts, to the End of the Year 1849* (Salem, Mass., 1911), 1:218, 404, 405; 2:226.

36. May 12, 1768. James Head, whom Peabody visited in Bradford on July 17, 1767, may also have been a maternal relation.

37. *Peabody Genealogy*, 20, 23–25.

38. The members of the Association for the Suppression of Vice were seniors Lemuel Cushing, Joseph Farrar, Jonathan Frost, Samuel Hancock, Moses Holt, William Mayhew, Nathaniel Merrill, Isaac Smith; juniors William Keous, Kenneth McKenzie, David Tenny; and sophomores William Bowers, Benjamin Bradshaw, Moses Dow, Elijah Fletcher, David Jewett, Alexander Scammell, and Peabody. Of this group, Peabody never mentioned six, and only Bowers, Jewett, Scammell, and Tenny appeared often enough to be considered intimate friends. All of these friends but Scammell were from within a day's ride from Andover, and both Tenny and Jewett attended Dummer Academy. Articles of an Association for the Suppression of Vice, College Papers, 2:22, Harvard University Archives.

39. Wright, *Revolutionary Generation*, 50.

40. March 9, 1768.

41. Peabody used the term "Sons of Liberty" twice—on March 8 and March 23, 1768.

42. Despite some minor factual errors, the most reliable work on the student upheavals of 1768 is Cohen, "Turkish Tyranny," 554–83. Clifford K. Shipton's account of Peabody's college years in *Sibley's Harvard Graduates* shows signs of his own biases as a Harvard administrator—the university archivist—writing in the early 1970s in the wake of the serious student upheavals of the Vietnam era. Convinced that Peabody was merely a troublemaker, Shipton dismissed the concerns of the students, took the faculty's side without reservation, did not exercise even modest skepticism in his use of student depositions critical of Peabody, and confused chronology, including the timing of Peabody's entrance into the Association for the Suppression of Vice. Shipton's portrait of Peabody in his later years shows him as mild and benign, a characterization completely inconsistent with his picture of Peabody during the spring of his junior year. *Sibley's Harvard Graduates*, 17:207–17.

43. Records of the Faculty Relating to Disorders, 1768–ca. 1880s, Student Disorders, 1768, no. 37, Harvard University Archives.

44. April 23, 1768.

45. See appendix 2. Note that most of Peabody's interactions with the other supposed ringleaders, especially Tudor and Varnum, came after the outbreak of the student strike.

46. May 5, 9, 1768.

47. *Sibley's Harvard Graduates*, 17:266.

48. Peabody tried to meet with Manning again on May 16 to talk further about transferring, but they failed to make connections.

49. April 16, 18, 23, 26; May 6, 7, 11, 12, 20, 1768.

50. John Hancock to Stephen Sewall, May 31, 1768, John Hancock Collection, 1754–92, Harvard University Archives, quoted in *Sibley's Harvard Graduates*, 17:117; Morison, *Three Centuries of Harvard*, 133.

51. Corporation Records, 2:228, Harvard University Archives; Wright, *Revolutionary Generation*, 54.

52. *Quinquennial Catalogue of the Officers and Graduates of Harvard University, 1636–1905* (Cambridge, Mass.: Harvard University, 1905), 131–32; *Sibley's Harvard Graduates*, 17:209–11.

53. *Sibley's Harvard Graduates*, 17:212; *Peabody Genealogy*, 138.

54. *Sibley's Harvard Graduates*, 17:190–207, 237–47, 219–32.

55. *Sibley's Harvard Graduates*, 17:593–605.

56. *Sibley's Harvard Graduates*, 17:214–15.

57. Samuel Gilman, *Contributions in Literature* (Boston, 1856), 190–230; quotations pp. 191–92, 201, 199, 200.

58. *Sibley's Harvard Graduates*, 17:217.

Short Titles of Works Frequently Cited

Andover Tax Assessments
Massachusetts Vital Records: Andover Tax Assessments, 1765–1774, microfilm, Memorial Library, Andover, Mass.

Arithmetick Vulgar and Decimal
[Isaac Greenwood], *Arithmetick Vulgar and Decimal* (Boston, 1729).

Bailey, *Historical Sketches of Andover*
Sarah Loring Bailey, *Historical Sketches of Andover* (Boston, 1880).

Barker, *Barker Genealogy*
Elizabeth Frye Barker, *Barker Genealogy* (New York: Frye, 1927).

Baumgarten, "Clothes for the People"
Linda Baumgarten, "'Clothes for the People': Slave Clothing in Early Virginia," *Journal of Early Southern Decorative Arts* 14 (1988): 27–61.

Bell, *History of the Town of Exeter*
Charles H. Bell, *History of the Town of Exeter, New Hampshire* (Exeter, N.H., 1888).

Bond, *Early Settlers of Watertown*
Henry Bond, *Family Memorials: Genealogies of the Families and Early Settlers of Watertown* (Boston, 1855).

Bond and Amory, *Printed Catalogues*
W. H. Bond and Hugh Amory, *The Printed Catalogues of the Harvard College Library, 1723–1790* (Boston: Colonial Society of Massachusetts, 1996).

Boxford Single Tax List, 1767
Tax and Valuation Lists of Massachusetts Towns before 1776, microfilm edn. (Cambridge, Mass.: Charles Warren Center, Harvard University, 1971), reel 7, Boxford.

Chase, *History of Haverhill*
George Wingate Chase, *History of Haverhill* (Haverhill, Mass., 1861).

"College Laws and Customs"
"College Laws and Customs: College Laws of 1767," *Publications of the Colonial Society of Massachusetts* 35 (1935): 347–83.

Corporation Records

Corporation Records, Harvard University Archives, Cambridge, Mass.

Currier, *History of Newburyport*

John J. Currier, *History of Newburyport, Mass.* (Newburyport, Mass.: The Author, 1906–9).

Descendants of George Abbot

A Genealogical Register of the Descendants of George Abbot of Andover (Boston, 1847).

Descendants of John and Joan Chadwick

Notes on Descendants of John and Joan Chadwick and Related Families, comp. Austin D. Kilham (Charlottesville, Va.: Bailey, 1966).

"Descendants of John Webster"

"Collection of Descendants of John Webster and His Wife Mary Shatswell of Ipswich, Mass.," comp. Henrietta Dolloff Johnson and George O. F. Caleff, typescript, 1932, New England Historic Genealogical Society, Boston.

Descendants of Thomas Hale

Robert Safford Hale, *Descendants of Thomas Hale of Watton, England, and Newbury, Mass.,* ed. George R. Howell (Albany, N.Y., 1889).

DNB

Dictionary of National Biography (London: Smith, Elder, 1908–9).

Endicott, "Peabody Family"

C. M. Endicott, "The Peabody Family," *New England Historical and Genealogical Register* 2 (1848): 153–61, 361–72.

Essex County Probate Files

Essex County Court House, Probate Court, Salem, Mass.

Essex County Probate Index

Essex County, Massachusetts, Probate Index, 1638–1840, trans. Melissa Lutz Sanborn, from the original by W. P. Upham (Boston: M. L. Sanborn, 1987).

Estes, "Therapeutic Practice"

J. Worth Estes, "Therapeutic Practice in Colonial New England," *Publications of the Colonial Society of Massachusetts* 57 (1980): 289–383.

Faculty Records

Faculty Records, Harvard University Archives, Cambridge, Mass.

Gozzaldi, *Supplement to Paige*

Mary Isabella Gozzaldi, *Supplement and Index to Paige, History of Cambridge* (Cambridge, Mass.: Cambridge Historical Society, 1930).

Greene and Harrington, *American Population*

Evarts B. Greene and Virginia D. Harrington, *American Population before the Federal Census of 1790* (New York: Columbia University Press, 1932).

Hovey Book

The Hovey Book (Haverhill, Mass.: L. R. Hovey, 1913).

Ingalls Family
Charles Burleigh, *The Genealogy and History of the Ingalls Family* (Malden, Mass.: Geo. E. Dunbar, 1903).

Kelley, *Wilmington Records*
James E. Kelley, *Wilmington Records of Births, Marriages and Deaths . . . 1898* (Lowell, Mass., 1898).

Kingsbury, *Memorial History of Bradford*
J. D. Kingsbury, *Memorial History of Bradford, Mass.* (Haverhill, Mass., 1883).

McCusker, *Money and Exchange*
John J. McCusker, *Money and Exchange in Europe and America, 1660–1775: A Handbook* (Chapel Hill: University of North Carolina Press, 1978).

Moody, *History of the Town of York*
Edward C. Moody, *Handbook History of the Town of York* (Augusta, Maine: York, 1914).

Morison, *Three Centuries of Harvard*
Samuel Eliot Morison, *Three Centuries of Harvard* (Cambridge, Mass.: Harvard University Press, 1936).

Morrison and Sharples, *Kimball Family*
Leonard Allison Morrison and Stephen Paschall Sharples, *History of the Kimball Family in America* (Boston, 1897).

NEHGR
New England Historical and Genealogical Register.

Noyes, *Noyes Descendants*
Harriette E. Noyes, *Genealogical Record of Some of the Noyes Descendants of John, Nicholas, and Peter Noyes* (Boston: N.p., 1904).

Officers and Students of Dummer Academy
Catalogue of the Officers and Students of Dummer Academy (Salem, Mass., 1844).

Osgood, *Descendants of . . . Osgood*
Ira Osgood, comp., *A Genealogy of the Descendants of John, Christopher, and William Osgood* (Salem, Mass., 1894).

Paige, *History of Cambridge*
Lucius R. Paige, *History of Cambridge, Massachusetts, 1630–1877* (Boston, 1877).

PCSM
Publications of the Colonial Society of Massachusetts.

Peabody Genealogy
Peabody [Paybody, Pabody, Pabodie] Genealogy, comp. Selim Hobart Peabody, ed. Charles Henry Pope (Boston: Charles H. Pope, 1909).

Perley, *History of Boxford*
Sidney Perley, *History of Boxford* (Boxford, Mass., 1880).

Phillips Genealogies
Phillips Genealogies (Auburn, Mass., 1885).

Pierce, *Foster Genealogy*
Frederick Clifton Pierce, *Foster Genealogy* (Chicago, 1899).

Pike, *Family of John Pike*
Allen Raymond Pike, *The Family of John Pike of Newbury, Massachusetts* (Carmel, N.Y.: Penobscot Press, 1995).

Princetonians
Princetonians: A Biographical Dictionary (Princeton, N.J.: Princeton University Press, 1976–91).

Pruitt, *Massachusetts Tax Valuation List*
Bettye Hobbs Pruitt, *The Massachusetts Tax Valuation List of 1771* (Boston: G. K. Hall, 1978).

Schutz, *Massachusetts General Court*
John A. Schutz, *Legislators of the Massachusetts General Court, 1691–1780: A Biographical Dictionary* (Boston: Northeastern University Press, 1997).

Sibley's Harvard Graduates
John Langdon Sibley et al., *Biographical Sketches of Graduates of Harvard University* [and revised titles] (Cambridge, Mass., and Boston, 1873–).

Siegel, "Governance and Curriculum"
Thomas Jay Siegel, "Governance and Curriculum at Harvard College in the 18th Century" (Ph.D. thesis, Harvard University, 1990).

Thomas, *History of Printing*
Isaiah Thomas, *The History of Printing in America,* 2nd edn. (1874; New York: Weathervane Books, 1970).

Tyler, *Smugglers & Patriots*
John W. Tyler, *Smugglers & Patriots: Boston Merchants and the Advent of the American Revolution* (Boston: Northeastern University Press, 1986).

Vital Records of Andover
Vital Records of Andover, Massachusetts, to the End of the Year 1849 (Topsfield, Mass.: Topsfield Historical Society, 1912).

Vital Records of Boxford
Vital Records of Boxford, Massachusetts, to the End of the Year 1849 (Topsfield, Mass.: Topsfield Historical Society, 1905).

Vital Records of Bradford
Vital Records of Bradford, Massachusetts, to the End of the Year 1849 (Topsfield, Mass.: Topsfield Historical Society, 1907).

Vital Records of Cambridge
Vital Records of Cambridge, Massachusetts, to the Year 1850 (Boston: Wright and Potter, 1914–15).

Vital Records of Dracut
Vital Records of Dracut, Massachusetts, to the Year 1850 (Boston: New England Historic Genealogical Society, 1907).

Vital Records of Methuen
Vital Records of Methuen, Massachusetts, to the End of the Year 1849 (Topsfield, Mass.: Topsfield Historical Society, 1909).

Vital Records of Newbury
Vital Records of Newbury, Massachusetts, to the End of the Year 1849 (Salem, Mass.: Essex Institute, 1911).

Vital Records of Rowley
Vital Records of Rowley, Massachusetts, to the End of the Year 1849 (Salem, Mass.: Essex Institute, 1928).

Weis, *Colonial Clergy*
Frederick Lewis Weis, *The Colonial Clergy and Colonial Churches of New England* (Lancaster, Mass.: Society of the Descendants of Colonial Clergy, 1936).

Worthley, "Inventory"
Harold Field Worthley, "An Inventory of the Particular (Congregational) Churches of Massachusetts Gathered 1620–1805," *Proceedings of the Unitarian Historical Society* 16 (1966–1969). Also published as *Harvard Theological Studies* 25 (1970).

Wright, *Beginnings of Unitarianism*
Conrad Wright, *The Beginnings of Unitarianism in America* (Boston: Beacon Press, 1955).

Wright, *Revolutionary Generation*
Conrad Edick Wright, *Revolutionary Generation: Harvard Men and the Consequences of Independence* (Amherst: University of Massachusetts Press, 2005).

PEDAGOGUES AND PROTESTERS

May 1767

Cambridge the 24th of May 17[67].

As the Day that I begin th[ese] Transactions of the ensuing yea[r] [of] the Lords, may I be excited to [be] in a continual Preparation for my exit into the other World, that [I] may be received to keep an everlasting Sabbath of Rest with God in his kingdom above.

I attended Prayers, & then went to Meeting & heard Mr. Appleton expound from the 1 of John 4th Chapt. & the 4 first Verses. P.M. he preach'd from the 15 of Proverbs 2V. I read to Day in Mr. Harvey's Contemplations on the Starry Heavens.

Stephen Peabody appropriately began this, his first known journal volume, on a Sunday with a prayer. A farmer from an agricultural family, he had received a call to the ministry several years before in his early twenties. His decision to attend college followed inevitably from his determination to seek ordination because New England Congregationalists expected their clergy to have a liberal education. Throughout the year this volume covers, he regularly devoted Sundays to worship and religious reading. Nathaniel APPLETON (1693–1784), A.B. 1712, was the minister of the First Church in Cambridge from 1717 to 1784. Rev. James HERVEY (1714–58), an Anglican devotional writer, was the author of two volumes of *Meditations and Contemplations,* including "CONTEMPLATIONS ON A STARRY NIGHT," in volume 2, first published in 1747. *Sibley's Harvard Graduates,* 5:599–609.

Monday the 25th of May.

To Day is very Pleasant. I attend[ed] Prayers & reciting to Mr. Hancock in Mane,[1] & then Tenny & I got leave to go out of Town. We got a Horse &

Chaise & went down over Charleston Ferry & through Boston, & did a little Business, & so up to Brookline to one Dana's a Relation to Tenny but he was not at Home so we made no stop but proceeded up to Waterton where we din'd at the Tavern. After some stop there we went to see Sr. [Bo]nd at his School-House. Sr. Bowman was there. We stop'd till [scho]ol was done & then went to Mr. [Fo]wles with Boman to see his Wife [and] Child. We made but little stop there but went with Bond to one Beemas's where he Bords, & stay'd till Evening. We drank Tea there & was treated very handsomly. We took a walk to a spring over the River where People go to get cured of their Diseases, & they have got very fine conveniences for drinking & Bathing.

We come back & took leave of Sr. Bond & Sr. Bowman came down to Cambridge with us in the Chaise. We had our Horse & Chaise home & then took our repose.

I got some Tobacco at Charleston for Mr. Hancock & carry'd it to him, & he said it was well & that I might stay out from reciting crass Mane.[2]

Classes at Harvard College were a combination of recitations, which the tutors, or junior faculty, conducted, and lectures by the professors. Although completing his twenty-fifth and final year on the faculty, Belcher HANCOCK (1709–71), A.B. 1727, remained a tutor. Peabody rarely left Cambridge on a class day; his visit to Brookline was the only one he would make there during the course of the year. David TENNY (1749–78), A.B. 1768, a close friend, was from Rowley and had attended Dummer Academy with Peabody. He became the minister of the First Church in Barrington, New Hampshire. DANA was Tenny's cousin George Dana of Brookline. Nathaniel BOND (1747–77), A.B. 1766, was a schoolteacher in Watertown following his recent graduation; the honorific "SIR" (abbreviated Sr.) indicated that Bond had received his bachelor's but not his master's degree. Joshua BOWMAN (1747–80), A.B. 1766, was preparing to move to North Carolina, which he did in June. His CHILD was his son Nathaniel (d. 1797), A.B. 1786. Edmund FOWLE was a cordwainer in Watertown. Bowman had married Fowle's daughter Abigail in April. Latin was a prerequisite for admission, but nowhere in this diary is there an indication that Peabody had mastered the tongue. His use of only short phrases such as IN MANE and CRASS MANE in this entry and throughout the journal reveals him to be a fledgling Latinist testing his wings. *Sibley's Harvard Graduates,* 8:137–40, 17:94, 16:325–26, 328; George Chandler, comp., *Chandler Family* (Worcester, Mass., 1883), 104–7, 209–10; Pruitt, *Massachusetts Tax Valuation List,* 488–89; Bond, *Early Settlers of Watertown,* 1:225–26.

1. In the morning.
2. Tomorrow morning.

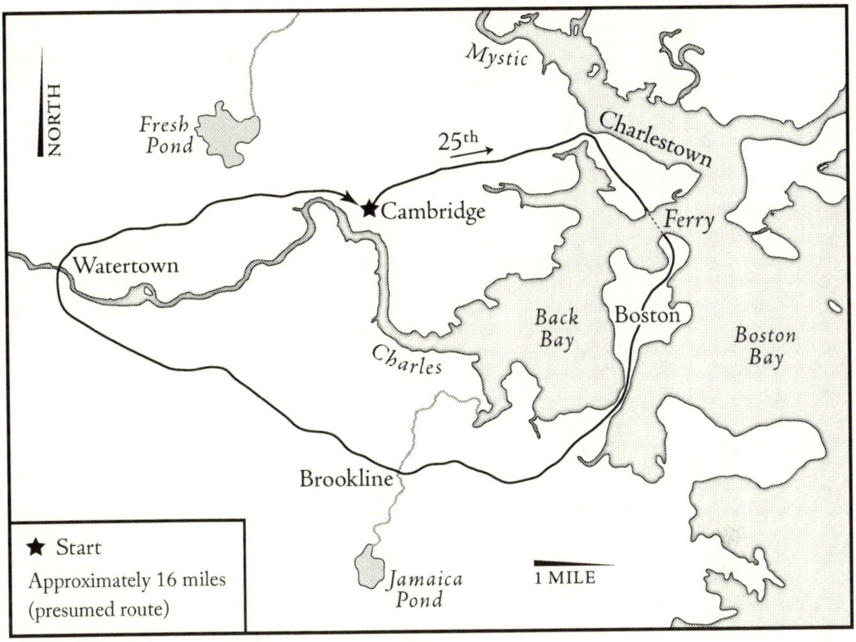

Peabody's Trip to Watertown, May 25, 1767.

Tuesday the 26th of May.

To Day is pleasant but toward Night there is a Shower. I attended Prayers & reciting. Made me a Journal & wrote some in it, & just at Night Ebenezer Webster, Lieut. Mulliken, Reuben Carlton & his Br. came here from Bradford. I went with them to Decn Prentices & got their Horses & then they came to my Chamber [. . .][1] the Evening & we had a little Fode of Bred & Chease & Bottled syder.

Adducerunt duas Epistalas Mihi a me[is] Amicis.[2] They bring no News only that Colo. Osgood is published to Huldah Frye.

The Carltons went & lodg'd at Decn. Prentices & I went [to] Warlands with Webster & Mulliken where they lodg'd. I came to my Chamber & wrote a little.

This entry identifies May 26 as the day Peabody actually began his JOURNAL. The two previous entries must have been retrospective. Although he was more than twenty miles from home when he was in residence at school, Stephen remained in frequent contact with his family and neighbors. EBENEZER WEBSTER

(1724–68) lived and farmed in Haverhill within a few miles of the Peabody family farm in Andover's North Parish, now the town of North Andover. His companions included Lt. Amos MULLIKEN and RUBEN CARLETON (1732–1818). Both men were from Bradford, immediately to the northeast of Andover. Carleton's BROTHER was either of two siblings, Benjamin (1745–1835) or Joseph (1748–1831). Both were farmers in Bradford. Henry PRENTICE (1693–1778), farmer and brickmaker, was deacon of the First Church in Cambridge, 1741–78. Col. John OSGOOD and HULDAH FRYE (b. 1737), who had announced their engagement, were from Andover. WARLAND was Owen Warland (1723–93) of Cambridge, a tailor. *Vital Records of Bradford,* 30–31, 164, 369, 121, 32, 300–301; Perley, *History of Boxford,* 59; Essex County Probate Files, nos. 4611, 4660; *Historical Data Relating to the Counties, Cities and Towns in Massachusetts* (Boston: Commonwealth of Massachusetts, 1966), 76; Paige, *History of Cambridge,* 629–31, 677; *Vital Records of Andover,* 2:256, 1:161.

1. Torn [one word].
2. They brought me two letters from my friends.

Wednesday the 27th of May.

To Day it is cool but very Pleasant & it is Election Day. My Company came & drank some Egg Rum with me in Mane & took a view of the Colleges & then Breakfast where they lodg'd. I went to Colo. Brattles with Webster. He wanted the Colo's Advise concerning his drinking of this spring Water, & he advises him to, & thinks it may do him good.

After Breakfast I got a Chaise at Bradishes & Webster put his Horse into it & my Chum & he & I rode to Charleston with the rest of the Company. We went over to Boston & I went to Meeting & heard Mr. Bridge preach a Sermon from the 33d of Deuteronomy & the 29th Verse. I din'd at Mr. Gridlees. I did a little business in Town & saw the Cadets exercised & they look exceedingly neat.

[. . .][1] met at Doctr. Scotts, & so came [ove]r the Ferry & up to Cambridge [. . .][2] at Night.

The Carltons went [fro]m Boston up to Lynn to a Relation of theirs, but Webster & Mulliken spent the Evening with me & lodg'd in Town. We put the horses up at John Hastings's & did not carry Home Bradishes Chaise for we are going to use it in Mane.

ELECTION DAY, the most important public event each spring in colonial Massachusetts, was the opening of the legislative session. Representatives gathered from across the province, presented their credentials, heard an address by the royal governor, were seated as members of the General Court, and then voted for the speaker and clerk of the House as well as for the members of the Governor's Council. Following these formalities, a clergyman chosen for the occasion delivered the annual Election SERMON, which traditionally included a discussion of the responsibilities of public officeholders. In 1767, Rev. Ebenezer BRIDGE (1716–92), A.B. 1736, of Chelmsford preached the sermon. Col. (later Gen.) William BRATTLE (1706–76), A.B. 1722, was a lawyer in Cambridge and one of the town's leading citizens. BRADISH was either Isaac Bradish of Cambridge, a blacksmith, or Ebenezer Bradish, the proprietor of the town's Blue Anchor Tavern. "CHUM" was not a familiar term for friend but more specifically a roommate. Evidence in this diary indicates that Peabody's "chum" in 1766–67 was Jacob Jewett (1747–1812), A.B. 1769, of Rowley. GRIDLEY belonged to an important Boston family, the most prominent of whose members, provincial attorney general Jeremiah Gridley, died later in 1767. Members of the Gridley family appear on many occasions in these pages, but Peabody does not offer enough clues to decode his cryptic references. The Company of CADETS was drilling for the observance of the birthday of King George III on June 4. Dr. Daniel SCOTT owned an apothecary shop. HASTINGS was probably John Hastings (1720–97), a brother of Jonathan Hastings, the college steward. Schutz, *Massachusetts General Court,* 9; *Sibley's Harvard Graduates,* 10:17–27, 7:10–23, 18:225, 17:126, 170, and below, January 20, 1768, where Peabody's by-now former roommate is identified as from Rowley, Jacob Jewett's hometown; Paige, *History of Cambridge,* 575; *Boston Gazette,* June 8, May 5, 1767, Jan. 7, Nov. 22, 1771.

1. Torn [one word].
2. Torn [one word].

Thursday the 28th of May.

To Day very pleasant & Mulliken, Webster & Chadwick set of with me a little after sun rise up to Waterton Spring. We drank of the Water & vomited a little & stay'd there some Time & there was some Company there & Sr. Bond amongst the rest. We came down to College again & Chadwick had Home the Chaise & we went & Breakfasted at Warland's, & they insisted upon paying for the Provision they had there & did. We came up to College & they stay'd but little while & took leave & set of on their Journey. Mittebam duas Epistolas ad meos Amicos.[1] We had no reciting to Day, but I wrote a little. Sr. Searl was here to Day & is going to Brookline to return tomorrow Morning. I received a letter from Bright to Day.

The pace of academic life at colonial Harvard was often languid, at least by later standards, as it was on this day, allowing Peabody to make another outing to take the spring waters. Humoral medical doctrines emphasized the importance of a balance among the four bodily fluids—blood, phlegm, choler, and black bile. Peabody and his friends VOMITED intentionally to restore bodily equilibrium. Benjamin CHADWICK (1745–1819), A.B. 1770, was from Boxford, adjacent to Andover, and had attended Dummer Academy. He eventually became the minister of the Second Parish in Scarborough, Maine. SEARLE was Jonathan Searle (1744–1812), A.B. 1764, who kept school for a time in Brookline. He later became the minister of the First Church in Mason, New Hampshire. He was originally from Rowley, not far from Andover, and was preparing for ordination. Henry BRIGHT (1744–74), A.B. 1770, entered Harvard with the class of 1769, but in March 1767, "he was rusticated for his part in keeping a woman in a college chamber." Bright won readmission in March 1768. Following graduation, Bright taught school in Watertown but died before settling on a career. *Sibley's Harvard Graduates,* 17:367–68; 16:90–92; 17:339.

1. I sent two letters to my friends.

Friday the 29th of May.

To Day is some rainy but P.M. it clears of. We had no reciting & I attended Prayers as Usual. I wrote a letter to Adams & sent it by Sr. Searl who was at my Chamber A.M. then I wrote some in Journal & after Commons I went up to Parsons's Chamber & Tenny, Thatcher & I desided a Case between Knowles & Parsons which was left out for a Bowl of Punch, & after hearing their Stories we desided it in Parsons's Favor. Nothing strange more to Day.

Peabody's role in adjudicating the dispute between Isaac KNOWLES (1741–1818), A.B. 1768, of Eastham, and probably Theophilus PARSONS (1750–1813), A.B. 1769, but possibly Obadiah PARSONS (1747–1801), A.B. 1768, both of Newbury and graduates of Dummer Academy, reflected the respect his fellow students accorded him. More mature than most of his classmates, he seemed to be an older brother to many of them. After college, Knowles became a trader, Theophilus Parsons a lawyer, and Obadiah Parsons a minister. Peter THACHER (1752–1802), A.B. 1769, was from Boston and had prepared for Harvard at Boston Latin School. He became a prominent minister in Malden and Boston. Joseph ADAMS (1749–68), a classmate of Peabody's at Dummer Academy as well as at Harvard, had returned home to Rowley on account of poor health. His illness, which ended in his death, is a continuing theme of this journal. *Sibley's Harvard Graduates,* 17:56–57, 78–82, 190–207, 237–47, 115–16.

Saturday the 30th of May.

To Day I attended Prayers & reciting as usual, wrote two Letters to Byfield, one to Judith Noyes, & one to Doctr. Kitridge, & I wrote one Letter to Sr. Pike at York & am going to send them to Bowmans, to send by Sr. Bond who is going eastward Monday.

I studied some in Xnophon & attended the private Meeting at Hitchbourns Chamber.

Willard sent for me after Prayers to enquire who made Distourbance & I very freely told him & he sent for them all.

Tenny & I went up to Bowman's after Dinner, & he spoke to me about taking a ride with him on Monday which I promised though with reluctance.

Saturday was a class day at colonial Harvard. During term time, Peabody spent most Saturday evenings at the PRIVATE MEETING of the Association for the Suppression of Vice. His encounter with tutor Joseph WILLARD following the prayer circle was the first of many such meetings recorded in this journal. Among the oldest of the undergraduates, Peabody seemed to identify with the faculty as much as with the students. Tutors often turned to him when there were disturbances, and he felt no compunctions about tattling on his schoolmates. JUDITH NOYES (1739–1816) was a sister of John Noyes (1750–1819), A.B. 1771, of Newbury. Dr. John KITTREDGE set up his practice in the North Precinct of Andover about 1741. Nicholas PIKE (1743–1819), A.B. 1766, was teaching school in York, Maine. He spent his career as a teacher and writer of arithmetic texts. XENOPHON (c. 430–357 BC) was a Greek general, disciple of Socrates, and writer. Harvard students read his *Cyropædia,* a biography of King Cyrus the Great of Persia, which also drew moral lessons and was highly regarded in educated circles in the eighteenth century. Benjamin HICHBORN (1746–1817), A.B. 1768, was from Boston. He became a lawyer. Joseph WILLARD (1738–1804), A.B. 1765, later served as president of Harvard College, 1781–1804. "College Laws and Customs," 353; Articles of Association for the Suppression of Vice, College Records, 2:22, Harvard University Archives, Cambridge, Mass.; *Sibley's Harvard Graduates,* 16:406–9, 17:36–44, 16:253–65; Noyes, *Noyes Descendants,* 1:61; Bailey, *Historical Sketches of Andover,* 157–58.

Sunday the 31 of May.

To Day is pleasant. I attended Prayers, went to Meeting & heard [o]ne Mr. Hemingway preach two sermons from the 26th Psalm & the 9th Verse. I wrote to Day for Tayler, & finish'd reading Harvey.

I receiv'd a letter from Sr. Pike to Day, which give Sargeant a very bad Caracter, which he had heard.

Congregationalist ministers frequently exchanged pulpits or otherwise filled in for one another on Sundays. In so doing, they reduced the number of sermons each had to prepare, since they ordinarily used ones they had already preached successfully to their own congregations. The practice also allowed parishioners to hear voices other than that of their own minister. This Sunday's preacher in Cambridge was Moses HEMMENWAY (1735–1811), A.B. 1755, the minister of the First Congregational Church of Wells, Maine. Hezekiah TAYLOR (1748–1814), A.B. 1770, was from Grafton, Massachusetts. He became the minister of the First Church in Newfane, Vermont. Winthrop SARGENT (1753–1820), A.B. 1771, may have owed his bad character, at least in Peabody's eyes, to religious heterodoxy. A little more than a decade after this entry, in 1779, Sargent's family played a leading role in the establishment of the first Universalist church in America in their hometown, Gloucester. Sargent had a distinguished career in military and government service, including the governorship of the Mississippi Territory. *Sibley's Harvard Graduates,* 13:609–18, 17:440–42, 614–26.

June 1767

Monday the 1 of June.

To Day it is very pleasant. I attended Prayers & reciting Xnophon A.M. to Mr. Willard. P.M. I got leave to go out of Town. I wrote two Letters Home, one to my Father, & one to Br. Oliver, & carry'd them down to Bradishes for Cobb to carry, & then went on to the Common & Mr. Bowman came along with a Chare and carry'd me up to Waterton with him & one Watson to Mr. Fowles's, to see if Watson and I could not be a Means of reconciling Bowman & Fowl respecting some Difficulties they have had concerning their Son and Daughter's marrying, but Fowl was going away & would say nor do nothing about it, & after some Jaw Bowman warn'd him not to entertain them any longer upon his Cost, before us two Witnesses, & so we came of & did not go in to the House.

I went up to Mr. Bowman's home & eat and drank & there was Garls there, & Tenny also trad[i] Epistolam ad Hannah,[1] & we did some set Dances & then I came to my Chamber & wrote a little, & came at what I heard Fowle say to writing.

Stephen Peabody's family worked a farm on the Andover side of the boundary with Boxford. His FATHER was John Peabody (1695–1780); OLIVER Peabody (1725–96), a farmer, was the second of Stephen's nine siblings. David COBB (1748–1830), A.B. 1766, who entered Harvard from Taunton and became a doctor there, was reading medicine in 1767 with Dr. Joseph Osgood of Andover. MR. BOWMAN was Noah Bowman of Cambridge, father of Joshua. HANNAH was Noah Bowman's daughter. A CHARE, or chair, was a light vehicle drawn by one horse. The SET DANCES Peabody enjoyed were country dances resembling contra or square dances. Endicott, "Peabody Family," 159; *Sibley's Harvard Graduates,* 18:275, 16:328, 337–51; Bond, *Early Settlers of Watertown,* 1:226; Joyce Van Cleef and

Kate van Winkle Keller, "Selected American Country Dances and Their English Sources," *PCSM* 53 (1980): 3–73.

1. I delivered a letter to Hannah.

Tuesday the 2d of June.

Today is Worm & Pleasant. I attended Prayers & reciting Xnophon & Greek Testiment as Usual. After Prayers I studied Xnophon some but Sr. Bowman came here & spent the Evening. I read the News to Day.

The *Boston NEWS-Letter,* published between 1704 and 1776, was the oldest surviving periodical in the American colonies in 1767. It was subsidized by the provincial government, which it supported in its editorial policy. Edward Connery Latham, comp., *Chronological Tables of American Newspapers, 1690–1820* (Worcester, Mass.: American Antiquarian Society, 1972), 2, 10; Thomas, *History of Printing,* 144.

Wednesday the 3d of June.

To Day is Hot. I attended Prayers and reciting as Usual. After Prayers I went to Scammels Chamber where there was some Company & had a sing. After that went to Tenny's Chamber & Sr. Bowman was there & spent the Evening.

Singing, a mark of gentility, was one of the students' favorite forms of entertainment. Over the course of the year this volume covers, Peabody took part in a SING more than sixty times. None of his daily entries specifies what music was performed. Although it is possible that some selections were devotional, almost all of the occasions Peabody reported took place outside of religious services. Ballads and other secular songs were the common fare at such times—as John Quincy Adams (1767–1848), A.B. 1787, later described them, "good, jovial, expressive songs such as we sang at College, 'when mirth and jollity prevail'd.'" Alexander SCAMMELL (1747–81), A.B. 1769, who hosted the evening's gathering, was from Mendon. A colonel in the Continental Army during the American Revolution, he died on October 6, 1781, one of the last casualties at the Battle of Yorktown. Carl Bridenbaugh, *Cities in Revolt: Urban Life in America, 1743–1776* (New York: Knopf, 1955), 191–92, 399; John Quincy Adams quoted in Cynthia Adams Hoover, "Epilogue to Secular Music in Early Massachusetts," *PCSM* 54 (1985): 771; *Sibley's Harvard Graduates,* 17:219–32.

Thursday the 4th.

To Day Hot Wind S.W. I attended Prayers & went in to reciting in Mane & Barns call'd me out, & then Willard went out of Town so that we did not recite. I went in to the Chappel & heard the Juniors have a forensick Dispute, & then wrote some. After Prayers I took a Walk to the River [sa]w them swim, & then came back to [. . .][1] Church & there was one Barrold [fro]m Boston there playing upon the Orgains & we went in & heard him [&] he play'd very neat.

I took a Walk towards Menotomy with Tenny. Lit of[2] Sr. Bowman with some Puiles[3] & we Walk'd as far as Waltons where we drank & then came Home.

Of all the subjects undergraduates studied in the eighteenth century, rhetoric was the most practical. Whether in the pulpit, the classroom, the courtroom, or the legislature, community leaders needed to be able to speak in public persuasively. FORENSIC DISPUTES such as the one Peabody attended were designed to develop this ability. Debates between two participants on assigned topics, these exercises cultivated a facility in argumentation that many students would draw on often during the course of their careers. Jonathan BARNS (1749–1805), A.B. 1770, was from Marlborough and was considering a clerical career; eventually, he became the minister of the First Congregational Church of Hillsborough, New Hampshire. The ORGAN was presumably the one at Christ CHURCH, the only one in Cambridge in 1767. Christ Church, within sight of Harvard Yard, was the town's Anglican congregation. BARROLD, the organist, has not been identified. MENOTOMY was the rural, western precinct of Cambridge. It later became West Cambridge and is now the town of Arlington. *Sibley's Harvard Graduates,* 17:336–38; Barbara Owen, "Eighteen-Century Organs and Organ Building in New England," *PCSM* 54 (1985): 678. On public speaking in the eighteenth century, see Christopher Grasso, *A Speaking Aristocracy: Transforming Public Discourse in Eighteenth-Century Connecticut* (Chapel Hill: University of North Carolina Press, 1999).

1. Torn [one word].
2. I.e., encountered (local idiom).
3. I.e., puellas—girls.

Friday the 5th of June.

Today very worm. I attended Prayers as Usual, wrote a Letter to Sr. Pike had one came from Bowmans to go with it to him, read some in Spectator, & wrote of my English for tomorrow Morning. After Prayers P.

Wadsworth & I walk'd down to Boston & back again. I deliver'd my Letter to Esq. Sayard to cary to Pike, & saw several of the Representatives, which I knew. I went to Gridlees but they were not at Home. I bought me a Box of Wafers, came over the Ferry, & got up to College at Ten o Clock. I saw Col. Jos. Frye going from Boston as I went down.

I got some sulpher at Doctr. Kneelands to take to drive out the Itch.

Proximity to Boston was one of the advantages of attending Harvard College in the eighteenth century no less than in the twenty-first. Peabody made frequent trips to Boston to do errands and see friends. The *SPECTATOR* was the genteel English periodical, published in 1711–12, by Joseph Addison and Richard Steele. Peleg WADSWORTH (1748–1829), A.B. 1769, was from Duxbury; during the American Revolution he served in the Continental Army, achieving the rank of general. After the war he settled in Portland, Maine, where he engaged in trade. Henry Wadsworth Longfellow was his grandson. Jonathan SAYWARD, merchant, was York, Maine's representative to the General Court, 1765–68. COL. JOSEPH FRYE of Andover owed his military rank to service as an officer during the Seven Years' War. Dr. William KNEELAND (d. 1788) of Cambridge, son-in-law of President Edward Holyoke, frequently treated the ailments of Harvard students. The ITCH, which afflicted Peabody, was scabies, a skin disease caused by parasitic mites. *Sibley's Harvard Graduates,* 17:291–303; Moody, *History of the Town of York,* 104; Bailey, *Historical Sketches of Andover,* 88, 239, 244, 245, 249–50, 257, 260–65, 272, 277, 279; *Vital Records of Cambridge,* 2:630.

Saturday the 6th.

To Day is Hot. I attended Prayers as usual. Wrote a Letter to Bright, read Spectator, & wrote in Journal.

Heard this week from Home by Chadw[ick] who has been up. All well. He brings [news] Jos. Pettengill & Tabathy Frye are marri[ed]. Hear likewise that Sr. Cobb has done his [. . .][1] with Dr. Osgood and is going to live in Boston.

In the Evening we had a fine Shower though with a great deal of Lightning.

Holt went Home on Thursday & I got put out of Commons & wait for the Tutors in his room.

Resident students took their meals in the college COMMONS. In 1767, Elizabeth Hastings, the wife of Jonathan Hastings, A.B. 1730, the college steward or business agent, oversaw the dining service. Much more concerned with controlling costs than providing edible or nutritious food, she produced generations of student protests in addition to meals. Undergraduates could apply to suspend Commons charges when they planned to be away for extended periods. TABITHA FRYE (b. 1746) was the daughter of Joseph and Mehitable Frye. She and Maj. JOSEPH PETTINGILL had at least six children between 1767 and 1781. Dr. Joseph OSGOOD (1718–97), A.B. 1737, practiced medicine in Andover. David COBB was apparently reading medicine with Osgood. Moses HOLT (1744–72), A.B. 1767, was from Andover; after college he became a schoolteacher. *Vital Records of Andover,* 1:163, 300–301; *Sibley's Harvard Graduates,* 10:219–20, 16:485.

1. Torn (but presumably refers to Cobb's medical training) [one word].

Sunday the 7th of June.

To Day is cloudy & worm in the Morning but the Wind came in to the East & it is cool. I went to Meeting & heard Mr. Appleton expound from the 1 of John 4th Chapter from the 5th to the 10th Verse. P.M. he preach'd from the 15th of Job 24th Verse. I wrote to Day for Stebbins & read two Nights in Doctor Young. In the Night it rained again a little.

Gad STEBBINS (1748–1826), A.B. 1771, entered Harvard from Springfield, where he became a physician after graduating from college and serving a medical apprenticeship. Edward YOUNG (1683–1765) was an English author and clergyman. In 1773, the catalogue of the college library reported a four-volume set of Young's works. Peabody was reading Young's multivolume devotional poem *Night Thoughts* (1742, 1745). *Sibley's Harvard Graduates,* 17:633–34; Bond and Amory, *Printed Catalogues,* B27.

Monday the 8th.

This Morning is cloudy but soon clear'd of. Attended Prayers but Mr. Scales was ex opido[1] so we did not recite. I wrote some & read in Spectator, & the News also. Did some Choares, & after Prayers my Chum went down to Doctr. Knelands & got him to give the President a Note that he had the Itch, so that it is probable when they meet Tomorrow they will give us leave to go Home. I took a [walk?] to see if I could get a Horse [if?] I do get leave, but could not. Senior [Pa]rsons is Sick & try'd to get leave to [go] home but could not, so he & Junior Parsons went off with out leave, & Scammel is not well likewise, & sent for Doctr. Kneeland but could not get a Note.

Harvard undergraduates of Peabody's era rarely appreciated the tutors who taught their recitation classes; logic tutor Stephen SCALES (1741–72), A.B. 1763, was a particular object of derision and loathing. Two years after this appearance in Peabody's journal, Scales was at the center of a student riot that inspired this description of him:

If too instead of politer grace,
The stiff logician wipes his greasy face,
Then spits his venom with sarcastick wit,
And grins in laughter at the object hit.

When Scales became a tutor in May 1767, he apparently planned a career in the ministry, but by July 1770 he had settled on the law when he resigned his appointment. He practiced briefly in Concord and Chelmsford before his death in 1772. Edward Holyoke (1689–1769), A.B. 1705, was the PRESIDENT of Harvard College, 1737–69. The college distinguished students of the same surname by their station within the ranking system. PARSONS SENIOR was Obadiah Parsons. PARSONS JUNIOR was Theophilus Parsons. *Sibley's Harvard Graduates,* 15:492–93; 5:265–78.

1. Out of town.

Tuesday the 9th of June.

To Day is clear & Cool wind East. I attended neither reciting, nor Prayers, but went & got the promise of a Horse at Cooper Prentices, & got my Things ready to go Home.

Scales sent for us at Eliven for not reciting but took our Excuse.

The President & Tutors met at 12 & sent for me & gave my Chum & me leave to go Home. After Commons, I got my Horse of Cooper Prentice though he was some put to it to find him, & we got our Things ready & set of on our Journey, & our Horses were very hard going over. We refresh'd ourselves at Wyman's & at Gowens, & in Woburn I got a Shoe set on to my Horse. We got to Father's a little after ten. Found them all well. I saw Dicr [?] Abbot, as I came a [. . .][1] & Sr. Lovejoy & George Abbot and [. . .][2] with them a while.

Samuel Chickring had been raising a Barn [&?] there was a great Company there [as?] we came a long.

Colo. Osgood was married to Huldah Frye this Even[in]g.

Travel between Cambridge and Andover was an all-day undertaking in 1767. Notwithstanding the effort involved, Peabody ordinarily went home once during term time as well as between sessions. Each trip took him from one landmark to the next—for example, from WYMAN'S to GOWEN'S, both taverns in Woburn. Henry PRENTICE (1711–97) of Cambridge made wooden casks. Nathaniel LOVEJOY (1744–1812), A.B. 1766, was from Andover. He served in the Massachusetts militia during the Revolution and rose to the rank of brigadier general in 1807. After the war he returned to Andover, where he was a trader. GEORGE ABBOT (1748–84) lived in Andover. Chickering may have been SAMUEL CHICKERING (1732–1814) of Andover, a farmer. Paige, *History of Cambridge,* 631, 633–34; *Sibley's Harvard Graduates,* 16:386–87; *Descendants of George Abbot,* 25; *Vital Records of Andover,* 1:104, 2:412.

1. Torn [one word].
2. Torn [one word].

Wednesday the 10th of June.

To Day is cloudy but little Rain. I went out and look'd of my Colt which has come since I have been gone, & I took my Mare & my Chum & I went up to Doctr. Kittridges & spoke for some ointment for the Itch which is to be got ready to Day. We went to Br. Oliver's where we din'd, & then we went up to see Osgood but he set of for Cambridge this Day. We came down to Samuel Johnsons, where we stop'd & drank Tea with a Number of People from Bradford. I carry'd up a Calfs Skin to Samuel Johnson & he cut me out a pair of Pomp's, & when I came Home Phinehas came with me & cut out the soles.

Thos. Webster & Sr. Barnard was here when I got Home & spent the Evening. Wm. Runnels & Ephraim Barker came here with the Garls & stay'd till late, & Barker stay'd all Night.

Although the Peabody family operated an active farm, Stephen relaxed during most of this mid-semester break from school. Samuel OSGOOD (1748–1813), A.B. 1770, was from Andover. He became the first postmaster general of the United States. Capt. SAMUEL JOHNSON, who was making Peabody a pair of shoes and appears frequently in these pages, lived near the Peabodys in Andover's north precinct. PHINEHAS (b. 1747) was his son. Thomas BARNARD (1748–1814), A.B. 1766, originally from Newbury, was reading theology with Samuel Williams, A.B. 1761, of Bradford. Barnard became the minister of the North Church in Salem. WILLIAM RUNNELS (1739–81) lived in Boxford. *Sibley's Harvard Graduates,* 17:412–19, 16:316–22; *Andover Tax Assessments,* Tax for 1768; *Vital Records of Andover,* 1:230; *Vital Records of Boxford,* 83, 261.

Thursday the 11.

To Day is wo[rm] & some cloudy. Wind high at S.W. My Chum & I took our Cambridge Horses & went up to Doctr. Kittredge, got our Ointment, & came Home. Breakfasted & Barker went from here after some talk My

Chum concluded to tarry & oint with me, so we went & got us some fever Bush & boil'd & fix'd up some old Cloths about the middle of the P.M. we ointed, looked & felt very bad.

James Stevens came Home to Night to be measur'd for some new Cloths.

FEVER BUSH was spice wood (*Laurus benzoin*). JAMES STEVENS (b. 1749) was Peabody's nephew, a son of his sister Sarah and her late first husband, James Stevens. Estes, "Therapeutic Practice," 343; *Vital Records of Andover*, 1:346.

Friday the 12th of June.

To Day worm & pleasant.

Jose Kimball came to Work here. My Chum & I studie'd. I wrote some in Journal read in Spectator & a Pamphlet Old Mr. Phillips sent down for the Boxford People to read which is very Pertinent to their case.

Just at Night we took a Walk & got a little Bark for my Sisters & in the beginning of the Evening we ointed again.

Timothy Jackman came to Br. John's to Night & lodged, & is going up to Furbushes with his Mare in Mane, & brings no News.

Kimball was Peabody's cousin JOSEPH KIMBALL (1727–1800) of Bradford, the second son of his aunt Abiel (Peabody) and her husband, Joseph Kimball. OLD MR. PHILLIPS was Rev. Samuel Phillips (1690–1771), A.B. 1708, the minister of Andover's South Parish. Peruvian BARK, or quinine, was used to control the effects of malaria. JOHN Peabody (1732–1820) was one of Stephen's older brothers. Charles FURBUSH, the only household head in Andover with that surname, lived in the town's south precinct. Morrison and Sharples, *Kimball Family*, 84, 148; *Sibley's Harvard Graduates*, 5:432–40; Estes, "Therapeutic Practice," 375; Endicott, "Peabody Family," 159, 367; *Andover Tax Assessments*, Tax for 1768.

Saturday the 13th of June.

To Day is clear & some cooler Wind out. Jackman went up the uper End of Andover & found that James Parker own'd the Horse, did his Business & came back here & tarry'd till about the middle of the P.M. & then he went off Home. I read in Spectator & wrote some. Br. John [. . .][1] some with our Cambridge Horses.

Just at Night we ointed again.

1. Torn [one word].

Lords Day the 14th of June.

To Day is very Worm. Our people all went to Meeting & my Chum & I tarry'd at Home. We read a Peice of Mr. Clap's & Mr. Smiths Peice against Mr. Parsons & then I read several Chapt.'s in Doctr. Doddridge. Just after our People ware gone the Bees sworm'd which we had to Hive but met with no Difficulty.

This P.M. we had two very fine Showers.

We ointed again this Evening & now we have done.

Orthodox doctrinally, Peabody did not approve of the theology of Rev. William Symmes (1729–1807), A.B. 1750, the liberal minister of the North Parish in Andover. Peabody found the writings of Thomas CLAP (1703–67), A.B. 1722, minister of the church in Windham, Connecticut, 1726–39, and president of Yale College, 1740–66, more edifying than church attendance when at home. Philip DODDRIDGE (1702–51), a famed dissenting clergyman and author, also taught a form of reformed Protestantism that Peabody found more comfortable than Symmes's Arminianism, the belief that human beings can influence their fate or at least prepare themselves for God to save them through their own works, and Arianism, the belief that Jesus, as the Son of God, is subordinate to God the Father. Trinitarianism, in contrast, does not subordinate the Son or Holy Spirit to God the Father but considers them one God in three persons. Hezekiah SMITH, *The Doctrine of Believer's Baptism by Immersion Only; Asserted and Maintained against the Attempt of Mr. Jonathan Parsons, A.M., to Invalidate It, in Two Sermons Preached at Haverhill Parish, Lord's Day April 28th 1765* (Boston, 1766), told one side of an ongoing ecclesiastical conflict over the nature of baptism. Smith (1737–1805), Princeton A.B. 1762, served as the minister of the Baptist church in Haverhill, 1766–1805. Jonathan PARSONS (1705–76), Yale A.B. 1729, was the minister of the First Presbyterian Church of Newburyport. *Sibley's Harvard Graduates,* 7:27–50; *DNB,* 5:1063–69; Wright, *Beginnings of Unitarianism,* 3, 4; *Princetonians,* 1:411–13; Franklin Bowditch Dexter, *Biographical Sketches of the Graduates of Yale College* (New York and New Haven, Conn., 1885–1912), 1:389–93; Weis, *Colonial Clergy,* 159.

Monday the 15th.

To Day is some cloudy & cooler. I wrote a little & read a little in Rollin, & finish'd the 3rd Vollum of Spectator. My Chum & I went out & mended a little Fence with Br. John, & Reuben Carlton was coming to us & we fled over into Barkers ground, & he stay'd with Br. some Time so we took a Circle round & came Home & had very lik't to have met Carlton as he was going away.

After that we took a Walk over onto Abraham Days Hill to take a View, & got some straburies & so came Home.

Mr. Osgoods Garls ware here this Evening but we ware not seen. James Stevens came Home to have his Cloths tried on & lodg'd.

I ointed a little at Night.

Charles ROLLIN (1661–1741), a Jansenist, was the rector of the University of Paris, after which he became the principal of the College of Beauvais. ABRAHAM DAY was either a farmer (1713–94) of Bradford or his son Abraham, Jr. (1739–1819), also a farmer of Bradford. Paul Harvey and J. E. Heseltine, comp., *The Oxford Companion to French Literature* (Oxford: Clarendon Press, 1959), 627; *Vital Records of Bradford,* 40, 308; Essex County Probate Files, nos. 7394, 7395.

Tuesday the 16th of June.

To Day is cool Wind North. I ointed [a] little this Morning & finish'd all my Ointment, then I went with my Chum out to howing a spell. Read some in Rollin & Spectator. P.M. my Chum & I compos'd each of us a Letter to Mr. Symmes & have some Thoughts of having one sent to keep him from troubling Boxford. Just at Night we went into Barker's Ground with my Sisters to Straburing & when we came back Uncle Kimball & Aunt ware here & stay all Night.

John Chadwick came here this Evening.

The West Parish of BOXFORD, which was seeking a minister, was considering Edward Perkins Sparhawk (1728–96), A.B. 1753. Sparhawk's religious orthodoxy appealed to Peabody, who worried that the liberal SYMMES would try to inject himself into the congregation's deliberations. UNCLE KIMBALL was Joseph Kimball. His wife was Abiel (Peabody) Kimball, youngest sister of Peabody's father. JOHN CHADWICK was Jonathan Chadwick (1720–97) of Boxford. He succeeded his older brother Thomas as deacon of Boxford's West Church in 1786. Chadwick's wife, Susannah (Peabody), was Stephen Peabody's second cousin. *Peabody Genealogy,* 20–22, 25; *Descendants of John and Joan Chadwick,* C12, C13.

Wednesday the 17th.

To Day is clear & very Pleasant wind N.W. We ware getting ready to wash up. I worsh'd a Pare of Breeches & Gloves & got all Things prepar'd & about three o Clock we clean'd up, & I felt in another World.

Capt. Parker & Andrew Foster came here to Day. Uncle Kimball & Aunt went from here, & after they ware all gone my Chum & I took a ride round by Mr. Osgood's down to Bradford, we went to Thomas Webster's to see Sr. Barnard & [. . .][1] was Mr. Barnard of Haverhill & [. . .][2] Mash. We stayed & drank Tea & eat Straburies till after Sun down & then my Chum had a mind to [go to] Haverhill so we rode down along belo[w] to the Meeting House, & went in to see Ebenezer Webster but he was not at Home, so we made but a short Stay, & after having drink'd a Glass of Wine and came Home. Lodg'd in a cleanly manner.

There were two CAPT. PARKERS in Andover, Peter (1714–95) and James, both militia officers in the South Parish. ANDREW FOSTER (1731–1803) was a yeoman of Andover. Osgood was a very common surname in Andover; MR. OSGOOD could have been any of a great many possibilities. Edward BARNARD (1720–74), A.B. 1736, was the minister of the First Church in Haverhill. Pierce, *Foster Genealogy,* 1042–43; *Vital Records of Andover,* 1:294, 2:438, 579; *Sibley's Harvard Graduates,* 10:4–11.

1. Torn [one word].
2. Torn [one word].

Thursday the 18th of June.

This Morning is pleasant. I got up early & went up to Doctr. Osgoods & got me some Physick to take to cary of the Itch, came Home & took it & took a Nap, & then my Chum had got his Things ready & set of for Home.

About ten o Clock it clouds up & rained till Night. My Physick work'd cleverly. I read in Spectator & Rollin finish'd the History of Egypt.

Charles ROLLIN wrote *Histoire ancienne des Egyptiens* (Paris, 1730–38). The college library's 1773 catalogue lists both Rollin's *Roman History* and others of his works, although it does not specifically mention the *Histoire ancienne des Egyptiens.* PHYSICK was a generic term for medicine. Bond and Amory, *Printed Catalogues,* B 22.

Friday the 19th.

To Day is pleasant. Wind S.W. I read some in Spectator & mended some of my Things for Cambridge (viz) Breeches gloves &c in A.M. P.M. I took a ride down to Bradford, went to Ebenezer Websters & there was some Company there, had a fine Dish of Tea & spent the rest of the Time in reading Spectator. At Evening came from there & came up to Jon. Chadwicks &c.

TEA drinking was a mark of urbanity. It is an indication of the circles in which Peabody was traveling that even in rural Bradford his acquaintances were affecting gentility. Richard L. Bushman, *The Refinement of America: Persons, Houses, Cities* (New York: Knopf, 1992), 184.

Saturday the 20th of June.

To Day is Pleasant. I went up to Samuel Johnson's & tarry'd there till almost noon, & eat grand & wrastled, & then I went up to Br. Olivers where I din'd & got my Camel shod at Tylers & so came Home & John Porter was here, & he tells me that Freshman Wetmore is degraded to the Bottom of his Class since I came from College, for breaking Mr. Danforths Windows. About 4 oClock Sally Martin & Hepz. Kimball came here. They have been over to the River. They all stop'd & drank Tea & I wrote a Letter to Mr. Sparhawk for my Father, & a little before sun down they went off.

DEGRADING was one of the college's most common punishments. At matriculation the faculty arranged each class in an order of merit that depended primarily on the social standing of the students' fathers. A degraded student was dropped from his assigned place in the class list to a lower position. It seems implausible that Peabody actually owned a CAMEL, so it must have been his pet name for his horse. JOHN PORTER (1748–1813), A.B. 1767, was from Boxford. He eventually settled in Portsmouth and Plymouth, New Hampshire, and practiced law. William WETMORE (1749–1830), A.B. 1770, was from Middletown, Connecticut. He later practiced law and served as a judge on several different courts. Thomas DANFORTH (1744–1820), A.B. 1762, was a tutor, 1765–68. A Loyalist, he became a lawyer then fled to England. SALLY MARTIN may have been Sarah Martin (b. April 22, 1747) of Andover, daughter of John and Hannah. HEPZ. KIMBALL was probably Hephezebah or Hephzibah Kimball (b. June 22, 1746) of Boxford, daughter of Jonathan and Mehetibal. Edward SPARHAWK, A.B. 1753, worked a farm in Lynnfield but regularly supplied pulpits throughout Essex County. *Sibley's Harvard Graduates,* 16:517–18, 17:447–51, 15:217–20, 13:360; *Vital Records of Andover,* 1:267; *Vital Records of Boxford,* 55.

Sunday the 21.

To Day is Hot though a fresh Air. James came Home & went to Boxford Meeting so I rode a Colt which he rode up to Meeting, & heard Mr. Sparhawk preach in A.M. from the 1 of John 2d Chapt. & 15th Verse.[1] P.M.

he preach'd from the 53d of Isiah & the 1 Verse.[2] I din'd with John Porter & we got to Meeting late. After Servise I came Home & it looked like a Shower, though we had not much Rain. I read in the Gospel Sonnets after Meeting.

Although Stephen Peabody's family now lived in Andover, their farm had been in Boxford until John Peabody successfully petitioned to relocate the town line. In order to avoid attending the uncomfortably liberal services in his home parish, Stephen often attended church in Boxford instead. The text of the morning sermon was particularly suited to orthodox teachings. JAMES was Peabody's cousin James Stevens. *GOSPEL SONNETS; or, Spiritual Songs* was a collection of verse by Ralph Erskine (1685–1752), a Scottish Presbyterian clergyman. A book-length poem, it was widely read in evangelical circles on both sides of the Atlantic. Bailey, *Historical Sketches of Andover,* 160.

1. Love not the world, neither the things *that are* in the world. If any man love the world, the love of the Father is not in him.
2. Who hath believed our report? and to whom is the arm of the LORD revealed?

Monday the 22d of June.

To Day is pleasant. I took m[y] Camel in the A.M. & took a ride o[ut] to Bradford. I called at Mr. Benj[amin] Carltons, & at Mr. Websters, & I lit of Benjn. Gage & rode Home with him. Got back here again to Diner. Videbam Puillas & dicunt veniuntur ad Andoveriam cras.[1]

P.M. I took Br. John's Horse & went down to Boxford to see their Managements at their Meeting. I lit of Stephen Runnelds, & went in to Decn. Chadwicks & drink half a Bowl of Punch with him then I stop'd at John Chadwicks with Mehitabel a while & when I got to the Meeting House their Church Meeting was over & their Parrish one they would not set upon, so broke up soon. They have appointed a Day for the Fasts & the Gentlemen to perform.

I went from there down to Gideon Tylers to see Mrs. Gridle & Mrs. Marshal, & Mr. Dexter & Wife who are there upon a Visit. I stayd & drank Tea & the Boston Ladies talk of coming to see me Tomorrow & to get me to lend a Horse for them to Boston.

I came from there & did an Arrand for Br. John at Asa Parkers, & so came Home & Sister Peabody had had a Quilting & I went in to that Room & such a Frolick as they had is no Ways Common. They stayd till almost twelve. I can think of nothing more to Day worth writing.

In most Massachusetts communities until 1833 the CHURCH and the PARISH shared responsibility for religious life. The church was a self-perpetuating body of pious men and women admitted to the communion table by virtue of their demonstrated faith. Many churches required signs of salvation from candidates for admission. The church took responsibility for calling a minister and for caring for the poor through the efforts of its deacons. The parish was a geographical and civic entity with bounds ordinarily coterminous with a town or a section of a town. Through the tax the parish levied, it paid for such public obligations as the salary of the minister and the maintenance of the meetinghouse. Samuel WEBSTER (1743–77), A.B. 1762, was candidating, or trying out for, pulpits in northern Massachusetts and southern New Hampshire in 1767. In 1771, he became the minister of the First Church in Temple, New Hampshire. BENJAMIN GAGE was either militia lieutenant Benjamin Gage (1699–1782) of Bradford or his son Benjamin, Jr. (1729–96), also of Bradford and a major in the Revolutionary War. STEPHEN RUNNELLS was the clerk of the West Parish of Boxford, 1763–71. Thomas CHADWICK was a deacon of the Second, or West, Church in Boxford. MEHITABEL was Stephen's sister Mehitabel Peabody Wood. GIDEON TYLER was from Boxford, where he died in 1800 at age eighty-seven. SISTER PEABODY may have been any of a number of relatives. Stephen had six sisters, of whom as many as five may still have been alive in 1767. He also used the term "sister" to refer to sisters-in-law. *Sibley's Harvard Graduates,* 15:332–34; *Vital Records of Bradford,* 50, 207, 313; Essex County Probate Files, nos. 10467, 10468; Perley, *History of Boxford,* 163; Worthley, "Inventory," 113; *Peabody Genealogy,* 25; *Vital Records of Boxford,* 269; Endicott, "Peabody Family," 159.

1. I saw the girls and they say they will be coming to Andover tomorrow.

Tuesday the 23d of June.

To Day is very Pleasant. I wrote [a] Note to get copied to cary to the President & Tutors, & some in Journal, & help'd our People draw away some Timber. Aunt Perley came up here. Just before noon John Chadwick, Mrs. Gridlie & Mrs. Marshal came here & din'd, & a little after two o Clock they went from here to see Mrs. Day.

After they ware gone I took Br. Johns Horse & did an Arrand for him at Asa Parkers & went up to Samuel Johnsons where I met my Sistors & a Number of Garls from Bradford. We went out a Straburing & Doctr. Baker & Jos. Osgood came to us & spent the Evening. After drinking Tea we had some Exercise, & my Chum came there (he came up 10 today with me to set of for Cambridge in Mane). We came from there & before I came Home I went & help'd the Garls Home in their Chare valedicebam Amicorum &c.[1]

Dr. Symonds BAKER of Methuen had recently married an Andover woman, Mrs. Lydia Gray. JOSEPH OSGOOD (1746–1812) was a son of Dr. Joseph Osgood of Andover. He later became a doctor himself and moved to Salem. *Vital Records of Andover,* 2:37; Abiel Abbot, *History of Andover: From Its Settlement to 1829* (Andover, Mass., 1829), 151; Osgood, *Descendants of . . . Osgood,* 70.

1. I wished [my] friends well.

Wednesday the 24th of June.

To Day is Pleasant & we fited our Things & we set off on our Journey. Call'd at Samuel Johnsons & waited till he had finish'd a pare of Shoes for me, stop'd at Doctr. Osg[oods] till Jos. wrote me a Note, then w[e] came up to Mr. Frye & John Kast ware came up. We stop'd [there?] & din'd & then proceeded on our Jour[ney]. I run over to see Jos. Frye a few of [Minu]tes who is just came from Pigwocket. We came up from there & call'd at two Tavarns & got to Cambridge a little bef[ore] sun down. We met Tenny & Osgood & they tell us that old Hancock has had his Chamber & Chest broke open & that he has lost Money & that he lays it to Frye & Kast & that it is very probable they will both be expell'd. I likewise hear of a good Many Erregularities since I went away.

This morning Miss Gridley sent a Horse to me to take down to Boston, & I rode him & led Cooper Prentice. Got him kept at John Hastings's.

OLD HANCOCK was tutor Belcher Hancock, A.B. 1727. Joshua FRYE of Andover was a hatter and father of John FRYE (b. 1750), class of 1770. John apparently died about 1770. PIGWOCKET, or Pequawket, now the town of Fryeburg, Maine, was granted by the Massachusetts General Court to Col. Joseph Frye in recognition for his military service during the Seven Years' War. Thomas KAST (1750–1820), A.B. 1769, was from Boston. After college he became a doctor. *Sibley's Harvard Graduates,* 8:137–40, 17:158–59, 172–73; Edward W. Hanson, ed., *The Papers of Robert Treat Paine,* vol. 3, *Collections of the Massachusetts Historical Society* 89 (2005): 82–83.

Thursday the 25th of June.

To day some Cloudy but no rain. I was not very well. Mr. Hancock sent for me & told me the Difficulties that Frye was in & that if it was carry'd before the President & Tutors they would certainly be expell'd, but that it was in his Power to settle it, & if they would come & make him Satisfaction it should go no farther, & told me to advise them to come & make up with him. I got leave to go out of Town & took Gridleys [ad]vise & rode round to Boston, & went [to] his House & din'd & soon after came out of Town. I saw Hannah Bayley & Polly Day in Boston. They came down Yesterday & talk a little of coming to see me Tomorrow as they go Home. I came up to College & Frye & Kast came & we a Number of us went to Kasts Chamber to advise them what to Do, & Mr. Hancock sent for them & what is done they will not tell, nor we cannot tell what will be the Issue. I came to my Chamber & lodg'd.

Peabody's role as an intermediary between the faculty and the students appears in his interchange with Tutor Hancock. Although faculty members sometimes threatened students with expulsion, the penalty was actually very uncommon. More often, undergraduates guilty of extremely antisocial behavior served a year of "rustication." Students who were rusticated went to live with a rural minister and consider their shortcomings. Upon successful completion of this sentence and offering an appropriate apology for their misconduct they were readmitted but to the class below the one with which they had entered. POLLY DAY (also called Molly Day, 1741–1829) was the daughter of Abraham and Mary Day of Bradford. She died unmarried. *Vital Records of Bradford,* 42, 309.

Friday the 26th of June.

To Day is pleasant. I was not well & studie'd but little, clean'd up my Room & P.M. went to Lecture & heard Mr. Appleton preach a Sermon from the 26th of Matthew & 22d Verse. Mr. Frye came down here to Day to see a little about his Son but he made but a short shop.

Holt had a Difference with Cheney on account of his treating the Butler ill to Day.

Holt got leave to go Home, so I got put out of Commons by Mr. Hancock & am to wait for him. Mr. Hancock told me to tell Frye to be at his Chamber this Evening. I talk'd to him about living with Tenny next year & about living in t[he] Chamber where Tudor & Austin & he says there is no Dan[ger] but we shall get it.

Just before Night Gridley came here with a Lady from Boston, & they stop'd & drank Tea & some other Things & then went Home. In the evening Tenny & I went up to Bowman & went tradere Literam[1] & return'd soon.

Note Stephen's role as an intermediary bearing a disciplinary message from the tutor. Samuel CHENEY (1745–1820), A.B. 1767, a future physician, was from Roxbury. The BUTLER, appointed by the college Corporation, kept a small store for the convenience of the students. In 1767, the butler was Nathaniel Ward (1746–68), A.B. 1765. William TUDOR (1750–1819), A.B. 1769, later a lawyer and judge, was from Boston. Jonathan Williams AUSTIN (1751–79), A.B. 1769, was from Boston; he settled in Chelmsford, where he practiced law. *Sibley's Harvard Graduates,* 16:451–53, 250–51, 17:252–65, 116–22; Corporation Records, 2:264.

1. To deliver a letter.

Saturday the 27th of June.

To Day is worm & dry. I am not very well. The President & Tutors met about Frye & Kast but could get no Proof against them so they dismiss'd it for the Present. I wrote a little & studie'd some in Xnophon & then Sr. Bowman came here & drank Tea & stay'd till Night & then we accompany'd him part of the Way Home. He is going next Week to set of for Carolina. I heard that the Catalogues are gone to be printed & that Porters Name is not sent by Reason of his not being down, & it is fear'd he will not have his Degree this Year.

The CATALOGUE was the *Catalogus eorum qui in Collegio-Harvardino, quod est Cantabrigiæ, Nov.-Anglorum, ab anno 1642, ad annum 1767, alicujus gradus laurea donate sunt* (Cambridge, Mass., 1767), the college's triennial alumni list. John PORTER, a senior, had been absent. On July 2, however, President Holyoke upbraided him in chapel, Porter apologized, and then he resumed his place in the class of 1767. *Sibley's Harvard Graduates,* 16:517.

Sunday the 28th.

To Day fair Weather & some cooler Wind out. I went to Meeting & heard Mr. Appleton preach two Sermons from the 3d of Acts 26th Verse.

[I] wrote to Day for Winthrop & [re]ad some in Doctr. Young.

WINTHROP, for whom Peabody WROTE, was presumably his classmate James Winthrop (1752–1821) of Cambridge, the son of John Winthrop (1714–79), A.B. 1732, the Hollis Professor of Natural Philosophy and one of the most prominent American scientists of his day. After graduation, James Winthrop served for many years as the college's librarian. *Sibley's Harvard Graduates,* 17:317–29; 9:240–64.

Monday the 29th of June.

To Day is Hot. Studie'd Greek & recited all Day to Willard, & he was very strict especially with a few of us who made a little Blundering. After

Prayers studied Xnophon & read the News, & we had a little Shower. I am pretty well again.

Tuesday the 30th.

To Day is some cloudy, Wind S.W. I attended Prayers & reciting unless at eliven when there was none. In the Morning Jones when we ware reciting was taken in a kind of Fit & went out of the Chappel & was out of his Head but it was not long before he got better. After reciting old Jewett & I went to Willard & got leave to go out of Town Tomorrow Morning to go up to the spring at Watertown & so went round after a Horse & Chaise & at last got the Promise of one of Bradish.

I came to my Chamber & wrote some, & we had a fine shower just at Night & it rain'd moderatly some Time.

Daniel JONES (1750–79), A.B. 1769, was from Boston. After college, he helped his father keep the family tavern. OLD JEWETT, David Jewett (1744–83), A.B. 1769, of Boxford, was two years older than Young Jewett, Jacob Jewett (1747–1812), A.B. 1769, of Rowley. Both Jewetts prepared for Harvard at Dummer Academy; David became a minister. *Sibley's Harvard Graduates,* 17:171, 168–69.

July 1767

Wednesday the 1st of July.

To Day is pleasant & Jewe[tt] & I got our Horse & Chaise & set [out?] early & Parsons & Austin went with us in another Chaise. We all Drank of the Water & some of us went in the Bath. I only div'd in & made no stop but after I came out I felt very Worm.

Parsons & Austin came right back but Jewett & I came round by Menotomy & got back about ten. I brought a Bottle of the Water with me. I did not recite to Day but had a bad Head-Ache. Sr. Bowman came here & spent the biger part of the P.M. Just at Night Holt came down & is going to wait, but I don't intend to be put in to Commons again.

Thursday the 2d of July.

To Day pleasant & cooler. Willard was out of Town so I did not recite. Breakfasted at Worlands, din'd in the Hall. Had a very bad pain in my Head & could not studie at all.

Porter read his Confession this Morning & was restor'd to his place in the Class. In the Evening I was at Thaxters Chamber with Sr. Bowman.

I can think of nothing strange to Day.

Joseph THAXTER (1742–1827), A.B. 1768, was from Hingham. He became the minister of the First Parish in Edgartown. *Sibley's Harvard Graduates,* 17:95–101.

Friday the 3d of July.

To Day is very Pleasant & [c]ool & it is Validictoria. We had Prayers at nine o Clock & Barnard pronounced the Oration did it as well as was expected. There was but little Company in Town.

Sr. Curtis was at my Chamber a few Minutes.

Porter came to my Chamber & is going to Boston tomorrow to get some stores for Commencement & he is to lend me some Money & I am going with him to get some Stores also, & other Things which I want. I spoke for a Horse & Chaise at Yanks. I have the Head Ache to Day, but toward Night am a little better, so that I wrote some.

Classes for the 1766–67 school year ended on July 3; "VALEDICTORIA," or farewell, referred to this milestone. The ORATION observed the end of the year. The speaker was Thomas Bernard (1750–1818), who ranked first in the graduating class by virtue of being the son of the royal governor, Francis Bernard. All that remained was to prepare for commencement on the third Wednesday of the month. Sir CURTIS was probably Samuel Curtis (1747–1822), A.B. 1766, originally from Stoughton, who was reading medicine, but possibly Charles Curtis (1744–1819?), A.B. 1765, of Scituate, later a Loyalist refugee. *Sibley's Harvard Graduates,* 16:316–22, 352–54, 137–38.

Saterday the 4th of July.

To Day is Pleasant. Read a little A.M. & there came a Man here from Boston on Foot who was a Stranger to me but upon some Inquiry I found it to be my Cousin Asa Peabody from Norwich. He has been to Cascowbay by Water upon Business & is now going Home by Land. I was very Glad to see him & he tells me our Friends are well in them Parts. He din'd with me [at] Warlands, & after some stop at [my] Chamber I accompany'd him up to [. . .][1] Br. Watsons where he is going to tarry over the Sabbath. I came b[ack] & took a Horse & Chaise at Hasting[s] & came to College & Porter & I [took?] some Bottles & went down to Bos[ton] & got us some Wine & Shugar for Commencement & did some other Business there & then came round to Cambridge & put the Liquor into my Cellar.

ASA PEABODY (b. 1717) was a son of Stephen's uncle Richard Peabody of Pomfret, Connecticut. Stephen's encounter with his cousin reveals the importance of relationships particularly forcefully, since he had apparently never met this member of his large extended family. CASCOWBAY is Casco Bay, Maine. Endicott, "Peabody Family," 159, 366.

1. Torn [one word].

Sunday the 5th of July.

To Day is Pleasant. I went to Meeting & heard Mr. Appleton expound A.M. from the 1 of John 5 Chapt. & 3 first Verses. P.M. I went but had such a violent pain in my Head I was oblig'd to come out of the Meeting House & came to my Chamber. Cousin Peabody din'd with me to Day at Warlands & stay'd with me at my Chamber 'till just Night. I read to Day Mr. Dana's A.M. Sermon & liked it as little as when I heard it preach'd. Read some likewise in Dr. Young. I got some Drops of Wales to smell of and my head is a little better.

James DANA (1735–1812), A.B. 1753, was the minister of the church in Wallingford, Connecticut. An Old Light, or opponent of the evangelical heirs of the Great Awakening, he was controversial in Connecticut, a stronghold of revivalism. Dana's views, expressed at Cambridge in *Two Discourses Delivered at Cambridge* (Boston, 1767), were popular among most Harvard students but anathema to Peabody, a strong Calvinist. WALES, whose first name has not been determined, was a local doctor. *Sibley's Harvard Graduates,* 13:305–22.

Monday the 6th of July.

To Day is Pleasant & cool. [I] went up to Mr. Watsons in [t]he Morning & Breakfasted & spent the forenoon there with Cousin Peabody & din'd, then we came from there & stop'd at one of his Aquaintance & drank & eat Mulburies & I made a little stop at Bowmans. We came to College & I drank & Cousin Peabody after having taken some Letters for the Students, took leave of me & set out on his Journey Home.

Porter, my chum, & I draw'd of our Wine, & after Prayer I carry'd a Pare of Breeches to Warlands to have some Knee bands put on, & so went into the Water.

KNEE BANDS were narrow strips of matching fabric gartering at the bottom of men's knee-length breeches. The breeches in question were apparently made of leather (see below, July 9), and Peabody may have been replacing worn knee bands on an old garment. For an image of knee bands on leather breeches, see Baumgarten, "Clothes for the People," 53–55. Personal communications, Linda Baumgarten, Colonial Williamsburg Foundation, Jan. 7, 11, 2008.

Tuesday the 7th of July.

To Day is a little Cloudy, but no Rain. I was not well & took a Vomit of Doctr. Wales. Osgood tended upon me & it work'd very well & strain'd me prodigiously but afterwards I felt Better, though I was able to do nothing. P.M. the Masters came after their Questions, & my Chum had Company. He had Lankester, Searl, & on[e] Hasselthin from Beverly.

We clean'd up our Things a little after they ware gone.

Away from home, without their parents to look after them, the students tended to each other's health problems, as Samuel OSGOOD, a fellow resident of Andover and alumnus of Dummer Academy, did when Peabody fell ill. The QUESTIONS were the printed list of *quaestiones.* In advance of commencement, each candidate for the A.M. proposed a question on which he was prepared to discourse. Thomas LANCASTER (1743–1831), A.B. 1764, originally from Rowley, was teaching school in Beverly as he read for ordination. In 1775, he became the minister of the Congregational Church in Scarborough, Maine. *Sibley's Harvard Graduates,* 16:69–70.

Wednesday the 8th of July.

To Day I am Pretty Well. The Masters are down Plenty & we ha[ve] a good Deal of Company. I read [the] News & Mr. Danas other Sermon which I like.

Benjn. Read was here with Lemmons & a Number of us Bought a Box & divided them, & Porter, my Chum & I took a Hundred & divided them. My Chum went with his Company to Worlands.

I wrote a Letter Home.

Scammel came to Town to Night & is going off early in the Morning.

James Dana's OTHER SERMON was the second of his *Two Discourses Delivered at Cambridge.* See above, July 5.

Thursday the 9th.

To Day is Pleasant & very dry Weather. My Chums Company went from here & I wrote some, & read in Spectator. Holt came here & shew me his Forensick Despute, & I think is pretty Well done. After Prayers I went down to Bradishes & saw Bright who is come down to try to git into his own Class again & he tells me he is Pretty Well.

Doctr. Barker was at Chadwicks Chamber & is going Home so I sent a Letter by him. Porter went with him.

Warland & I had some Despute about sewing a Leather Breeches seam, & he offers to set on a Pare of Kneebands for me if [I] can find out & will shew him how & after I left him I believe I did find out but am not certain.

Moses HOLT was preparing a speaking part for presentation at commencement. He participated in a forensic dispute with his classmate Daniel Johnson (1747–77), originally from Bridgewater and later the minister of the First Church in Harvard. Dr. BARKER was Dr. Symonds Baker; see above, June 23. The SEAM on

LEATHER BREECHES sometimes differed from that on cloth garments, with a welt worked into it, possibly leading to the DISPUTE over the proper method to employ. *Sibley's Harvard Graduates,* 16:485–89; personal communication, Linda Baumgarten, Colonial Williamsburg Foundation, Jan. 11, 2008; Baumgarten, "Clothes for the People," 53–55.

Friday the 10th of July.

To Day is Worm & clouds up some & I attended Prayers as usual, but we are out of Commons so I went to Warlands, & Warland told me he would venture a Bowl of Punch that I did not know how to sow that Seam, & would leave it to a Tailor who understood it. So we did, & I sow'd some, & gave it to Mr. Jones who is going down to Boston to Night.

I went to Hancock's & Holts Chambers & had some Despute concerning Mr. Dana's Sermons but Holt inclin'd to say but little about them. I walk'd down to the River to see them swim & then came & helped Holt drink a Bowl of Punch, & so down to Diner. P.M. I wrote some & read some in Spectator, & Tenny & I drew up a little Piece to put into the News Paper to shew the World our Opinion of Dana's Sermon.

Theodore Parson was down here & came to my Chamber, & Bright also came in the Evening & made a short stop & our Class talk of puting in a Petition to the Authority to have him received again. It rains a little toward night, Wind S.W.

The LITTLE PIECE Peabody and David Tenny, A.B. 1768, drafted was a disclaimer. James Dana's supporters had indicated they were publishing his *Two Discourses Delivered in Cambridge* in response to "the general desire of the students," but this was not the case as far as Peabody and Tenny were concerned. They disagreed with Dana, who seemed to them to grant human agency a role in salvation, a position in contradiction to Calvinist orthodoxy but acceptable to religious liberals, or Arminians. In a letter signed *Amicus Societatis* in the *Boston Evening-Post* of July 20 they wrote,

> The general desire it was not, there being many who were very averse to its being published, and were, and still are of opinion, that the Faith there described is no more than every unregenerate man may have, who is born in a land of light, and even the devils themselves not excepted.—By the personal acquaintance I have had with a considerable number of that society, I can affirm that the discourse is not agreeable to their sentiments; and I would not have the world suppose that all of the Seminary are in such gross errors as to expect to be justified by the deeds of law, either in whole or in part.

THEODORE PARSONS (1751–79), A.B. 1773, was from Byfield. A brother of Peabody's classmate Theophilus Parsons, Theodore was a student at Dummer Academy in July 1767. He became a doctor. *Sibley's Harvard Graduates*, 17:208; 18:273–75.

Saterday the 11th of July.

To Day is Hot & towards Night w[e] had a little Shower. I attended P[ray]ers as usual. Spent the chief of the Day in writing & reading.

I pay'd Cooper Prentice for his Horse Home, a Dollar.

Warland told me that the Leather I got for knee Straps would not do so I sent it to Boston by Osgood & got it chang'd & I sent what Tenny & I drew up, & the Printer would not insert it unless there was a Name to it, so he brought it back again.

Jones came from Boston & tells me the Tailers there say that that seam which I sent is right. I talk'd with Mr. Elot concerning living with Tenny & he speaks very incouraging.

Tutor Andrew ELIOT (1744–1805), A.B. 1762, taught Latin. He became the minister of the First Church in Fairfield, Connecticut. *Sibley's Harvard Graduates*, 15:224–29.

Sunday the 12th.

To Day is Hot & I went to Meeting & heard Mr. Appleton Preach two Sermons from the 15th of Proverbs 2d Verse. Validictoria Sermons they ware.

I read in Mr. Marshel to Day. Wrote for Townsend.

After Service Sr. Pike came to my Chamber. He came to Town Yesterday. Nothing remarkable to Day.

Nathaniel Appleton's VALEDICTORIA, or farewell, SERMONS reflected the ongoing relationship between the First Church and Parish in Cambridge and Harvard College. Although Appleton served the hundreds of men, women, and children who lived in the First Parish, the members of the college community—approximately two hundred students, faculty, and staff—who attended his services distinguished his congregation from every other in Massachusetts. His farewell, which must have been an annual event, recognized the departure each year of dozens of familiar faces. MARSHEL was Walter Marshall (1628–80), a Presbyterian minister of Gosport, England, whose most important work was *Gospel Mystery of Sanctification*, published posthumously in 1691. David TOWNSEND (1753–1829),

A.B. 1770, was from Boston, where he became a physician. *DNB*, 12:1134–35; *Sibley's Harvard Graduates*, 17:442–45.

Monday the 13th of July.

Today is Pleasant & after Breakfast I set of to go down to Boston. I had gone but little Way & Pike & Miss. Hannah over took me & I rode down in a Chare with them, & went over to Boston with one Mr. Greenoughs with them where I din'd. I did my Business in Town, got me some Velvoit for a pare of Breeches, & triming for them & for a Jacot. I went to another Place with Pike & drank Tea. I got my Wotch, & went to Gridleys, & went to the Printers & talk'd with him, & he says he will insert that Peice which he saw on Saturday for 30/. I came over the Ferry & rode up with Pike & his Miss. to College again, & in the Evening I carry'd two Petitions to the Presidents, one for the Waitership & another for a Chamber for Tenny & I to live together next Year.

Miss HANNAH Bowman was Nicholas Pike's future wife. Peabody recorded their elopement below, beginning with his entry for October 3. The PRINTERS of the *Boston Evening-Post* were brothers Thomas Fleet, Jr., and John Fleet. Undergraduate WAITERS served daily at Commons. Through these and other jobs the college enabled students to earn a portion of their school expenses. *Sibley's Harvard Graduates*, 16:406; Thomas, *History of Printing*, 142–43.

Tuesday the 14th.

To Day is Worm & very dry. I got Things in a little Preparation for Commencement & P.M. Mr. Moody came down with his Scholars. He offers 13 this year & they came to my Chamber so that I had Company all the rest of the Day. Just at Night old Jewett & I took a Walk to see [if] we cou'd get some Lodging for [them?] but when we came back we [comited?] to lodge them all ourselves so Phillips, Moses Hale & Cheswell lodged in our Bed & my Chum & I lodgd [in] Chadwicks & Osgoods Chamber.

We had a great sing in the Yard before nine & the Freshmen behav'd very well & rejoic'd very much when their freshmanship was up.

Each year at commencement, the school teachers and clergymen who had prepared candidates for the college's admissions examination brought them to Cambridge to be tested. Under the stern eye of two of the college's tutors, the candidate translated a Latin passage into English, rendered a shorter English piece into Latin, and demonstrated an acquaintance with Greek. The tutors passed those who successfully met this modest quiz to the president for his *pro forma* certification. In the late 1760s and early 1770s, Dummer Academy, Peabody's preparatory school, trained more than one-sixth of the college's students. Samuel MOODY (1726–95), A.B. 1746, was the master of Dummer Academy. Samuel PHILLIPS (1752–1802), A.B. 1771, of Andover; MOSES HALE (1749–86), A.B. 1771, of Newbury; and Wentworth CHESWILL of Newmarket, New Hampshire, were all students of Moody. Cheswill never matriculated at Harvard. Phillips was the founder of Phillips Academy Andover and became lieutenant governor of Massachusetts; Hale became the minister of the Second Church in Boxford. Freshmen were subject to hazing during the eighteenth century, leading to a sense of relief when the first year, or FRESHMANSHIP, ended. *Sibley's Harvard Graduates,* 12:48–54, 17:593–605, 523–24; James Duncan Phillips, "Harvard College and Governor Dummer's School," *Proceedings of the Massachusetts Historical Society* 69 (1947–51): 199; *Officers and Students of Dummer Academy,* 10.

Wednesday the 15th of July.

To Day is Hot & very Dry. We had not a great Commencement, but I had a good deal of Company of allmost all Sorts. I went into the Meeting House, & heard their Performances which ware not Extraordinary.

I had a fine sing with Messrs. Osgood & Adams.

Doctr. F. Kitridge sent me down a Horse & I got him kept at Frosts.

At Night we had a great Deal of Sport seeing three Negroes handle a Squaw. Kittridge, & Phillips brought me some Money.

Harvard's commencement was an annual festival day in eastern Massachusetts in the eighteenth century. At the formal exercises in the morning and afternoon, members of the graduating class and candidates for the master's degree offered orations and other spoken pieces. At the same time, outside the college grounds, men, women, and children with no connection to the school gathered to eat, drink, dance, and enjoy a wide variety of entertainments. Religious services took place in New England's MEETING HOUSES, which also accommodated other public functions. Isaac OSGOOD (1724–91), A.B. 1744, was a merchant of Haverhill. Phineas ADAMS (1743–1801), A.B. 1762, was teaching school in Rowley in 1767; in 1769, he became the minister of the West Church in Haverhill. No details survive about the SPORT between the THREE NEGROES and a SQUAW that Peabody reported, but whatever it entailed, it occurred near the close of a day of drinking, rowdiness, and carousing. KITTRIDGE was Dr. Francis Kittredge, who later served as the surgeon of the American army's general hospital in Roxbury during the siege of Boston. Several men with the surname FROST, all related to one another, lived in Cambridge in 1767: Ebenezer (1697–1768), a currier; Edmund (1715–77), a blacksmith; and Gideon (1724–1803), a blacksmith. *Sibley's Harvard Graduates,* 11:472–73, 15:150–51; Philip Cash, *Medical Men at the Siege of*

Boston (Philadelphia: American Philosophical Society, 1973), 51; Paige, *History of Cambridge*, 553–54.

Thursday the 16.

To Day is a little Cloudy. Master Wigglesworth breakfasted with me, & I had Porters Company at my Chamber & many others. I got my Things ready to set of Home. I left that Peice for my Chum to get put into the [pa]per. Just before I came away, I [s]wop'd Watches with Cheswell & he gave me 5 Dollars to Boot. I came from there up to Bowmans where [I] din'd & then had a fine sing with Pike Master Adams Fogg & Tenny & then Master Webster came along & we all set of & went Andover Way. We stop'd at Woburn at Fowles's and then at Gowens, got into Andover just at Dark & it look'd like a Shower. Mr. Adams & Tenny stop'd at the uper end of Andover. We rode pretty Fast & Master Webster proceeded to Bradford & Fogg stop'd with me all Night. I found our People all Well. Just after we got Home it rain'd smartly & was hard Thunder.

Edward WIGGLESWORTH (1742–1826), A.B. 1761, had taken his A.M. the previous year. He became a merchant. Daniel FOGG (1743–1815), A.B. 1764, had taken his A.M. the previous day. An Anglican, he later served as the minister of his denomination's church in Brooklyn, Connecticut. MASTER WEBSTER was Samuel Webster (1743–77), A.B. 1762, who had just begun to candidate at the First Church in Northborough, which called him to its pulpit in September. The FOWLES Tavern stood near Woburn's town center. *Sibley's Harvard Graduates*, 15:129–33, 332–34, 16:46–49; Samuel Sewall, *The History of Woburn* (Boston, 1868), 612.

Friday the 17th of July.

To Day is rainy & Fogg stay'd here till after noon & we spent our Time in singing & play & Jos. Simmons is at Work here. P.M. I took Br. John's Horse & rode as far as Bradford Meeting-House to accompany Fogg & parted with him & went down to Uncle Kimball's where I stay'd till Night & drank Tea & then Francis came with me to James Heads where we spent the Evening. The People are [. . .][1] Francis gave me some Money to g[et] him a Dictionary at Boston & I am to bring it up when I come, he giving me 4–15–0. It rains the chief of the Night. Formosissima[2] &c.

Andover and its environs were close enough to Boston to be in regular contact with the metropolis but sufficiently distant that residents waited for friends to

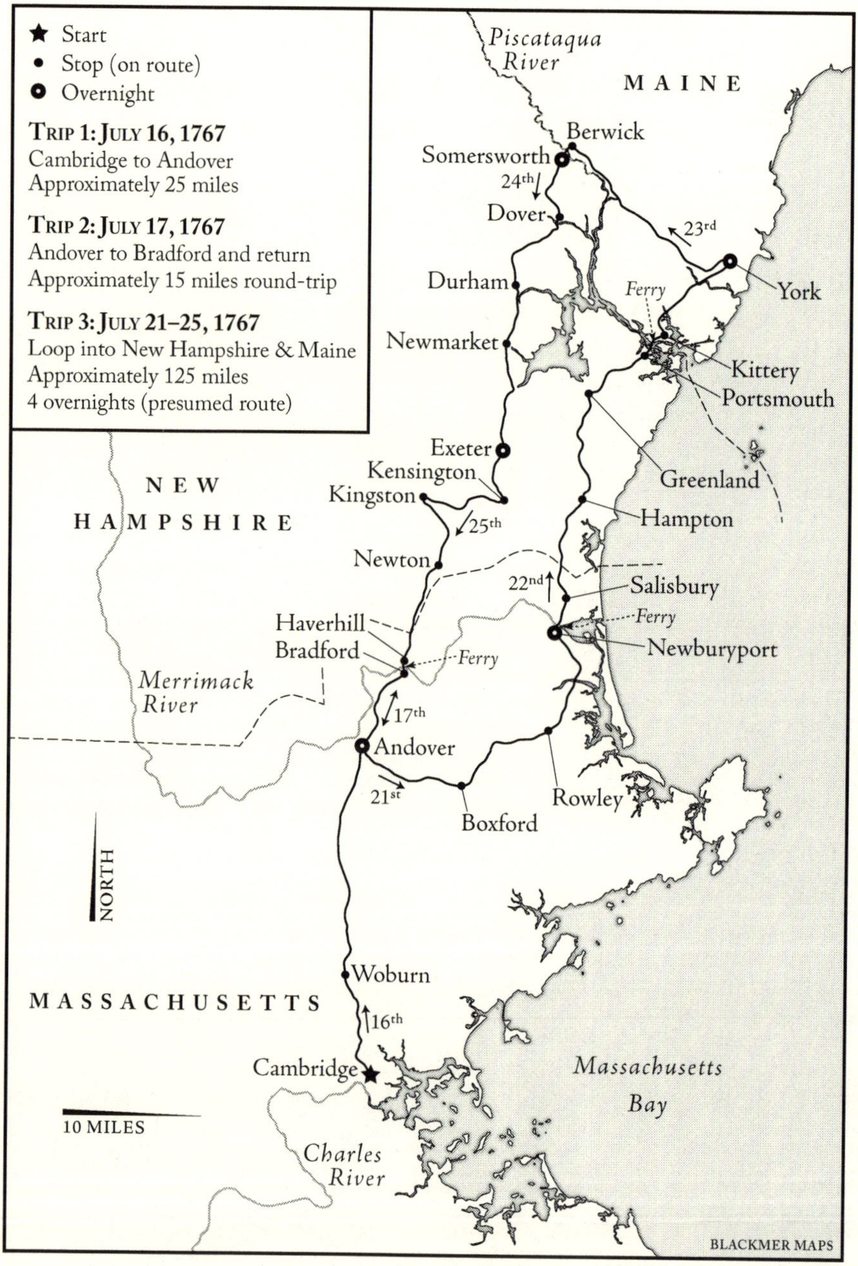

Peabody's Travels, July 16, July 17, and July 21–25, 1767.

travel to town to do their errands. Here, Stephen agreed to do an errand for his cousin FRANCIS Kimball (1742–1822) of Bradford, a blacksmith and farmer. Francis was the ninth child of Peabody's aunt Abiel (Peabody) Kimball and her husband, Joseph. JAMES HEAD may have been a relative through Stephen's mother, but he has not been identified. Morrison and Sharples, *Kimball Family,* 84, 151.

1. Torn [one or two words].
2. Very strongly.

Saterday the 18th of July.

This Morning it clears off Worm & I took the Chaise & went up to Tylers to get him to mend it, & my Father came there, so just before Night I took the Horse which he rode up & came Home. I call'd at Samuel Johnsons & stay'd a while, & Moses Hale & John White came along & they tell me that they are got into College & that all Mr. Moody's scholars have likewise that he offer'd. Simmons went from here. Careo [. . .].[1]

Without regular chores to perform now that he was a student living away from home, Stephen had discretion over how he would make use of his vacation time. He helped his family by handling errands for which no one else had time, such as taking the family chaise to be repaired. He also networked with friends and acquaintances such as incoming freshmen (and former students at Dummer Academy) MOSES HALE of Newbury and JOHN WHITE (1752–1816), A.B. 1771, of Haverhill, where he became a merchant. *Sibley's Harvard Graduates,* 17:523, 672–73.

1. I am without [illegible, one word].

Sunday the 19th.

To Day is Cool. I went to Andover Meeting & I heard one Mr. Chevers preach in the A.M. from the 5 of Galatians 4 Verse. P.M. he preach'd from the 14th of Proverbs & the 15th Verse. I din'd with Lovejoy, saw Samuel Phillips & gave him an Advertisement to put up at Braggs some time this week for Sister Wood. After Servise I came Home & read some in Dr. Doddridge.

Upam was at Andover Meeting to Day.

Whenever William Symmes was not conducting the service, Peabody felt free to attend Andover's North Church. The preacher on July 19 was probably Edward CHEEVERS (1717–94), A.B. 1737, the minister of the church in Eastham. Born in

Lynn, Cheevers had local connections, having previously served in Saugus. SISTER WOOD was Stephen's sister Mehitabel, who had married Solomon Wood of Andover and Boxford in 1761. Timothy UPHAM (1748–1811), A.B. 1768, a rising senior, was originally from Malden. He served as the minister of the First Church in Deerfield, New Hampshire. *Sibley's Harvard Graduates,* 10:124–26, 17:101–3; *Vital Records of Andover,* 2:264; *Vital Records of Boxford,* 180.

Monday the 20th of July.

To Day fair Weather though at Night it clouds up. I wrote some & A.M. Upam, John Frye & Osgood came here but they made but a short stop. P.M. I help'd our People unlode a Lode of Hay & Sr. Pike & Holt came Here. Sr. Pike from Cambridge to Day & he tells me there are 49 Freshmen accepted 2 turn'd by for the Vacation & seven for the Year. They stop'd & drank Tea & then Holt went Home & Pike stayed with me all Night & we had a sing.

Samuel Johnson was here this Morning.

In the absence of relevant official records, this entry provides the best surviving indication of how easy or difficult it was to gain admission to Harvard College in the 1760s. The class of 1771 eventually numbered sixty-four members. *Sibley's Harvard Graduates,* 17:466–67.

Tuesday the 21st.

To Day is a steady Rain & Sr. Pike was in a Hurry to go a long so I got my Fathers Mare & set off with him to go to York. We went down through Boxford to Rowley to Mr. Adams's & to my great Sorrow I found my Class Mate Adams in exceeding low Circumstances, & I very much fear he will live but little While. We tarry'd there & din'd with Master & had a very Pleasant sing, & then we proceeded on our Journey. We call'd to see Tenny & something expected him to go with us but he could not so we made but a short stop. We went f[rom] there directly to Newbury Port & it ra[ined] very Fast. We left our Wet Things at Davenports & Stearns came there & brought the Papers & I saw that Peice in there which Tenny & I have been trying to g[et] in, & was very glad of it.

I got the Hands of my Watch alter'd a little & went to see Parsons & Traze & parted with Pike & went & lodg'd with Lemuel Noyes (Phebe Coburn keeps his House) & was treated very handsomely. It is a very rainy Night.

Peabody devoted much time during his vacations to maintaining ties with those Dummer and Harvard schoolmates who lived near his home in Andover. The first stop on this circuit with Nicholas PIKE, A.B. 1766, was in Rowley at the farm of Abraham ADAMS, the father of Stephen's mortally ill classmate Joseph. Here they dined with MASTER Samuel Moody. Next, in Newburyport, Peabody and Pike stopped at the inn of William DAVENPORT, who commanded a company during the Seven Years' War, then returned home and opened a tavern, which he ran until his death in 1773. STEARNS was either Jonathan Stearns (1751–98) or William Stearns (1749–83), both A.B. 1770 and both of Lunenburg. Both later became lawyers; Jonathan, a Loyalist, became solicitor general of Nova Scotia. Peabody's Harvard classmate Nathaniel TRACY (1751–96), A.B. 1769, was from Newburyport but prepared for college at Boston Latin School. Tracy became a merchant. LEMUEL NOYES (b. 1743) of Newbury was the brother of John Noyes, A.B. 1771. PHOEBE COBURN (or Colburn) was presumably the elder sister of Peabody's brother-in-law Moses Coburn. *Sibley's Harvard Graduates,* 17:115, 434–38, 247–51; Currier, *History of Newburyport,* 1:387; Noyes, *Noyes Descendants,* 1:61, 72; *Vital Records of Dracut,* 42.

Wednesday the 22d of July.

To Day the Rain is over, & I came from Noyes & lit of Pike & we went over the Ferry & through Salsbury into Hampton. I call'd at Doctr. Emery's & at Jona. Lovets where we refreshed ourselves & Horses. Saw Mr. Thayer & Sr. Moulton & was strongly invited to stop but could not with conveniency. We saw Sr. Hale who was keeping School at Greenland. We din'd at one Mastine at Greenland, & then went into Portsmouth & made some stop. I saw my School Mates Gilman & Folsom who live there. I went to several Places with Pike & to one where there was a set of House Orgains which I play'd upon some Time after a Fashion. We went from there over the River & through Kitery & so into York, got there a little before dark, went to Capt. Stones where Pike bords where we lodg'd & take his Situation well & find that the eastern Country far surpasses my Expectation.

Although Peabody never explains the reason for this circuit, his remarks about the EASTERN COUNTRY—that is, York County, Maine—show that he was evaluating all the communities through which he passed. An aspiring clergyman, he would need to find a congregation within a few years; probably he wondered whether he would find this rapidly growing part of the country suitable for settlement. Anthony EMERY (1713–81), A.B. 1736, was a physician in Hampton, New Hampshire, where Jonathan LEAVITT was a tavern keeper. Rev. Ebenezer THAYER (1734–92), A.B. 1753, was the minister of the First Church in Hampton. Josiah MOULTON (1749–96), A.B. 1767, a native of the town, was planning to go into trade there. Samuel HALE (1747–87), A.B. 1766, was teaching school while he decided what to do with his life. He settled on the law, eventually fleeing to England as a Loyalist. MASTINE was probably an unidentified member of the locally prominent Marston family. Peabody's spelling reveals his pronunciation of the name absent an "r" sound. Nathaniel GILMAN of Exeter, New Hampshire, was a former student at Dummer Academy. During Samuel Moody's tenure there were three students from New Hampshire named FOLSOM: Nathaniel and Jonathan of Exeter, and Simeon of New Market. Capt. John STONE was a merchant and farmer in York. *Sibley's Harvard Graduates,* 10:32–34, 13:363–67, 16:512–13, 368–71; Joseph Dow, *History of the Town of Hampton, New Hampshire* (Salem, Mass., 1893), 2:813–14; *Officers and Students of Dummer Academy,* 12–13; George Ernst, *New England Miniature: A History of York, Maine* (Freeport, Maine: Bond Wheelwright, 1961), 72, 83, 184, 232.

Thursday the 23 of July.

To Day is some cloudy. We took Capt. Stones Horse & Chaise & rode down to the Beech & then to Esqr. Sawards where we had a Sing & to Mr. Limans & Lawyer Sewels where we sang again & to many Places so we spent the chief of the A.M. We din'd at Capt. Stones & then took our Horses & set of from there to Summersworth. We call'd at Mr. Tompsons School & another House when we had a Shower. We went through Barwick into Summersworth & got to Mr. Pikes before Day Light down where we lodg'd. Mr. Pike tells me he has seen Mr. Danas Sermon & does not like it and is affraid it will be a great Disgrace to the College, & upon our telling him of there being a Piece in the Paper about it he was very Glad to hear it.

I like the Eastern Country very Well.

It is not certain whether Peabody already knew most of the men he visited on his tour or followed a network of acquaintances, passing from one to the next on the strength of his standing as a Harvard student and prospective clergyman. In either case, leading residents of the new towns in northern New England clearly accepted him as one of them and provided him with hospitality. Group singing was an indication of social acceptability. Rev. Isaac LYMAN (1725–1810), Yale A.B. 1747, was the pastor of the First Church in York. David SEWALL (1735–1825), A.B. 1755, was a lawyer in York. Mr. TOMPSON may have been Ezra Thompson (1735–98), A.B. 1756, who was supplying pulpits in northern New England in 1767; he later settled in Arundel, Maine, where he taught school. Rev. James PIKE (1703–92), A.B. 1725, was the minister of the church in Somersworth, New Hampshire, and father of Nicholas Pike, A.B. 1766. Moody, *History of the Town of York,* 55–56; *Sibley's Harvard Graduates,* 13:638–45, 14:95–96, 7:550–53, 16:406–9.

Friday the 24th.

To Day is Worm. We got our Horses & went to see Wentworth & stay'd a While & then he got his Horse & rode over to Barwick with us. We went to see Pelatiah March & stay'd [&] drank with him & then I called to see Doctr. Parsons but he was gone from Home, & they tell me likewise that Wood is not at Home neither. We came ov[er] into Summersworth & stop'd & drank & sang there with one Marshall a while & then came to Mr. Pikes & din'd & had another cleaver Sing.

After Diner I set of Homewards & Pike & Wentworth accompany'd me as far as Dover. We went up on to a very high Hill to view the Land, & lit of People mending the high Ways, by the Way. I parted with them & proceeded, came up to Durham stop'd & oated my Horse, came from there through new Market & got into Exeter a little before dark. I brought some Catalogues for Sr. Pike to Mr. Gilman. I saw Theodore Carlton & he has lately lost his Wife & is very Melancholy & Lonesome & invited me very strong to tarry with him all Night which I accepted & he treated me exceeding Handsomely. I am realy anamer'd with the eastern Country & like things vastly better then what I expected to have done.

PELATIAH MARCH and Dr. John PARSONS, both of Berwick, Maine, each owned the covenant of their town's First Church, thus recognizing their obligations to God and fellow church members. John WENTWORTH (1745–87), A.B. 1768, a graduate of Dummer Academy, was from Somersworth, New Hampshire. He settled in Dover, New Hampshire, where he practiced law. WOOD was probably Abraham Wood (1748–1823), A.B. 1767, who was teaching school and reading for the ministry in New Hampshire. He later became the minister of the First Church in Chesterfield, New Hampshire. THEODORE CARLETON, a leading citizen of Exeter and later a patriot during the American Revolution, had recently lost his WIFE, Deborah, and a baby son. *Sibley's Harvard Graduates,* 17:104–6, 16:550–52; Joseph Crook Anderson II, ed., *Records of the First and Second Churches of Berwick, Maine* (Rockport, Maine: Picton Press, 1999), 97–99, 102, 105, 127, 144; Bell, *History of the Town of Exeter,* 80, 85, 86, 88, appendix p. 6.

Saturday the 25th of July.

To Day is Hot & after Breakfast I went to see Mr. Parsons & Mr. [Poor?] & then Mr. Carlton set out with me & came to Kansington where I parted with him & I went to Mr. Fogg where I stop'd & din'd & had a very agreeable Chat & Sing & saw Sr. Potter & his Lady. He is keeping school there. About three o Clock Jeremiah Fogg took [a] Horse & we came from there. He accompanyd me & we went up to Kingston. We called to see Webster & he is better. Fogg stop'd at Kingston & Webster took a Horse & accompany'd me to New Town. We stop'd at Mr. Eames's & drank Tea & Webster came to his Sisters & I parted with him & came to Haverhill & so over the Ferry & made a little stop at Bradford & then came Home, & I hear nothing strange since I have been gone.

Peabody's circuit of northeastern Massachusetts, eastern New Hampshire, and southern Maine lasted five days and took him approximately 125 miles. Traveling through a young and growing corner of New England, he must have met people who were struggling to establish themselves, but if he did, it would be impossible to discern that from his diary. As he considered where to settle after college and preparation for the ministry, the people on whom he commented were almost invariably community leaders and often college graduates. Mr. POOR was probably Enoch Poor, shipbuilder, merchant, and later Revolutionary War general. Rev. Jeremiah FOGG (1712–89), A.B. 1730, was the minister of Kensington, New Hampshire, and the father of JEREMIAH FOGG (1749–1808), A.B. 1768, a future military officer. Ebenezer POTTER (1745–1822), A.B. 1766, was keeping school when Peabody visited him in 1767, but he eventually ended up a tavern keeper. Peabody's reference to Mrs. Potter is apparently the only surviving mention of her. She does not appear in the local vital records, and the entry for her husband in *Sibley's Harvard Graduates* only knows of her through Peabody's reference here. Nathaniel WEBSTER (1749–1830), A.B. 1769, was a schoolmate of Peabody's at Dummer Academy. During Webster's sophomore year he became so sick that the faculty instructed Stephen to accompany him home. He became the minister of the Second Church in Biddeford, Maine. Rev. Jonathan EAMES (1730–1800), A.B. 1752, was the minister of the church in Newtown, New Hampshire. Bell, *History of the Town of Exeter*, 80, 81, 86, 87, 245, 394; *Sibley's Harvard Graduates*, 8:710–14, 17:21–24, 303–5, 16:410, 13:227–28.

Sunday the 26th of July.

To Day is Hot. I went to Bradford Meeting & heard Mr. Sparhawk preach A.M. from the 8th of Romans & the 30 Verse.[1] P.M. he preach'd a very superior Sermon upon Faith but the Chapt. & Verse is out of my Mind. I din'd at Gideon Tylers. Read some in Doctr. Doddridge & Dickinsons Letters.

Hipsabah Kimbal told me something about Sally Martins Cantharides[2] which I was Stupiditalicimus.[3]

Edward SPARHAWK's sermon text selection, an important support for the Calvinist doctrine of predestination, was in keeping with Peabody's theological positions. Sparhawk preached from the same text the following two Sundays and again on January 31. Ensign GIDEON TYLER (c. 1713–1800) served as a Boxford selectman in the early 1760s. DICKINSON'S LETTERS refers to Jonathan Dickinson, *Familiar Letters to a Gentleman upon Subjects in Religion* (Boston, 1745). This reference could not have been to John Dickinson, *Letters from a Farmer in Pennsylvania to the People of America,* which did not begin to appear as a newspaper serial until the end of the year. Perley, *History of Boxford,* 379; *Vital Records of Boxford,* 269.

1. Moreover whom did he predestinate, them he also called: and whom he called, them he also justified: and whom he justified, them he also glorified.

2. Spanish fly.

3. Very stunned.

Monday the 27th of July.

To Day is clear & Worm & I took my Camel & went down to Jesse Kimball's & got the Promise of him to come and make me some Cloths next Week. I call'd to see Asa Sherwine & sang a while with h[im] & then went up to Frazers & got m[e] some things & went to Br. Peters's where I din'd & then I came to Jona. Holts & stop'd to see Sr. Holt who was there, & so he went with me to Esqr. Phillips's & Mr. Holt of Danvers was there & several others. I stayed a while & got some Things & then I came Home round by Br. Olivers, call'd at Curtis's & Ingalls's & did some Arrands for Br. John. Stop'd a Minute at Samuel Johnsons & then he came along with me. He is going to Bradford. I came Home & stop'd till Dark & then I took a little Excurtion & met Samuel Johnson & went Home with him nihil majus strange &c.

Peabody appropriately concluded this account of a day devoted to visits and errands with the assessment "NIHIL MAJUS" (or MAGUS)—nothing important. JESSE KIMBALL (1738–1814) lived variously in Boxford and Andover. ASA SHERWIN (b. 1744) was a neighbor from Boxford. John PETERS was the second husband of Peabody's sister Sarah. Jonathan HOLT of Andover was the father of Moses Holt, A.B. 1767. Samuel PHILLIPS (1715–90), A.B. 1734, was an Andover shopkeeper, public official, and the father of Peabody's future roommate Samuel Phillips, A.B. 1771. Nathan HOLT (1726–92), A.B. 1757, was the minister of the South Parish of Danvers (later Peabody). Morrison and Sharples, *Kimball Family,* 110, 202; *Vital Records of Boxford,* 85, 198; *Vital Records of Andover,* 2:269, 316; *Sibley's Harvard Graduates,* 16:485, 9:431–36, 14:175–76.

Tuesday the 28th of July.

To Day is Hot. Eram in Somno partum Temporis[1] A.M. & then wrote some. P.M. I went out & plow'd among Corn for Br. John & there was a smart Shower but I did not stop for that but went on & finish'd the Peice & when I had done I was very Wet & looked like seven Furies. I came up & shifted my Cloths & took Br. Johns Horse & rode down to John Days & there was some Company there. I stayd till sun Down & then I came from there & went up to Samuel Johnsons & there was a young Company there & they had a Dance & then we had a little play & so dispers'd. Samuel Osgood & Benjn. Chadwick was there with others & B.C. sistebat cum H. Frye sistebam in Parte[2] &c.

1. I fell asleep for a while.
2. B.C. stayed with H. Frye and I stayed awhile.

Wednesday the 29th of July.

To Day is pleasant. The chief of the A.M. I spent in writing & P.M. I went up to Samuel Johnsons videre Puillas[1] & found some eorum in Somne[2] & they got out of the Window. I went from there to the River where I met our Garls & went over to see James Frye with them. I found them in a very Great Hurry a Reeping. Mr. Bodwill was there and we had a long Talk upon Religion. We drank tea & then went out to Blackburying & stay'd till past Novem,[3] & James Frye & Thos. Croos had a Quarril & began to fight & after that was over Frye set us over the River & we came Home.

BODWILL may have been Henry Bodwell of Methuen. See below, February 10, 1768. Col. JAMES FRYE of Andover was an uncle of John Frye, who entered Harvard with the class of 1769 but left without a degree. *Sibley's Harvard Graduates,* 17:158–59.

1. To see the girls.
2. Of them asleep.
3. Nine.

Thursday the 30th.

To Day is Pleasant but some Cloudy. I got up very early & mow'd for Jona. Stevens who is at Work here till he brought Br. Johns Horse & then I took him & went down to Nathaniel Peabodys & got him shod, & went round by the Pond & got Br. a little Sand & then came home & wrote some in Journal & Samuel Johnson came here & got [a] Barrel of Syder to make Vinegar of. Mr. Ingalls is a Reeping here with so[me?] Hands for Br. John. A little after [. . .][1] 1 o Clock Jos. Osgood came down her[e] & made a short stop & I took my Cam[el] & our Garls & we went down to John Days & there was considerable of a Company. We drank Tea & then Doctr. Baker came there & we walk'd down to the River & after we came back we had a Dance & some Play. Broke up seasonably & each one went his Way. Ego[2] [. . .][3] accompany'd unam Puillam in Via,[4] & it is cloudy & looks like Rain &c.

I help'd my Father in with a little Wheat to Day.

Peabody's awkward next to last sentence suggests that he did not know the Latin for "ACCOMPANY'D." JONATHAN STEVENS was Peabody's nephew, a son of his sister Sarah and her first husband, James Stevens. NATHANIEL was probably Peabody's cousin, a son of his uncle Ephraim. Nathaniel lived in Boxford. *Vital Records of Andover,* 1:347; Endicott, "Peabody Family," 159, 366.

1. Torn [one word].
2. I.
3. Illegible [one word crossed out].
4. One girl along the way.

Friday the 31 of July.

To Day is some Cloudy & very Hot. Fere mortuus sum.[1] I wrote two Letters for Br. John to St. Johns & one for myself to Br. Coburn. Br. John is going to Boxford to carry them. Old Abner Hariman & Amos Kimball ware here. P.M. I wrote some & just at Night I help'd move a Peice of Fence to save some Apples, & we had a plentiful Shower.

Moses COBURN was the husband of Peabody's sister Betty. OLD ABNER HARIMAN was probably Abner Harriman (1699–*ante* Apr. 13, 1770) of Haverhill, Massachusetts, and Plaistow, New Hampshire. AMOS KIMBALL (1707–88) was a farmer in Boxford. Endicott, "Peabody Family," 159; *Vital Records of Andover,* 2:264; Lois Ware Thurston, comp., *The Harriman Family: Research in Progress* (Chelsea, Maine, 1992), 19–20, typescript, New England Historic Genealogical Society, Boston, Mass.; Morrison and Sharples, *Kimball Family,* 66, 109–10.

1. I am almost dead.

August 1767

Saturday the 1 of August.

To Day is Clear & very Pleasant, wind N.W. I went out & mow'd for Br. John the bigger Part of the A.M. P.M. I took my Camel & went up to Andover & call'd at Doctr Osgood. Sr. Barnard & Sr. Lovejoy came [t]here, we stay'd a while & then Jos. took his Horse & we all went up to Frazers & I got me some Lining for a Coat & some Silk Hair, then we went Home with Lovejoy & drank Tea & it was after sun Down when we came from there. I rode down to Br. Peters's in the interim. I rode from town with Barnard & got Home about Dark.

Lords Day the 2d of August.

To Day is Pleasant. I went to Boxford Meeting & heard Mr. Sparhawk preach A.M. from the 8th of Romans & the 30th Verse. P.M. he Preach'd from the 2d of Petter 1 Chapt. & 1 Verse. I din'd at Deacn. Chadwick's after servise. I came Home & read in Mr. Meed.

MR. MEED was Joseph Mede, or Mead (1586–1638), an English biblical scholar whose most important writing, *Clavis Apocalyptica,* or *Key to the Apocalypse,* attempted to discern the millennial meanings of the Book of Revelation. *DNB,* 13:178–80.

Monday the 3d.

To Day is clear & Hot. I wrote a Letter & did some Choers & mow'd with Br. John the Bigger Part of the A.M. P.M. I took Br. John's Horse

& accompany'd our Garls down to Thos. Websters & there we stay'd till Night & drank Tea & Mr. Williams was there. Just before dark my Sisters came Home & I took a walk with Mr. Williams & Sr. Barnard down [to] Town. We stop'd a few moments at Decn. Kimball's & I parted with them at Mr. Webster's. I stop'd to see my Class mate Sargent who was th[ere]. The Weather is very Hot. We stay'd there till something late & then he came home with me. Somnum ignotus est ad Sally Webster[1] &c.

Samuel WILLIAMS (1743–1817), A.B. 1761, who served as Hollis Professor of Mathematics, 1780–86, had been ordained and installed at the First Church in nearby Bradford. Aaron KIMBALL was a deacon of the First Church in Boxford, 1759–74. Christopher SARGEANT (1747–78), A.B. 1769, was from Methuen. He became a lawyer. *Sibley's Harvard Graduates,* 15:134–46, 17:218; Worthley, "Inventory," 112.

1. Sleep is unknown to Sally Webster.

Tuesday the 4th of August.

To Day is Hot & Sargent stay'd with me the bigger Part of the A.M. & then he went from here. P.M. John Hovey came & stay'd till Night & we had some singing.

I rak'd after the Cart for Br. John to Day. In Vespere[1] Sally Osgood & Phebe Russell came here.

JOHN HOVEY (1727–1807) was a farmer in Boxford. *Hovey Book,* 166–67.

1. In the evening.

Wednesday the 5th of August.

To Day is cooler Wind out. I help'd Br. John unlode a Lode of Hay & then spent the Chief of the A.M. looking over my old Journals. P.M. I took a Ride. I called to see Asa Parker a few Minutes & then went down to John Chadwicks where I stay'd till just Night & drank Tea & there was a Shower. I came from there & stop'd a Minute at the Decn's & came to Nathan Barkers to see Jesse Kimbal & he says he will come to work for me tomorrow. I stop'd & drank a Bowl of Toddy with the Doctr. & so came Home.

This entry suggests that Peabody kept JOURNALS before the one printed here, but he may have been referring to previous signatures of the present work.

NATHAN BARKER was one of as many as three men of that name possibly active in Andover in 1767: Nathan (*post* 1726–89), Nathan (1709–74), or Nathan (b. 1713). Barker, *Barker Genealogy*, 269–71.

Thursday the 6th of August.

To Day is some Cloudy A.M. but clear'd of Hot. Jesse Kimball came to Work here & I help'd my Father reep a little Wheat. P.M. I took a ride down to Bradford to Mr. Williams where I stay'd till Night & drank Tea & heard him read what the Church had done to Wm. Eastman for his absenting himself from them. I came from there to Mr. Websters & then took a Walk over to Jacob Kimballs where I spent the Evening &c.

Peabody's frequent visits during his vacation helped him to keep up with the latest local news and gossip. William Easman, or EASTMAN, here subject to ecclesiastical discipline, had been a member of the church in Bradford since November 29, 1741. JACOB KIMBALL was one of three possible men of that name: either a blacksmith of Andover (1700–1787); his son (1731–1810), a blacksmith of Andover and Topsfield; or a resident of Bradford (1741–97). Kingsbury, *Memorial History of Bradford*, 46; Morrison and Sharples, *Kimball Family*, 66, 88, 108, 109, 160, 199.

Friday the 7th of August.

To Day is some cloudy. I was at Home all Day. Just before Noon Capt. Coffin & his Uxor[1] & the Doctr. came here from Boston, & stay'd & din'd & so proceeed to Newbury. P.M. Benjn. Chadwick came here & stay'd till just Night & drank Tea, & his Horse got away so he took mine to ride part of the Way Home & is to turn her out in the Evening. Soror Polly & ego went down to Thos. Osgood & stayed till late. I read a Sermon there which Wm. Ingals sent to my Father to read & it is to be sent to Lieut. Parsons. It was preach'd by Mr. Hutchinson at Newbury Port & is a very smart Peice. We came Home & it is cloudy.

SOROR POLLY was Peabody's sister Mary (b. 1739). Osgood was probably THOMAS OSGOOD (1721–98) of Andover. Ingalls was WILLIAM INGALLS (1737–98) of Andover. Rev. Aaron HUTCHINSON (1722–1800), Yale A.B. 1747, preached *Valor for the Truth* to the Presbyterian Church in Newburyport in 1767. A denunciation of the theological moderation of liberal, often Harvard-educated ministers, it triggered a controversy pitting Calvinist and Arminian spokesmen against one another. Peabody's approval of Hutchinson was to be expected in view of the diarist's theological orthodoxy. Endicott, "Peabody Family," 159; Osgood,

Descendants of . . . Osgood, 46; *Vital Records of Andover,* 2:516; *Ingalls Family,* 53; *Sibley's Harvard Graduates,* 12:174–75.

1. Wife.

Saturday the 8th of August.

To Day is some Cloudy & Worm. I wrote some & read Mr. Hutchininson's Sermon again & like it much & P.M. Sr. Barnard came here & I took a ride with him up to Andover to see Lovejoy & then we all went up to see Holt & there was a smart Shower. Stay'd there till it slack'd & so came off down Lovejoy's where we drank Tea & came Home. Barnard is going to stay there over the Sabbath. I call'd at Esqr. Phillips's & at Br. Oliver's & I came Home.

Sunday the 9th.

To Day is fair Weather. I took Br. Johns Horse & let him have mine, & went to Meeting & heard Mr. Sparhawk preach a sermon in A.M. from the 22d of Luke & the 19th Verse. It was the best discourse I ever heard upon the Subject. P.M. he Preach'd from the 8th of Romans & 30th Verse. I din'd with Sr. Porter, after Servise. I set of down to old Boxford call'd at Uncle Fosters a spell, got to Sister Woods just at Night & found them all well there.

Jonathan FOSTER was the husband of Peabody's aunt Hannah. Endicott, "Peabody Family," 156.

Monday the 10th of August.

To Day pleasant but Showery. Sister is going to have a Vendue to sell some of her Household stuff. I look'd over the Inventory & took an Account of what she determin'd to sell & what she wanted to keep & went down to John Hales to get him to come up to it & bid of some things for her. I lit of Jewett & he came with me, & tells me that my worthy Class-Mate Adams is thought to be near his end.

My Father & Mother & Br. Peters & Sister came down, & there was a number of People came, & things went of pretty briskly though cheep. I stood Clark of the Vendue till almost nine o Clock & then I got Doctr.

Hales to stand in my Room & being our People are going to stay I came away & rode about Seven Miles & put up my Horse & tarry'd all Night. Nihil magus &c.

Note the subterfuge used to inflate prices at Peabody's sister's auction. JOHN HALE was probably John Hale (b. 1745) of Boxford, a son of Cousin Priscilla (Peabody) Hale. Peabody's MOTHER was the former Sarah Head. She was probably the daughter of Henry and Joanna Head born in Newbury on March 27, 1702. SISTER PETERS was Peabody's sister Sarah. Dr. HALE was probably William Hale of Boxford. George R. Howell, ed., *Genealogy of Descendants of Thomas Hale of Watton, England, and of Newbury, Mass.* (Albany, N.Y., 1889), 215, 223–24; *Vital Records of Newbury*, 1:218; *Peabody Genealogy*, 25; *Vital Records of Boxford*, 43, 153.

Tuesday the 11th of August.

To Day is Pleasant. After Breakfast I tarry'd the bigger Part of the A.M. & then validecabam Amicorum & accipio paucos Pyros,[1] & set of for Home. Stop'd a few Minutes by the Way, got Home a little before twelve, spent the chief of the P.M. fiting my Things for Cambridge. Kimball finish'd my Jacot & Bree[ches] & I determin'd to have the making the Coat defer'd till I come up again. Just at Night my Father & Mother came Home, & I went up to Br. Olivers for Money but got none. He is to have it soon & will send it to me at Cambridge. I drank Tea there & stay'd till in the Evening & then came Home by Wm. Copper's & did an Arrand for Br. John. When I got home & found Fogg there who stayed all Night & is going to Cambridge Tomorrow.

Peabody's college education required the commitment of his entire immediate family. Not only did his parents have to do without the farm labor he would have provided if he had remained at home, but sisters, brothers, and even more distant relatives did what they could to make his liberal education possible. Cash was short in an economy that depended heavily on credit and barter as in New England. The efforts of Stephen's brother Oliver reflected both the commitment of relatives to facilitate Stephen's education and the difficulty New Englanders encountered when they needed to convert credit into cash.

1. I wished my friends the best and accepted a few pears.

Wednesday the 12th of August.

To Day is Pleasant & I got my Things ready & Esq. Webster & his son came & my Father is going with me to bring back my Horse so we all set off togather. I call'd at several Places in the Town & at Fryes there ware more Scholars going down. We proceeded on our Journey stop'd at Jacoes & call'd & din'd at Wyman's at Woburn, got to Cambridge a little before five o Clock. I called at Bowman's see David Tenny & left some Things that I had for Hannah which I brought from the Eastward, got to College & found my Chum & I have continued in our old Chamber, & that I have not got the Waitership, but am Moniter which is an unthankful Post. Found Things all safe, but a vast deal of uneasiness about Chums & Chambers. I put our Horses out at Frosts & my father did some Business with [. . .][1] for Nathaniel Peabody & came up & spent party of the Evening at my Chamber, & then I accompany'd him to Warland's where he lodged.

They tell me that Mr. Elot is chosen Tuter in the Room of Mr. Hancock.

Because Peabody's family was of modest means, he depended in part on student jobs to pay his own way. While more affluent undergraduates would have found a WAITERSHIP in the college Commons menial, it was desirable for someone such as Peabody who needed the support. The monitorship Stephen received instead was particularly undesirable. MONITORS took attendance at church and chapel, a policing function that invariably made them unpopular. From the faculty's perspective, however, Peabody was an obvious choice for the post because he had already shown himself to be perfectly willing to report misbehaving scholars. WEBSTER was probably Jeremiah Webster of Kingston, New Hampshire, father of Peabody's classmate Nathaniel. En route, Peabody stopped in at the farm of Samuel Jaques or Jaquis (JACOES), the only adult male resident of Wilmington with that surname. FROST was probably Edmund Frost (1715–77), a blacksmith who lived on what is now Kirkland Street in Cambridge. *Sibley's Harvard Graduates,* 17:303–5; Kelley, *Wilmington Records,* 48, 148, 231; Pruitt, *Massachusetts Tax Valuation List,* 294–95; Paige, *History of Cambridge,* 553, 554.

1. Illegible [one last name].

Thursday the 13th of August.

To Day is Pleasant. We ware in an unsettled Posture, so there was but very little done. Mr. Noyes was down to bring John, & at my Chamber some Time.

I found so many Inhabitants in my Bed Sted, I was oblig'd to take it down & get it scalt by Mrs. Pierce.

My Father could not get all his Business done for Peabody but expects to come down again. He went from here to Day about Eight o Clock.

Roommates customarily shared a single bed, but preferably not one with other INHABITANTS like bedbugs. Joseph NOYES of Newbury was the father of JOHN NOYES (1750–1819), A.B. 1771, whom he was delivering to college to start his freshman year. John prepared for Harvard at Dummer Academy; he became a merchant in the coastal trade and eventually moved to Lumberton, North Carolina. MRS. PIERCE, or Pearce (her first name is unknown), was a sweeper, one of two women who maintained the dormitories. Her responsibility was the north end of Stoughton Hall and all of Hollis Hall. *Sibley's Harvard Graduates,* 17:567; Faculty Records, 3:208.

Friday the 14th.

To Day is some Cloudy & at Night Rains some. The President & Tutors met to examine Six Scholars & they accepted five & turn'd one by who was turn'd by for the Vacation. My Chum moved out of College to Mr. Warlands. Esqr. Phillips came here & stay'd some Time & tried to get his son in to live with Osgood but could by no Means prevail with them; he went from here just before Night, & Osgood & I took a Walk to Bowman & I took two Letters there to send to York.

Kast ow'd [. . .][1] 15/ & he could not get it, & he said he would give it to any one for 4/6 so I took him up & asked Kast for the whole & he readily paid me.

Roommates lived in such close circumstances that the prospect of a randomly assigned chum was unpalatable to Peabody when Jacob Jewett decided to move out of college housing. Thus Stephen took the initiative to control the outcome. OSGOOD was either Samuel Osgood (1748–1813), A.B. 1770, or David Osgood (1748–1822), A.B. 1771. Both were natives of Andover and acquaintances of Peabody. Samuel Osgood had also attended Dummer Academy. *Sibley's Harvard Graduates,* 17:412–19, 570–80.

1. Illegible [one last name].

Saturday the 15th of August.

To Day fair Weather. I made my Bill & fitted a little to oversee the scholars, corded up my Bed, & fitted up my Things a little, & the President & Tutors met concerning settling some Chambers & I went (as I had no Chum) & petitioned hard for Samuel Phillips & to my surprize obtained him, though much to my Joy.

Doctr. Thom. & Esq. Vernier was at Sargents Chamber so I wrote a

Letter to Esqr. Phillips, & sent it by the Doctr. informing him what I had done & for his son to bring down Furniture. I read a little in Lock this P.M.

Although classes had not yet begun, Peabody apparently got a head start on his assignments. The work by John LOCKE may have been *Essays on Human Understanding,* which the college adopted as a text in 1743. Dr. Isaac THOM resided in Methuen between 1769 and 1781, but his whereabouts are otherwise unknown. Siegel, "Governance and Curriculum," 388; *Vital Records of Methuen,* 278.

Sunday the 16th of August.

To Day Pleasant & cool. I went to Meeting & heard Mr. Appleton expound A.M. from the 1 of John 5 Chapt. 10. 11. 12. & 13th Verses. P.M. he preach'd from the 6th of Hebrews 7th & 8th Verses. I wrote for Townsend & read Mr. Marshal. I went into the Butery to Day noon & talked with Frensh a spell & find him to be a very Sensible Person.

At the start of the school year, Peabody made an effort to get to know the new students, including freshman Jonathan FRENCH (1740–1809), A.B. 1771, who eventually became the minister of the South Church in Andover. French relied on college aid throughout his undergraduate career and was serving as "Butler's Freshman," in effect a work-study job in the BUTTERY, a small shop presided over by the butler that sold the undergraduates sundries such as paper, ribbons, and cider. *Sibley's Harvard Graduates,* 17:514–20.

Monday the 17th of August.

To Day is Pleasant. We had no reciting. I read some Leters & wrote a Leter to Pike, & did some other writing & at Night I read Lock. There was one Bangs a Freshman lodg'd with me to Night.

The school year began slowly. Without a rigid academic calendar, the faculty waited for the students to trickle into Cambridge. Isaac BANGS (1752–c. 1780), A.B. 1771, of Harwich, became a doctor. He died in military service. *Sibley's Harvard Graduates,* 17:480–84.

Tuesday the 18th.

To Day is cool & very Pleasant & Austin & I got leave to go out of Town & walked down to Boston. I went Home with him & din'd & drank Tea

& was very handsomely treated, & I find Mr. Austin to be a very sensible Man. I did my Business in Town. Got a Wards Mathematicks & a Cyphering book & Bayleys Dictionary for Fransis Kimball & it cost 60/ & left my Watch to get clean'd. I borrow'd a book of mr. Austin which is a Preface to the copysign of Faith & I saw some Sermons that were put out by Mr. Davis which I think by so short a view of them are fine.

We came over the Ferry & got up to College just in the Evening. I went to Fleets & spoke for the News Papers another Year.

Nihil majus only there was a scholar examined to Day & accepted which makes 55 Freshmen.

Since students were still arriving for the new year, Peabody had an opportunity to socialize and do errands in Boston. Jonathan Williams AUSTIN (1751–79), A.B. 1769, eventually moved to Chelmsford, where he was a lawyer. His father was Samuel AUSTIN of Boston. WARD'S MATHEMATICKS was John Ward, *The Young Mathematicians Guide: Being a Plain and Easie Introduction to the Mathematicks* (many editions). BAYLEY'S DICTIONARY was Nathan Bayley, *Dictionarium Britanicum; or, A More Compleat Universal Etymological English Dictionary Than Any Extant* (London, 1730). DAVIS'S SERMONS was Samuel Davies, *Sermons on the Most Important and Useful Subjects* (many editions); Davies, who was briefly president of Princeton, preached the warm Calvinist doctrine that Peabody favored. *Sibley's Harvard Graduates,* 17:116–22.

Wednesday the 19th of August.

To Day is Pleasant. I recited & desputed publickly in A.M. & just a noon my Chum Phillips came down & brought his Things & likewise Freshman Osgood from Andover. They bring no News. I wrote a Letter to Br. Oliver & sent it by the Man who has back my Chum's Horse & Cart.

I accompany'd my new Chum to Diner & he spoke to Manning for some Chairs. I helped him fit up his Things a little & in the Evening I read Locke.

Samuel PHILLIPS, Stephen's new roommate, was only fifteen years old at the start of his freshman year, more than a decade younger than Stephen. His parents, Elizabeth and Samuel, Sr. (1715–90), A.B. 1734, a wealthy Andover merchant, must have found it comforting to think that a mature and responsible roommate would be looking after their son. FRESHMAN OSGOOD was David Osgood. MANNING was either Edward (1698–1774) or John (1725–1814) Manning, father and son, both chairmakers of Cambridge. *Sibley's Harvard Graduates,* 9:431–36; Paige, *History of Cambridge,* 602–3.

Thursday the 20th.

To Day Pleasant. I attended the Exercises of the College as Usual. I compos'd a Peice to put into the Paper in Answer to one which Mr. Dana put in against our first Peice, & old Jewet has composed another. After Prayers there was a Ring of wrastling & there are some smart Fellows in the Freshman class.

By custom, the sophomores challenged the freshmen to a WRESTLING tournament near the beginning of the academic year. A test of the new students' manhood, it was intended to put them in their place. The response by James DANA to the disclaimer Peabody and David Tenny had placed in the *Boston Evening-Post* of July 20 appeared in the same newspaper's August 17 issue. Dana took offense at Peabody's and Tenny's assertion that he had not published in response to the "general desire" of Harvard's student body, noting that of 167 undergraduates, between 130 and 140 had petitioned him to publish his *Two Discourses Delivered at Cambridge.*

Friday the 21st.

To Day is Pleasant. I attended Prayers & made me a Bill for another Week, & took Jewets Peice & mine & fitted a Peice out of them both for the Paper & sent it down by Jewett but Fleet would by no Means print it unless there was a Name to it, for he [sa]ys he was much blam'd for printing the other, so Jewett brought it back again. P.M. I went to Lecture & heard Mr. Appleton preach a sermon from the 5 of Matthew 47th. After prayers they wrastled again, & in the Evening had a Feast of boil'd Corn, & then I studied Wolebious a while.

At noon we had a butiful sing with Master Wadsworth at Knowles's Chamber.

The text Peabody studied was WOLLEBIUS, *Compendium theoligiæ christianæ* (many editions). WADSWORTH was presumably John Wadsworth (1739–77), A.B. 1762. *Sibley's Harvard Graduates,* 15:329–31.

Saterday the 22d of August.

To Day it clouds up & looks like Rain. I attended Prayers & reciting. After Breakfast, Osgood, Gill, my Chum & I went after wild Charies but could get none. We came back & I wrote some & studie'd a little in Euclid.

There was a Number of us put in a Petition to the President to set by ourselves behind the Freshmen in the Chappel to sing & to Night we went in & made out pretty well in Vespers. We went to Bowers's Chamber & had a private Meeting & Crosby join'd us.

The chapel singers probably included many of the more pious undergraduates. Their musical contributions to college services both annoyed and challenged some of those students who did not share their religious commitment. John GILL (1750–1804), A.B. 1771, was from Cambridge. He settled in Princeton, Massachusetts, where he manufactured potash. The college used various geometry texts drawn from EUCLID beginning in the seventeenth century. William BOWERS (1744–1820), A.B. 1769, of Billerica, became a physician in that town. Aaron CROSBY (1745–1824), A.B. 1770, from Shrewsbury, became a missionary to the Oneida Indians and then served as the minister of the Congregational church in Dummerston, Vermont. *Sibley's Harvard Graduates,* 17:521–22, 125, 381–83; Siegel, "Governance and Curriculum," 434.

Sunday the 23d.

To Day is Hot. I went to Meeting & heard Mr. Appleton A.M. from the 6 of Galations 14th. P.M. he preach'd from the 6th of Hebrews 7th & 8th Verses. I read [to] Day in the Preface to the Confession of Faith & like it well.

We sang by ourselves in the Chappel again tho we had some Intruders, & we had a little soft Sing at my Chamber in Vespere.

CONFESSIONS OF FAITH refers to William Dunlop, *A Collection of Confessions of Faith, Catechisms, Directories, Books of Discipline and of Public Authority* (Edinburgh, 1719–22).

Monday the 24th of August.

To Day is clear & Hot. I attended Prayers & reciting in Euclid all Day. After Prayers they had another Wrastle & the Freshman Tyler threw Osgood & Chadwick, & so the Freshman Class have concur'd the Sophomores in Wrestling. I came to my Chamber & studied Euclid. Sr. Wood was to see me to Day.

If the implicit purpose of the annual wrestling tournament was to establish the sophomore class's dominance over the freshmen, then it was not a success in 1767. The winner was freshman Daniel TYLER (1750–1832), A.B. 1771, of Canterbury,

Connecticut, a future trader in his hometown. During the last day of the competition he defeated sophomores Benjamin CHADWICK and Samuel OSGOOD. *Sibley's Harvard Graduates*, 17:651–53.

Tuesday the 25th.

To Day is Hot. I attended Prayers & reciting in Euclid all Day. After Prayers they had another wrestle on the Common & I took hold of Tyler & never threw any Body easier nor much quicker. We had a drink at Knowles's Chamber & Cushing inebriabatur.[1] I came to my Chamber & studied Euclid a little.

Yesterday the Seniors chose their Oriter & Thesis Collectors. Greene has the Latin Oration, although Henshaw had allmost as many Votes for it, & as he expected it & was disappointed it almost killed him. Wentworth, McKenzie, West, & Jones ware Thesis Collectors.

Before the advent of class officers, the seniors expressed both respect and popularity when they voted for the principal commencement ORATOR and four THESIS COLLECTORS, the students who arranged for printing the day's program, paid for by the graduating class. The drunken Roland CUSHING (1749–88), A.B. 1768, of Scituate later became the register of probate of Lincoln County, Maine. David GREENE (1749–1812), A.B. 1768, the Latin orator, was from Boston, where he later became a merchant. Andrew HENSHAW (1752–82), A.B. 1768, of Boston, became the clerk of the Supreme Judicial Court of Massachusetts. Kenneth McKENZIE (1746–98), A.B. 1768, was from Edenton, North Carolina; during and after the Revolution he held a variety of civil and military posts. Benjamin WEST (1746–1817), A.B. 1768, from Martha's Vineyard, became a lawyer in Charlestown, New Hampshire. John Coffin JONES (1750–1829), A.B. 1768, from Newbury, became a merchant in Boston. *Sibley's Harvard Graduates*, 17:13–14, 27–29, 34–36, 59, 106–12, 49–54.

1. Was drunk.

Wednesday the 26th of August.

To Day is very Worm. I attended Prayers & reciting Euclid & the Lectures as usual. Went into Wigglesworths private Lecture for the first Time. After Prayers I went to Austin's Chamber to see his Pater & Mater & after they were gone had a little sing there. I saw old Jewett & he told me of an old affair of Varnums about his killing a Goose which he is lik'd to be found out in, & it distourbs him very much for there is a Rumer of a

Warrant being out after him, but it is without ground I believe. I studed Euclid this Evening.

Harvard professors offered two kinds of lectures: public lectures, which provided elementary introductions to subjects, and PRIVATE, or advanced, LECTURES for upper classmen, for which they paid the faculty members an extra fee. Jonathan Austin's MATER was his mother, Mary, of Boston. James Mitchell VARNUM (1748–89), from Dracut, left Harvard later in the school year. He graduated from Rhode Island College, now Brown University, in 1769. During the American Revolution he rose to the rank of brigadier general in the Continental Army. *Sibley's Harvard Graduates,* 17:116, 266–79.

Thursday the 27th.

To Day is Worm. I attended Prayers & reciting as usual. We had a Class Meeting at Cooledges Chamber, & voted when we go into Willard to get but 40 Lines in Xnophon & chose two Persons to speak to Mr. Willard when we are in a reciting not to exact so much of us, (the Persons are Tudor & me) inasmuch as we have so many Lectures to attend & are taking Books out of the Liberary.

This day's CLASS MEETING is the first indication in Peabody's journal of discontent with the recitations the students attended. It would not be the last. Samuel COOLIDGE (1751–90), A.B. 1769, came from Watertown. He became a schoolmaster in Dorchester. Students were not permitted to take books from the LIBRARY until their junior year. Peabody emphasized the time the privilege would consume because it was new to his class. *Sibley's Harvard Graduates,* 17:138; "College Laws and Customs," 371.

Friday the 28th of August.

To Day is Hot. I attended Prayers & read Mr. Dunlop. Just after noon my Father came down here on some Business for Nathaniel Peabody. He brings word that People are generally well, only my sister Rebecca is Poorly. He says likewise that there was a Clap of Thunder there this Week which struck Jona. Martin, Ephraim Swan, & some others who ware together, & stunded them but that they are all likt to do well.

I accompany'd him to Warland's to Diner then he went to Jewets to get his Business done & I came up & went in to Winthrops to begin Cyphering & he instructed us as far as our Division. I got my Father's Horse kept at Frosts. After Prayers I went down to my quondam[1] Chums Chamber &

my Father came there, & after some stay we all come up to my Chamber & spent the Evening. Frye call'd here again to Day. There was some Thunder & Lightning in the Night but there was but little Rain. My Pater lodg'd at Warlands. Br. Oliver sent me about 40 Pounds of Money.

REBECCA Peabody (b. 1746) was Stephen's youngest sibling. JONATHAN MARTIN lived in Andover's North Parish. EPHRAIM SWAN (1739–77) was from the town's South Parish. Swan was a farmer, and Martin was probably one too. FROST was probably the blacksmith Edmund Frost. Endicott, "Peabody Family," 159; *Andover Tax Assessments,* Tax for 1768; *Vital Records of Andover,* 1:357, 2:322; *Essex County Probate Index,* 2:894; Paige, *History of Cambridge,* 553–54.

1. Former. Peabody sometimes referred to his former roommate, Jacob Jewett, simply as his "quondam."

Saterday the 29th of August.

To Day is very Pleasant & cool wind N.W. I wrote two Letters to my Sisters, & my Father got his Business done & got his Horse & set of for Home. I sent all my dirty Linin by him. After my Father was gone I got leave to go to Boston & went down with Austin & went to his Fathers & din'd again. P.M. went & got my Watch & inquir'd into the Price of Books a little & came to Mr. Austins & he lent me one Vollume of Mr. Davis's Sermons to Read. We came from there between four & five & came to Cambridge. Thacher came up with us. I receiv'd two Letters from Pike & duo nam ejus Puilla.[1] They came by Lawyer Sewall.

I attended Private Meeting at Bowers's Chamber again.

Last Thursday old Jewett came to my Chamber & copy'd of that Peice we try'd to get into the Paper, & sign'd it by the Name of Enoch Prentice & sent it down by Osgood & he left it there, & whether it will be printed or not, is uncertain.

Peabody took advantage of his father's visit to send his DIRTY LINEN home for his sisters to wash. At the start of each term they washed twelve sets for him. He wore each set one week, returning it no later than the end of the term to be washed in time for the next term. On Peabody's newspaper PIECE, see below, August 31. Samuel Gilman, "Reminiscences of a New-England Clergyman and His Lady, Living at the Close of the Last Century," in *Contributions to Literature* (Boston, 1856), 196.

1. Two for his girlfriend.

Sunday the 30th of August.

To Day is cool & very Pleasant. I went to Meeting & heard Mr. Appleton expound from the 1 of John 5 Chaptr 14, 15, 16, & 17th Verses. P.M. he preach'd from the 14th of Proverbs 12 Verse. I heard read some of Doctr. Dodridge, & read myself two of Mr. Davis's Sermons which I like very Well, a Sermon of Mr. Chandlers which is good, & some in Mr. Dunlop who writes very well.

Nothing remarkable more to Day.

Peabody probably read a recently published sermon by James CHANDLER, the minister of the Congregational church in what is now Georgetown, Massachusetts, and was then a section of Rowley: *Ministers of the Gospel, Gifts of the Lord to His Churches* (Boston, 1767).

Monday the 31st of August.

To Day is very Pleasant. I attended Prayers & reciting as Usual. I went down to Mr. Sewalls & got some Books which Pike sent up to be deliver'd to H.B. After Prayers I went up tradere Literas[1] & cary'd the Books & got the two first Vollumes to read myself. They are the History of Clarysa Harlowe. I came to College again & our Paper was come up & to my joy I found the peice which was sent down against Dana printed Verbatim. I went to Osgoods Chamber & feasted upon boil'd Corn & then came to my own & studie'd a little in Ceasars Commentaries.

The debate over James Dana's *Discourses* ended with the publication in the August 31 *Boston Evening-Post.* Peabody maintained that the undergraduates who asked Dana for his discourses for the press "knew of a considerable number [of students] at that very time who shewed their utter aversion to the publication of it." He went on to contend that the petitioners, aged twelve to sixteen, were too young "rightly to distinguish between truth and error." He also questioned unpersuasively whether most of the large majority of undergraduates who signed the petition to Dana actually favored the sermons' publication. H.B. was Hannah Bowman, later Mrs. Pike. Peabody was reading *CLARISSA HARLOWE; or, The History of a Young Lady,* by Samuel Richardson (1747–48, many editions), for pleasure and moral instruction. In class, the text was CAESAR'S *COMMENTARIES,* which the college added to the curriculum in 1767. Siegel, "Governance and Curriculum," 357.

1. To deliver letters.

September 1767

Tuesday the 1 of September.

To Day is very Pleasant. I attended Prayers & reciting to Mr. Elot in Cæsars Commentaries & Horace, wrote a Letter to Pike; after Prayers Tenny & I went up to Bomans & I drank Tea there & after some time accipiebam Literam[1] & came down to College again & studied some in Cæser. Went into the Butery as I came along.

There is great inquiry about College who Enoch Prentice is but there can no such Man be found. Some judge one Thing & some another. Some think it was a Scholar who wrote & some mistrust perhaps the right Person, but nobody knows certain who did it.

Lieut. Putnam & James & one Kay ware at my Chamber to Day. They had been to Pomfret and bring word that my Friends are well there. Legebam Literas hæc Nocte.[2] Last Night about 10 o Clock Jon. Searl came to my Chamber from Rowley with Capt. Gardner. I was got to Bed but got up & let them in, & they made a short stop. Searl is going to keep Brookline School. He brings News that Adams grows worse fast. Malancholy News to me!

Yesterday I received a Letter by Parsons from Oliver. He is well & concludes to have some second Handed Books which I sent up to him.

Peabody sometimes acted surreptitiously, a fact that would have surprised classmates who came across his diary. His quiet pleasure at the puzzlement over the newspaper contribution by "ENOCH PRENTICE" anticipated his later satisfaction at the failure of his schoolmates to realize that he was turning in miscreants. In 1767, Harvard began to teach the works of Quintus Horatius Flaccus, or HORACE, the Roman poet, as part of the year's curricular reforms. JAMES may have been Peabody's nephew James Stevens, a son of his oldest sister, Sarah.

CAPT. GARDNER may have been his neighbor Jonathan Gardner of Andover's North Parish. It is not clear to which of the PARSONS Peabody was referring. There were three in school in September 1767: Obadiah (1747–1801), A.B. 1768; Theophilus (1750–1813), A.B. 1769; and David (1749–1823), A.B. 1771. All three had attended Dummer Academy. Siegel, "Governance and Curriculum," 357; *Andover Tax Assessments,* Tax List for 1768; *Sibley's Harvard Graduates,* 17:78–82, 190–207, 590–93.

1. I received a letter.
2. I read letters tonight.

Wednesday the 2 of September.

To Day is rainy & I studie'd & attended Exercises as Usual. Went in to the Library & took out Doddridges Life, & Lows call to a devout & holy Life & read some in the former.

After Prayers I read some, & made me a Book to take down particular sentences from Authors. My quondam & Osgood spent the Evening here. My chum & I made some Ink.

Ready-to-use products were much less common in colonial New England than they later became. Note that Peabody and Samuel Phillips made their own INK and Peabody made a BOOK. Such commonplace books were used to copy passages a reader wanted to remember. DODDRIDGE'S LIFE was probably the Boston 1766 edition, printed for John Mein, of Job Orton, *Memoirs of the Life, Character and Writings of the Late Reverend Philip Doddridge, D.D., of Northampton.* The book attributed to LOW was William Law, *A Serious Call to a Devout and Holy Life* (London, 1728).

Thursday the 3.

To Day it clears of. I attended Prayers & reciting in the Morning, but not after. I got ingag'd in reading which prevented it. I read in Dunlop upon Confessions of Faith, & like him well only he condemns the Marrow of Modern Divinity as a da[n]gerous Peice. I read in Doddridge & he does not like Confessions of Faith, & there seems to be a difference in the Judgments of good Men. I read a little in the Spectator likewise. After Prayers I went down & settled Accompts with Warland & pay'd him, & stay'd a little while with my old Chum, & then came to my Chamber.

In preparation for his intended life in the ministry, the most important intellectual work Peabody did took place not in the classroom but in the library and the study, where he read both religious and secular writings. Over the course of the year Peabody sampled many of the texts he believed he would need to master in preparation for ordination, including Edward Fisher, *THE MARROW OF MODERN DIVINITY* (London, 1645). When Peabody SETTLED ACCOUNTS with Owen Warland he performed a common act in colonial New England. Perpetually short of currency, New Englanders routinely transacted business on credit.

Friday the 4th of September.

To Day is cool & very Pleasant. Wind N.W. I attend Prayers & forgot my Punishing Book & was forst to come out in Prayer Time. Read some in Spectator & made me a Number of Bills & attended Mr. Winthrop in Cyphering & did through Division. Wrote a little & in the Evening studied in Wolebious.

As a monitor, Peabody kept a list in his PUNISHING BOOK of students who had missed chapel or Sunday services.

Saterday the 5th.

To Day is clear & pleasant. I attended Prayers & finished reading Mr. Dunlop. Upon the whole like it well. Read some in Spectator. At Noon took a Walk around the Square with Osgood & then old Jewett came to my Chamber & we studie'd Xnophon. In the Evening after having taken a short walk we attended private Meeting at Fletchers Chamber & read part of a Discourse of Doctr. Doddridges. I came to my Chamber & Hunt & Cushing came in there & staid some time.

Peabody's WALK AROUND THE SQUARE may be an early and surprising mention of Harvard Square, but it probably refers to Hollis Square, the open quadrangle bounded on three sides by Harvard and Hollis Halls and Holden Chapel. Elijah FLETCHER (1747–86), A.B. 1769, of Westford, became the minister of the First Church in Hopkinton, New Hampshire. HUNT was William Hunt (1750–1804), A.B. 1768, of Watertown, who practiced law there. *Sibley's Harvard Graduates,* 17:46–48, 156–58.

Lords Day the 6th of September.

To Day is Pleasant. I went to Meeting & heard Mr. Appleton expound from the 1 of John 5th Chapt. from the 18th verse to the end. P.M. he preach'd from the 14th of Proverbs 12th Verse. I wrote for Ballantine.

I heard some of Doctr. Doddridges rise & Progress read to Day, & read some of his Life & three of Mr. Davis's Sermons which are excellent. Things are set in a clear & most allarming Light, & what I have read & heard to Day, together with Consideration seem'd to have more than common Aspect upon me.

William Gay BALLANTINE (1751–1820), A.B. 1771, from Westford, became the first minister of the Congregational church in small, isolated Washington, Massachusetts. *THE RISE AND PROGRESS OF RELIGION IN THE SOUL* (many editions) was by Philip Doddridge. *Sibley's Harvard Graduates*, 17:478–79.

Monday the 7th of September.

To Day is clear & very pleasant. We recited to Mr. Willard. He was very high in Mane because we have got but 40 lines in Xnophon, & we all that ware in told him we could get no more now we had so many other Things to do & desir'd he would eleviate our Task, which upon Consideration he did after trying to Cow us a while, & telling us what the Sophamores get, & it was best for him, for we ware determin'd to get no more, & let him have done his worst. There was a large Number of our class did not come in to reciting in Mane pretending they expected to have reci[tation] in the old Chappel but however he punished in all, about two Dollars and a half for not coming in.

We did not recite i[n] P.M. I read some in Spectator.

Mr. Jos. Moody was in Town & at my Chamber in Vesperi.[1] He goes Home tomorrow.

Osgood was taken Sick this Evening.

It is difficult to overstate the extent of the tension between the undergraduates and the tutors. Many of the instructors were so young that they struggled to secure and maintain the respect of their students. Greek tutor Joseph Willard was twenty-eight in September 1767, and at least a few years older than his students, but he still bridled whenever he perceived a challenge to his authority. Controlling a classroom consisting largely of adolescent boys is often difficult, and the hierarchical model that governed social relationships sensitized Willard—and most other faculty members—to any apparent threat to his station. JOS. MOODY was probably Joseph Moody, brother of Samuel Moody, A.B. 1746, the master of Dummer Academy. Joseph and his wife were responsible for the academy farm, where the students also lived. *Sibley's Harvard Graduates*, 12:50. On student-tutor tensions, see Kathryn McDaniel Moore, "The War with the Tutors: Student-Faculty Conflict at Harvard and Yale, 1745–1771," in B. Edward McClellan and William J.

Reese, eds., *The Social History of American Education* (Urbana and Chicago: University of Illinois Press, 1988), 39–51.

1. In the evening.

Tuesday the 8th of September.

To Day is very Pleasant. I attended Prayers but not reciting till afternoon. Mr. Moody came to my Chamber, & I wrote a Letter to send to Master, & one to my Cousin Oliver & sent them by him. Osgood took a Vomit to Day and has considerable of a Fever, so that he is not able to sit up. My Chum watch'd over him to Night. In the Evening Jewett came here & studie'd with me Xnophon, & we had a Foderation of boil'd Corn.

Yesterday the Corporation met & chose Mr. Moore Librarian in the Room of Mr. Elot, & Mr. Danforth was chosen one of the Corporation.

Chadwick lodg'd with me hac Nocte.[1]

The care that Peabody's CHUM Samuel Phillips gave OSGOOD offers a particularly good example of the close sense of mutual responsibility among undergraduate friends. Peabody's COUSIN OLIVER (b. 1726), A.B. 1745, had died in 1752. In this entry Stephen may be referring to his nephew Oliver (1752–1831), A.B. 1773. Jonathan MOORE (1739–1814), A.B. 1761, originally from Oxford, Massachusetts, had been living in a college chamber, reading theology, and supplying local pulpits when the college's Corporation appointed him librarian in place of Andrew ELIOT, who had been promoted to tutor. Moore eventually became the minister of the First Church in Marion, Massachusetts. *Sibley's Harvard Graduates,* 11:563–64; 18:275–83; 15:80–82.

1. Tonight.

Wednesday the 9th.

To Day is fair Weather Wind out. I attended Prayers & reciting in Mane & then got leave to go out of Town but did not. I wrote some read a little in Spectator & began to read the History of Clarissa Harlowe.

P.M. Gridley & John Chadwick came here from Boston but did not make a very long stop. In the Evening I studied Xnophon with Guild, & then I watch'd with Osgood who seems to be a little better. I borrow'd two singing Books of French, & picked out one Anthem & one Tune more to Night. Read a little.

A popular novel that everyone of refinement must have read at some point, Samuel Richardson's *CLARISSA Harlowe* was also extraordinarily long, well over a thousand pages depending on the edition. Peabody revealed considerable persistence, chipping away at the book until he finished it on January 29. Benjamin GUILD (1749–92), A.B. 1769, was from Wrentham. He eventually became a bookseller in Boston. *Sibley's Harvard Graduates,* 17:161–66.

Thursday the 10th of September.

To Day is rainey & I attended Prayers & reciting as usual except at eliven when I was asleep.

In the Evening I went to John Fryes Chamber where they had a little Vendue & sold some old Books. I bought one which had two Sermons in it upon Election & Free Grace which I like very well. I give eighteen pence old Tennor for it.

Peabody's purchases at JOHN FRYE'S auction show him building a professional library in anticipation of ordination. The doctrine of ELECTION taught about how God saved sinners. The doctrine of FREE GRACE instructed that the Lord saved sinners out of His own goodness, and not in recognition of personal merit. OLD TENOR, first introduced in Massachusetts in 1690, was the province's paper currency until inflation forced the return to silver as the circulating medium in 1750. Thereafter, provincial law established a ratio of 7.5 Old Tenor (which remained in use) to 1 Lawful Money. McCusker, *Money and Exchange,* 132–33.

Friday the 11th.

To Day it clears of Pleasant. I attended Prayers as usual. Osgood is some better & got leave to go Home & I got leave to go with him, when Colo. Brattle shall think proper for him to go. Chadwick is not well took a Vomit.

In the Morning Peter Osgood, Daniel Hardy & some others came here from Concord Corts went to Boston & are going Home to Day. Pater did not know his Br. was sick, but he says he can do nothing towards getting him Home but when he is well enough & can get leave, he would have him come.

I went in to Mr. Winthrop to Day & we did Reduction. I wrote some & read my two Sermons & a little in History. I heard by Peter Osgood that John Porter lay very Bad wi[th] the Nerves Fever.

The level of mathematics taught at colonial Harvard is apparent in Peabody's comment that Professor WINTHROP had spent a session teaching the junior class REDUCTION—rewriting a mathematical expression in its simplest form. Winthrop was teaching his students how to restate fractions. PETER OSGOOD was a brother of sophomore Samuel Osgood of Andover. DANIEL HARDY was probably the resident of Bradford of that name born in 1743. Claude Hardy and Edwin Noah Hardy, *Hardy and Hardie, Past and Present* (Syracuse, N.Y.: Syracuse Typesetting, 1935), 425.

Saturday the 12th of September.

To Day is some cloudy & some cool. Wind pretty high at West. I expected to go Home with Osgood & got ready but Colo. Brattle came up & told him it would not do for him to go out, but if the Day was good tomorrow he might go. I went to several Places to get a Horse & Chaise, & at last am to have one of Stedman. Read some in Clarissa Harlowe & a little in Spectator to Day. In the Evening I attended the private Meeting at Fletchers Chamber. Read in Doddridge.

Whenever possible, the college sent students who were sick home for their families to care for them. Since students who lived nearby customarily accompanied the invalids, the practice provided an opportunity for a home visit. Ebenezer STEDMAN (1709–85), Cambridge selectman, kept a tavern on the present Mount Auburn Street near Dunster Street. Paige, *History of Cambridge,* 662–63.

Sunday the 13th of September.

To Day is clear & Pleasant. Colo. Brattle came up & gave Osgood & me a Pass & we got our Horse & Chaise & took our Things & set of for Home. We stop'd at Woburn & refresh'd ourselves & got to Capt. Osgoods just at 2 o Clock & Osgood held out very Well. We met with no Opposition only the Wardien at Wilmington inquir'd the Occation of our riding. I din'd there & then went to Meeting [P.]M. there in Singing Time heard Mr. Symmes preach from the 1st of Peter 2 Chapt. & the 7th Verse. I told Joshua Frye I had left some of John's Things at Capt. Osgoods. I called at Esqr. Phillips's & left some things for my Chum, & then I went down to Br. Olivers where I sup'd. Heard that John Porter was exceeding Bad & that he had wanted to see me very much. They say he has been in remarkable Horror of Conscience & raving Destracted also. I came to my Father's & found all as well as I expected. Rebecca is better.

My coming Home was very unexpected.

I read to Night Mr. Tuckers Peice against the Counsel.

Puritan Sabbath laws still prevented unnecessary Sunday travel in eighteenth-century Massachusetts. The PASS Colonel Brattle provided was a certificate authorizing the trip. The inquiry of the WARDEN in Wilmington was to make sure that Peabody and Osgood were traveling with a legitimate excuse. By the time Peabody and Osgood reached Andover, there was no time to make other arrangements, so Stephen heard William SYMMES preach, a rare occasion when he attended the liberal's service. John TUCKER (1719–92), A.B. 1741, was the minister of the First Church in Newbury. When New Light parishioners attacked Tucker for denying the doctrine of original sin, they called a council of representatives from nearby churches to consider the charge. Tucker responded with *A Brief Account of a Council* (Boston, 1767). CAPT. Peter OSGOOD, farmer of Andover, was Samuel Osgood's father. *Sibley's Harvard Graduates,* 11:78–91; 17:412.

Monday the 14th of September.

Today is very Pleasant. I took a Ride call'd & Decn. Chadwicks to tell them Benjn. was not well. I went to see Porter & he has his Senses but is very weak & sleepy so that he talk'd but little, appear'd to be very Glad to see me. There seems to be a little Hope of his living.

I came from there stop'd a few Minutes at Gideon Tylers, & at Uncle Fosters & then went down to Sister Woods where I din'd. Found them well. She tells me Mr. Williams of Bradford Corts Jenny Kilbourne, after the Old Woman had us'd her utmost Afforts she brought it to pass.

I went from Sisters down to see my Class-mate Adams who is very low & expects soon to leave the World. He was exceeding Glad to see me & said it was what he never expected.

Jos. Hale & his Wife ware there. I stop['d] & talk'd with Master & my Class-mate till dark & they both talk very well.

I had a considerable talk with my Class-mate alone & he told me the Troubles he had had in his mind for his Sins but seems to be comfortable now, & to have a good Hope that his Sins are pardon'd. He talk'd very plain to me & when we came to part he took me by the Hand, told me he was going to take his last farewell of me, that he should never see me, he believ'd more, wish'd me to be extensively useful in the World, & that I might be a means of doing much good & have many for my Crown of Rejoicing in the great Day. I wish'd him the best of Heavens Blessings, & so left him with a Heart breaking Parting I never had with any one. Oh! what a faiding Flower is human Life!

I came from there up to Bradford where I tarry'd all Night. People generally as well as Common &c.

The continuing story of Joseph ADAMS, suffering from a lingering and ultimately fatal illness, allows a glimpse of Peabody in two capacities. As a friend of his mortally ill classmate, Stephen offered support and consolation. As a would-be clergyman, he also assumed the role of confessor, urging on Adams the need to prepare for death. MASTER Samuel Moody of Dummer Academy was presumably visiting Adams for the same purpose. Rev. Samuel WILLIAMS of Bradford married JENNY (or Jane) KILBORN of Boxford on May 5, 1768. Joseph HALE (1688–1778) had served as deacon of Boxford's First Church, 1759–65. His WIFE in 1767 was the former Lydia Brown of Topsfield, Hale's third wife. Perley, *History of Boxford,* 405; *Vital Records of Bradford,* 285; *Sibley's Harvard Graduates,* 15:134–46; *Vital Records of Boxford,* 152, 240.

Tuesday the 15th of September.

To Day is some Cloudy & looks like a Storm. I went to Breakfast & then went cum meam[1]—down to Chandlers, & I went over to Haverhill to Master Whites to git some Books to bring down to John & got them. I went to Webster's to look of some Kerseys for a great Coat but did not like them much. I went up to see Chase in his School & he is surrounded by a great Multitude. I came over the River, stop'd at Chandlers a while & validicabam Amici[2] & came up to Ebenezer Websters whare we had an excellent Diner. Benjn. Gage & Daniel Jequish & their Wives were there & several others. We smok'd a Pipe & a little after three I got my Horse & came Home & John Robinsons wife & Betty ware there, & in the Evening he came & when they went away it was dark & Rainey. Rebecca Perley & Rebecca Varnum were at Br. Johns but he was gone to the Mash.

Peabody's unexpected visit home afforded him an opportunity to perform errands both for himself and for some of his schoolmates, including JOHN WHITE, A.B. 1771. John's father, also JOHN WHITE (1725–1806), A.B. 1751, was a merchant in Haverhill. KERSEY is a twilled woolen fabric, sometimes made with a cotton warp, typically used for coats. Simeon CHASE (1745–1831), A.B. 1767, became the schoolmaster in West Newbury. Daniel JAQUES (1728–75) of Bradford was with his second WIFE, Sarah (Dunston) Jaques (b. 1728). JOHN ROBINSON worked a farm in Boxford. BETTY was Peabody's older sister Elizabeth (Peabody) Coburn. REBECCA PERLEY (1734–1813) lived unmarried with her father and then with her brother Aaron in East Boxford. REBECCA VARNUM (c. 1742–1810) lived in Andover. *Sibley's Harvard Graduates,* 13:154–56, 16:449–51; William Morris, ed., *American Heritage Dictionary of the English Language* (Boston, 1970), 718; Roger Jaques and Patricia Jaques, eds., *Jaques Family Genealogy* (Decorah, Iowa: Jaques Family Association, 1995), 161–62; Boxford Single Tax List, 1767, North Parish; *Peabody Genealogy,* 25; M. V. B. Perley, comp., *History and Genealogy of the Perley Family* (Salem, Mass.: The Compiler, 1906), 32, 54; *Vital Records of Andover,* 2:562.

1. With my girlfriend (or perhaps girl friend).
2. I wished [my] friends well.

Wednesday the 16th of September.

To Day is very stormy so that I could not set out on my Journey. Stay'd at Home. Eat a plenty of Rost Corn & Water Mellions. Got sauce for Dinor, & fitted my Things for Cambridge. Br. John came Home & I shew him over our last Peice against Dana & had a Sing with him.

Thursday the 17th.

To Day is cloudy but not a great Deal of Rain. Our People with my help fitted me out with some Eatables & drinkables & I took leave & set out on my Journey. I call'd & paid Samuel Johnson for a pare of Shoes he had made for me, then call'd at Capt. Osgood & Samuel is Better. I had a sing with him & his Uncle from Haverhill who was there. I saw Doctr. Osgood & did an Arrand for him from Sr. Curtis to him. I stop'd at Esqr. Phillips's & din'd, took my Chum's Things & proceeded, left a Catalogue at Lovejoys to be sent to Sister Paters, call'd at Mr. Fryes to bring down Johns Things but he has been down this Week & cary'd them. I came from there to Wymans & refresh'd me & my Horse & paid the [owner?] for sabbath Day & then proceeded & got down to College about Eight & it is dark. I took my Things out of the Chaise & my Chum had it Home. Chadwick is poorly but they have no News since I went away.

SAMUEL Osgood's ability to join in a sing is a clear indication that his health had improved. His UNCLE FROM HAVERHILL was Isaac Osgood, A.B. 1744, who represented Haverhill in the General Court. Osgood, *Descendants of . . . Osgood,* 46; *Sibley's Harvard Graduates,* 11:472–73.

Friday the 18th of September.

To Day is very Stormy. I attended Prayers as Usual. When I came to go out in the Morning there was upon the Elm Tree the Effegies of Mr. Willard Executed. It was drest to the Life. On his Forehead there was the Greek Word Φιλοκακος.[1] Out of his Mouth hang those Words, cary it through the cognate tenses. There was upon the tree a Paper starchd containing a detail of his Life with his dying Speach which is a spirited Peice. An Advertizement was put up also to give Notice of a Vendue to be at his Chamber to sell every great Variety of Greek Authors to defray Funeral Charges.

Mr. Danforth order'd Cato to take it down, & he put it into the Brew House, & we hear nothing certain whether Willard takes any Notice of it or not. After Prayers they took it out of the Brew House & naled it to Willards Door, set a Bottle by it with a burning Candle in it & when he came to his Chamber he found it in that situation, he threw it out at the Window, but we hear nothing from him yet. The Steward sent to Knowles & I to come & dine with him to Day. We went & had a genteal Diner & was treated very handsomly by his Sons.

I went up to Bomans & received a Letter from Pike, took one to enclose to send to him. I came to my Chamber & Doctr. Russel came here & lodg'd. I eat a fine Water Melion to Day at my Chamber which I brought from Home, & in the evening we had boil'd Corn.

Undergraduate protests against Joseph WILLARD took an ironic turn when the students conjugated the caption for their effigy of the Greek tutor. CATO is unidentified but was presumably an African (or African American) slave or servant. Jonathan Hastings (1709–83), A.B. 1730, was the STEWARD, in effect the college's business manager. Hastings's SONS were Jonathan, A.B. 1768; Walter, A.B. 1771; and John, A.B. 1772. Dr. Edward RUSSELL (1735–85), A.B. 1759, preached in North Yarmouth, Maine. *Sibley's Harvard Graduates,* 8:720–23; 14:493–94.

1. *Philokakos:* lover of the nasty.

Saturday the 19th of September.

To Day is stormy. I attended Prayers as Usual. Read some in Clarissa Harlow. Doctr. Russel spent the chief of the Day here. I wrote a letter to Pike, & in the Evening attended private Meeting at Fletchers Chamber, read in Doddridge.

Sunday the 20th.

To Day is clear & very Pleasant. I went to Meeting & heard Mr. Scales preach two sermons if I may be allow'd the Expression from the 119th

Psalm & 59th & 60th Verses. I wrote for Allen. Read to Day three of Mr. Davis's Sermons which are excellent. In the Evening took a Walk with Tenny up to Bowmans & left my Letter to be sent to York. Chadwick is not so well to Day.

Once again, Peabody expressed disrespect for Tutor Stephen SCALES and his preaching ability. Ebenezer ALLEN (1748–1806), A.B. 1771, was from Tisbury. He became the minister of the Congregational church in Wolfeboro, New Hampshire. *Sibley's Harvard Graduates,* 17:471–73.

Monday the 21st.

To Day is very Pleasant. I attend Prayers & reciting Euclid as Usual, wrote a Letter to my Class-mate Adams, & some in Journal. At Evening took a Walk with Scammel round the Square. Heard tha[t] Mr. Willard said he did not Vallue the good or ill Will of 170 Boys, that they ware not worth minding.

Peabody's hearsay evidence suggests that Joseph WILLARD had as little use for Harvard's undergraduates as they had for him. His tenure as a tutor afforded him interesting preparation for his presidency between 1781 and 1804.

Tuesday the 22d of September.

To Day is Clear & Worm Wind aft. We recited in Mane as Usual & I attended Prayers as Usual. The overseers ware up to Day & we went into the Chapel & Chipman, Jones, Varnum, Thatcher, Henshaw, & Hunt Deliver'd each of them an Oration, & Tuder & Austin had a Dialogue, & they all preform'd Pretty well. We did but little studie to Day. Chadwick & Guild got leave to go Home & Tenny & Fisher went with them. They are sick. In the Evening I studie'd a little in Euclid.

Performances such as this day's afforded the faculty a chance to gauge the progress of the students. The OVERSEERS, the larger of Harvard's two governing boards, met periodically to consider matters of policy. In the eighteenth century the smaller governing board, the Corporation, dealt with more operational matters. By a Corporation vote in June 1766, at the Overseers' semi-annual visitation, selected students "exhibited," or made public presentations, an opportunity for the board to exercise quality control. Ward CHIPMAN (1754–1824), A.B. 1770, was from Marblehead. A Loyalist during the Revolution, he became a lawyer and eventually the chief justice of New Brunswick. Joseph HUNT (1750–1812), A.B. 1770, of Concord, became a doctor. Elias FISHER (1749–1831), A.B. 1769, was from Wrentham. He became the minister of the Congregational church in Lempster, New Hampshire. Corporation Records, 2:259; *Sibley's Harvard Graduates,* 17:369–79, 396–97, 155–56.

Wednesday the 23d.

To Day worm & after Prayers, reciting & Breakfast in the Morning Parsons & I got leave to go out of Town. (I got Coolidge to keep Bil). We walk'd down to Charleston where I parted with Parsons, & went over the Ferry & did my Business, & then I went to Gridleys whare I din'd & John Chadwick was there. After diner I played Chekers with Gridley & got the better of him, then Chadwick walk'd with me. I lit of Amazie Kyse & his Father in Town & they tell me People are generally well at Pomfret. I never saw my cousin Kyse before, & he tells me he shall [n]ot have Time now to come & see me though he talks of bring his Wife down this fall to see all his Relations. I lit of Esqr. Phillips who has been to my Chamber since I came down. He tells me he left our Friends well at Andover. He says he will come to Cambridge again before he goes Home if he has Time.

Chadwick & I went to see Mrs. Marshal & then to Mr. Harris's & it Rains steady. I borrow'd a great Coat there & came to Mrs. Robins's & Capt. Peter Osgood was there. His Wife & Daughter are over at Charleston. It rains stedy & we stay'd & went to Supper & then it slack'd raining & I left my great Coat to be sent back & Capt. Osgood & I came from there over the Ferry & before we got over it rain'd again fast. We went in to Trombles & the Wind blew & the Rain encreased very fast & was exceeding dark & thunder'd & lightn'd & so held on till midnight & I concluded not to try & go to Cambridge to Night. I lodg'd with the Capt. in Charleston. I left a Head Flower for Mrs. Osgood to carry up for my Sister Pol.

Peabody's encounter with his cousin AMAZIE KYSE—that is, Amasa Keyes (b. 1744)—and Keyes's father, Stephen, reveals how strong the sense of family was in colonial New England. Peabody's cousin Abigail (Peabody) had married Stephen Keyes in 1741. He was originally from Chelmsford, but in 1735 had removed to Pomfret, Connecticut, where the newlyweds settled and raised their children. Although Stephen indicated that heretofore I NEVER SAW MY COUSIN KYSE, the meeting was obviously meaningful to him. This was the second time within twelve weeks that he had met a cousin for the first time; on July 4 he met his cousin Asa Peabody. Peter Osgood's WIFE was Sarah (Johnson) Osgood (1719–1804); the DAUGHTER who accompanied them was probably Susannah

Osgood (1753 or 1754–1846). SISTER POL was Peabody's sister Mary. *Peabody Genealogy,* 20, 24, 25; Asa Keyes, *Robert Keyes of Watertown, Mass., 1633, Solomon Keyes of Newbury and Chelmsford, Mass., 1653, and Their Descendants* (Brattleboro, Vt., 1880), 83–84; *Sibley's Harvard Graduates,* 17:412; *Vital Records of Andover,* 1:288; Osgood, *Descendants of . . . Osgood,* 45.

Thursday the 24th of September.

To Day is clear & cool. I got up early & parted with Capt. Osgood & came up to Cambridge. Got there before Breakfast, & went to studieing Euclid, & at Eliven when we went to recite he would not let me say with the Class but would make me bring what I was behind up first, & so he Serv'd Parsons & Jones & several others, & after the Class had done we all went up to Battle him & Parsons talk'd very plain to him & a little impudent & [we] all had a slant at him & he was uncommon mad, & insisted upon our bring our Lessons up, & we are determin'd not to unless he makes all who have mised any.

In the afternoon we none of us went in reciting. He sent for us & told Parsons that he was in a Passion at noon, but that it was very necessary we should say every Lesson in this Book, & all that ever had been absent should bring it up as well as we, & talk'd handsomely.

Amazie Kyes call'd upon me a few Minutes this afternoon.

I went to see Wheton who is sick.

In the Evening I had College Company.

My Chum has been to Boston & says he has met with fine Luck & that his Father has bought him all he ask'd to set out our Chamber.

Tenny came down & brought me a Letter from Chadwick & he is better, & he says Porter is better, but that poor Adams is worse & is but just alive.

Most eighteenth-century Harvard students were not persuaded of the practical importance of the material they covered in class. They were in school to acquire the social polish and connections that every gentleman required, and in the case of prospective clergymen such as Peabody, to earn a necessary professional credential. Stephen shared these doubts, as he reveals in his resistance to his tutor's insistence that he make up the work he missed while at home. George WHEATON (1751–73), A.B. 1769, was from Norton. After professional study he briefly served as the minister of the Congregational church in Claremont, New Hampshire. *Sibley's Harvard Graduates,* 17:305–6.

Friday the 25th of September.

To Day is clear & cool. I attended Prayers as Usual. Tenny & I each of us receiv'd a Letter from Pike pregnent, so after Breakfast we went tradere eas.[1] I came to my Chamber & wrote two Letters Home.

I studie'd a little in Vulgar Fractions & attended Mr. Winthrop. My Chum had some old Maps & Pictures come up to Day.

We want to get Hill to come up & do something to our Chimney & white wash our Chamber, & he says he will next Week. In the Evening I came to my Chamber & wrote in Journal.

The President began to publish a new set of College Laws.

In a VULGAR FRACTION, as opposed to a decimal fraction, the numerator is placed above the denominator. Aaron HILL was the college mason. President Holyoke's decision to publish the COLLEGE LAWS probably reflected his concern at the incivility of relations between the tutors and the students and the resistance of the latter to the former. Corporation Records, 2:277. For the new laws, see "College Laws and Customs."

1. To deliver them.

Saturday the 26th of September.

To Day is some cool. I attended Prayers as usual read some, & studie'd & wrote some upon Fractions. P.M. my Chum went to Boston & got a new set of Maps. In the evening I attended private Meeting in Bowers's Chamber. Read in Doddridge. I went to see Sr. Smith A.M., & had a long talk with him.

Every year a few recent graduates preparing for the ministry remained in residence in the college dormitories while they read theology on their own in preparation for ordination. When an opening arose in a junior teaching or administrative position these men formed an available pool of candidates from which the faculty would choose. Tutorships were the most prestigious of these openings, followed by the positions of librarian and finally butler. Some graduates worked their way up the hierarchy from butler to librarian to tutor. Isaac SMITH (1749–1829), A.B. 1767, a cousin of Abigail Adams, was a resident graduate in 1767. After a European tour he became a tutor in 1774, but his unreliable politics forced him to flee to England after the Battles of Lexington and Concord on April 19, 1775. He eventually returned to Massachusetts, where he served as Harvard's librarian, 1787–91, and as the master of Dummer Academy, 1791–1809. *Sibley's Harvard Graduates,* 16:523–30.

Sunday the 27th.

To Day is cool. I attended Prayers & went to Meeting as usual. Heard Mr. Appleton expound from the 2d Epistle of John from the 7th Verse to the End. P.M. he Preached from the 20th of Matthew 6th & 7th Verses. Some breveramus [?][1] at Meeting. I read to Day in Mr. Davis & in the Evening part of Mr. Tuckers answer to Mr. Chandler which is witty.

Doctr. Wales brook a Tooth for Thatcher at my Chamber to Day, & at Night I went to see him & he tells me he has a good Deal of pain. Willard call'd me up about Disorder at Meeting & I told him what I knew.

Although Stephen's journal reveals frequent confrontations between the tutors and the students, it also makes it clear that the faculty often consulted with him after student DISORDERS. Peabody's evening reading was John TUCKER, *A Letter to the Reverend Mr. Chandler* (Boston, 1767).

1. Possibly "we shortened."

Monday the 28th.

To Day is pleasant but at Night clouds up. I attended Prayers but not reciting, finish'd reading Mr. Tucker's Peice, then wrote a Letter to John Porter, pen'd down some sentences out of Mr. Davis's Sermons, attended Mr. Sewall's Lecture, wrote a little in Journal, & perus'd the News Papers, found two of the smartest Peices in Edes & Gill upon Liberty that I ever saw. I can think of nothing remarkable more.

Peabody commented in his diary only occasionally on the political issues of his day. However, his appreciation for the articles on LIBERTY in the September 28 issue of the *Boston Gazette,* published by Benjamin EDES (1732–1803) and John GILL (d. 1785), makes it clear in no uncertain terms that he shared the fear of most New Englanders that a corrupt and oppressive administration threatened the freedom of Englishmen both at home and in the colonies. Stephen SEWALL (1734–1804), A.B. 1761, was the first Hancock Professor of Hebrew and Other Oriental Languages. Thomas, *History of Printing,* 134–38; *Sibley's Harvard Graduates,* 15:107–14.

Tuesday the 29th of September.

To Day is Stormy. I attended Prayers & reciting A.M. as usual. P.M. attended Wigglesworths Lecture & then I was taken with the Teeth Ache

& went up to Wales & he dug out two Roots which have long troubled me & he pull'd out one which he broke of last Winter.

I went to Tuders Chamber & heard him read a very pretty Sermon in Favor of Swearing. I wrote a little upon Cyphering, & a little in Journal, & in the Evening read a Chaptr. of Doddridges Life.

By the 1760s, specialists had begun to appear in Boston to treat TEETHACHES such as Peabody's. Most patients, however, still went to general practitioners or folk healers and craftsmen (including Paul Revere) who pulled teeth as an adjunct to performing other services. James Wynbrandt, *The Excruciating History of Dentistry: Toothsome Tales and Other Oral Oddities from Babylon to Braces* (New York: St. Martin's Press, 1998), esp. 88–92.

Wednesday the 30th.

To Day is Pleasant. I attended Prayers but no reciting for Hill came & white washed my Chamber & built a stone Chimney & we give him 55/ for doing the Chimney. In the Evening I went up to Wentworths Chamber & there was a Number there ploting against Knowles. Then I went into Knowles's Chamber & he was very much inrag'd with them, but he was in feeble circumstance, could make but a poor shift in talking, so I left him & they did nothing to him.

I went in to Cushings Chamber & Sr. Cushing came there, & after a while they both came to my Chamber & smok'd a Pipe & drank a Glass of Wine.

I read to Day in D. Doddridge's Life.

SR. CUSHING was probably Lemuel Cushing (1746–76), A.B. 1767, of Scituate but possibly John Cushing (1744–1823), A.B. 1764, of Shrewsbury. Lemuel eventually became a doctor; in 1768, John was called to the pulpit of the First Church in Ashburnham. *Sibley's Harvard Graduates,* 16:454–55, 36–40.

October 1767

Thursday the 1 of October.

This Day Pleasant. I attended Prayers & reciting in Mane & then Mr. Elot went out of Town & we had no reciting. My Chum & I fitted up our Maps & put up the Pictures, clean'd our Chamber & got Things in very good Order.

P.M. Tenny & I went up to Bowmans to meet [C]apt. Stone & his Lady from York. We found them there with some others but they are all in a great hurry & did not stop long. We drank Tea & Wine in plenty. Tenny & I spent part of the Evening there & sang some, then came to College.

Joshua Bowman's Wife was there.

Langdon has got leave to go Home & John Noyes is going to carry him Tomorrow, so after I came to my Chamber, I wrote two Letters to Byfield, & a little in Journal.

Distractions often interrupted undergraduates' education in the eighteenth century. Many of the tutors, including Andrew ELIOT, were less interested in teaching than in preparing themselves for the ministry, a process that often led them to skip classes as they supplied pulpits several days' ride from Cambridge. In 1774, Eliot accepted a call to the First Church in Fairfield, Connecticut. It is fortunate that the students rarely resented the cancellation of classes. STONE and his LADY were Capt. John Stone of York, Maine, and his second wife, Martha (Greenough), formerly of Boston. Abigail (Fowle) Bowman was the WIFE of JOSHUA BOWMAN, who had recently left Watertown for North Carolina, where he had settled. Paul LANGDON (1752–1834), A.B. 1770, of Portsmouth, became the first preceptor of Fryeburg Academy in Maine. Lester MacKenzie Bragdon and John Elbridge Frost, trans., *Vital Records of York, Maine* (Camden, Maine: Picton Press, 1992), 73, 150; *Sibley's Harvard Graduates,* 16:328, 17:402–4.

Friday the 2d. of October.

To Day is Pleasant. I sent my Letters by John Noyes, & then I went to studieing Fractions & P.M. I attended Mr. Winthrop. Just at Noon Mr. Phillips of Boston came here & is going to Andover. I sent two Letters by him Home, & just after Commons I coppy'd of a Letter to John Porter & sent it by Cabot who is going up to Haverhill.

I went down to see my quondam a little spell, & I left my Hat with Jones to be drest.

In the evening I went to Parsons Chamber to a Vendue of Books but there was nothing very valuable sold.

I came to Scammel's Chamber studie'd Wolebious, & then came to my own.

Because the college did not test its applicants for admission on arithmetic, to say nothing of higher mathematics, many of the undergraduates arrived in Cambridge with at best a rudimentary knowledge of the subject. Mathematical instruction consequently included many basic subjects such as decimals and FRACTIONS. Mr. PHILLIPS was probably William Phillips (b. 1722), merchant of Boston, Andover native, and an uncle of Peabody's roommate, Samuel Phillips. George CABOT (1752–1823), A.B. 1770, of Salem, became a sea captain, merchant, and U.S. senator. Tyler, *Smugglers & Patriots*, 270; *Vital Records of Andover*, 1:304.

Saturday the 3d.

To Day is very Pleasant. After Prayers, reciting & Breakfast Jewett, Webster, John Frye & I went out a nuting. We found a great many Nuts but they ware hard to shell so we got but a few. We divided them at Fryes Chamber, & helped him drink some [Rum] & then came to my Chamber. After diner Wentworth cut my Hair & Jewett & I began to studie Xnaphon & Sr. Pike came here (he has been to Boston) & he stayed till Night. He told me privatly he is going to enter into a conjugal State in a very private Manner, & strongly invited me & Tenny to take a Ride with him on Monday as far as Dunstable. I was Amaz'd at it, & could not give him an Answer, but we are to think of it & tell him another Time.

He went from here & I attended the private Meeting at Fletcher's Chamber, & came to mine wrote a little.

Nicholas PIKE's secret marriage to Hannah Bowman of Cambridge, first hinted at here, was remarkable because elopements were extremely uncommon in colonial New England, and certainly among the alumni of Harvard College. New

Englanders almost always postponed marriage until they were settled and their careers begun. Only then did they believe that they had reasonable prospects for supporting a family. Wright, *Revolutionary Generation*, 73–74.

Sunday the 4th of October.

To Day is Pleasant & at Night a little Rain. I went to Meeting & heard Mr. Appleton expound from the beginning of the 3d Epistle of John. P.M. he preach'd from the 20 of Matthew 6 & 7 Verses. At noon I smok'd a Pipe with Thacher & Austin. Read two of Mr. Daviss Sermons & finished the 3d. Vollume; they are the best Sermons I ever read. Pike was here after Meeting & insists on Tenny & my going with him but Tenny is not well, & Pike says he will be here early tomorrow Morning.

Monday the 5th of October.

To Day is exceeding Pleasant. I attended Prayers, & Pike came here & was very urgent with us & we concluded to go with him. I got leave & fix'd up as soon as possible & we got a Horse & Chaise at John Hastings's & went up to Newells & Pike & Hannah ware there. We drank & went to Breakfast & set off from there about nine. Went through Woburn into Bildraca where we stop'd & Drank & oated our [Ho]rse. From there we went to Chelmsford where we din'd at the Tavern & oated our Horse & our Horse was Lame & began to faulter. We went from there up into the upper Part of Dunstable to one Pike's, a Relation of Sr. Pike & when we got there our Horse could hardly set his Foot to the ground. There was a good Deal of Company there & ware going to have a great Husking. Pike let his cousin know the secret & he told us he would go with us, so he let us have a Horse for our Chaise & left the lame one there, & we went over to one Esqr. Lovills & there was one Esqr. Chase there who married Mr. Nicholas Pike to Miss. Hannah Bowman. We came back to Mr. Pikes & after they had done husking we had a very genteal Supper, though we had a Dish of tea as soon as we came back. Spent the Evening conversing & singing. The huskers had a very great Frollick so we did not get to Bed till late. They had so much Company the Bride & Bridegroome lodg'd appart.

Despite the sensational beginning of Nicholas and Hannah Pike's marriage, their families eventually accepted it. By March 21, 1768, as Peabody reports below, Hannah's father, Noah Bowman of Cambridge, had begun to treat Nicholas well. The

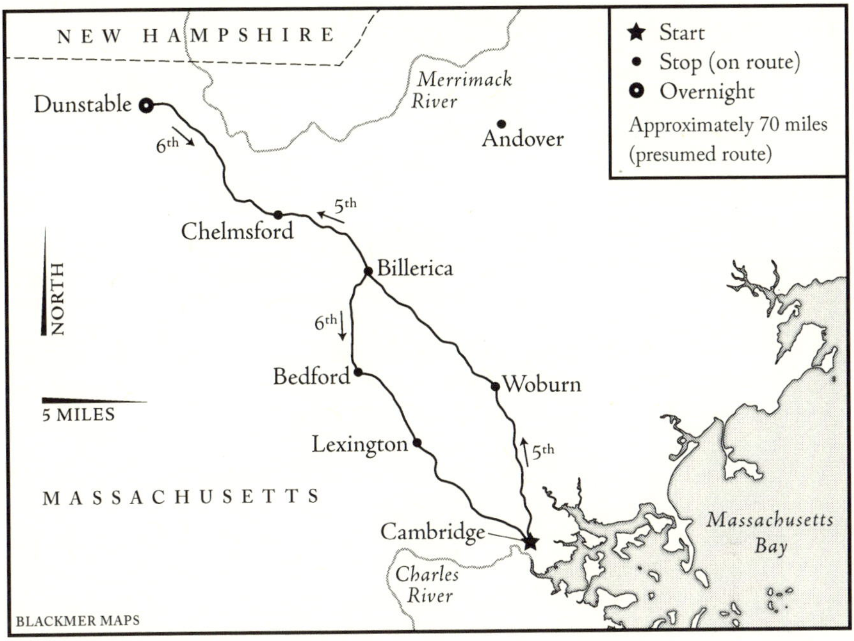

Peabody's Trip to Dunstable, October 5–6, 1767.

couple remained married until Hannah's death on July 7, 1778. Jonathan NEWELL (1749–1830), A.B. 1770, of Needham, became the minister of the First Parish in Stow. Pike's RELATION was either of two brothers, his cousins Benjamin (1723–1803) and Daniel (1725–91), sons of his uncle Joseph. LOVILL was a member of the Lovewell family of Dunstable, which included Col. Zaccheus (1701–72) and Col. Nehemiah (1726–1801), both militia officers, and Jonathan (1713–92), who held a number of civil offices. *Sibley's Harvard Graduates,* 16:406–7, 17:409–12; Pike, *Family of John Pike,* 54, 85–86, 89–91; Ezra S. Stearns, *Early Generations of the Founders of Old Dunstable* (Boston: G. F. Littlefield, 1911), 39–43.

Tuesday the 6th of October.

To Day is Pleasant but our Horse was exceeding Lame so that we could not use him, & Mr. Pike concented to let us have one till Saturday & take Care of our Lame One, so after Breakfast we came from there & stop'd at some of Pikes Relations a little While & then proceeded. We came to Chelmsford again & din'd, & I saw Jona Sherwine there. He has been at Work up Country. We came from there thro' Bildrica, & they had a training there. We came through to Bedford & Pike & Hannah his new Wife stop'd there. Tenny & I ca[me] down to Lexington & oated our Horse & drank some Oringe Water & then came to Cambridge. Had our Horse & Chaise to Hastings's & told him how it was. We came to College & I find I have been punish'd for not reciting but I went up to Willard & told him how it was & he order'd the Punishment to be taken off & treated me like a Gentleman.

Peabody's judgment that Willard TREATED ME LIKE A GENTLEMAN reflects the expectations of colonial college students for whom a liberal education was primarily about acquiring social status. SHERWINE may have been Jonathan Sherwin (m. 1755) of Boxford. *Vital Records of Boxford,* 198.

Wednesday the 7th of October.

To Day is very Worm & some showery, Wind S.W. I attended Prayers & reciting A.M. as Usual. P.M. went up to Bowmans & Pike & Uxor is coming to my Chamber. I came down to College & went & invited some others to come but some of them could not, but at last I got Fessenden, Tenny & Porter, Ponds, Wyeth & Anna Warland; they came & drank Tea & spent a very pleasant Evening. I borrowed Palmers Fiddle & play'd a little for them to dance, & we had some singing, & just before nine they went off.

The presence of a young woman, ANNA WARLAND (1750–1835), daughter of Owen, a tailor, and Sarah (Stearns) Warland of Cambridge, at a party at Peabody's reveals the freedom undergraduates had to entertain in their dormitory rooms. Anna's brother was Owen Warland (1752–75), A.B. 1770, of Cambridge, who became a doctor in Boston. William FESSENDEN (1750–1805), A.B. 1768, became the first minister of the church in Fryeburg, Maine. Joseph Pearse PALMER (1750–97), A.B. 1771, of Braintree, became a merchant and teacher. *Sibley's Harvard Graduates,* 17.445, 17–20, 584–90; Paige, *History of Cambridge,* 677.

Thursday the 8th.

To Day is Pleasant. I attended reciting all Day. Got call'd out in Mane & prodigiously curs'd. Pike was here a few Minutes A.M. After reciting my Chum & I took a Walk to Boston with out leave. We got there a little after Sun down & I got my Watch & my Chum bought me a pare of Snuffers to carry Home. I lit of Austin & drank a Glass of Wine with him & then we went to Mr. Crooswell's Evening lecture & heard him begin a Sermon from the 12 Chapt. of John from the 27 to the 32 Verse. We stayed as long as we could & get over the Ferry, but what I heard of his Sermon I think is nihil ad Rem orat[1] most but very little. We came over the Ferry & got to College a little after nine & it is very Pleasant indeed.

In preparation for ordination, Peabody made a point of listening to as many prominent preachers as he could. Andrew CROSWELL (1709–85), A.B. 1728, minister of the Eleventh Church in Boston, had a controversial career that included itineracy in the manner of the evangelist George Whitefield and aggressive opposition to the theological moderates and liberals who were dominant in Boston. Croswell's theology and manner made him *persona non grata* among Boston's other clergy. *Sibley's Harvard Graduates,* 8:386–407.

1. It does not speak to the point.

Friday the 9th of October.

To Day is very Pleasant, & I attended Prayers as usual. Spent the chief of the Day in preparation for a ride I am going to take to Night. I bought some Trifles at Marrets to Day.

At Prayer Time Osgood came down from Andover & is going to keep a Horse here till the Vacation. He brings Word they have given Mr. Sparhawk a Call at Boxford & he is to give his Answer tomorrow but there is so many against him they think his Answer will be in the Negative. He says also that Porter is better. He likewise brings News that Jonathan Parker fell of from a Stage at Lovejoys & kill'd himself instantly.

I got leave of Mr. Danforth to go out of Town & went to Hastings's & got my Horse brought up & got all Things ready, & went to Bed & Tenny & John Noyes set up in order to wake me about one oClock.

New Englanders valued consensus in both their civil and ecclesiastical affairs, and candidates for ordination or installation rarely accepted a call from a seriously split church. In view of the division in the West, or Second, Boxford Church, Edward Perkins SPARHAWK, A.B. 1753, declined its invitation. MARRET was probably Edward Marrett (1713–80), tailor, militia captain, and Cambridge selectman, 1769–77. He lived on the corner of the present Mount Auburn and Dunster Streets. JONATHAN PARKER died in Andover in his sixtieth year on October 7, 1767. *Sibley's Harvard Graduates,* 13:360; Paige, *History of Cambridge,* 604, 605; *Vital Records of Andover,* 2:518.

Saterday the 10th.

To Day is little cloudy & a little Rain. Tenny & Noyes call'd me just before one oClock & I got ready & they went with me to get my Horse & then I set off.

Went through Woburn & got to Bildri[ca] just at Day & left some things at Capt. Bowers's for my Class-mate & I went up to Chelmsford where I went to Breakfast at Capt. Barns's Tavern (went out of my Way a little). I went from there to Dunstable to Mr. Pikes & found the old Horse almost as lame as ever. I made but little stop, paid him for his Horse & his trouble 50/ which I think very Reasonable, & came from there & drove my Steed. I stop'd at his Brothers & Fathers & the old People search'd for the lameness & found it to be in the Huff where it gravel'd & was working out above that Hair & had fastend almost all Round. I came from there & came on Foot the biger Part of the Way. Came the back Way through Chelmsford, call'd at Bildrica & eat & drank & oated at the Tavern, came to Capt. Bowers's where I took some Things for my class-Mate, eat part of a Rost Chicken & then proceeded (I call'd to see Jona. Stevens but he was not at Home.) I came through Bedford & Lexington into Manotomy. Let of a man whom I rode a little way with. I got to Cambridge between 10 & 11 & left my lame Horse at Hastings's. Came to my Chamber & was faithfully tired.

Note how early Peabody arose for his trip. Capt. William BOWERS was the father of William Bowers, A.B. 1769. When Peabody returned to Dunstable to retrieve the injured horse he had left earlier in the week, his stops included visits with both Pike brothers, Benjamin and Daniel, and their father, Joseph (1696–1788), Nicholas Pike's father's oldest brother, who owned a farm there. Oliver BARRON, a militia captain and selectman, kept a tavern in Chelmsford in the late 1760s. *Sibley's Harvard Graduates,* 17:125; Pike, *Family of John Pike,* 54, 89–91; Wilson Waters, *History of Chelmsford, Massachusetts* (Lowell, Mass.: Town of Chelmsford, 1917), 401, 174, 760.

Sunday the 11th of October.

To Day is Pleasant. I went to Meeting & heard Mr. Appleton expound from the 3d. of John from the 9th Verse to the End.

P.M. he preach'd from the 32d. of Deuteronomy 29th Verse. In the Evening Sr. Cobb came in here & we sang a little, & after he was gone Wentworth & Tenny & I went up to see Sr. Pike who is going Home

Tomorrow. We had a pleasant Sing & then parted & I came to College. I am not very Well.

Monday the 12th of October.

To Day is some cooler. I did not attend Prayers nor reciting. Was not very well. I went to Smith's Chamber & he gave me a Sermon in Praise of Swearing & I borrow'd of him Sherlock on Death. I read my Sermon to Day & some in Doddridge's Life. Like them both well. Wrote some, & read the Paper. Bought a Load of Wood to Day. Had a little Quarril with Bill Hunt for some of his extraordinary Freedoms. Osgood told me an odd Storry about Richard Kimbal & Br. Olivers Wife, but he says he did just hear of it, so he cant tell the particulars.

Too sick to attend prayers or class, Peabody stayed in his room and read. Under the circumstances, he felt free to choose whatever book he wanted. It speaks to his priorities that he selected a religious text that served his career aims but had nothing to do with his formal education. SMITH was either Jonathan Smith (1748–1829), A.B. 1768, of Hadley, later the minister of the First Church in Chilmark, or Abner Smith (1744–c. 1843), A.B. 1770, of Springfield, who became the minister of the Great Hill Church in Derby, Connecticut. William SHERLOCK wrote *Practical Discourse Concerning Death* (many editions). KIMBAL was probably Richard Kimball (1728–c. 1809), third child of Stephen's aunt Abiel (Peabody) Kimball and her husband, Joseph. BR. OLIVER'S WIFE was Sarah (Robinson) Peabody, mother of Oliver Peabody, A.B. 1773. *Sibley's Harvard Graduates,* 17:91–92, 429, 18:275; Morrison and Sharples, *Kimball Family,* 84, 148–49.

Tuesday the 13th.

To Day is cold. I did not attend Prayers or reciting but kept my Chamber. Wrote some & read in Doddridge's Life. Osgood was with us a little to Day.

Wednesday the 14th.

To day is Cool. I did not attend Prayers or reciting. I finish'd reading Dr. Doddridge's Life & began reading Law's Call to a devout & holy Life. There are several Scholars gone Home to Day with leave from the President & Tutors. I wrote a Letter & sent Home by Dow to my Father, wrote another to Obadiah Parsons.

Wentworth, Parsons, my Quondam & Osgood ware here in the Evening, & Parsons tells me that Mesrs. Elot & Willard drank Tea with him to Day which is very Remarkable.

Harvard's hierarchical social order made cordial interactions between students and members of the faculty relatively uncommon. PARSONS'S invitation to take TEA with tutors Andrew ELIOT and Joseph WILLARD was worth recording precisely because it was VERY REMARKABLE. LAW'S CALL is William Law, *Serious Call to a Devout and Holy Life* (many editions). Moses DOW (1747–1811), A.B. 1769, of Plaistow, New Hampshire, became a lawyer in Haverhill, New Hampshire, a leading New Hampshire legislator, and in 1793 a major general in the state's militia. *Sibley's Harvard Graduates,* 17:140–41.

Thursday the 15th of October.

To Day is cool. I kept my Chamber. Read in Mr. Law all Day. In the Evening I stept into Osgoods Chamber with Tenny a little While.

Friday the 16th.

To Day is cool. I kept'd my Chamber again. Finish'd reading Mr. Law & upon the Whole like him well. Wrote a little in Journal. Emerson came in here & mimick'd old Mr. Woster to very great Perfection to Day, & he has been afflicting Dole & has made him really believe he can raise the Devil. A sad Chap he is! I saw Dole & told him not to mind him.

This evening there came a Man here who has bought some Wood from Doctr. Russel from the Estward, & he sent word for us to have a Cord of it if we chose it. The Man is to be at the Vesel tomorrow when we are to go down & look of it.

Undergraduates heated their own rooms, at their own expense, using fireplaces. Students of modest means, such as Peabody, kept a close eye out for inexpensive WOOD for burning. Joseph EMERSON (1751–1822), A.B. 1771, of Topsfield, became the postmaster in Alfred, Maine. Greenleaf DOLE (1751–1829), A.B. 1771, of Rowley, became a schoolteacher in Georgetown. *Sibley's Harvard Graduates,* 17:510–11, 506.

Saturday the 17th.

To Day is cool. I got out & went down to the Wharf to look of our Wood. Like it pretty Well but it cant be got out of the Vessel till Monday. I came to my Chamber & read some in Clarissa Harlow & borrow'd Mr. Willards dying speech of Tracy & wrote it out, & studied a little in Euclid & Danforth has told some of the Class that we all go in togather on Monday & that we are not to bring it up as he said we should, since he has consider'd of it he thinks it will not do, so we have got our Will of him.

I attended private Meeting in Bowers's Chamber, finish'd reading Doddridges Sermons.

The "last words & DYING SPEECH of Josseph WILLARD who was executed in Hollis Square near Union Hall for high Crimes & misdemeanors committed against the Sons of Harvard Sept. 1767" was a satirical confession prepared for Willard's hanging in effigy on September 18. The manuscript address by an unnamed undergraduate purports to be the final statement of the tutor, accused by students of maltreatment. The previous year, a student protest against rancid butter served in the college Commons had caused the walkout of almost all the undergraduates. Student-faculty relations continued to deteriorate and resulted in March 1768 in the most serious college uprising of the colonial period, discussed below. TRACY was John Tracy (1753–1815), A.B. 1771, of Newburyport, later a merchant. "Collection of Humerous Verses and Sketches Relating to Harvard College, 1769," Harvard University Archives, Cambridge, Mass.; *Sibley's Harvard Graduates,* 17:646–49.

Sunday the 18th of October.

To Day I attended Prayers & went to Meeting & heard Mr. Appleton A.M. & Mr. Scales P.M. The Texts are out of my Mind but Scales's Sermon was nihil ad Rem.[1] At noon I went and smok'd a Pipe with Thacher. Read to Day in Marshal on Santification & am afraid he is a little of the Antinomion Principle.

ANTINOMIANISM is the belief in justification by faith alone without reference to moral law. It is the obverse of Arminianism. Puritan New Englanders and their eighteenth-century heirs struggled to balance the two views. Many worried that Antinomianism encouraged libertine behavior by absolving sinners from any responsibility for their outcome, while others saw Arminianism as an assault on predestinarianism, a characteristic tenet of the Calvinism of New England's leading English settlers. Wright, *Beginnings of Unitarianism,* esp. 15.

1. Not to the point.

Monday the 19th.

To Day is Wormer. I attended Prayers & reciting Euclid all Day. We got Chandler to bring up our Wood from the Whorf for 10/0 & Richardson & his Boys cut, saw'd & brought it in for 15/0 & it makes a large Heep of it.

Mr. Williams was here from Bradford & stayed a few Minutes. Brings no News. John Chadwick was here also from Boston & talks some of coming here to go Home with us.

I read some in Clarissa Harlow.

RICHARDSON may have been Moses Richardson (1722–75), a Cambridge housewright. Paige, *History of Cambridge,* 640–41.

Tuesday the 20th.

To Day is worm & looks like Rain. I attended Prayers & reciting. Finished reading the first Volum of Clarissa & went up to Bowmans with Tenny & got two more of them. I did a good many Choers to Day, prick'd a Tune, wrote Willards Advertizement, got one of Dana's Sermons for Mr. Williams. Jona. Searl was at College to Day.

The Scholars go of plenty & Horses are coming plenty.

John Day has come to Boston to Day with his Wife & has sent me Word by Mr. Wheeler he is coming here tomorrow to cary me Home, so that our People are not coming down which is a very good Chance.

In order to help each other out, the students' parents sometimes cooperated on dropping off and picking up their sons. Moses WHEELER was the father of Samuel Wheeler (1748–1817), A.B. 1771, a graduate of Dummer Academy. Deborah Day was the WIFE of JOHN DAY of Bradford. The couple entered the Bradford church together on February 9, 1766. *Sibley's Harvard Graduates,* 17:671–72; Kingsbury, *Memorial History of Bradford,* 48.

Wednesday the 21st of October.

This Morning is a very smart Rain. I attended Prayers & the Bill was call'd over & we had Breakfast early but the Rain continu'd till almost noon. The Scholars are chiefly gone. I got my Things Ready & waited impatiently & about Eliven o Clock John Day came here with my Fathers Chaise, & I put my Things in the Chaise & we set of as soon as possible with other Company. We came round by Mistick to get some Bisquit &

came up to Woburn & stop'd at Wymans where we din'd but they ware got before us, so we overtook them no more. We made a little stop at Esqr. Fords, & just stop'd at my Chums & Osgoods who had just got Home. We got to Fathers between Eight & nine. Find them all well.

They tell me Wm. Fosters wife is dead since I had been gone.

And that Anna Gage has got a Child & lays it to Peter Johnson who is a Child himself.

Cadwallador FORD (c. 1703–90) lived in Wilmington. Sarah (Eames) FOSTER of Boxford died either October 2 or 3, 1767. The birth of ANNA GAGE's child does not appear in local vital records. Anna was probably the daughter of Joseph and Anna Gage of Bradford, born April 5, 1741, and twenty-six years old in October 1767. PETER JOHNSON may have been either of two eighteen-year-old boys born in Andover in 1749, one the son of Obadiah and Dorothy, the other the son of Samuel and Elizabeth. Kelley, *Wilmington Records,* 224; Pruitt, *Massachusetts Tax Valuation List,* 292–93; *Vital Records of Boxford,* 238; *Vital Records of Bradford,* 50–54; *Vital Records of Andover,* 1:230.

Thursday the 22d.

To Day is very Pleasant. Simmons is at Work here & took my Camel & went up to Andover. I call'd at Samuel Johnsons where I din'd & spoke to him to make me a pare of Boots & after Diner he took his Horse & rode up to Colo. Osgoods & look'd me out the best Calfs skin I ever saw, & then I parted with Johnson & he cary'd the Skin to Pearson to curry, & I went to Frazers to look of some Kersey but his Goods ware not come. I went to Br. Peter's & did several Arrands & then came Home. I call'd to see my Chum & Osgood. When I came Home Br. Peters was at Fathers. I got my Things fitted up a little & between seven & Eight set of to see Mr. Moody. I went but part of the Way, made one stop & stay'd all Night. Found all Well &c.

At a time before ready-to-wear clothing, every piece of apparel not made at home had to be ordered specially. Stephen Peabody's journal records several such instances, the most involved of which were his orders for BOOTS and a winter coat, both concerns of his this day.

Friday the 23d of October.

To Day is very Pleasant. After Breakfast I took my Camel & went to see David Tenny where I din'd. Went up to see Wm. Chandlers & had a beautiful sing. P.M. Tenny & I went up to Mr. Adams & Master is better, but my Classmate is a great Deal worse. To an Eye of reason he seems to be but very little While for this Life. We stop'd a little While & came from there & call'd Mr. Fisher at his School & went in to Mr. Chandlers & drank with him & heard him give Sr. Merril a Caracture. We all came from there to Mr. Tennys & Fisher & Dow took a Walk down to Byfield & Mr. Jackmans where we spent the Evening & Tenny & I stay'd all Night & Fisher went & lodg'd with Isaac Pearson. They are all well there.

William CHANDLER lived in Andover's South Parish. SIR MERRILL was Nathaniel Merrill (1743–91), A.B. 1767, originally from Newbury and in October 1767 a candidate for the pulpit of the Congregational church in Boscawen, New Hampshire. MR. TENNY was David Tenny's father, Lt. John Tenny, of Rowley. MR. FISHER may have been Nathaniel Fisher (1742–1812), A.B. 1763. Fisher's whereabouts in October 1763 are unknown, but for a period in 1766–67, he taught in Dedham; he later taught in the southern colonies before receiving Anglican Holy Orders in 1777. ISAAC PEARSON (1728–1805), a clothier and miller, was born in Newbury, lived in Rowley, then moved to Boscawen. *Andover Tax Assessments,* Tax for 1768; *Sibley's Harvard Graduates,* 17:94, 15:387–92, 16:504–6; Noreen C. Pramberg, *Four Generations of the Descendants of John and Dorcus Pearson of Rowley, Massachusetts* (Newburyport, Mass.: N. C. Pramberg, 1994), 80–81; *Vital Records of Rowley,* 157.

Saturday the 24th of October.

To Day is very Pleasant & after Breakfast I came from there to Mr. Parsons's where I stop'd & din'd upon rost Goose & then Obadiah walk'd with me to Decn. Colmans & stop'd a few Minutes, then I went to Mr. Noyes's & turn'd out my Camel. Found them all well. John walk'd with me down to see Mr. Moody where we stop'd & drank Tea & the old Gentleman was very full of Discourse about Mr. Willard but did not blame the Scholars so much as I expected. He went & shew us the new School Houss & it is a very neat one. Things are alter'd there vastly for the Better since I came away. I came from there & went to Jos. Hales & stay'd there about an Hour & had read my Swearing sermon & lik'd it very much. I came to Mr. Noyes's again & lodg'd. The old Gentleman tells me he is going to marry.

Constructed sometime shortly after Peabody left Dummer Academy in 1765 and restored in 1938, the Little Red SCHOOLHOUSE remains a symbol of the school and a connection with its past. Presumably Peabody's SWEARING SERMON affirmed the values of the Association for the Suppression of Vice, which proclaimed in the preamble to its bylaws that "Rash & Profane Swearing" was an offense "of so heinous a Nature & of such dangerous Tendency" that it had to "fill every pious breast with Concern." Over the following months he passed the piece to friends repeatedly for their approval. MR. William PARSONS was the father of Obadiah Parsons. DECN. COLMAN was Deacon Benjamin Colman of Byfield, the father of Thomas Colman (1751–81), A.B. 1770. JOSEPH HALE was probably either Capt. Joseph Hale (1712–76) or his son Joseph, Jr. (1743–1818), both cordwainers of Byfield. JOSEPH NOYES was the father of JOHN NOYES (1750–1819), A.B. 1771, a former student of Moody at Dummer Academy. John W. Ragle, *Governor Dummer Academy History* (South Byfield, Mass.: Governor Dummer Academy, 1963), 13; "Articles of an Association for the Suppression of Vice," College Papers, vol. 2, item 22, p. 1, Harvard University Archives, Cambridge, Mass.; *Sibley's Harvard Graduates,* 17:78, 380–81, 567; *Descendants of Thomas Hale,* 154, 267–68.

Sunday the 25th.

To Day is Pleasant. Went to Meeting & heard Mr. Parsons preach two Sermons from the 10th of Proverbs 9 Verse. Din'd very genteally at Mr. Noyes's & then took leave of them.

After Servise I went to Mr. Parsons's & stop'd till Night & drank Coffee. Heard Moses give Holt a shocking Caracter for attempting to dispute with Mr. Marsh.

I took my leave of them & came up to Mr. Tennys whare I stop'd & eat & drank & then came to Mr. Adams's & [st]ay'd till after nine & then I believe I took a final Leave of my worthy Class-Mate & came up to Boxford to Master Woods & they ware abed. They got up & let me in & I tarry'd all Night, & they are Well.

Stephen's visit to Byfield allowed him, once again, to indulge his pre-professional practice of sampling the preaching of local ministers. MR. PARSONS was Moses Parsons (1716–83), A.B. 1736, the minister of the Congregational church in Byfield. MOSES was Parsons's son Moses Parsons (1744–1801), A.B. 1765, later a lawyer in Haverhill. HOLT was Moses Holt, A.B. 1767, who was teaching school in Newburyport. Christopher Bridge MARSH (1743–73), A.B. 1761, was one of two rival candidates contesting the open pulpit of the North Congregational Church of Newburyport. Marsh received the call; he was ordained and installed in early 1768. John WOOD (1708–73), A.B. 1731, was the master of the school in Boxford. *Sibley's Harvard Graduates,* 10:52–59; 16:196, 485; 15:71–73; 9:112–14.

Monday the 26th of October.

To Day is rainy. Wind ashore. I spent part of the A.M. at Sisters & Jenny Kilbourne was there. I came from there up to Uncle Fosters stay'd a While & then came up to see Sr. Porter who is poorly but in a likely way to recover. He is civil but does not incline to talk any thing concerning his Concern in his Sickness. I read my swearing Sermon to him & din'd there.

It is said he is to be married shortly.

I came from there & made some inquiry after Jesse Kimball & find he is so engag'd he cant come to work for me till next Week notwithstanding he engage'd firmly which I don't well like. I came Home, & my Chum Phillips came here & stay'd a little While & borrow'd my Willards dying Speech, & is to bring it to Fosters tomorrow Morning.

There was one Roe came here & lodg'd at Night. I wrote some in Journal & read my swearing Sermon.

On October 10, John PORTER had announced his intention to marry Sarah Martyn of Boxford. *Sibley's Harvard Graduates,* 16:517.

Tuesday the 27th.

To Day is cloudy but no Rain. I went up to Tailers & meet my Chum there, but I find Tailer will not go out to Work, so I believe I shall not employ him. I came from there & call'd at Samuel Johnsons & he measur'd me for a pare of Boots. I came from there & went down to Bradford & din'd & then had a little Talk about Ordination. I came Home & stay'd till just Night & then went up to Doctr. Kittridges where ware John Noyes, Emerson, Judith Noyes, & Betty Jackman. We drank Tea & I spent the chief of the Evening there. They are going to Ordination. I came from there to Br. Olivers & stay'd till late. Read him my swearing Sermon & Willard's dying Speech, & talk'd with him a little about Money, & getting a Piece of Cloth for a great Coat at Frazers on his Accompt.

I came Home & it Rains very fast.

Elizabeth (BETTY) JACKMAN (b. 1739) was from Rowley. The ordination did not take place. See October 28 and 29, below. EMERSON was Joseph Emerson, A.B. 1771. *Vital Records of Rowley,* 104.

Wednesday, the 28th of October.

To Day is a very Smart Storm Wind N.E. I stay'd at Home till after twelve & there ware some People come by, going to Ordination, & at last Br. John, Simmons, & I concluded to go. We set out & went over Herricks Ferry & it Rain'd exceedingly, but before we got to the Meeting-House we heard there was to be no Ordination, but we proceeded & I went to one Websters where there ware a Number of Scholars whom I knew. We stop'd there till just Night & had an exceeding Good Entertainment, & the Storm turns to Snow & is very Cold. I came from there with Jewett by the Tavern, & saw two Men fighting in a Mud Puddle.

We hear'd the Counsel had adjourn'd acting any Further upon Affairs till Tomorrow, so Jewett & I came directly down to Haverhill Town, & came over the River, & he went & lodg'd at Capt. Thurstins & I stop'd at the first good Harber I could light of. After I had got a little Dry & comfortable, I went to Mr. Benjn. Carlton's where spent the Heal of the evening. Nihil majus &c.

As a break from routine, an ORDINATION might attract a regional audience. Clergymen and men such as Peabody who intended themselves for the ministry were particularly likely to attend because they could count on the event as a reunion of friends, acquaintances, and colleagues. Capt. Daniel THURSTON (1720–1805)—architect, housewright, and farmer of Bradford—later served as a colonel in the American Revolution and as a Massachusetts state senator. Brown Thurston, comp., *Thurston Genealogies,* 2nd edn. (Portland, Maine, 1892), 30–31; *Vital Records of Bradford,* 278.

Thursday the 29.

To Day it clears off & is some Cold. I stay'd & went to Breakfast with some other Company & then Swett came & call'd me & I fix'd up a letter & set of with him over the River again. Met Smith Noyes & Betty Jackman going Home. They have had news Timothy Jackmans Wife is dead. I saw a great Deal of Company that I knew. I went & put my Camel up at Websters again & then went up to Hasseltines where the Counsel are, & at last it is concluded upon that there should be no Ordination because of the great Opposition, not for any thing that appear'd against the Man. I went down to Websters & din'd & had a little Sing. Lost one of my Gloves by the Way, & after I came away I lit of Holt & there was a Number of us agreed to Meet at Osgoods at Town & have another Sing. I lit of some unexpected Company at the Tavern and stayd with them a little While. There was a banter struck up about Wrastling & Samuel Johnson & Phinehas & I wrastled but the last Man & I neither of us threw. Samuel Osgood & I left the Company & came down to Mr. Osgood's & had a very pretty Sing. (I brought a pare of saddle bags for Master Fuller) & then we came over the River, stop'd at Chandlers a few Minutes, & then came to Jacob Kimball's where we made a little longer stop, & upon the whole I concluded to come Home with Company who ware coming to Andover. Holt came with me but would not stop.

Because New England's Congregational churches operated on the basis of consensus, they rarely proceeded to call a minister in the face of substantial, albeit minority, opposition. The West Church of Haverhill had called tutor Joseph Willard as its minister, but when local opposition arose, the ordaining council concluded that it was imprudent to proceed. John Barnard SWETT (1752–96), A.B. 1771, of Marblehead, later a doctor, was being rusticated for his role in keeping a woman in a college chamber, so by college law Peabody should have had no contact with him. Mary JACKMAN, of Newbury, died of consumption on October 27, 1767. Chase, *History of Haverhill,* 568; *Sibley's Harvard Graduates,* 17:635–38; *Vital Records of Newbury,* 2:624.

Friday the 30th of October.

To Day is Clear. I was at Home the chief of the Day. Did a pretty many Choers. John Noyes & Emerson came here & made a little stop, & then Hitchbourn came here & is going to Rowley. I put up his Horse & he stop'd & drank Tea & then I rode with him almost to Capt. Spoffords (for he would not stay all Night) & I directed him to Tennys & parted with him, & came back to Jesse Kimbals & he confesses he has served me wrong but says he will come early on Monday Morning. I came Home a little before nine. Nathan Eames was here to Day from Pigwocket.

NATHAN EAMES, or Ames, was one of the settlers who moved from Andover and environs to PIGWOCKET in search of fertile farmland in the early 1760s. When the new town established its own government in 1777, at the first town meeting he was chosen a fence viewer. Eames was probably born in Boxford in 1738, although another man of the same name was born in Bradford in 1746. John Stuart Barrows, *Fryeburg, Maine: An Historical Sketch* (Fryeburg, Maine: Pequawket Press, 1938), 28, 30, 31, 79, 105; *Vital Records of Boxford,* 32; *Vital Records of Bradford,* 44.

Saturday the 31st of October.

To Day is very Pleasant. I wrote a little in Journal & coppy'd an Evidence of old Mr. Hovey's for Nathaniel Peabody & then took a ride to Andover. I carry'd some Thred to Samuel Johnsons to make my Boots with, & went to Br. Olivers but he was not at Home. I did some Arrands there & went to Esqr. Phillips's & Nathaniel Peabody came there to get the Esqr. to go & give old Capt. Stevens his Oath concerning Bradford Line & he is going so we went along before & din'd there & talked with the Capt. & I wrote his Evidence & then the Esqr. came & swore him. I went from there to Jos. Stevens's & got my Hat drest & one for Br. John. Went to Frazers to get some Things but his Goods ware not come. Lit of Lovejoy there & went Home with him & drank Tea with Ephraim Swans Wife & took a View of Lovejoys new House, & saw Jos. Frye.

I went to Br. Peters's & stay'd a few Minutes & sister tells me her little son Jos. has got Fitts.

I came from there down to Pearsons & got my Leather for Boots & left it at Samuel Johnson, & he told me an Acknowledgement had lately been made [con]cerning his having his Horse turn'd away. I came Home & Br. Oliver & Daniel Ingals ware here & stay'd a while & I read my swearing Sermon to them & they went Home.

OLD CAPT. STEVENS was Capt. James Stevens (c. 1686–1769) of Andover, the father of James Stevens, Jr. (1721–59), the first husband of Stephen's oldest sister, Sarah. His oath concerning the BRADFORD LINE presumably referred to one of the boundaries of the town of Bradford, but the specific issue has not been identified. Joseph Peters (1764–1843) of Andover was the SON of Peabody's sister Sarah and her second husband, JOHN PETERS. DANIEL INGALLS (b. 1714) lived in Andover. EPHRAIM SWAN'S WIFE was either Sarah (Poole) Swan, the wife of Ephraim, Sr., or her daughter-in-law Martha (Farrington) Swan, the wife of Ephraim, Jr. Because Martha Swan was closer in age to Stephen than her mother-in-law, she seems the more likely possibility. *Vital Records of Andover,* 1:346, 2:264, 316, 322, 523; Edmond Frank Peters, comp., *Peters of New England: A Genealogy, and Family History* (New York: Knickerbocker Press, 1903), 102–3, 109–10; *Ingalls Family,* 51–52.

November 1767

Sunday the 1 of November.

To Day is very Pleasant. I went to Boxford Meeting & heard Mr. Sparhawk preach A.M. from the 53 Chapt of Isaiah & the 1 Verse. P.M. he preach'd from the 2d of Peter 1 Chapt. & 3d Verse. I din'd at John Chadwicks. After meeting I came Home & in the Evening went down to Sister Woods to bring Rebecca Home, & stay'd there all Night. They are all Well.

REBECCA was Stephen's sister Rebecca Peabody.

Monday the 2d of November.

To Day is very Pleasant. Got up early. Read a Piece upon the Marrage State under the Semilitude of a Dream which is very pretty. Went to Breakfast & came from there Home & Kimbal came here to make me a Coat. Nathaniel Peabody & Luke Hovey came here & Father & Br. John went to Moses Gages with them where An Arbitration is to settle the Affair between Peabody & the Bradford Men to Day. P.M. I took my Camel & went down to Gages & made a little stop & then went down in Town with Wm. Hasseltine of Penicook. I put up my Mare at old Mr. Websters & went over to James Hasseltines & from there to see Mr. Williams where I stop'd & drank Tea & spent part of the Evening with him & S[r.] Barnard & he read my swearing Sermon & he's very much Pleased with it. I gave him Mr. Danas Sermons & then came from there. Call'd a few Minutes at Benjn. Warths & then came to James Hasseltines again &

I spent the Evening & there was Company there who had a Dance. There ware some People from Penicook.

I came from there & hear there was a pretty Deal of talk concerning Ordination & a good Many Reflections cast.[1]

In "THE SIMILITUDE OF A DREAM," perhaps the most famous passage in John Bunyan's *Pilgrim's Progress,* Christian, "crying, *What shall I do to be saved?*" despairs that his soul is lost. Evangelist consoles him, however: "All manner of sin and blasphemies shall be forgiven unto men; be not faithless, but believing." Peabody's appreciation of this passage, while hardly unique, underscores his religious piety. LUKE HOVEY was one of several related men of the same name in Boxford, possibly a selectman in that town in the 1750s and 1760s. PENACOOK, where WILLIAM HASSELTINE had settled, was a village in what is now Concord, New Hampshire. Hasseltine was still there in 1776 when he signed New Hampshire's Association Test. Perley, *History of Boxford,* 379; James O. Lyford, ed., *History of Concord, New Hampshire* (Concord, N.H., 1896), 282.

1. Following this entry three lines are crossed out and unreadable.

Tuesday the 3d of November.

To Day is very Pleasant. Esqr. Varnum & Roe lodg'd at Br. Johns last Night. I breakfasted with them at Brs. Read my swearing Sermon to the Esqr. which pleas'd him, & he insisted upon my Accrostick upon our Varnum which I give him, & sometime in the A.M. they went of & I spent the Day gitting my Things ready for Cambridge. Try'd my Coat on & Kimbal work'd almost all Night upon it. In the Evening Br. Oliver & Wife Hipsabah Kimbal, Jeremiah Eames, Nathan Jos. Frye & one Story came here & spent it, & after Supper a little aften ten they all went of. Br. Oliver & I look'd over our Accompts a little & I find I am a smal Matter in his Debt.

I have nothing Remarkable to write to Day as I can Think.

ACROSTICS were a popular form of wordplay among eighteenth-century New Englanders, who wrote poems or other passages in which a letter from each line, usually the initial letter, taken in sequence formed a name, motto, or proverb. ESQ. VARNUM was John Varnum (1705–85) of Dracut, where he had a substantial farm. John Marshall Varnum, *The Varnums of Dracutt* (Boston: D. Clapp and Sons, 1907), 48–66; Pruitt, *Massachusetts Tax Valuation List,* 202–3.

Wednesday the 4th of November.

To Day is some Cloudy but no Rain till Night. John Day came along pretty early & I got my Things ready & Kimball finish'd my Coat, & I took leave of my Friends & we set of for Cambridge. I call'd at Samuel Johnsons & took my Boots which he had done, & so at Jos. Stevens's & he iorn'd my Hat a little. Lit of David Foster & I went in to the Captns. with him & drank & they show me a new Almanack which had come out lately, & I read to them my Swearing Sermon & they ware exceedingly pleased with it so I left it with the Capt. as a Present.

We came from there through Wilmington & saw Emery & Frye, & came down to Wymans in Woburn & Mr. Scales was there. We stop'd & din'd & Doctr. Barker came there. Is going to Boston for Medicines. We came from there & got down to College a little after dark & my Chum had got there. I took my Things out of the Chaise & Mr. Day stop'd & drank some Kelly with me & then went down to Boston.

In November 1767, Boston newspapers carried advertisements for two competing ALMANACS, *Bickerstaff's Boston Almanack* and *Ames's Almanack.* Thomas EMERY (1750–70), A.B. 1768, a graduate of Dummer Academy, was from Newbury. At the time of his premature death he was studying medicine. KELLY was an alcoholic drink with a rum base. *Boston Post-Boy,* Nov. 9, 1767 (supplement), Nov. 16, 1767; *Sibley's Harvard Graduates,* 17:17.

Thursday the 5th.

To Day is very Worm & Foggy. After Prayers & Breakfast I got leave to go to Boston. Rode a Horse for Parsons to Charleston. Went to Mr. Trumbles & Mr. Day & his Wife & Children ware come over & are going to set out Home. I parted with them & went over the Ferry to Mrs. Robinsons. Stay'd a while & then went to Mr. Harris's where I din'd. The old Gentleman was sick. Doctr. Barker din'd there. After having smook'd we ca[me] from there & it rain'd. I went to several of Vendue Rooms to see if I coud get nothing for a great Coat but could see nothing which suted me. I got some Magaziens at Meins for the Scholars, & Parsons's watch mended at Jacks [?] & bought 100 of Nedles for our People. Saw Amasa Kyes. I went to Churches Vendue. Lit of Wm. Porter, John Chadwick. Porter bid of a very Large Glass there for 12 Dolers ½. We all went to Gridleys (where was Polly Adams) & drank Tea. They stay in Town to Night. I came from there & there was a Cry of Fire. One Mr. Goldthrit had a Barn burning. There was a concourse of People & 6 or 7 Ingines immediatly there, & they play'd to admiration, & after having beat in the Roof with their Axes they extinguished it. I came down to the Farry & the Boats had done going so I was obliged to give 9/0 to get a Cross & then I came up to Cambridge. Got the News Papers by the Way.

John MEIN, a Scotsman and recent immigrant to Boston, was a partner in the firm that published the *Boston Chronicle.* He also sold books and periodicals at his print shop. Benjamin CHURCH (1704–81), A.B. 1727, an auctioneer, held VENDUES in Boston on Thursdays. WM. PORTER was William Porter (1744–1822) of Boxford. He and Mary (POLLY) ADAMS (b. 1745) had recently announced their intention to marry. The BARN belonged to Ezekiel Goldthwaite, Esq., of Boston. Goldthwaite held many public offices; in 1767, he belonged to his town's board of auditors. Bostonians used a combination of public fire companies with hand-pumped ENGINES and private mutual-benefit fire societies to fight blazes like Goldthwaite's. Thomas, *History of Printing,* 210; *Sibley's Harvard Graduates,* 8:125–29; *Boston Gazette,* Oct. 5, 12, 26, Nov. 9, 1767; *Vital Records of Boxford,* 7, 79, 191; *A Genealogical History of Robert Adams of Newbury, Mass., and His Descendants, 1635–1900* (Rutland, Vt.: Tuttle, 1900), 32; Robert Francis Seybolt, *The Town Officials of Colonial Boston, 1634–1775* (Cambridge, Mass.: Harvard University Press, 1939), 323, 327; Carl Bridenbaugh, *Cities in the Wilderness: Urban Life in America, 1625–1742* (New York: Ronald Press, 1938), 209–12, 367–68.

Friday the 6th of November.

To Day is Pleasant. I attended Prayers as usual. Got our Room clean'd, fitted our things for studie. I read two News Papers & there is Accounts that there are Officers sent over here from England to receive the Duties lately lay'd upon several Sorts of Goods, & that the Inhabitants of Boston are determin'd to send for no More of them Goods, but as much as possible to encourage manufacturing of Necessaries in New-England.

I cast the interest of Br. Oliver's Note & find I am indebted to him about £9–17d–0 Old Tenr. In the Evening Osgood came down [&] his Br. Peter came with him & we all went to Parsons's Chamber & had a Sing. There came Word to me there was Company wanted me so I came to my Chamber & Wm. Porter & his Paramor & Doctr. Barker was come. They stay'd & drank with me & then went of intending to go to Woburn to Night. I spent the rest of the evening at Parsons's Chamber.

It is in the Paper that Thanksgiving will be the 3d of December.

Peabody never found imperial politics as interesting as ecclesiastical politics, but in 1767 the tensions that eventually led to the outbreak of the American Revolution were already in the air, and they were impossible to ignore. The Townshend Act of 1767, referred to here, imposed a three-pence DUTY on tea as well as taxes on glass, lead, paper, and painters' colors. The date for THANKSGIVING varied from place to place and year to year until Abraham Lincoln fixed it by presidential proclamation in 1863.

Saturday the 7th of November.

To Day is Cool & towards Night looks like fowl Weather. I attended Prayers as usual. Peter Osgood & others drank with me & then he went of to Boston. I wrote some & went into the Library & took out Shackford on Mans fall. After Commons I went with Tenny up to Bowman's & made a short Stay. Came down to College & read Mr. Chandlers Letter against Mr. Tucker which I like well in general. In the Evening I attended private Meeting at Bowers's Chamber & we read a sermon of Mr. Wadsworth's against keeping bad Company.

Yesterday I was sent for before the President & Tutors for staying over a Night when I went a Journey with Pike, & I told my story to them & came of.

I receiv'd a Letter from Pike, & Wentworth told Tenny & I in a very private Manner that he was married, upon our promising not to tell of it.

Peabody's reading, which continued to reveal his theological orthodoxy, included Samuel SHUCKFORD, *The Creation and Fall of Man* (London, 1753), and James CHANDLER, *An Answer to Mr. Tucker's Letter to Mr. Chandler* (Boston, 1767). The private meeting read Benjamin WADSWORTH, *Faithful Warnings against Bad-Company Keeping* (Boston, 1722).

Sunday the 8th.

To Day some cool. I went to Meeting & heard old Mr. Appleton expound from Jude from the 5th to the 9th Verse. P.M. he p[reach]ed from the 32d of Deuteronomy & the 29 Verse. I read to Day in Marshel, smok'd a Pipe with Osgood at noon, drank Tea with Hunt at Night.

HUNT was Joseph Hunt, A.B. 1770. *Sibley's Harvard Graduates,* 17:396–97.

Monday the 9th of November.

To Day is cool. I attended Exercises as Usual. Read a little in Clarisa Harlowe. Took a Walk with Osgood. Had a long Talk upon serious Matters. In the Evening went & drank Tea with Emerson & Noyes. Came to my Chamber & studied in Cæsar.

Tuesday the 10th.

To Day is pleasant in the fore Part of it but towards Night Rains. I attended Exercises as usual. Wigglesworth had a Lecture nihil ad Rem. Had some College Company after Lecture, & in the Evening. Studie'd a little in Cæsar.

Edward WIGGLESWORTH, the Hollis Professor of Divinity, exasperated many of his more pious students by treating theology as an academic subject, deserving of analysis, and not devoting his lectures to more catechetical ends. Peabody probably dismissed Wigglesworth's LECTURE for being too dryly analytical.

Wednesday the 11th of November.

This Day new Stile I am 26 Years of Age. I attended Prayers as usual. Got leave to go out of Town though I did not. Carry'd my Bill to Wigglesworth. Went to Warlands Shop talk'd a little with him about a great Coat but he asks dear for making one. Went up to Scales to desire him to speak to the Freshmen to set in their Order in the Chappel.

I receiv'd two very pretty Letters from Master Adams to Day giving me a very perticular Account of his Brs. Circumstances, by which it seems the Lamp of his Life is just extinguished. I wrote to Day some in Journal & some Letters Home. Just before Commons I had [so]me of my College Friends here to drink Kelley with me & after Commons we went to Osgoods Chamber & drank Cyder & smook'd a Pipe, & then went in a Hurry up to Tennys Chamber & had a crack of Nuts. Eat & drank at Osgoods Chamber to Night.

Peabody was born in Boxford on November 11, 1741, making this day his twenty-sixth birthday. Although the British Empire adopted the Gregorian, or NEW STYLE, calendar at the start of 1752, he translated the date here from the Julian calendar, which was still in force at the time of his birth. The adoption of the new calendar advanced the year eleven days and introduced new rules for leap years to improve its alignment with the earth's annual revolution around the sun. As one of the oldest of the undergraduates, Stephen found the immaturity of many of his schoolmates especially irksome. The disorder of the freshmen in chapel was a particular affront to his piety. MASTER ADAMS was Phineas Adams, A.B. 1762, brother of Peabody's classmate Joseph Adams. Stephen implies here that Joseph had died, but he lived until January 1, 1768. Note Peabody's collective term "A CRACK OF NUTS." *Sibley's Harvard Graduates,* 15:150–51.

Thursday the 12th of November.

To Day is exceeding Pleasant. I attended Prayers & reciting in the Morning & then Eliot went out of Town. Webster is going Home. I fitted 3 Letters & sent by him, then I spent the chief of the Day in reading Clarissa Harlowe.

Just before Diner there was a very grand Wedding at Church. I went over & saw William Pepperrell married to one of Collo Royals Daughters in the Church Way. When it was over my Chum & I went to my Quondams chamber & drank Kelley & stayed almost too late for Commons.

I had no Company in the Evening but heard a very great Noise in Fishers Chamber occasioned by Butery Syder.

Christ Church was the Anglican outpost in Cambridge, an otherwise strongly Congregational town. Today's wedding IN THE CHURCH WAY united WILLIAM PEPPERRELL (1746–1816), A.B. 1766, of Kittery, the heir to a vast Maine estate, to Elizabeth ROYALL of Medford, daughter of Hon. Isaac and Mary (McIntosh) Royall and herself a child of privilege. Congregationalists objected that the Anglicans cared more about an elaborate liturgy than true faith, but this reservation did not prevent Stephen from taking in the show. BUTERY SYDER was hard apple cider purchased from the college butler. *Sibley's Harvard Graduates,* 16:397–403; 17:170.

Friday the 13th.

To Day is fair weather. I attended Prayers, read in Clarissa went to Mr. Winthrop to Cyphering. In the Evening, went to Osgoods Chamber to drink some Kelley I had won of him, & then came to my own & studie'd Volebious.

Saturday the 14th.

Is very stormy & rainey. I attended Prayers made me a Bill, wrote some in Journal, & read in Clary & just before Night I got Hastings Cyropedia & Guild & I studie'd Xnophon. In the Evening attended private meeting at Fletcher's Chamber, read Cole on Election & I lik'd so far as was read very wel[l].

Peabody probably received his copy of Xenophon's *CYROPÆDIA* from senior Jonathan HASTINGS, who was through with it, having used it in 1766–67. Hastings, a son of the college steward, later became Boston's postmaster. COLE ON ELECTION was probably either a work by Thomas Cole (1627–97), Independent minister of London, the author of *Discourse on Regeneration, Faith, and Repentance* (many editions), or Nathaniel Cole, *The Godly Man's Assurance* (London, 1615).

Sunday the 15th of November.

To Day is clear'd of & is pretty Cool. I attended Prayers & went to Meeting & heard Mr. Marret preach A.M. from the 10th of Romans 4 Verse. P.M. he Preach'd from the 2d of Cor 5 Chapt. & 17 Verse. His Way of Delivery is poor but his Sentiment[s] are Exceeding Good I think. I drank a Glass of Wine with Nathll. Tracy at noon. In the Evening eat & drank with Scammel. I read some in Marshel to Day & in the Evening.

MARRET was John Marrett (1741–1813), A.B. 1763. He was in residence at Harvard as a Hopkins fellow while he read divinity. He eventually became the minister of the First Church in Burlington. *Sibley's Harvard Graduates,* 15:437–39.

Monday the 16th.

To Day is clear wholsome Weather. I attended Prayers & reciting all Day to Willard. Drank Tea with Thacher. In the Evening went to Thaxters Chamber eat, & drank Kelley with him, came to my own & Webster was just come down. He brought a letter from Br. John which informs me that our People are well but that Hananiah Barker is dead & Sarah Peabody, since I came down, & that John Robinson is sick. What a mortal dying World is it that we live in, & yet how little is Death contemplated upon by the Children of Men.

Peabody's piety led him inevitably to draw an orthodox lesson from the deaths of acquaintances, as he did here based on news from home about two deaths and a third apparently near at hand. Of these deaths, SARAH PEABODY's reveals the extent of the family connections Stephen kept track of; she was his second cousin once removed. Born in Boxford in 1748, the daughter of Stephen's second cousin Lt. Thomas Peabody and his wife, Ruth, Sarah died in Newburyport on November 12. HANANIAH BARKER of Andover, a farmer, died the same day in his eighty-third year. *Vital Records of Boxford,* 67; *Vital Records of Newburyport, Massachusetts, to the End of the Year 1849* (Salem, Mass.: Essex Institute, 1911), 2:745; *Vital Records of Andover,* 2:385; *Essex County Probate Index,* 1:53.

Tuesday the 17th.

To Day is Pleasant. I attended Prayers as usual. Studied Xnophon. Esqr. Phillips came down here from Andover & went to Boston. Brings no News. In the Evening studied Xnophon & Parsons came here & told me he had Company at his Chamber who wanted to see me so I went there & there was a Master Wigglesworth & Sr. Colman. We drank & spent the Evening & had two Fiddles which we play'd upon. Rais'd Scales but soon lay'd him again.

COLMAN was Dudley Colman (1745–97), A.B. 1765, of Newbury, eventually a lieutenant colonel in the Continental Army. At various times Colman made his living as a tavern keeper, a chocolatier, a tallow chandler, and a tobacconist. "RAIS'D SCALES" is a pun referring both to tutor Stephen Scales and to fiddle music. *Sibley's Harvard Graduates,* 16:131–34.

Wednesday the 18th of November.

To Day is Stormy. Wigglesworth & Colman came here & drank with us in Mane & then they went to Boston.

Willard sent for me for having so much Company and not being in to reciting, but treated me well. I got leave to go out of Town & got Sayers Horse to go for doing a small Arrand for him. I went to Gridley, & din'd & his Wife was just brought to Bed. I drank tea there also & intended to have heard Sandiman but his lecture was sooner than I expected. I went to Mr. Phillips's & see the Esqr. & he took me to his Brs. Sumer House & every Thing there is Butiful. He went with me to Miens & bought my Chum two Books & sent them by me & then I parted with him. I look'd of several Peices of Kersey but see none which I lik'd. Went to Abots & he say'd he would use me well so I am to go there again when I go down.

I attended Deshons Vendue a little while but bought nothing so I came over the Ferry & came Home. Had Sayer's Horse to Hastings's.

Peabody's interest in the preaching of Robert SANDEMAN (d. 1771) reveals the breadth of his planned professional training. Like most contemporaries intended for the pulpit, Peabody believed that he needed to have a wide acquaintance with the prominent ecclesiastical figures of his day and their teachings. Sandeman, a Scottish preacher, led a small sect that observed a legalistic form of Calvinism and practiced such primitive Christian rites as the kiss of charity and foot-washing. There was a congregation of Sandemanians in Boston, although Sandeman himself lived in Danbury, Connecticut. Thomas COLMAN (1751–81), A.B. 1770, of Newbury, a graduate of Dummer Academy, became a lawyer in Groton, Massachusetts. Ebenezer SAYER (1751–78), A.B. 1768, of Wells, Maine, served in a variety of public offices, including militia colonel and member of three Provincial Congresses. MR. PHILLIPS was probably Hon. William Phillips. ABBOT may have been Samuel Abbot, a dry-goods merchant. Moses DESHON held public auctions at the west end of Faneuil Hall Market. William G. McLoughlin, *New England Dissent: The Baptists and the Separation of Church and State* (Cambridge, Mass.: Harvard University Press, 1971), 2:740–41; *Sibley's Harvard Graduates,* 17:380–81, 87–89; *Phillips Genealogies,* 26–27; Tyler, *Smugglers & Patriots,* 258–59; *Boston Gazette,* Nov. 30, 1767.

Thursday the 19th.

To Day is very stormy the fore part of the Day but clear'd of toward Night. I attended Prayers & reciting all Day. Hear nothing strange. In the Evening wrote a Letter to Br. John.

Friday the 20th of November.

To Day is very Pleasant. I wrote a Letter to my Sisters & after Prayers & breakfast Webster & I walk'd down to Boston. I went with Webster & din'd with one Decn. Boynton & then went in persute of a great Coat, look of a great many pieces, went to Abbots but a[t] last traded with Gyer. Gave him 55/ pr yd for a Piece which was better than I could have at Abbots. I got Trimming there & it all cost me almost a Joannes. I did some other Arrands in Town & then came over the Ferry & came up to Cambridge alone. Call'd at Mr. Samsons & left a letter for Esqr. Phillips from my Chum & one for me to be cary'd to Andover. Saw Painter White there.

I saw Jos. Hale as I went over to Boston & he told me he was coming to

Cambridge & when I came up I expected to see him but he was gone to Charlston again which I was very sorry for. I eat & Drank with Osgood to Night & went to Noyses Chamber a few Minutes. Nihil majos.

Richard BOYNTON was a deacon of the Sixth Church in Boston. GYER may have been Frederick William Geyer, a dry-goods merchant and wharfinger. A JOHANNES was a Portuguese gold coin, roughly equivalent in value to £1.80 in 1766. Worthley, "Inventory," 75; Tyler, *Smugglers & Patriots,* 264–65; McCusker, *Money and Exchange,* 5, 6, 12.

Saturday the 21st.

To Day is cloudy & after Prayers & reciting I took my Kersey & went to Bowmans to get them to let me wet it there & so went over to Mrs. Goddards to see if she could make it for me before Thanksgiving but she could not. I came back & put the Cloth a sooke & they contrived to have it made there & sent of to one Cook a young Woman to come to work there, but I came down to College before the Word came back. In the afternoon wrote & read some. In the Evening I attended private Meeting at Bowers's Chamber & Sr. Smith was there. Read a little in Cole on Election. He talk'd to us very handsomely & wish'd us success.

It snows this Evening.

There were at least two and possibly three married women named GODDARD in Cambridge in 1767: Elizabeth (1713–86), widow of John; Hannah (1718–99), wife of Thomas; and possibly Mary (c. 1744–98), wife of Stephen. Paige, *History of Cambridge,* 553, 560–61, 567.

Sunday the 22d of November.

To Day is a very Smart Storm of Snow. I went to Meeting & heard Mr. Eliot A.M. from the 4 of Proverbs 18th. P.M. he preach'd from the 1 of Peter 2 Chap & 21 Verse. I read to Day & in the Evening in Mr. Marshal.

I wrote to Day for Esterbrook. After Servise Sr. Cobb came here & gave me some Pills to help my Stomuck, which I recon I have hurt by Singing.

Jedidiah ESTABROOK (1741–82), A.B. 1771, of Lunenburg, may have practiced medicine after graduation. *Sibley's Harvard Graduates,* 17:511–12.

Monday the 23d.

To Day is clear'd of but is not very Cold Wind N.W. I attended Prayers & Sewall's Lecture but we had not reciting. Mr. Scales was out of Town just before Prayers. I went up to Bowmans to take Care of my Cloth but they had taken it out of the Water & it was almost dry so we took it & brush'd it & they say they will hang it out again tomorrow. They have been to this Cook young Woman & she says she will come & make it there. I stay'd there & went to Supper & spent the chief of the Evening & then came Home & it is bad going. I studie'd a little upon Cyphering to Day & read my Lesson at Night in Fordice. I learn it is out of my Chums Preseptor.

Notwithstanding Stephen SEWALL's title, the Hancock Professor of Hebrew and Other Oriental Languages often lectured on points of English grammar. David FORDYCE wrote *Elements of Moral Philosophy* (many editions). *Sibley's Harvard Graduates,* 15:107–14.

Tuesday the 24th.

To Day is pretty Cold. I attended Prayers & reciting all day only at 11 when there was none. I got leave to go out of Town but the going was Bad so I did not. Scales desird me to call at Charlestown & bring him his News-Paper.

In the Evening my Chum & I went up to Bowmans to get my Cloth and have it cut out, & Jenny & John Noyes ware there & there was 2 or 3 garls there a quilting a Bed Quilt so we[nt] down & help'd them some Time, & then came Home & it was yet Bad going. We had a pretty little Sing there.

After I came back I read my Lesson in Fordice.

Wednesday the 25th of November.

To Day is very pleasant. I attended Prayers & reciting in Mane. Got leave to go out of Town again being I did not go Yesterday & he wanted to have his Paper brought up yet but I saw Wetmore going so I sent by him & thought I would not go, but at Night he came back but never thought to call for Mr. Scales's Paper & when I see him I expect to be cow'd horridly. I carry'd my Cloth to Capt. Marrets to have it cut out & it is shrunk so he is affraid there will not be anough but he is to try & I am to go down again after Diner, so he measur'd me. After Diner I went down & he has cut it out but he was obliged to Peace it some & he says he believes there will be hardly anough to face it left. I give him a Pistolean for cuting it out & brought it up to College. I wrote me a Declamation to Day, & made my Forensick Arguments. After Prayers I cary'd my Coat up to Bowmans & when I had got there I had lost my Peaces for facing & we could not find them. As we came back, Tenny & Noyes were there again & then came Home with me. They had just finish'd their Bed Quilt. It is wormer some cloudy, & the Wind southerly.

My Chum had some of his Class-Mates meet here to Night.

After I got back I wrote some in Journal.

Thursday the 26th of November.

To Day is Pleasant. After Prayers I went up to Bowmans but could not find my Peaces, & the Garl was come there to make my Coat, but they said they should not want the facing very soon so I came down to College again & went down to Bradishes to see Bright who was there, & is not well. It is fear'd he is inclining to a Consumtion. I went from there to Capt. Marrets & there found my Peaces of Cloth very unexpectedly. We had no reciting, so Tenny went with me to Bowmans & I went to try to get some Cloth for facing but could get none & Mrs. Bowman says she will try to make it do without. I came to College & wrote of a Declamation & copy'd of my Arguments & Peter Osgood came here from Andover. Brings no News.

Last Night we saw a Fire at a Distance & heard to Night there was a very fine House burnt at Brantree which belonged to Fresh Man Pamers father.

BRIGHT's illness was probably the reason he was out of college housing and at Ebenezer BRADISH's tavern. CONSUMPTION is now called tuberculosis. Gen. Joseph Palmer of Braintree was the FATHER of Joseph Pearse PALMER, A.B. 1771. Gozzaldi, *Supplement to Paige,* 69; *Sibley's Harvard Graduates,* 17:584.

Friday the 27th of November.

To Day is Thawry. I declaim'd in Mane. Peter Osgood went from here. I wrote a little in Journal & a letter to Master Adams. Just before Night I went up to Prentises & cary'd one of Osgoods Boot Straps for a Pattern to have me a Pare made by. I call'd at Bowmans & had my Coat try'd on & it is lik'd to be finish'd to Night, & they are to pay for the making & I to pay them. I drank Tea there & in the Evening Came home. It rains a little.

William PRENTICE (1708–71) of Cambridge, a cordwainer, probably made Peabody's bootstraps. Paige, *History of Cambridge,* 630, 632.

Saturday the 28th.

To Day is Pleasant. I attended Prayers & in Mane went up to Tennys Chamber to see Sr. Fisher, who is come down. He says Adams is yet alive though exceedingly Low. Fisher is going Home to see his Friends. Sr. Searl came here & is going Home & I sent my Letter by him to Mr. Adams. I wrote some to Day & made some Bills & read a little in Clary Harlowe. P.M. Doctr. Russell came here stay'd a few Minutes talks of going to Andover to Day. In the Evening I attended private Meeting. We read a Peice upon the Truth of the Scripture. I shew my Chum our Articles & he talks of Joining our Society.

Voluntary associations were relatively uncommon in colonial New England, although their numbers grew rapidly after the American Revolution. For Peabody and his contemporaries, such organizations amounted to a new social technology that they had to learn how to employ. The use of ARTICLES of organization for their Association for the Suppression of Vice, a small, private student club, reveals the formalism with which New Englanders often approached such societies before they became at ease with them. Joshua FISHER (1748–1833), A.B. 1766, of Dedham, taught in Rowley for two years after graduation. A defective palate so affected his speech that he gave up plans to enter the ministry. After reading medicine in Hingham, he became a physician in several towns in Essex County. *Sibley's Harvard Graduates,* 16:355–58.

Sunday the 29th of November.

To Day clouds up & snows a little. I attended Prayers & when we were in at Breakfast Colo. Brattle came to the kitchen & sent for me & invited me to dine with him to Day. I except'd of the Invitation. The Old Gentleman look'd like seventeen Furies. He invited my Chum also.

I went to Meeting & hear'd Mr. Appleton expound A.M. from Jude from the 10th to the 14th Verse. P.M. he preach'd a Sermon to encourage People to contribute largely to the Poor on the approaching Thanksgiving, but his Text I have forgot.

My Chum & I din'd at Colo. Brattles with Mr. Willard, Master Marret, Sr. Hall, Hutchinson & Saltonstall. Had a very great Variety for Diner. We had an Indian Pudding, soup, Hogs Liver, fry'd with aple, cold Beef, Neats Tongue, a rost Goose & rost Ducks & Chicken Pye with a plenty of Wine & Cider.

For oddities the Diner & Man much alike. After Servise came to my Chamber & read Marshel & heard my Chum read some in Sherlock on Death. I drank Tea with Tenny.

Scammel Wadsworth, & Osgood came & eat Chese with us to Night. Talk'd of giving Fisher some Butery Cider.

Attendance at Harvard provided students with entrée into a level of New England society that otherwise would have been unattainable for many of them. The opportunity to take Sunday dinner with Col. William BRATTLE, A.B. 1722, of Cambridge, the scion of one of the leading families of Massachusetts, would have been unimaginable for Peabody if he had not left his family's farm for college. SIR HALL was either Stephen Hall (1743–94), A.B. 1765, of Westford, or William Hall (1745–1823), A.B. 1766, of Methuen. Both men, recent graduates, were in Cambridge as Hopkins fellows reading for the ministry. HUTCHINSON was either Aaron Hutchinson (1754–1843), A.B. 1770, of Grafton, a future lawyer, or William Sanford Hutchinson (1752–80), A.B. 1770, of Milton, a son of Gov. Thomas Hutchinson, A.B. 1727, and soon to be a Loyalist refugee. Gilbert SALTONSTALL (1752–97), A.B. 1770, of New London, became a merchant and officer in the Marines. INDIAN PUDDING, a traditional New England dish, consists of cornmeal, molasses, sugar, and spices. William SHERLOCK wrote *A Practical Discourse Concerning Death* (many editions). WADSWORTH was either Benjamin Wadsworth (1750–1826), A.B. 1769, of Milton, who became the minister of the First Church in Danvers, or Peleg Wadsworth, also a member of the class of 1769. *Sibley's Harvard Graduates,* 16:165–69, 371–73; 17:397–401, 426–28, 286–91.

Monday the 30th.

To Day is Pleasant. In the Morning there was a large Pitcher of Butry Cider hung on Fishers Door, & two Advertizements put up about it, but not much said. I attended Prayers & reciting in Euclid to Danforth.

Went into the Library & took out Allen on the Lord's Supper & the 5th Volume of Spectator. Saterday I received a Letter from Pike & unum ad ejus Uxorem[1] & after Prayers this Evening took a Walk & deliver'd it, got my Boot Straps & like them well. Give 25/0 for them. Went to one Tapleys & spoke for a Horse to go Home if I git leave. I took my great Coat at Mr. Bowmans but don't recon with them till I [c]ome again.

Pikes Wife tells me that the Wedding is lik'd to be found out, & is in trouble about it.

I drank Kelly at my chamber at noon.

DANFORTH was tutor Thomas Danforth. William ALLEN wrote *De sacramentis in genere; de sacramento eucharitiæ, et sacrificio missæ* (Antwerp, 1576). TAPLEY was probably Mansfield Tapley (d. 1787), the only adult male with that surname in Cambridge at this time. *Vital Records of Cambridge,* 1:690; 2:384, 758.

1. One to his wife.

December 1767

Tuesday the 1 of December.

To Day is cloudy but no falling Weather. I attended Prayers & reciting as usual, & Lecture likewise. The President & Tutors met to give leave to go Home on Thanksgiving. I went & obtain'd leave to be gone till Friday Night from Tomorrow noon.

I intended to have had a Dish of Tea but could get no Body to drink with me. The President made a Butiful Speech to the Scholars about talking in at Prayers.

In the Evening it Rains. I wrote some in Journal, look'd a little in Euclid & partly wash'd my Breeches.

Because drinking TEA was a social experience, the fact that Peabody COULD GET NO BODY TO DRINK with him undermined the central reason for the beverage.

Wednesday the 2d of December.

This Morning it rains a while but soon clear'd of. I attended Prayers & reciting A.M. & got my Things fitted to go Home immediately after Commons, & my Chum went up to Tapley's & got my Horse & I set of & find it some cool & pretty wet riding. I came to Wyman's where I stop'd & refresh'd myself & Horse & just after I came from there I lit of George Abbot who was going Home to keep Thanksgiving so I rode with him to Andover. Got to his Fathers a little after Sun Down. Stop'[d] & worm'd & drank a Dram & then proceeded. Came to Br. Peters's, stop'd

& eat & drank & they tell me John is come Home & that my Cousin Kyse & his Wife have been down & paid a Visit. I am sorry I could not have seen them. I came from there call'd & left some Things for my Chum at his Fathers, & so call'd again at Capt. Osgoods & left a letter & Mr. Isaac was there, so I rode Homewards with hi[m]. I parted & went to my Fathers & find them all well there. Sister Wood is here with her Famaly. Br. John tells me he is likt to get but about 40 Pound in Money for me at present which will not answer.

My Father tells me that Nathaniel Peabody has made up with the Bradford Men for about 50 Pound.

Nihil majus.

Abbot's FATHER was Col. George Abbot (1724–75) of Andover. MR. ISAAC was probably Isaac Osgood of Andover. *Descendants of George Abbot*, 25.

Thursday the 3d of December.

To Day is clear & cool. James came Home & is lame. He Cut his Heel with an Ads. We got ready as soon as we could & I went to Meeting to Boxford & heard Mr. Sparhawk preach from the 47th Psalm 1 Verse. The latter part of his Sermon was the most allarming I ever heard & the Congregation was the most affected I ever saw one. May such seasonable & moving Discourses move & affect my Heart & be a Means of rousing me from my carnal Security, & fiting me for the more immediate Servise of God in his Zion above.

I deliver'd a Letter to Chadwick from his Chum, & he is yet poorly. I came from Meeting with him & call'd at his Fathers a few Minutes, & so at Uncle Robinsons & then came Home, & had a fine Supper. I stay'd there till in the Evening & nobody came to see us, so I took my Camel & went down to Bradford to old Mr. Websters & put her into the Barn, & took a walk cum Amico[1] down to Edmund Kimbals where was S. Johnson & Wife & some others, & in the other Room some young Company. They ware looking of Mr. [T]uckers answer to Mr. Hutchinson & they had a Mind I should read it, so I did, & such a Peace of Wit, Blackguard, & Error I never saw. As soon as I was done reading I came from there & went in at Jacob Kimbals a few Minutes & then the other Room. Folks came along & accompany'd us Home.

People are generally in Health &c.

Benjamin CHADWICK (1745–1819), A.B. 1770, of Boxford, became the minister of the First Church in Dunstan, Maine. Chadwick's CHUM was Samuel Osgood, A.B. 1770. His FATHER was Deacon Thomas Chadwick (1712–88) of West Boxford. Samuel Johnson's WIFE was Elizabeth (Gage) Johnson (1723–96). EDMUND KIMBALL (1716–95) was a prominent farmer in Bradford. John TUCKER wrote *Remarks on a Sermon of the Rev. Aaron Hutchinson* (Boston, 1767). *Sibley's Harvard Graduates*, 17:367–68, 412; *Vital Records of Boxford*, 22, 229; *Vital Records of Andover*, 2:201, 479; *Vital Records of Bradford*, 51, 208; Morrison and Sharples, *Kimball Family*, 62, 86, 100.

1. With [my] friend.

Friday the 4th.

To Day is Stormy. I Breakfasted with Mr. Ebenezer Webster with some others & he told me Jeremiah Kimbal had 40 Pound in Money to let. After a while I got my Camel & went cum Amico ad Edmund Kimballs illa est apud Operam ibi.[1] I stay'd a while & then set of for Home. I call'd at Kimbals & he said if I would come down at Night he would let me have the Money. I call'd at John Days & left a pare of Scissurs which Mrs. Robins sent to her. I din'd at Home & then went with my Sisters in the Slay to Stephen Barkers & Uncle Robinson & Mr. Sparhawk came there. They stay'd but a little While. Chadwick came there also & brought me some things to bring to his Chum. I walk'd with Mr. Sparhawk to Uncle Robinsons & stay'd till in the Evening & drank Tea. Mr. Sparhawk seems a good Deal destourb'd & at a Loss what to do, whether to stay with them or not at Boxford, but they desire he will not give his Answer till they have seen whether those who are against him will not be reconcil'd, & if they will not he says he shall by no Means settle, & I believe they will build a new Meeting-House directly if they remain against him. Br. Oliver, Richard Kimball, their Wives with some others came to Uncle before I came away. I came to Mr. Barker & there was Abraham Poor, & my Sisters got ready & we came Home, & I took my Camel & went down to Jeremiah Kimbals & got 40 Pound in Money & gave him a Note. At last I went to Edmund Kimbal where I went to Supper & made a little stop. It clear'd of about Midnight & is cold. Validicebam Amici[2] &c.

Peabody needed cash to pay his college expenses—including tuition, room, board, books, clothing, firewood, and incidentals—but cash was in short supply in Andover, a farming community where most business was conducted on credit. Securing the money to cover anticipated costs was thus a predictable problem for him. Stephen may be referring to EBENEZER WEBSTER (1724–68) of Bradford, a brother of Thomas Webster. JEREMIAH KIMBALL (1735–1808) lived in nearby Bradford. STEPHEN BARKER (1724–1811) was a farmer in Andover. The WIVES of Brother Oliver and Richard Kimball were Sarah (Robinson) Peabody of Andover and Annie (Robinson) Kimball of Andover. ABRAHAM POOR (1742–1819) was a laborer in Andover. "Descendants of John Webster," 39, 75; Morrison and Sharples, *Kimball Family*, 90, 165–66, 148–49; Barker, *Barker Genealogy*, 270, 276; *Peabody Genealogy*, 36–37; *Vital Records of Andover*, 1:306, 2:275, 527.

1. With [my] friend near to where Edmund Kimball was working.
2. I wished my friends well.

Saturday the 5th of December.

To Day is clear. Br. John had got some Money for me. I give him a Note, wrote some Receipts for Sister Wood & then she & her Fama[ly] went Home. I got all Things ready & din'd & so set out. Oliver came there & I settled Accompts with him & he came along with me.

I call'd at Samuel Johnsons & borrow'd a pare of Taps for my Shoes. Came from there & parted with Oliver. Stop'd at Capt. Osgood. Took a pare of Stockins & a Dictionary for Samuel. Came to Esq. Phillipses. Took some Things for my Chum. Came to Br. Peters's swop'd Horses. James rode mine up there yesterday. Stop'd & talk'd with John a while, & then proceeded. It is pretty Cold. I got to Wyman's about dark refresh'd myself & Horse, then proceeded & got to Cambridge about Eight o Clock. Find all well. My Chum had Home my Horse, & after a little Chat, took our Repose.

CAPT. OSGOOD was either Capt. Isaac Osgood or Capt. Peter Osgood, both of Andover.

Sunday the 6th.

To Day went to Meeting & heard Mr. Appleton expound A.M. from Jude from the 14th to the 18th Verse. P.M. John Wyeth attempted to preach from the 11th of Romans 33 Verse & such insipped Stuff I never heard nor such Actions I never saw nor so much Distourbance in the Meeting-House I believe never was known. Tenny repeated the Heads of the Sermon for Emerson just as it was deliver'd. I finish'd reading Marshal, & in the Evening went & eat Commons with Scammel & Wadsworth.

JOHN WYETH (1743–1811), A.B. 1760, was briefly the minister of the First Church in Gloucester when he delivered this sermon. Peabody regularly derided liberal preachers for what he considered to be their theological errors, but in Wyeth's case there seems to have been widespread agreement that he lacked both the talents and the personality to be an effective preacher or pastor. *Sibley's Harvard Graduates*, 14:676–77.

Monday the 7th of December.

To Day is cloudy, foggy & thawey. I attended the Exercises of College. In the Evening wrote some & went down to the Presidents & talk'd with him about the Disorders at Prayers & he says there shall be some other Method taken in punishing that shall prove more affectual if we will let him know who those are who do make the Noise. I told him he should know.

Tuesday the 8th.

To Day is Cloudy. I attended the Exercises, cast up my Quarter Bills & wrote some. In the Evening I cary'd my Shoes to Mannings to be tap'd, borrow'd a pare of Osgood to ware, lent my boots to Goodhue to Day to ride a little Way in.

Went over & paid the Steward some Money & the Gold fell short. Was urged to sup but chose not for I have an Invitation at College. I came over to College & went to Osgood's Chamber & John Noyes had a fine Turky rosted there which Judith sent him. They got all Necessaries & we had a very fine Super & a Glass of Wine after it. Nihil majus.

Settled accounts with Doctr. Wales to Day.

The value of coins made of precious metals depended on their weight, not on the amount stamped on them. Prudent participants in transactions weighed the coins they received to make sure that they were not underweight. Unscrupulous traders occasionally clipped coins, making them SHORT, thereby reducing their weight and value. The resulting fragments were negotiable as precious metal. MANNING was either William Manning (1700–1778) or his son Samuel (1729–1824), both cordwainers of Cambridge. William GOODHUE (1747–82), A.B. 1769, of Waltham, became a physician. Paige, *History of Cambridge*, 602–3; *Sibley's Harvard Graduates*, 17:160.

Wednesday the 9th.

To Day it clears away Pleasant. I attended Prayers & Mr. Eliot as usual. We finish'd the Turky at Osgood's Chamber for eating. Had some exercise. After Commons my Chum & I went down in Town. I got my shoes at Mannings & went to see my Quondam & drank a Glass of Cider with him, & my Chum got a Joannes chang'd for me at Mores's.

Came up to the College & I translated a Peace of English into Latin. In the Evening went down to the Presidens & inform[ed] him of Bradish, Moors, & Colman who talk at Prayers, & told him who to send for if they deny it. He thank'd me for the Information. I see Stearns, Stone Burnap & Osgood who say they will not be backward in telling if sent for.

We had a pleasant Sing at Scammel's Chamber & then by Mr. Honeywill's Desire we went [to] his House & had another. He had some Compa[ny] there. Mr. Hancock sent us in a mug of Flip for our good Sing. We came from there in a pretty high Gail & Wadsworth Scammel & I had a travil back & forth wishing one an other good Night & then a Correspondence by Letters till very late, then I went in a very humble Manner & wished them good Night & then Scammel jumped out of bed & follow'd me upon the Run naked to my Chamber thro the Mud & I drove him Home again, so we took our Rest.

Peabody's informing was an example of the Association for the Suppression of Vice at work. STEARNS was either Jonathan Stearns (1751–98), A.B. 1770, of Lunenburg, later a Loyalist and lawyer, or William Stearns (1749–83), A.B. 1770, of Lunenburg, later a lawyer. STONE was Isaac Stone (1748–1837), A.B. 1770, of Shrewsbury, later the minister of the First Church in Douglas. Jacob BURNAP (1748–1821), A.B. 1770, of Reading, became the minister of the First Church of Merrimack, New Hampshire. OSGOOD was Samuel Osgood, A.B. 1770, of Andover. The miscreants were Ebenezer BRADISH (1746–1818), A.B. 1769, of Cambridge, a future lawyer; Thomas MOORE (1745–96), A.B. 1769, of Boston, later the minister of the First Church in Wiscasset, Maine; and Thomas COLMAN (1751–81), A.B. 1770, of Newbury, who became a lawyer. HONEYWELL was either William Hunnewell (b. 1735) or his brother Richard (1734–98), both of Cambridge. FLIP, in colonial New England, was a heated, frothy drink made of beer, rum, and sugar. Later versions also included eggs. *Sibley's Harvard Graduates*, 17:434–39, 412–19, 126–28, 187–88, 380–81; *Vital Records of Cambridge*, 1:369, 2:615.

Thursday the 10th of December.

To Day is pleasant & after reciting in Mane Mr. Eliot went out of Town & Tenny & I went up to Mr. Bowmans & I pay'd for the making of my great Coat & settled Accompts there & then came to College just before Commons & my Chum tells me Colo. Osgood has been here, but he made no Stop. I spent the afternoon in writing a Letter to Sr. Pike & some in my Journal. After Prayers Tenny complain'd of some indecent Behaviour at Prayers, to the President. In the Evening we a small Number of us had a pleasant Singing Meeting at Foggs Chamber & are going to have them every Week.

Friday the 11th of December.

To Day is Pleasant. I attended Prayers as usual. Sent my Letter to Boston by Tenny. Went down to see my quondam. Got a peice of black Led of him. Came to my Chamber. Read a little in Spectator & some in Clarissa. Made my Theme for tomorrow Morning. There was some Scholars complain'd of for Disorders at Prayers & punished sevearly. Tenny & Dole had some Difference because Dole would not have Home the Horse & Chaise which Noyes had rid in. I thought Dole was right.

Saturday the 12.

To Day is pleasant. I attended Prayers & reciting as usual. Tenny was mad at me about Dole but we made Matters up & so did he & Dole. I read Clarissa & a little in Spectator. In the Evening I attended private Meeting in Bowers's Chamber. I came to my Chamber & Mr. Scales had sent for me, so I went to him & he examined me concerning some Disorders at Prayers & I told him freely. It Snows a little this Night.

Sunday the 13th.

To Day is Clear. I was a little indispos'd & got leave to stay at Home. I have had a cold & have been a little stif & have had a little of the Rhumatism. I read to Day Allen on the Lords Supper & some very excellant Maxims in it, & finish'd the Book. Webster was at my Chamber at Noon

& talk'd without Sense & at Night he was there with a Number of others & we black him remarkably & he went off.

There was some complain'd of for behaving ill at Meeting to Day.

Monday the 14th of December.

To Day is cloudy & snows fast. P.M. I kept to my Chamber, & Sr. Cobb came in to see me. I read a little in Spectator, & finished the 3d Vollume of Clarissa. Received a Letter from Webster & he is Angry at being treated as he was at my Chamber last Night. I wrote him an Answer & irritated him in it as much as lay in my Power. Sent it by Frye.

In the Evening we had a very smart Rain. There is a considerable Number punish'd to Day heavily for bad Behaviour at publick Worship which I rejoice to hear of.

There is a Rumer that they determine to Mobb Stearns & Stone whom they suspect inform'd of them, but it is a Question whether they will or no.

Peabody was mistaken about PUNISHMENTS. The faculty records list more than twenty fines for absence but none for misbehavior in chapel. Faculty Records, 3:65–66.

Tuesday the 15th.

To Day is clear. Wind high at West & some cool. I kept my chamber began the 4th Vollume of Clarisa Harlow & read a little in Spectator. There was two punish'd for playing at Meeting. A great Talk about there's being Informers but they cant find out who they are. Nothing strange to Day.

The faculty records contain no evidence of punishments FOR PLAYING AT MEETING.

Wednesday the 16th of December.

To Day is Cool. I kept my Chamber. Read in Clarissa. Webster came here & seems to be good Stuff again. In the Evening there was a Number here who had been over to Munrows to Sing. French told me to Day they had got a Notion that I am against the Informers. Let them enjoy their Opinion. I set up late & read.

MUNROW may have been James Munroe (1735–1804) of Cambridge, a blacksmith and later a deacon of the local church. He lived on what is now Brattle Street between James and Mason Streets. Note that some of the students, instead of confining themselves to the college community, were apparently socializing here with residents of Cambridge. Paige, *History of Cambridge*, 613–14.

Thursday the 17th.

To Day cold but Pleasant. I kept my Chamber, finished the 4th Vollume of Clarissa, read some in Spectator, wrote some in Journal.

My Chum tells me that Isaac Farnam is gone along to Roxbury with a Drove of Cattle for Colo. Osgood & will call here tomorrow. In the Evening I went up to Wentworths Chamber & we had a Singing Meeting & then I came to my own & wrote a Letter Home &c.

ISAAC FARNAM (1742–1823) lived in Andover's North Parish. Russell C. Farnham, *The New England Descendants of the Immigrant Ralph Farnum of Rochester, Kent County, England, and Ipswich, Massachusetts* (Portsmouth, N.H.: Peter Randall, 1999), 1:467–68; *Andover Tax Assessments*, Tax for 1768.

Friday the 18th.

To Day pleasant. I wrote three more Letters Home but Farnam never call'd so I have no Opportunity to send them. I read a little in Spectator & made some Bills. In the Evening my Chum & I got Tenny, Osgood & Noyes here & had a drink of Kelly & a Supper of the Thanksgiving good Chear which I brought from Home & from the Esqrs. & they spent the Evening here. There is a very great Stur about College concerning a riotous Noise there was at Kasts Chamber & at Fryes last Night & it is said that Samuel Hastings had his Windows broke & there was a great Distourbance made up at Prentices & the Persons concerned ware Kast, Frye, & Watson, & several Others knowing to it. It is thought Frye & Kast will be rusticated.

Thomas KAST (1750–1820), A.B. 1769, of Boston, became a physician. Samuel HASTINGS (1724–85), a glazier of Cambridge, lived on the eastern side of North Avenue near Mellen Street. The faculty decided to rusticate John FRYE for disorderly conduct on December 22. The sentence was imposed on December 24. Samuel PRENTICE (1753–1815), A.B. 1771, of Cambridge, taught school and became the postmaster of Gorham, Maine. Abraham WATSON (1752–1804), of

Cambridge, became a physician. *Sibley's Harvard Graduates*, 17:172–73, 606, 670; Paige, *History of Cambridge*, 575, 576; Faculty Records, 3:67.

Saturday the 19th of December.

To Day is snowey. I kept my Chamber. Heard of some very blasphemous Talk of Fryes & that there was Prof of it. So all Things well consider'd I thought it my Duty, as well as for the good of the Society to let a Tutor know of it, & accordingly wrote a few Lines to Mr. Danforth & told him where he might have Information & he has sent round to them, & what will be the issue I can't tell but I believe the Punishment will be very heavy.

My Chum had a Relation come from Boston to see him. His Name is Bromfield & stay'd till after noon. He is soon to sail for London to serve aprentiship there. Is a pretty Youth.

I wrote a little, & read some in Spectator, & in the Evening read in Sherlock on Death. I hear Frye blames me for advising Wheten what to say to the Tutors, & that Wheten has told of more than I have said, & Webster has had a say upon it, so I sent for Wheten & he says there is nothing to what Webster has said, but I determine to see them togather for I believe there is lying somewhere.

Bowers came here & was affraid Frye would mob or kill him if he is expelled for something he has said.

BROMFIELD was a relation of Peabody's roommate, Samuel Phillips. Samuel's uncle William married Abigail, daughter of Edward Bromfield, Esq., of Boston. *Phillips Genealogies*, 26.

Sunday the 20th of December.

To Day is cold. I stay'd at Home, read Sherlock. I saw Wheton & Webster to Day seperately & they give each other the Lye about what they have said.

In the Evening Sargent, Webster, & Frye came here & I did not known whether I should have another Opportunity to see Frye to have any Talk with him, so I made some Kelly & told Frye what I advis'd Wheten, & he said if so he had no hard Thoughts of me, then I sent for Wheten & he confirm'd what I had said & contradicted Webster & they give each other the Lye then too, & upon the whole I believe they have both Lyed, but the Matter shall rest for the Present. Frye expects to be expelled.

Just at Night my Chum saw Bristow going by the College so he hail'd him & brought him in & we sent some Letters by him to Andover. He has been to little Cambridge with some Oxen for Colo. Osgood.

SARGENT could have been either Christopher Sargent (1747–78), A.B. 1769, of Methuen, a future lawyer, or Winthrop Sargent (1753–1820), A.B. 1771, of Gloucester, later an artillery officer in the Continental Army and the governor of the Mississippi Territory. LITTLE CAMBRIDGE was the present-day Brighton. *Sibley's Harvard Graduates*, 17:218, 614–26.

Monday the 21.

To Day is very Cold. I got out a little, went up to Mr. Danforth to Desire my Name not to be mentioned in Fryes affair & he says there will be no occation for it.

The President & Tutors meet. I wrote & read a little. P.M. I went to Bowers's Chamber & told him how Frye blamt him & advis'd him to git him to his Chamber & make Matters up, so he has agree'd to it. In the Evening I Went to Fryes Chamber & he & a Number of others came to Bowers's Chamber & we had a drink of Kelly & they made up so I came to my own Chamber. Sr. Smith, Greene, Thacher & Austin drank Tea with me this P.M. Hear nothing what the President & Tutors have done.

Tuesday the 22 of December.

To Day is stormy. It snows in the Day & at Night Rains. The President & Tutors met & determin'd the Affair they have been upon but don't tell how. We agree'd to send to Fryes Father if he is rusticated or expelled. Sargent went to Mr. Eliot but he would not tell him. Fogg went to Scales but he could not find out but Scales tells him to come to him again tomorrow. I read some in the 5th Vollume of Clarissa though but little. Had College company all Day talking upon this Affair.

Wednesday the 23d.

To Day is clear & not cold. I attended Prayers & Mr. Sewall was up & it seems the punishment was to have been inflicted this Morning but the President did not come up so it is defer'd but by one of the Professors being there it appears that there is to be Rustication or Expulsion. After reciting I got leave to go to Boston, & we agreed that Fogg should go to Mr. Scales as he had orderd & then that Osgood should go to Andover & cary the News to Fryes Father.

My Chum & I walk'd to Boston & I went to Gridley's & din'd & then went & pay'd for the News Papers & drop'd them. Got Mien to send me the Chronicle instd of my Chum. Bought me a Watch Chain & several other small Articles & went to hear Sandiman but his Sermon was almost over so I cant judge how he preach'd.

I met my Chum at the Ferry & came over. Saw Isaac Robinson. He was waiting for the coming in of a Vessel lode of Lumber, & he is very Sociable.

We came up to Cambridge & they tell me Osgood is gone Home though he meet with some Difficulty to get leave but Scales help'd him away & thay say Frye, Kast, & Watson is order'd in to Prayers in the Morning. Frye came here & seems to be chearly & says he has been to Boston and has got a berth to go of to sea immediatly, & he intends to be gone directly after his Sentence is pass'd & he little thinks News is gone to his Father.

The first issue of the weekly Boston CHRONICLE appeared on December 21, 1767. John MEIN, the publisher, aimed for a sophisticated readership, but before long his support of the crown became apparent and he began to lose subscribers. The paper ceased publication with the June 25, 1770, issue. ISAAC ROBINSON (b. 1741) lived in the North Parish of Andover. Thomas, *History of Printing*, 263–65; *Vital Records of Andover*, 1:319; *Andover Tax Assessments*, Tax for 1768.

Thursday the 24th of December.

To Day is Pleasant. I attended Prayers & Frye was Rusticated. As soon as the Sentence came out, he pronounc'd Amen with an audable Voice & put on his Hat & left the Chappel. The Amen was an imitation of Wigglesworth & it made a good deal of Laugh in the Chappel. Kast was degraded 20 in his Class & Watson 5. The President talk'd very well to us afterwards.

When the President & Professors cam[e] into the Yard Frye went to them with his Hat on very bold & it is supposed talked very Impudent but it is not known what he said. Just at that Time Colo. James Frye came to cary him Home. He was surprised to see him but on the whole (the Colo. being very resolute) concluded to go Home. The Colo. tells me Osgood got there about eight o Clock last Night & that Mr. Frye & his Wife are exceedingly affected.

Frye got his Things ready & Webster is going with him to bring back his Horse. They came & drank some Kelly with me & then went of. He, to outward appearance is but very little affected with it.

I attended Forensick Dispute & then Colo. Osgood came here, & we told him the News. P.M. I read some & Osgood came back & says he met Frye, & then he knew how his Uncle came to come. Brings no News which is new. The President sent for me to know whether anybody was come for Frye. I was at my Quondams Chamber this Evening. I had an invitation to greet Dana but had rather not go.

John FRYE's behavior after the pronouncement of his rustication was an intentional affront to the college and its officers. Under similar circumstances, students were ordinarily more contrite. By wearing his hat in the Yard, he was disrespectful of the faculty and in violation of the college laws, which required students to remove headwear in the presence of their superiors. John Frye's MOTHER was Sarah (Frye) Frye (c. 1711–81) of Andover. Faculty Records, 3:67–68; "College Laws and Customs," 350; *Sibley's Harvard Graduates*, 17:158–59; *Vital Records of Andover*, 2:448.

Friday the 25th of December.

To Day is Cold. I attended Prayers as Usual, read in Clarisa & made me a Bill. Just at Night my Father came down here & at seeing him I was affraid of some bad News but he brings none. He is come down for Uncle Kimbal about Francis's Case & Ebenezer Websters, to speak to Mr. Sewall about it. He brought me a short Letter from my Sisters but no News. He stay'd part of the Evening here, & then I went with him to Mr. Warlands where we sup'd & he lodg'd. I went to Mr. Sewalls & [h]e says he will wait upon my Father in Mane. Sr. Searl was at Mr. Warland's. It is Christmas to Day & we went to Church & heard the Orgains go butifully, & heard Mr. Sargent preach from these Words, & they hated me without a Cause.[1] The Sermon was ingenious but not very good.

Webster came down & says Fryes Parents are very kind to him, & make him good Offers but are very much grieved. My Chum went up to Prentices to Night & got me a Gallon of Rum, & had my Fathers Horse to Frosts.

Until the early nineteenth century, New England Congregationalists did not celebrate CHRISTMAS. Given the opportunity to do so, though, Peabody was happy to take in a Christmas service. Unlike the Congregationalists, the Anglicans observed the holiday. Winwood SERJEANT (1739–80) was the rector of Christ Church, 1767–74. SEARL was Jonathan Searl (1746–1818), A.B. 1765, of Rowley; he eventually became the minister of the First Church in Salisbury, New Hampshire. Weis, *Colonial Clergy*, 182; *Sibley's Harvard Graduates*, 16:213–14.

1. John 15:25.

Saturday the 26th of December.

To Day is cool. I attended Prayers & wrote to my Sisters & to John Frye & my Father did his Business & set of for Home about ten o Clock. I spent my Day in reading Clarissa & Spectator. In the Evening I attended private Meeting at Bowers's Chamber.

Sunday the 27th.

To Day is cold & cloudy & at night snows. I attended Prayers & Meeting. Heard Mr. Appleton begin to Expound the Revelations which he did three Verses of it A.M. P.M. he preach'd from the 2d of Titus 10 Verse. I smok'd a Pipe & eat Apples with Osgood at noon, & drank Labradore Tea with Scammell after meeting & I like it about midling. I read in Shearlock. Don't like some of it. I received a Letter from Pike to Day & one ad Uxorem[1] which I sent by Tenny. He writes he is well.

1. To [his] wife.

Monday the 28th of December.

To Day is cloudy & cool & a little Rain. I attended Prayers & reciting in Euclid all Day & Mr. Sewall's Lecture also. Read a little in Spectator. Nihil Majus. Only read my Chronicle whch is pretty good.

Tuesday the 29th.

Is clear & grows cold. I attended Prayers Mr. Wigglesworths Lecture & finished Euclid, finished the 5th vollume of Clarissa, had a little pritty sing & then wen[t] to Foggs Chamber where he had a Vendue of Books. I set up Homer but it did not go to the Worth of it, so my Chum bid it of for me. I came to my Chamber & borrow'd a Gravesand of Knowless for this Week. We are going to learn it to Mr. Danforth.

Peabody borrowed a work by Willem Jacob 's GRAVESANDE, a Dutch mathematician and philosopher, possibly his *Mathematical Elements of Natural Philosophy* (many editions), of which the college library owned three sets in 1790. Bond and Amory, *Printed Catalogues*, C138.

Wednesday the 30th.

To Day is very cold. I attended Prayers & reciting in Gravesande & like it pretty Well. Read a little in Spectator, & wrote in Journal. Sold my Euclid to Rogers for 60/ & in the Evening read in Clarissa & studie'd in Gravesand.

Peabody's book sale is evidence of a market in used texts among Harvard undergraduates. Much as on November 14 he had purchased the copy of the *Cyropædia* that senior Jonathan Hastings no longer needed, Peabody himself had no further use for EUCLID's geometry text and was willing to pass it on to freshman Daniel ROGERS (1749–1804), A.B. 1771, of Littleton, a Loyalist during the Revolution who became a farmer. *Sibley's Harvard Graduates*, 17:609–10.

Thursday the 31.

To Day is more moderate. I attended Prayers & reciting in Mane but no more. Spent the Day in reading Clarissa & Spectator. In the Evening I went up to Bowmans & cary'd my great Coat to have some Buttons set on to it, & they tell me Sr. Pike has sent a Letter to Mr. Bowman leting him know that he was married to his Daughter which displeases Mr. Bowman very much & they seem to be in a good Deal of Trouble about it.

I came to my Chamber & read a little.

Considering that Nicholas PIKE had married Hannah Bowman almost three months before on October 5, Noah BOWMAN may have been as upset by the delayed notification as by the message.

January 1768

Friday the 1st of January 1768.

To Day is Pleasant but cool. I spent my Day (after attending Prayers) in reading & in making a Bill, & a Theme for tomorrow morning. I got out the 6th Vollume of Clarissa. Esqr. Phillips was here to Day from Boston & is going to Andover & says he does not determine to come again till Tuesday, when our Horses are to come.

I drank tea with Greene.

As a monitor, Peabody had to submit a BILL to report the violations of the college laws he had identified.

Saturday the 2d.

To Day is pleasant. I attended Prayers & then read in the 7th Vollume of Clarissa. After Diner I went up & paid Tapply for his Horse to Andover 40/. I stop'd at Bomans & Mrs. Pike had set on my Buttons & got out some stains which ware in my Coat but she could not quite finish it. She wanted some quolity to set over where they were set on.

I stay'd & drank Tea & she desired me to talk with her Father about her Affairs, which I did & he is very much displeased about their being married & blames Tenny & I for going with them, & seems, as though he would hardly ever be reconcil'd so I left him & came to College & attended private Meeting as usual. Read one of Mr. Davis's sermons which I borrow'd of Austin.

MRS. PIKE was Hannah (Bowman) Pike, Noah Bowman's daughter.

Sunday the 3d.

To Day is cloudy & grows more moderate & at Night it rains. I went to meeting & heard Mr. Appleton expound from the 1 of Revelations from the 4th to the end of the 8th Verse. P.M. he preach'd from the 2nd of Titus 10 Verse. Mr. Sewall had his first Child Christien'd to Day & his name was Stephen.

I finis[hed] reading Sherlock on Death to Day.

STEPHEN, son of Professor Stephen Sewall and his wife, Rebecca, was born in Cambridge on December 30, 1767. *Vital Records of Cambridge*, 1:632.

Monday the 4th of January.

To Day is Worm & rains a little but soon cleard of very pleasant. I attended Prayers & reciting in Mane, then got leave to go out of Town but did not go. Return'd my Books to the Library borrow'd the 6th Vollume of Spectator of Pason to carry Home. Got my quarter Bill & did some choars & read some in Clarissa. In the evening went up to Bowmans with Tenny & Mrs. Pike finish'd my Coat & we had a long talk about affairs & he is very much cast down about it.

The Horses begin to become plenty for the Scholars. There is a Letter come that my worthy Classmate Adams is Dead! He Dyed last Fryday Morning. The nearest Friend must part, & how weighty it is to part so as to meet again in the Relms of Light. A Person of greater Worth I don't know than he was, & it is to be hop'd he made a bless'd Change. He has been poorly so long that seems to be not so shocking as otherwise it would have been.

PASON was probably John Payson (1746–1804), A.B. 1764, who was preparing for the ministry. Less than a week after this entry, on January 9 he accepted a call from the First Parish in Fitchburg. Joseph ADAMS, class of 1769, died in Rowley on January 1, 1768. *Sibley's Harvard Graduates*, 16:84–87; 17:115–16.

Tuesday the 5.

It clouds up & rains. I attended Prayers & reciting in Mane. I wrote a Letter to Mein to keep my Chronicles till after the Vacancy. Wrote a Letter to Sr. Pike. Received a very pretty Letter from Master Adams giving an Account of his Brs. Death.

Lemuel Noyes is down here for his Br. & came & drank some Kelly with me, & then Esqr. Phillips came here & had brought Osgood & I each of us a Horse. He says my Father was coming but the going was good & the Horses led so well he ventur'd alone & so my Father went back. He din'd here & we got a few of us here togather & had a pleasant sing & then he went to Charlston, & my Chum went down & brought up the Horse to ride back tomorrow.

There was a blind man at College with [a] Harp & play'd upon it & it is midling pritty Musick. I could play any Psalm tune upon it as I found by experience.

I wrote some in Journal & clean'd my Breeches & got things fitted for Home. I drank coffee with Sr. Smith, return'd his Sherlock.

Mr. Chandler sent a Piece down here for Tenny & I to alter to our Mind & put into the News paper concerning Adams's Death which we did. They say Austin is writing a Piece of Poetry upon it.

I heard to Day there was fault found with me by the Scholars for keeping a strict Bill & that Varnum is offended which does not disturb me at all.

Tenny has been up to Bowmans to Day & says the old man is reconcil'd & they are all much pleas'd. I wrote a few Words to Pike about it. It holds on raining.

The faculty had made Peabody a monitor because they trusted him to maintain order among the undergraduates through measures such as a STRICT BILL. Mr. CHANDLER was presumably James Chandler (1706–89), A.B. 1728, the minister of the West Parish in Rowley, where Joseph ADAMS lived. The death notice appeared in the *Boston Evening-Post*, January 11, 1768. AUSTIN's poetry has not been found. *Sibley's Harvard Graduates*, 8:375–81; 17:266–79.

Wednesday the 6th of January.

To Day is cloudy & some Rain. We got up early & fitted our Things & after Breakfast I went down to Mr. Dana & left Holtons Note with him. We drank with Osgood & secured our Chamber & set of for Home. I call'd at Mr. Bowmans & left 2 Vollumes of Clarissa & Miss. Hannah looks the better for her Fathers being reconcild to her. We proceeded & stop'd at Wyman's, & Gowens & drank & oated our Horses, & there is a considerable Number of Scholars comes through Andover. Wentworth & Osgood & I called to see F[rye] & he look'd miserably & seems to be far forsake[n] & his Mother also. I never saw such an Alteration as in that House. Frye blames us for sending to his Parents.

We came from there & Wentworth & I stop'd at my Chums till Evening & was entertain'd exceedingly Well. We came from there & just call'd upon Osgood & then came to my Fathers & found them all Well. It clears of cool.

They tell me they are not going to have the school kept here till Spring.

HOLTON may have been James Holton, who lived in Little Cambridge. Paige, *History of Cambridge*, 446.

Thursday the 7th of January.

To Day is cold. After Breakfast Wentworth went from here & Uncle Robinson was here & went with him as far as Haverhill. I spent the Day in reading a little & Wm. Runnels was here. In the Evening I took a ride over to Haverhill to Doctor Hucar [?] & got some senting for Pomatum & it is very slipery Riding. I call'd at Jeremiah Kimballs & left word how much the Gold I had from him fell short in wait & made some other stops. Found the People all well. Nihil majus &c.

WILLIAM RUNNELS, or Reynolds, lived in both Andover and Boxford between the late 1760s and the early 1780s. He married Rebecca Foster of Andover on May 3, 1768, and may have been the William Runnels of Boxford who died "in the Army" in 1781. POMATUM, or pomade, is a perfumed ointment for dressing hair. DR. HUCAR, or possibly Hooker, as a pharmacist as well as a physician, dispensed scented additives. He has not been further identified. *Vital Records of Andover*, 2:290; *Vital Records of Boxford*, 261.

Friday the 8th.

To Day is cool. I did some choars & just before Night I went up to Samuel Johnson & stay'd & drank Tea & so till in the Evening. I borrow'd a thing of him to run Pomatum in. Came from there down to Asa Robinsons where Br. John & Wife met me, & there was a number of others there. We spent the evening agreeably in Singing & reading my Swearing Sermon & talking & had a very fine Supper & when we come Home it was late.

ASA ROBINSON (b. 1732) lived in Andover, but the births of his children appear in the records of the West Parish of Boxford, strongly suggesting that, like Stephen

Peabody, he belonged to different civil and spiritual communities. Peabody's reason for attending church in Boxford was his disdain for the liberal theology of William Symmes of Andover's North Parish. Robinson may have acted for similar reasons, although he may have had different justifications, including existing family ties to the Boxford congregation. Brother JOHN Peabody's WIFE was Mary (Perley) of Boxford, whom he married on June 28, 1764. *Vital Records of Andover*, 1:319, 320, 2:288; *Vital Records of Boxford*, 81; *Peabody Genealogy*, 37.

Saturday the 9th of January.

To Day it clouds up & grows wormer. I went up to Andover & called to see Osgood but he was not at Home. I see my Chum & then went up to Br. Peters where I din'd. Sister is not well. She mentioned having a Town Library & I think it would be a very good Scheme & determine to use my influence to bring it to pass if I can get some of the Gentlemen in Town to contribute towards it, & any one to keep it. I came to Lovejoys & drank Tea & stay'd till Night. The Town is full of Talk concerning Frye. I came from there Home & in the Evening it rains. I read a sermon of Mr. Davises.

Residents of the North Parish established the Andover Social LIBRARY, a lending collection for members, no later than 1770. LOVEJOY may have been Nathaniel Lovejoy (1744–1812), A.B. 1766, although one would have expected Peabody to call him Sir Lovejoy because he held a bachelor's but not a master's degree. See below, February 7. Bailey, *Historical Sketches of Andover*, 531; *Sibley's Harvard Graduates*, 16:386–87.

Sunday the 10th.

It clears of & grows cold, the ground is glased & is very slipery. I went to Boxford Meeting & heard Mr. Sherman of Woburn Preach two excellent Sermons from the 3d Chapt. of Romans & A.M. from the 28th Verse.[1] P.M. he preach'd from the same Chapter & 31st Verse.[2] The afternoon Sermon I think was very excellent. I din'd with him and Decn. Chadwick, & he gave me an Invitation to call & see him as I go along. Benjn. Chadwick is poorly but as well as usual. I came Home & at Night & read two of Mr. Davises Sermons.

It grows colder.

There was a good many Andover People at Boxford to Day whom I was glad to see.

The religious fracture in Andover's North Parish was the reason why THERE WAS A GOOD MANY ANDOVER PEOPLE AT BOXFORD. Both in the morning and in the afternoon, the sermon text suited orthodox doctrines on justification by faith. Josiah SHERMAN (1729–89), Princeton A.B. 1754, was the minister of the Congregational church in Woburn. He was taking part in a common custom in New England among clergymen, an exchange of pulpits for a Sunday. *Princetonians*, 1:116–18.

1. Therefore we conclude that a man is justified by faith without the deeds of the law.
2. Do we then make void the law through faith? God forbid: yea, we establish the law.

Monday the 11th of January.

To Day is pretty cold. I wrote a Letter to Mr. Sparhawk concerning the Stewards Serving a Writ upon him, & one to David Tenny, & some in Journal & then I went over to Hoveys & went to see all those of the Families & got some Tallow of Johns Wife to make Pomatum. Then I came Home & in the Evening read a little in Spectator & then took my Camel & took a Ride to Bradford. I saw Master Webster to Night at his Uncles. Nihil majus &c.

Samuel WEBSTER (1743–77), A.B. 1762, was supplying pulpits in the area. He was eventually called to the Congregational church in Temple, New Hampshire. *Sibley's Harvard Graduates*, 13:360; 15:332–34.

Tuesday the 12th.

To Day is cool. I made me some black Ball, & did some Choars & Elizabeth Barker sent up here for my Sisters & I to come down there. They went & I was going up to Town & went that Way. There was considerable Company there. I stop'd & drank Tea & then I went to Andover. John Parker went with me part of the Way. I went to Capn. Osgood & my Chum met me there. Stay'd a while & talk'd with the Capt. about the Library & he likes it & says he [wi]ll think more upon it.

Osgood & my Chum & I went over to Miller Parkers to a Singing Meeting & met Br. John there, & after he had done instructing of them we had a pretty good sing. We came from there Home & it was late. I sup'd with Br.

BLACK BALL was a blacking compound used by shoemakers. JOHN PARKER lived in Andover's North Parish. *The Oxford English Dictionary* (Oxford: Oxford University Press, 1933), 1:891; *Andover Tax Assessments*, Tax for 1768.

Wednesday the 13th of January.

To Day is Pleasant. I was at Home all Day. Made me a fine store of Pomatum & read a little in Clarissa & Spectator. Phebe Osgood & Abiah came here & spent the Evening.

Sisters PHEBE (b. 1746) and ABIAH (1747–1825) OSGOOD were the daughters of Timothy and Phebe Osgood of Andover. Phebe apparently never married, but Abiah's late marriage to Parker Varnum of Dracut when she was fifty-four or fifty-five reflects the social ties that connected these towns. *Vital Records of Andover*, 1:282, 287, 2:254; *Vital Records of Dracut*, 297.

Thursday the 14th.

To Day is Pleasant. I went up to Br. Olivers & spent the Day there & at Kimballs & they ware reconing concerning their Vessel. I saw Doct. Osgood & talk'd a little with him about the Library but he does not incline to join. I came Home & in the Evening, Benja. Gage, Nathaniel, Daniel Jequish, Stephen Carlton with their Wives came to Br. Johns, & Wyman, Samuel Osgood, my Chum & Elizabeth Barker came here, & they stay'd till very late. We spent the Time in talking & Singing & supp'd in both Rooms. I read my Swearing Sermon & then they all went of but Elizabeth Barker who stay'd all Night, which is very strange. I had a shocking peace of work digging up a Cabbage. Osgood, my Chum & I agreed to go to Byfield next Week.

DR. Joseph OSGOOD (1718–97), A.B. 1737, was a physician in Andover. DANIEL JAQUIS (b. 1728) lived in Bradford. *Sibley's Harvard Graduates*, 10:219–20; *Vital Records of Bradford*, 90.

Friday the 15th of January.

To Day is wormer but at Night grows cold. I was at Home till just Night. Read some in Clarissa. Stephen Runnels & Lise Rolins came here. Rolins came to get some Eye-Bright for Mr. Mullikin who had hurt one of his Eyes & my Father went with him to get some, & then Ebenezer Kimball came here & made considerable stop. After he was gone I yok'd the Oxen & had them to Br. John to bring up some Wood with, & then took my Camel & went down to Mr. Williams's & call'd at Ebenezer Websters as I went along, & made a small stop. I drank tea at Mr. Williams's & ibi erat meam Puillam.[1] We stay'd till after Eight & then went to Mr. Websters & there was Company. We all went into Ebenezers Room & sup'd & they stay'd till Late. They were Mr. Hall & Thos. Webster & their Wives &c.

This entry indicates that Peabody had a MEAM PUILLAM, possibly a girlfriend. If this was the case, the diary provides no way to identify her. EYE BRIGHT, genus Euphrasia, is a plant sometimes used medicinally as an eyewash. Mr. WEBSTER was probably Samuel Webster, A.B. 1762, whose temporary positions included pulpit supply in Boxford before his call to Temple, New Hampshire. Mr. HALL may have been Willard Hall (1703–79), A.B. 1722, minister of Westford. His wife was Abigail (Cotton) Hall. THOMAS WEBSTER may have been Thomas Webster (1726–1804) of Bradford. His wife was Sarah (Kimball) Webster (1731–96). Frederic G. Cassidy and Joan Houston Hall, eds., *Dictionary of American Regional English* (Cambridge, Mass.: Harvard University Press, 1985–2012), 2:327; *Sibley's Harvard Graduates*, 15:332, 7:78–82; "Descendants of John Webster," 67–68.

1. My girlfriend was there.

Saturday the 16th.

To Day is cloudy & cool. I read a little in Clarissa & then Richard Gage & Nathaniel, meet John Robinson here & swop'd stears though they ware some Time about it.

I went over into the Woods & cary'd some Diner for Br. John & Stephen Runals & Wm. who ware cutting Staves there. After I came back I help'd John up with a Load of Wood, & in the Evening I read a Sermon of Mr. Davises. Nihil majus.

RICHARD GAGE (1727–70) lived in Bradford. *Vital Records of Bradford*, 54, 209, 314.

Sunday the 17th of January.

To Day is clear & cold Wind West. Br. John & I went over to Haverhill to Meeting. Heard Mr. Webster A.M. preach from the 6th of John 27th P.M. he preach'd from the 12th of Ecclesiates 5th. We din'd at Decn. Ayers's. My class-mate Dow was there keeping School & Bords & Haynes's. I went there with him after Meeting & drank Tea & stay'd till after Sun Down & heard Haynes extal Sandimans Works.

I came from there & call'd Br. John at Decn. Ayres's & we came over the River to Ebenezer Kimballs where Mr. Smith preach'd. Br. John had a very bad fall from his Horse.

We went in & heard Mr. Smith from the 10th of Jeremiah 23d & he spoke out to somebody who laugh'd in Sermon Time.

When Servise was over we came Home. I like Mr. Webster Well & Mr. Smith no ways extraordinary.

MR. WEBSTER was presumably Samuel Webster, A.B. 1762, but possibly his father, Samuel (1718–96), A.B. 1737, minister in Salisbury. John AYERS was a deacon of the First Parish in Haverhill. *Sibley's Harvard Graduates,* 10:250–59; Worthley, "Inventory," 275.

Monday the 18th.

To Day is cool. I read a little & then Mr. Ingals, Mr. Nutt & Br. Oliver came here. Mr. Nutt read my Swearing Sermon & lik'd it & then he read some of his proceedings since he has been gone at England in order to get the eastern Country settled, & that he had got the Governor of Hallifax turn'd out & shews a willingness to assist my Brs. in gitting them New Lots at St. Johns.

Richard Kimbal came here & we all went into Br. John's Room & drank Tea & they stay'd & spent the Evening, but we ware engaged to go to John Robinsons this Evening, so I took Br. John's Wife & Horse in the Slay & went down there & it looks like foul Weather. There was a Number of People & we spent the Evening very agreeably, & had a very genteel Supper. Br. John came there after his Company was gone, & we stay'd there till after Midnight & Sang & Chatted & I read my Swearing Sermon & then came Home.

Jonathan Belcher served as lieutenant GOVERNOR (the governor was nonresident) and chief justice of Nova Scotia from 1760. In 1763, under fire for his harsh dealings with subjugated Acadians, he resigned the lieutenant governorship. Col. Montagu Wilmot succeeded him. John Mack Faragher, *A Great and Noble Scheme: The Tragic Story of the Expulsion of the French Acadians from Their American Homeland* (New York: Norton, 2005), 418–22.

Tuesday the 19th of January.

To Day is Pleasant but cool. I got ready pritty early & set of to go to Byfield & my Father went with me to the lower End of Boxford. We call'd at Decn. Chadwicks & met Osgood & my Chum there. We went to new Rowley & stop'd at Mr. Adams's & din'd & they went along to Tennys. Master Adams gave me a perticular account of his Brs. Death & I had an agreable visit. We viewed the Eclipse while I was there.

I came from there to Tennys & there was my Company & my quondam, & Tenny had just received a Letter from me. We made but a short stop, & they agree'd to come up to Andover some Time next Week. My quondam went with us to Byfield. We went to see Wheeler & we stop'd there till I went to Capt. Pearsons & got some Cloth of my Fathers. I came back & we drank with Wheeler & then came down to Mr. Parsons's & stop'd a While & from there came to Mr. Noyes's & he was gone & so ware Judith & a House full there but nobody but Oliver who us'd to be there. John was gone to Port. Osgood & I had our Horses put up & then we went down Mr. Moodys all of us. (We met Judith as we went along.) We found Master in good health & stay'd there & sup'd & spent the Evening. Mr. Moody examin'd pritty closely about them Peaces which ware put in the News-paper some time ago, but we did not resolve him. We stay'd till late & then we came to Mr. Noyeses & my Chum stay'd at Mr. Moody & my quondam went to Jos. Hales. We set up pretty late & then took our repose.

NEW ROWLEY was Rowley's West Parish, now the town of Georgetown. MR. ADAMS—Abraham Adams of Rowley—was the father of Joseph Adams, class of 1769. MASTER ADAMS was Phineas Adams (1743–1801), A.B. 1762, older brother of Peabody's late classmate Joseph. Nathaniel Ames (1741–1822), A.B. 1761, predicted a solar ECLIPSE for Boston on January 19 beginning at 12:58:40 P.M. and ending at 3:31:24 P.M. Samuel WHEELER (1745–1817), A.B. 1771, of Byfield, was a graduate of Dummer Academy. In college he planned to enter the ministry, but unsuccessful in pursuing this calling, he passed most of his life as a small-time trader. CAPT. PEARSON was either Capt. Benjamin Pearson or Capt. John Pearson, both of Newbury. MR. NOYES was probably Joseph Noyes of Newbury, father of John Noyes, A.B. 1771. *Sibley's Harvard Graduates*, 17:115, 567, 15:150–51; *An Astronomical Diary; or, Almanack, for the Year of Our Lord Christ 1768* (Boston, 1767), 4; *Vital Records of Newbury*, 1:380, 2:683.

Wednesday the 20th of January.

To Day is Wormer. After breakfast I got two of the Scholars to git my Mare shod at Jewetts which they did & Osgood & I went down to see Jos. Hale who is confin'd with a very bad sore on his Leg. We stay'd there till almost noon & just came in to the School as we came back & are to wait upon Mr. Moody after Diner. We came to Mr. Noyes's & he was just came home from courting. My Class-Mate Parsons came there & we had a fine Diner & then we got our Horses & came from there to the School, & Mr. Moody & I went into the Chamber & had some private Discourse & then all the School came up & we had a sing. I shew'd Mr. Moody a Letter that Austin sent me which he lik'd, & kept it to take a Coppy of it.

We took a view of the School Library & then took leave of Mr. Moody & set of down to Port. My quondam did not go with us but went Home.

We call'd to see Lem Noyes & John but could find neither of them. We call'd upon Moses Frazer & then at Capt. Tracys where we drank Tea & was very handsomely treated. We went to Doctr. Sawyers to see Sr. Curtis & Kittridge & sent for Sr. Holt, & we spent the biger Part of the Evening there. We came away & Kittridge went up t[o] Byfeld with Osgood & my Chum & I par[ted] with them & went over the Bridge to Rowley to my Quondams where I lodg'd. Got there a little after nine.

Vacations were a time for refreshing acquaintances, and for Stephen Peabody none was more important than his connection with Samuel MOODY, the master of Dummer Academy. Genuinely liked by his students and former students, Moody was also a man of influence. In the decade before the Revolution, no one prepared more students for Harvard than Moody, who possessed a well-earned reputation as one of New England's most capable educators. Jeremiah JEWETT (d. 1785) of Rowley may have reshod Peabody's horse. MOSES FRAZER was a merchant of Newburyport. CAPT. TRACY was either Capt. Patrick Tracy or Capt. Nicholas Tracy, Newburyport merchants and importers. DR. MICAJAH SAWYER (1737–1815), A.B. 1756, practiced medicine in Newburyport, where Moses HOLT, A.B. 1767, was teaching school. *Essex County Probate Index*, 1:485; Pruitt, *Massachusetts Tax Valuation List*, 116–17; Currier, *History of Newburyport*, 2:216–18; *Sibley's Harvard Graduates*, 14:85–86, 16:485.

Thursday the 21 of January.

To Day is very Pleasant. After breakfast we went over to see Mr. Jewett & heard him converse a little abot Merril. We came back & din'd & took our Horses & came to Mr. Lesslies & found him not well but some better than he has been. He was very glad to see us & diverted himself a good deal with my swearing Sermon & a peice in the News paper about Jemmy Otis.

We came over to Jewett's School & then went to see Hannah & Ruth Fosters where we spent part of the Evening & drank Tea, & chatted with

Thos. Foster, & then we all came over to Mr. Lesslies where we lodg'd. Set up almost all Night & lay'd awake almost the other part.

MR. JEWETT was probably Ezekiel Jewett of Boxford, father of Peabody's classmate David Jewett. George LESSLIE (1727–1800), A.B. 1748, was the minister of the Linebrook Branch Parish in Ipswich. James (JEMMY) OTIS (1725–83), A.B. 1743, was a lawyer and patriot activist in Boston. The PIECE IN THE NEWSPAPER has not been identified, but during the winter of 1767–68, Otis was leading Boston's opposition to the Townshend Duties. HANNAH (1726–1802) and RUTH (1734–1806) FOSTER were unmarried sisters of THOMAS FOSTER (1724–89). The sisters lived in Topsfield until the deaths of their parents, then moved to Ipswich, where they stayed with Thomas. *Sibley's Harvard Graduates*, 17:168, 12:284–89, 11:247–87; John J. Waters, Jr., *The Otis Family in Provincial and Revolutionary Massachusetts* (Chapel Hill: University of North Carolina Press, 1968), 170–73; Pierce, *Foster Genealogy*, 140, 163, 165.

Friday the 22.

To Day is very pleasant. My quondam & I stay'd at Mr. Lesslies till almost noon, & then we took our Horses & took leave of Mr. Lesslie & came over to Jewetts School. I call'd a Minute at Fosters again & then went in to school [&] heard Jewetts Scholars read & spell, & then he dismiss'd them & went to his lodging & my quondam went with him. I parted with them & came up to Abraham Hows where I din'd & had a little Sing with Nathaniel & then came up to Boxford, call'd at John Hales dore a Minute, came to Sister Woods & found them all well. I stay'd till Night & drank Tea & then I came from there.

I went to Bradford, call'd to see Jos. Kimball & Daniel but they ware neither of them at Home. I proceeded & put up my Horse & went to Jacob Kimballs where was a little Company of old People & I stay'd till some late &c.

JEWETT was Peabody's classmate David Jewett (1744–83) of Boxford, a fellow graduate of Dummer Academy. Some of the more needy undergraduates took advantage of the longer school vacations to make money by teaching for a few weeks. DANIEL KIMBALL (1736–1802) of Bradford was the son of Stephen's aunt Abiel (Peabody) Kimball and her husband, Joseph, and a brother of JOSEPH KIMBALL (1727–1800). *Sibley's Harvard Graduates*, 17:168; Morrison and Sharples, *Kimball Family*, 84, 149–50.

Saturday the 23d of January.

To Day is very Pleasant. I stay'd & went to Breakfast & spent the bigger Part of the A.M. Saw Peter Parker. Came from there up to Ebenezer Sherwines where I din'd, & so to John Chadwicks & got half a Pound of Tea, & stay'd there & drank Tea, & then John came with me to the Decns. where was Mr. Sparhawk & the Comittee talking about his giving his Answer which is to be done on Monday but they cant find out which way it will be. Mr. Sparhawk says he is obliged to me for writing to him but he knows of nothing due to the Steward from him.

I came Home & it is exceeding bad riding.

Our People tell me Mr. Williams has sent for Mr. Davises Sermons.

I heard to Day some of Mr. Symmes's People were trying to find find [*sic*] out somthing which my Father has said against Mr. Symmes.

JOHN CHADWICK (1720–97) of Boxford was married to Stephen's second cousin Susanna (Peabody) Chadwick (1721–94). EBENEZER SHERWIN (b. 1728) lived in Boxford. WILLIAMS was Rev. Samuel Williams, A.B. 1761. *Peabody Genealogy*, 22; *Descendants of John and Joan Chadwick*, C13; Cora (Sharon) Leukhart, comp., *Sherwin/Sharon Genealogy from John Sherwin of Ipswich, 1644–1726, to Charles Willard Sharon of Winchester and Norfolk, 1884–1966* (Arlington, Va.: C. S. Leukhart, 1993), 28; *Sibley's Harvard Graduates*, 13:360.

Sunday the 24th of January.

To Day is lowery. I went to Boxfor[d] Meeting & heard Mr. Sparhawk A.M. from the 2 of Ephesians & 3d Verse. P.M. he preach from the 2d of Peter but the Chapt. & Verse is out of my Mind. I din'd at John Chadwicks. As I came Home I call'd in at Uncle Robinsons with Br. Oliver & went to super.

Came Home & the riding is very bad. Read some in Mr. Boston on the Covenents.

LOWERY, as pertains to weather, means dark or threatening. Thomas BOSTON (1677–1732), a Scottish Presbyterian clergyman, wrote *A View of the Covenant of Grace from the Sacred Records* (many editions).

Monday the 25th.

To Day it is cloudy & the later Part of it snows. I read in Clarissa & get out the 7th Vollume & wrote a good Deal in Journal. In the Evening Jos.

Stevens came here, & John Barker was here & told us that Mr. Sparhawk had given his Answer to Day in the Negative. It rains this Night.

JOHN BARKER was probably Lt. John Barker (1721–92), yeoman of Andover, but possibly John Barker (d. 1799), yeoman of Methuen. Barker, *Barker Genealogy*, 269, 272, 275, 279.

Tuesday the 26th.

To Day the fore part of it is a storm of frozen Rain & in the Later Part of it snow'd very fast. I took my Camel & went up to Samuel Johnsons & there is a sharp Crust on the Snow. I got him to alter my Boots & made up a reconing with him. Din'd there & stay'd till past Night, & then went up to Lieut. Parsons where there was to have been a Singing Meeting but nobody came so I spent part of the Evening & read my Swearing Sermon & then I came Home, & worse riding I should not desire to be out in. I read a little in the 8th Vollume of Clarissa Harlowe. It clears of.

Wednesday the 27th of January.

To Day is clear the fore part of it. I read in Clarissa & wrote some in Journal & went into the woods with Br. John to help him break a Path. P.M. I took my Mare & went down to Mr. Days & Mehitabel is sick. I stay'd there & drank Tea & till Evening & then I went farther. Determin'd to have come back part of the Way directly but I lit of Master Webster & some others which detain'd me. I saw Pol. Chandler to Night &c.

Thursday the 28th.

To Day clouds up & at Night Snows. We had several of the Neighbours came down here & help'd us up with our lame Ox, & some of them talk of coming to see Br. John to Night but none came but Asa Robinson & Wife & they spent a good long Evening. I supp'd with them with Br. John. Read some in Clarissa & it snows very Fast. When they went away, there was one Hariman had come from Haverhill.

Asa Robinson's WIFE was Margaret (Hovey) Robinson, whom he married on May 4, 1756. *Vital Records of Boxford*, 194.

Friday the 29th of January.

To Day is cold & blustering. I finish['d] Clarissa & read a little in Spectator & some of that over again to Br. John & help'd our People make some things to raise the Ox with, & in the Evening I too[k] my Camel & went & made a Visit at Stephen Barkers. He was gone from Home in the forepart of the Evening but when he came Home I could hardly get away he was so good stuff. I was treated exceeding Handsomly & came Home between 11 & 12. It is bad riding.

Saturday the 30th.

To Day is cold. Our People fitted their Things & we got up the Ox twise & kept him up some Time. I spent the Day fitting up some of my Things for Cambridge, wrote a little in Journal, & in the Evening read a little in D. Doddridge.

D. DODDRIDGE was a slip of the pen. Peabody is referring to Philip Doddridge.

Sunday the 31 of January.

To Day is wormer Wind SW. Is cloudy & in the latter Part of the Day snows & melts as it falls. Uncle Robinson came up here to tell us Mr. Sparhawk is to preach at Boxford to Day so we set out & went to Meeting & heard him A.M. from the 8th of Romans 30th Verse. P.M. he preach'd from the 4th of Galatians 5th Verse. Excellant well he preach'd. I din'd with Sr. Porter at his Grandfathers. The traveling is very Bad. In the Evening went in to Br. Johns Room & read in Mr. Boston on the Covenants.

Edward SPARHAWK returned for his text to Romans 8:30, the same text on predestination that he had used on July 26, August 2, and August 9. His focus on predestination, especially immediately after he declined the West Boxford church's call, suggests that divisions over the doctrine were what undermined his candidacy. As the liberal and orthodox wings of Massachusetts Congregationalism struggled between the 1740s and the early nineteenth century, the doctrine of predestination was a central point of controversy. See Wright, *Beginnings of Unitarianism*, passim.

February 1768

Monday the 1 of February 1768.

To Day is worm & cloudy. I read a little, wrote some, & our people ware killing Hogs & I assisted them a little, & P.M. I took my Camel & went down to Bradford to Uncle Kimballs & stay'd & drank Tea. Pay'd Francis some Money I ow'd him, then I came up to Mr. Williams's but he was gone to Boston. I came from there & accipiebam meam Puillam & illa veniebat cum meo, ad Patrem eius in Loge ubi sistiebamus omne Nocte.[1] Was very handsomly treated. The old people ware gone in primo parte Vesperis[2] &c.

1. Got my girlfriend and she went there with me to her father's place where we stayed all night.
2. In the first part of the evening.

Tuesday the 2d.

To Day is worm & pleasant. I stay'd ubi eram donec pere.[1] 11 o Clock breakfasted. Rode a Colt there that was not broke & then came from there up to Br. Olivers. He was not at Home so I went to Tylers where I din'd & then went up to town to Joshua Freys to see John but he was gone to Salem. His parents are very much troubled by their sons Misfortune but his Mother seems to be willing to think as light of his Faults as possible. I came from there to the Colos. where was Br. Oliver & we stay'd some Time & the Colo. read my swearing Sermon. Lik'd it much. We came from there down to Esqr. Phillips's & my Chum take a Horse & came with me to Lieut. Parsons where there was a singing Meeting. After the

Instructions ware over we had over a Number of Tunes which went pretty Well.

It grows Cold. We came home & met Benjn. Poor & Ebenezer & talk'd with them about the Library & they like it.

Br. tells me that Asa Parker, John Robinson & their Wives ware to see him last Night. I am sorry I want[2] at Home. I heard last Night they wanted to send a Horse to Esqr. Mallakin at Boston & if I could get him to ride it would be a good Chance.

The FRYES were one of Andover's leading families, and two of its members were militia colonels. One can make the case for Peabody to have visited either of them. Col. (later Maj. Gen.) Joseph Frye (1712–94) was an uncle of John Frye, the student who had just been dismissed. In 1768, he was in the process of settling Pigwocket, later Fryeburg, Maine, and was traveling back and forth between Massachusetts and Maine. Col. James Frye (1711–76), farmer and tavern keeper, was less prominent but more present in Andover. Peabody probably encountered the POOR brothers, BENJAMIN (b. 1728, m. 1752) and EBENEZER (b. 1732, m. 1757), both of Andover. The Poor brothers married sisters Phebe and Susanna Varnum of Dracut. Sarah Marbel Parker was the wife of ASA PARKER. Ellen Frye Barker, *Frye Genealogy* (New York, 1920), 50–56, 61–62; *Vital Records of Andover,* 1:306–7, 2:275–76, 259.

1. Where I was as long as about.
2. I.e., I wasn't.

Wednesday the 3d of February.

To Day is cool. I took the Slay & went to Boxford to bring up Molly. Stop'd at Decn. Chadwicks as I went along. When I got to Sister Woods she told me she had pay'd in all her Money last Monday & she believed it was gone from me by Reason of Johns not coming down at the Time which was last Monday. I was much concern'd about it & went down to Uncle Farleys to cary Aunt a Hat & to do some Arrands & he told me the Money was all let, & that he kept it as long as he possibly could expecting Br. Down. Such a horrid Disappointment I never had a[t] all by confounded Carelessness in his forgittng the Day. I came up to Sister Woods & she came up in the Slay with us to her Br. Nathans. She says she will do her utmost to get me a little Money before I go down. We came from there & call'd a few Minutes at Uncle Fosters & then came home & Br. Oliver & Wife, Bagley, & Hipsabah Kimball. Benjn. Chadwick & Doctr. Barker was here. Bagly & Hepsabah went of soon. The rest stay'd

& spent the Evening. I told Br. John of the Disappointments (I believe with some Anger,) he try'd to throw the blame on Sister Wood, or at least of from himself, but could not & it seems to discompose him not a little, as I am sure it does not me.

Col. Jonathan FOSTER had married Peabody's aunt Hannah Peabody. HEPZIBAH KIMBALL (1746–1824) lived in Boxford. *Peabody Genealogy,* 20, 36–37; Pierce, *Foster Genealogy,* 148; Morrison and Sharples, *Kimball Family,* 174.

Thursday the 4th of February.

To Day is very pleasant. I was at Home all day. Had the Teem to Br. John in the Wood once & coming down the Hill one of his stears escap'd very narrow of being kill'd. We came up & ware all going down to Jeremiah Eames's but Luke Hoveys Garls & Jos. Stevens & Benjn. & their Wives & Jos. Harrad came here & we could by no Means go. They drank Tea in our Room, supp'd in Br's. spent a pretty long Evening in dancing & play childrenlike. I wrote a Letter to Jeremiah Eames telling him the Cause of our not coming.

LUKE HOVEY (1708–87), farmer of Boxford, had four daughters in 1768: Hannah (b. 1736), Elizabeth (b. 1739), Abigail (b. 1742), and Olive (b. 1743). Of the Hovey daughters, at least one, Hannah, was married and probably living away from home at the time of the entry. *Hovey Book,* 104–7.

Friday the 5th.

To Day it Snows. I help'd our Folks load some Ashes & get up the Ox & then I wrote in Journal A.M.

P.M. I took some Leather & went up to Samuel Johnsons to get him to make me some Shoes. Carry'd a side of Sole leather to him. I came from there to Thos. Osgoods where I drank Tea & stay'd till the Evening & there was some Garls there who ware going to Haverhill West parrish & ware afraid of meeting with some Difficulty so I went down to the Cove with them & help'd them on to the River & then I proceed'd call'd at Thos. Websters to see James who is lame though not so bad as I expected.

I call'd at Jerh. Kimbals & he tells me he will pay me what the Gold I had of him fell short. I went to Mr. Williams's & got Mr. Davises Book which I lent him & he likes it much. I came there. Call'd at Lieut. Mallikens & he tells me they want to send a Horse to Boston for his Father,

& if he does not come up before they will send a Horse to me on Tuesday Night to convey to him after I have return to Cambridge which is a good Chance to me. I made but one Stop more till I got Home &c.

JAMES was probably Peabody's nephew James Stevens. See above, June 11, 1767.

Saturday the 6th of February.

To Day snows moderately all Day. I wrote & read a little & did some Choers for our People. Obadiah Parsons came here from Andover A.M. & stay'd here & din'd & then went Home & my Father went away with him to Boxford so that I had the Things to do at Night. In the Evening I read a Sermon in Mr. Davis.

Sunday the 7th.

To Day is very Pleasant. My Father went to Stephen Barkers to see if Mr. Sparhawk was come up but he was not so we went to Andover Meeting & heard Mr. Scales preach two Sermons (I think they call them) from the 119 Psalm 59th and 60th Verses. I have heard the Substance of them before. I asked him after Meeting to come & see me but his Horse is sick & he cant come. I saw Colo. Osgood & he ask'd me to come & dine with him Crass. I din'd with Sr. Lovejoy. Came Home at Night & read all the Evening in Mr. Davis.

Peabody heard Stephen SCALES preach on the same two texts on September 20, 1767. Nathaniel LOVEJOY, A.B. 1766, of Andover kept the local school between 1768 and 1773. He then became a trader. Lovejoy served in the militia as a captain on April 19, 1775, and in 1807 he became a brigadier general in the state militia. *Sibley's Harvard Graduates,* 16:386–87.

Monday the 8th of February.

To Day is some Stormy. Jesse Kimball came to Work here for my Father. I help'd up with the Ox & then took my Camel & went up to Andover to Colo. Osgoods where I din'd & read a Discourse upon Usery & part of Mr. Davis's Curse of Courage & borrow'd the Book of him & it is an Animating Peice as I ever saw. After Diner I went with the Colo. & tasted of some Syder which he is going to bring to Cambridge & it is pretty good & I am to try to get a Market for it. He treated me very well & was full of his Encomiums upon Learning & wanted to have his Children taught & gave me an Invitation to come & live with him & teach his Children in the Vacations & he would give me just what I ask'd & such short of talk in plenty.

I came from there & call'd at Capt. Osgoods & took Samuel & we went up to see my Chum & Frye was there. We stay'd a while & then went over to Mr. Symmes & he was gone from Home but Mr. Scales was there & we stay'd a considerable Time & then came back again & Mr. Scales came over there, & Br. John & Mr. James Bridges came & we had a very pretty Sing. Mr. Scales & Br. John went of about Eight & we stay'd & had a very genteal Supper indeed. We stay'd a while after Supper & then Osgood & I came from there & it rains. I parted with him & rode six or seven miles. Found People just going to bed. &c.

Either inadvertently or ironically, Peabody's mention of CURSE OF COURAGE refers to Samuel Davies, *The Curse of Cowardice: A Sermon Preached to the Militia of Hanover County in Virginia, May 8, 1758* (many editions). Peabody used the correct title on February 15.

Tuesday the 9th of February.

To Day is pleasant. I went down to Sister Woods to see if she had got me any Money but she had not. I din'd there & look'd over some of her Notes & then came homewards. Call'd at Lieut. Fosters but he was not at Home. Came to Gideon Tylers & drank Tea with Sr. Porter & Hipsabah Kimball. Stay'd till Evening & John Hale & his Br. from Brookfield came in & stay'd a while & then I came Home & Mr. Fogg & his son ware at Fathers & lodg'd. There was a Singing Meeting at Br. Johns & we all went in & had a Sing, & Mr. Fogg was much pleas'd with it, as also he was at hearing the Fiddle & at reading my Swearing Sermon. I heard they ware not going to send for Esqr. Mallikin by me.

Daniel Jaquish told me.

There were two Lieutenant FOSTERS in Boxford in 1768. Peabody probably visited Lt. Jonathan Foster (d. 1813), the husband of his aunt Hannah (Peabody) Foster. The other possibility was Lt. Jeremiah Foster (1732–85). *Peabody Genealogy,* 20; Boxford Single Tax List, 1767; *Vital Records of Boxford,* 36, 236, 237.

Wednesday the 10th.

Is a Pleasant Day. I got ten Dolers of Br. John which Henry Bodwill sent him last Night & fitted my Things & took my Camel, & after Breakfast took leave of Friends & we set of for Cambridge. I called at Samuel Johnsons & took [a] pare of Shoes he had made for me, and at several other Places in Town. I saw Joshua Holt & he wanted I should befriend him about selling some Sydar again this year at College which I told him I would. We stop'd at Jacoes & Osgood overtook us & after having refresh'd ourselves we proceeded to Wyman's at Woburn where we din'd. From there we came to Cambridge time enough to attend Prayers. Found all Things safe. Osgood & I put up our Horses at Frosts. There are plenty many scholars come.

HENRY BODWELL lived in Methuen. In 1775, he married Mary Robinson of Andover. JOSHUA HOLT (1730–1810) was a farmer and a deacon of the South Church in Andover, 1766–1810. Pruitt, *Massachusetts Tax Valuation List,* 110–11; *Vital Records of Methuen,* 150; Schutz, *Massachusetts General Court,* 253–54.

Thursday the 11th of February.

To Day is very pleasant. I got leave to go to Boston & the President sent for me to go to the Treasurers for him to receive his quarter Salary, so a little before noon Osgood & I went & took our Horses at Frosts & went to Charlston & left them at Trumbles & went over the Ferry. I carry'd some Things to Mrs. Robins from Mrs. Day & then went to the Court House & deliver'd some Letters to Colo. Garrish, & one to Esqr. Phillips from his Son & he had wrote to him (by his unbounded Kindness & complisance to me) the Disappointment I had met with about Money, & the Esqr. says he will come up to Cambridge & there seems to be a fair Prospect of his leting me have some. I saw Capt. Osgood & he was soon going out of Town & he is to take my Camel, & I sent some Letters by him to Andover.

I got some books at Meins for Parsons & the Chronicles at the printing Office. Din'd at the Tavern with Osgood & he went from there before me to do some Business, & I saw no more of him till I got to Cambridge. I lit of a Man there who had got a very pretty look'd Watch he had been getting mended & I swop'd with him & give him quarter Dolers to boot. Went to the Watchmaker & got him to alter the Chanes.

I went to the Treasurer & got the Presidents Money & gave a Receipt, & then came over the Ferry to Mr. Trumbles where I drank Tea & there was Colo. Frye, Capt. Parker & Doctr. Peabody going to Boston. I parted with them & was coming up on foot & Samuel Hastings overtook me & invited me to ride up in a Slay with him & his Daughter which I gladly excepted. I Cary'd the Money to the President & I think there was 20 Joannes which I brought for him. I had some Talk with Esqr. Saward in Boston about Pikes being married.

After I came to my Chamber at Night I made a Bill & my Chum made me a Present of a black Silk Handkerchief. My Heart glow'd with a kind of pleasing Gratitude to him for his unparralel'd Bounty & Generosity to me, which lays me under the strictest Obligations to him in every Respect wherein it is in my Power to serve him.

He pretended it for the servise I had done him in the Rules of Singing, which is no great. This seems to have been a prosperous Day.

President Holyoke's request to Peabody to pick up his quarterly salary payment from Thomas Hubbard (1702–73), A.B. 1721, a Boston merchant and provincial commissary general as well as Harvard's TREASURER, is a clear indication of the faculty's trust in him. Peabody's great pleasure at the gift of a handkerchief from his CHUM, Samuel Phillips, underscores the emotional bond between these roommates. CAPT. OSGOOD was probably Capt. Isaac Osgood of Andover, father of Samuel Osgood, A.B. 1771. HASTINGS'S DAUGHTER was Sarah Hastings (1749–91), whose father was Cambridge glazier Samuel Hastings (1724–85). *Sibley's Harvard Graduates,* 6:490–95, 17:570; Paige, *History of Cambridge,* 575–76.

Friday the 12th of February.

To Day is pleasant. I attended Prayers as Usual, made a Bill, went into the Library, took out Fordices Art of Preaching. P.M. I went down to Town to enquire the Price of Syder but could not find out. Talk'd with old Mr. Manning about Singing, went to Mr. Dana's to see what he had done with Holtons Note & he says he has just sent to him but has had no Return. I saw at Bradishes the Man I swop'd watches with Yesterday & he likes mine pretty well, & I his. I heard Goddard read part of Mr. Hutchensons reply to Mr. Tucker which I think is pretty smart. At night it Rains. I came to my Chamber had some College Company & wrote some.

Peabody borrowed David FORDYCE, *Theodorus: A Dialogue Concerning the ART OF PREACHING* (many editions). OLD MANNING was probably Edward Manning (c. 1698–1774) of Cambridge, a chairmaker. Nathan GODDARD (1747–95), A.B. 1770, of Shrewsbury, became a lawyer. He was reading Aaron HUTCHINSON, *A Reply to the Remarks of the Rev. Mr. John Tucker* (Boston, 1768). Paige, *History of Cambridge,* 602; *Sibley's Harvard Graduates,* 17:386–88.

Saturday 13th of February.

To Day is a lowery wet day. I attended Prayers as usual. Went up with Tenny to Mr. Bowmans. Read a little in Spectator A.M. P.M. I cut Jewetts Hair & then he & I studied Xnophon togather. In the Evening I went to Bowerss Chamber to private Meeting. Read one of Mr. Davis's Sermons.

I wrote a little this Evening.

Nihil Majus.

Sunday the 14th.

To Day is pleasant. I attended Prayers & Meeting & heard Mr. Appleton A.M. expound from the 2 of Revelations from the 12 Verse to the end of the [ ].[1] P.M. Mr. Scales pretended to preach from the 3d of Romans 19 & 20 Verses. I borrow'd the first Volume of Mr. Davis of Austin, read the Preface & Mr. Finleys Sermon on his Death. In the Evening I went to Thachers Chamber & we talkd a Number of us of meeting every Sunday Night to talk upon abstruse Points in Religion.

Doctr. Cobb was in here this Evening.

Since Nathaniel Appleton would preach from verses 18 through 23 the following week, presumably he preached here from verses 12 through 17. Peabody's Sunday reading included Samuel FINLEY, "The Disinterested and Devout Christian: A Sermon, Preached at Nassau-Hall, Princeton, May 28, 1761, Occasioned by the Death of the Rev. Samuel Davies, A.M., Late President of the College of New Jersey," printed in the frontmatter to Samuel DAVIES, *Sermons on the Most Useful and Important Subjects* (New York, 1766). DR. SAMUEL COBB (1717–81), A.B. 1737, was a prominent physician in Tolland, Connecticut. *Sibley's Harvard Graduates,* 10:126–27.

1. Blank in manuscript.

Monday the 15th.

To Day is very pleasant. I attended Prayers & reciting to Mr. Willard all Day. Studie'd with old Jewett at Tennys Chamber. Read one of the Chronicles which was printed in the Vacation. In the Evening Jewett & Osgood & P. Wadsworth ware at my Chamber. I lent Wadsworth the Curse of Cowardise to read.

Tuesday the 16th of February.

To Day is Worm & very Pleasant. I attended Prayers & reciting all Day & Wigglesw[o]rth's Lecture. Studied with Jewett. Read one of the Chronicles. Was troubled with Dady Bowers Cyropedia which I let Scammel have & so we dec[ei]ved him & he saw it no more.

Wednesday the 17th.

To Day is exceeding Pleasant. I attended no reciting. We had none at Eliven. Studie'd A.M. with Jewett in Xnophon. P.M. read some in Spectator & in Chronicle. I attended Winthrop's Lecture & went to see my Classmate Winthrop.

Thursday the 18th.

To Day very Pleasant. I attended Prayers & reciting in Mane & then got leave to go out of Town but did not go. I read some in Chronicle & wrote a Letter to Joshua Holt & one to Colo. Osgood about their Syder & just as I had done the Colo. came, & tells me he has got some of his Sydar to Newells and I am to send Scholars up to Newells to taste. He stop'd & drank some Kelly & then went over to Roxbury. P.M. I attempted to compose a Peace of English & then I drank a glass of Wine with Wentworth. He came last Night & brought me a Letter from Pike. In the Evening we went up to Tennys Chamber & had a Sing.

Friday the 19th.

To day is very worm. I attended Prayers, studie'd some in Cyphering, went in to Mr. Winthrop did through Practice. Read some in Chronicle. Made a Bill.

It rains a little to Night & continues Worm. Nihil majus.

Saturday the 20th of February.

To Day is worm & Foggy. I attended Prayers & reciting in Volebious, finished all my Chronicles read a little in my Library Book, wrote some in Journal. Colo. Osgood call'd here in Mane & I sent my Letter to Holt by him.

Esqr. Phillips came here A.M. & talk'd of going Home but the riding was bad so he concluded not to but went up to Watertown & so came back her[e] just before Night & return'd to Boston. He was so very Kind as to let me have £90 old Tenr of Money which is anough to answer my present Neccesaty. In the Evening I attended private Meeting & we read in Mr. Davis's first Vollume of Sermons. It remains worm.

The value that New Englanders placed on personal connections when making credit transactions is apparent in the loan Samuel PHILLIPS, Esq., the father of Stephen's roommate, made to Peabody. The Andover network of acquaintances made the deal possible.

Sunday the 21st.

To Day is very pleasant. I attended Prayers & went to Meeting & heard Mr. Appleton expound from the 2d of Revelations from the 18th to the 23d Verse. I wrote after him. P.M. he preach'd from the 2 of Philipians 4 Verse. I wrote for Johnson. I read a Sermon of Mr. Gibbins's on the Death of Mr. Daves & some of both their Poetry. In the Evening I had Company at my Chamber. We Talk'd upon Gods foreknowledge & the Freedom of the Will & upon Mans Fall. Those of us who meet are Tenny, Thacher, Austin, Jewett, Osgood, French, & myself.

Peabody and his company spent the evening puzzling over one of the thorniest questions for Calvinists. If God was all-knowing, and thus knew the future, which was predestined, then how could men and women be held responsible for their own sins? The crux of the issue was whether or not a sinner possessed freedom of the will, and thus in some measure was willfully sinful. Orthodox Calvinists went to great lengths to demonstrate that predestination and freedom of the will might coexist, a conclusion that the day's religious liberals had difficulty accepting. Given the topic, it is no surprise that most of those involved in the discussion became ministers. If one assumes that JEWETT was David Jewett, A.B. 1769, and not his classmate Jacob Jewett, Peabody's former roommate, whom Stephen now typically called his "quondam," five of the seven participants became clergymen. Only Jonathan Williams AUSTIN, who became a lawyer, and Samuel OSGOOD, a government official, followed a different calling. Four of the seven were former students at Dummer Academy. This same group also met on February 28 and March 13 and 27. Moses JOHNSON (1751–73), A.B. 1771, died in Falmouth, Maine, while reading law in preparation for a career as an attorney. Peabody was reading Thomas GIBBONS, *Divine Conduct Vindicated; or, The Operation of God Shown to Be the Operation of Wisdom* (London, 1761). Wright, *Beginnings of Unitarianism,* 91–114; *Sibley's Harvard Graduates,* 17:546.

Monday the 22d.

To Day is Worm & rains some. A.M I attended reciting twise, wrote three Letters Home. In the Evening read my Chronicle. I went to pay the Steward and three of the Joannes which I had of Esqr. Phillips fell short so I did not pay him all. We ha[d a] little Fun with Bowers in a reciting. In the Evening I was at Parsonss Chamber a little While. I attended Newall's Lecture to Day.

Tuesday the 23d of February.

To Day is very Pleasant. I attended Prayers & reciting, wrote a Letter to Pike. At noon we took a Walk a Number of us & we hier'd P. Wadsworth to wade through a Pond Hole which made us a great Deal of Sport so we came to his Chamber & dra[nk] a Bottle of Wine with him & what added to the Fun Bowers was one that hired him.

I drank Coffee with my Chum & Benjn. Call was here from Charlston. After Prayers we had a high Gail round the College gitting one & others Hats. Bowers's was got which mad'd him & he talk'd of hoisting some of them, which made them treat him ill & hiss him. In the Evening Sayer was here & spent the biger part of it.

Peabody may be referring to BENJAMIN CALL (c. 1748–85), son of Caleb and Rebecca (Stimpson) Call, of Charlestown. Benjamin was a baker. Thomas Bellows Wyman, *The Genealogies and Estates of Charlestown, Massachusetts, 1629–1818* (Boston, 1879), 172.

Wednesday the 24th.

To Day is clear & cool Wind West. The Weather is much alter'd. Such a spell of Worm Weather I never knew at this Time of Year as we have had now, so long & so worm. I attended Prayers & reciting in Mane & then got leave to go out of Town, but did not go. I wrote upon a Peace I have

Thoughts of puting in the News Paper, & wrote two more Letters Home & read some. I attended Wigglesworth's private Lecture & Winthrop's publick.

Thursday the 25th.

Is some cool. I attended Prayers & forensick Dispute & no other reciting. Attended Wigglesworths catikistical Lecture. My Chum went to Charleston & cary'd some Things & my Letters [t]o send Home by his Father. P.M. I went down in Town & got my Shoes mended & so to see my quondam who came down Yesterday. Stop'd & drank a Glass of Wine with Buckley who is newly come down.

After Prayers Parsons came to my Chamber & then my Chum & I went to Chadwick's Chamber & had a set down there eating sasigies & spent the Evening.

A CATECHETICAL LECTURE inculcated reformed Protestant doctrine, as opposed to Edward Wigglesworth's usual presentations, which focused on the science of theology. John BULKLEY (1749–74), A.B. 1769, was briefly a lawyer in Groton, his hometown, before his early death. *Sibley's Harvard Graduates,* 17:131–32.

Friday the 26th of February.

To Day is a pleasant Day. I attended Prayers as usual & Mr. Winthrop, & we work'd through part of the Single Rule of three & the double Rule. I made Tea & had Coffin, Tracy, Scammel & Wadsworth to drink with me. Read a little in Fordice on preaching. Just after Prayers, I was call'd out of my Chamber, & Richard Kimball was come down here upon some Business with Mr. Sewall, & just at the same Time Mr. Dana sent up for me to come down to see him. I sent Kimballs Horse to Frosts & we went down to Sewalls togather. Kimball cant have his Business done to Night so he left his Papers & is to call for them in the Morning. Dana tells me he has sued Holton & has got the Money which I may have next Week. Kimbal says he saw Holton in Boston to Day & he told him of his being sued & seem'd to think hard of me for doing it, but I can't help it if he does.

Kimbal spent the Evening with me & sup'd & lodg'd. He brings News of a general Time of Health, & that his Br. Francis is married & had a large Wedding, which it is probable I should have been at had been at Home.

The SINGLE RULE OF THREE offered a means for determining an unknown fourth term when three other terms of either a direct or an inverse proportion of two ratios were known. The DOUBLE RULE of three showed how to answer proportional questions in two steps, each of which required the calculation of a proportion. Peter COFFIN (1752–1821), A.B. 1769, of Gloucester, a graduate of Dummer Academy, became a merchant. Henry SEAWALL (1750–72), A.B. 1768, of Brookline, died before pursuing a profession. FRANCIS KIMBALL of Bradford married Bettee Head on February 18, 1768. *Arithmetick Vulgar and Decimal,* 91–94, 99–103; *Sibley's Harvard Graduates,* 17:135–36, 91; *Vital Records of Bradford,* 237.

Saturday the 27th.

To Day is Pleasant. I attended Prayers & Kimball did his Business & breakfasted with us at our Chamber & I wrote a Letter Home by him & sen[t] some dirty Things. He is down in persute of an old Deed which if he can find he thinks will be of vast servise to him.

He w[ent] from here about nine o Clock, & I wrote & read [a] little A.M. P.M. I took a Walk with Parsons & went to see my Class-Mate Bradish & drank a Glass of Wine & spent a considerable part of the P.M. with him, Williams, Chad[wick] & Sr. Cobb. Came up to College & drank Tea with Thacher & Austin. Austin's Father was here with another Gentleman from Boston. I got some more Trade to take of Doctr. Cobb. In the Evening I attended private Meeting at Bowers's Chamber. Read in Mr. Daves'. We had some Talk of the Difficulties we labour under by having Wigglesworth set over us here & talk of trying to get him turn'd out by a Petition to the Overseers, which when I came to my Chamber I began to write one, to see whether I could do it if we concluded to try. My Chum lodg'd with Pain who is not well.

BRADISH was Ebenezer Bradish, A.B. 1769. WILLIAMS was either John Williams (1751–1816), A.B. 1769, of Deerfield, or Nehemiah Williams (1749–96), A.B. 1769, of Hadley. John read law but became a trader in his hometown. Nehemiah became the third minister of the church in Brimfield. AUSTIN'S FATHER was Samuel Austin of Chelmsford, father of Jonathan Williams Austin, A.B. 1769. PAIN was probably Samuel Paine (1754–1807), A.B. 1771, but could be his older brother William (1750–1833), A.B. 1768. William became a physician, Samuel became a minor public official, and as Loyalists both fled to England after the outbreak of the Revolution. William returned to Massachusetts in 1787 and took up practice in Salem. Samuel returned to Worcester in 1793 but eventually moved back to England. *Sibley's Harvard Graduates,* 17:126–28, 310–17, 116, 67–75, 580–83.

Sunday the 28th of February.

To Day is some stormy & worm. I did not wake up to Prayers in Mane which I have not done but once before since I came to College.

I went to Meeting & heard Mr. Appleton expound from the Remainder of the 2d Chapter of Revelations & P.M. he preach'd from the 1 of Proverbs 22. I wrote all Day. I read two of Mr. Daves's Sermons. After Prayers our Company met at Tennys Chamber & talk'd upon Faith & upon the whole have Thoughts of going to Mr. Wigglesworth to inquire of him concerning those Things.

I put my Watch out of order to Night winding it up.

Monday the 29th.

To Day is worm & rainy the chief of the Day. I attended Prayers & reciting twise though I had no Book to study in. There is no Gravesends to be borrow'd in College nor to be bought in Boston. I read some in Fordice & wrote in Journal. Rogers was here the Chief of the P.M. In the Evening I read my Chronicle.

We went to Foggs Chamber a Number of us after Diner & drank a glass of Wine & had a genuine sing.

March 1768

Tuesday the 1 of March 1768.

To Day is Pleasant. I attended Exercises as Usual. Parsons wanted me to write a Letter for him to send to a Br. he has, who is in a discourag'd frame, & he determines to have it inonimous so he gave me a general Plan which he would have persu'd & I wrote one & sent it to him in a rough Draught & he likes it well, so I am to coppy it at my Leisure. After Commons we took the other Bottle of Wine & sing with Fogg.

Wednesday the 2d.

To Day is very Pleasant. I attended College Duties, wrote a Letter to Sister Wood & did a little other Writing. Receiv'd a nonsensical Letter from Webster. Colo. Osgood was here from Andover. Brings nothing new. In the Evening Parsons Junior & I went down to Mr. Appletons & spent the Evening there very agreeably. The old gentleman has heard of the noise which is made by the Scholars at Wigglesworths Lectures, & we talk'd with him largely upon it & told him the universal Dislike which the Scholars had to Mr. Wigglesworth, & how he dwelt upon one Text, & that he said very li[ttle] to the purpose upon it & the old Gentleman seem'd to think a good Deal of it, & appear'd to b[e] very sorry. He talk a good Deal upon the points of Religion & was glad to see us. Lent me one of his Sermons to read, & invited us to come & see him again. I cam[e] to my Chamber & Hill was come, & had brought me a Letter from Pike. He writes is well.

Peabody placed substantial stock in the affirmations of men such as Nathaniel APPLETON whenever he complained about the college and its faculty. Stephen's ready assumption that everyone else agreed with his carping left him susceptible in March and April when many nonstudents sided with the college against the undergraduates over new policies regarding class preparation. The college identified undergraduates who shared the same surname according to their class and position within the class. In March 1768, PARSONS JUNIOR was Theophilus Parsons, A.B. 1769. Parsons Senior was Obadiah Parsons, A.B. 1768. David Parsons, A.B. 1771, was Parsons Tertius. Samuel HILL (1750–69), A.B. 1768, of Boston died at nineteen shortly after graduation and before settling on a career. *Sibley's Harvard Graduates*, 17:190–207, 78–82, 590–93, 44.

Thursday the 3d of March.

To Day it Clouds up & rains. In the Evening my Chum went to Boston & I sent my Letter to be cary'd to Sister Wood & my Watch to Peck. I got leave to go out of Town but did not. Read some in Fordice. Wrote a little. After Commons went over to see Jewett who is not very Well; came back & read a little & then drank Tea with my Class-Mate Parsons. After Prayers went up to Thaxters Chamber & saw Sr. Bond & borrow'd Seneca's Morrals of Thaxter. Came to my Chamber, & my Chum was come from Boston & says Peck thinks the main spring of my Watch is broke so he left it. I sent them Joannes to Boston but they all fell short so my Chum brought two back, & I went over to the Steward & paid him & they all fell short 19/ which my Chum made it up to me.

Osgood & Chadwick came here & we had a pretty set down eating sasigis.

Moses PECK was a watchmaker in Boston. Lucius Annaeus SENECA wrote *Morals* (many editions). *Inhabitants and Estates of the Town of Boston, 1630–1800* (CD-ROM; Boston: Massachusetts Historical Society and New England Historic Genealogical Society, 2001), no. 48947.

Friday the 4.

To Day is clear & Cold Wind N.W. I attended Prayers in Mane & then I went [&] carry'd a Bill to Mr. Winthrop & made me some Bills A.M. P.M. I went into the Library. Took out Fordice [a]gain the Al Koran & Homes essay one Vollume of it upon Criticism, then had a Number here to drink Tea with me, & Bowers among the rest, whom we had some sport [wi]th trying to get him Tardy to Prayers. They all went into Prayers but Parsons [. . .][1] & we stay'd out.

Just at Night Russel came here whom we had our Wood of last year, & stay'd a little while.

In the Evening Hill & I went up to Bowmans, & stay'd a little while & Bowman tells me he has heard from his son Joshua at Carolina & that he has been sick almost the whole Time he has been gone. I heard to Night a bad story about Judith Noyes & one of the Borders there (who is Frost) about their being a little too sociable.

I finish'd Fordices Art of preaching, drank a Glass of Wine with Thacher after Diner & sang some songs.

The decision by JOSHUA BOWMAN, A.B. 1766, to move to North Carolina was unusual. Before the Revolution hardly any Harvard graduates from New England moved anywhere else after completing their studies. Bowman may have been seeking a new start in life after having been accused of theft as an undergraduate. The charge was withdrawn, but the allegation so humiliated him that he challenged his accuser to a duel with pistols. The challenge was rejected. Henry HOME, Lord Kames (1696–1782), legal thinker, philosopher, and major force within the Scottish Enlightenment, was the author of *Elements of CRITICISM* (many editions). *Sibley's Harvard Graduates*, 16:328.

1. Torn [one word].

Saturday the 5th of March.

To Day is cold. I attended Prayers as usual, fix'd my Peice for the News Paper. Began to Coppy Parsons's Letter. Wrote some in Journal. Read a little in Spectator. In the Evening attended private Meeting in Bowmans Chamber, & read in Mr. Davis. I drank tea with Austin.

Sunday the 6th.

To Day is Cold. I attended Prayers & went to Meeting & heard Mr. Appleton Expound from the 3d of Revelations & the 6 first Verses. P.M. he preach'd from the 1 of Proverbs 22d Verse. I read two of Mr. Daves's Sermons & h[eard] my Chum read some of Mr. Hopkins's Peice against Doctr. Mahew which is very smart. I drank tea with Tenny, & in the Evening he was at my Chamber with Thacher. We disappointed of having our Meeting to Night by Reason of Osgood having Company for we ware to have met there.

Jonathan MAYHEW (1720–66), A.B. 1744, the minister of Boston's West Church at the time of his death, was one of his generation's leading Arminians. Peabody despised Arminian teachings, which suggested that a sinner could prepare him- or herself for salvation. Samuel HOPKINS (1721–1803), a Yale graduate, was the minister in Great Barrington in 1768. A student of Jonathan Edwards, he played an important role in the development of the New Divinity, a neo-Calvinist systematic theology. He wrote *An Inquiry Concerning the Promises of the Gospel* (Boston, 1765). *Sibley's Harvard Graduates*, 11:440–69; Wright, *Beginnings of Unitarianism*, 116, 288.

Monday the 7th of March.

To Day is cool. I attended Prayers & reciting & Mr. Sewalls Lecture, & finish'd Parsons's Letter. Drank Tea with Parsons. In the Evening I went up to Bowers's Chamber & we drank the Wine which had been ventured about Fryes being punished, & eat Bisquit & Chese, & when Bowers sent for his Bottle, it was stole from the Freshman, which made us a great Deal of inward Diversion, & offended Bowers highly for he thought we ware some of us knowing to the affair, & so we ware, but after a long debate we persuaded him to send for another Bottle, which came from him like his Hearts Blood & then we told him in a friendly Manner what the scholars thought of him, that he had the Name of a nigardly Fellow, & we suppos'd the Wine was taken from him on that account. I understand the Wine is to be return'd again. So I came to my Chamber.

Tuesday the 8th.

To Day is Pleasant. I attended Prayers & reciting in Mane then read some in my Chronicle, but there was very little study done for there was a Man came into the yard with a load of wood sold it to Knowles & when it came to be thrown down the Middle of it was hollow & Knowles would not stand to his Bargain. The fellow was very high & impudent about it, & went to the President & Tutors but could get no relief. He is a noted cheat. After Prayers the Scholars [su]rrounded him, & he was push'd from one side [to] the other in a remarkable Manner, & it rained brick Bats & Chips on him & his Team till they drove him out of the Yard. Afterwards he came, in order to load up his Wood but his Team could not be stop'd, his linchpins ware taken out, & he hiss'd out of the Yard. By this Time some began to pitty him, & Nathaniel Chandler bought his Wood at a low prise, & got him to his Chamber & pay'd him, & when he came out he attempted to defend himself with his Whip & struck several Scholars, & they had him down in an Instant & jam'd him faithfully & persued him with an amazing Noise & Clamour down as far as Colo. Brattles & then his Wheel came of. When he saw that, he acknowledg'd to the Scholars he had treated them ill in bringing such Wood, & ask'd their Pardon, & they help'd him on with his Wheel & some of them gave him some Money, & sent him of. Colo. Brattle inquir'd of the Cause of the Distourbance & being told say'd if he had known of it he would have drove him into Jail. The Scholars generally resented Chandlers buying the Wood, & being true Sons of Liberty, when it grew dark they assembled & took it & carry'd it all out on the Common & made a large Fire & had a very high Frolick round it but broke up seasonably. Chandler resents it some but cant help himself. There was a Number of us went over to Mr. Honeywills to a singing Meeting which the Town People had, & after they had done singing, we had a pretty good one & it was much admir'd, & we ware treated ver[y] Well. There was one Russel here to Day to get a Market for Syder & we gave him som[e] incouragement, to get one for him, he went to Boston to Night & is to be here tomorrow agai[n.] Varnum sent me a line yesterday which I answer'd, & to Day I receiv'd another from him. [He] is offended at something I wrote to Jewett I believe.

Peabody's assessment that his schoolmates showed that they were TRUE SONS OF LIBERTY when they lit a bonfire with Nathaniel Chandler's disputed wood reveals Harvard's political leanings as the imperial crisis festered in early 1768. If Stephen's diary is a fair measure of the school's political temperature, most students sympathized with resistance to the British administration led by the Sons of Liberty, a patriot group best known today for organizing the Boston Tea Party in 1773, but opposition to the crown was still in the backs of their minds. CHANDLER (1750–1801), A.B. 1768, of Worcester, became a lawyer. *Sibley's Harvard Graduates*, 17:9–11.

Wednesday the 9th of March.

To Day is exceeding Pleasant & quite worm. I attended Prayers but not reciting. After the Morning, I had the Head Ach[e]. We went in to a private Lecture to Wigglesworth & he gave us a horred Lecture about our making a Noise at his former Lectures & went on to tell us if we did not like to attend we must get Notes from our Parents that they do not want us instructed in Theology, & he would present them to the Overseers. A

Stupid Vilian did he think that could be done? The Students resented it in a very high Manner & talk of Petitioning to him, or the Overseers to see if they could get us some Redress. After Commons I took a Walk with Parsons up to Mr. Bowmans, wrote a Letter to Varnum in Answer to his, & attended Mr. Winthrops Lecture.

Russel came here from Boston & he is to bring a Load of Syder soon. Colo. Osgood was here to Day from Andover but brings no News. In the Evening I went to see my Class-Mate Parsons & talk'd about Wigglesworth & he seems to think it will do to Petition. I heard to Day by Emerson that Mr. Noyes was married & had got his Wife Home, & Judith is mad.

Edward WIGGLESWORTH's chastisement of the junior class for disorderly conduct in theology lectures marked the renewal of tensions between the undergraduates and the faculty. Unlike the academic year's previous confrontations, in which Peabody regularly sided with the faculty, either overtly or silently, now for the first time he identified with the students. Joseph NOYES married Bethia Dodge of Rowley on February 29, 1768. *Vital Records of Rowley*, 357; Noyes, *Noyes Descendants*, 1:61.

Thursday the 10th of March.

To Day is worm & very Pleasant & at Night clouds up & rains. I attended Prayers & reciting in Mane & then Eliot went out of Town. I went & talk'd with Leonard about attempting to get rid of Wigglesworth & he thinks it will not answer [to] put in a Petition, but amagines an [a]nonimous Letter might do Servise to let him know the true State of the Case.

I receiv'd a Letter from Varnum & sent it back to him without opening which I hear offanded him. After Diner Bowers's Wine made its appearance on the Butery Hatch with a Paper stack'd onto it to show whose it was, which was discover'd first by Gove & Bowers so they took it in to the Buttery & sent for me & drank it rejoicing, but the Beuty of it was those who had got it went to Bowers's Chamber expecting it would come there that they might have a Share, & mist of it. We had a hearty laugh with them afterwards. I spent what little Time I had in writing. Heard Knowles was in search after Truth last Night. In the Evening I went to Wellingtons Chamber where they had a Vendue of Books, but I bought none.

I drank Tea with Tracy.

In the Evening I wrote something which might do to send to Wigglesworth.

The proposal to petition for the termination of Professor WIGGLESWORTH revealed both the degree of the students' animus and the extent of their delusions. It is difficult to imagine that either President Holyoke or the college's Corporation would even have considered such an action. Thomas LEONARD (1744–72), A.B. 1768, of Plymouth, became a physician. Jonathan GOVE (1746–1818), A.B. 1768, of Weston, also became a doctor. Palsgrave WELLINGTON (1748–1808), A.B. 1770, of Waltham, became a farmer. *Sibley's Harvard Graduates*, 17:58, 25–26, 446–47.

Friday the 11th.

To Day is Worm & Showery. I attended Prayers then studied Arethmatick all Day. I borrow'd some Books, studied in Fractions & Alogation.

Drank Tea with Thacher. In the Evening studied in Volebious, wrote a letter & read a little in Spectator. Walk'd & sang with Fogg at noon.

The rule of ALLEGATION concerned "the Mixture or Composition of several sorts of the same kind of Merchandize, with another; such as *Corn, Wine, Metals, Medicines*, &c. and teaches how to proportion the Quantity of each Ingredient, and determine the *Price* of the Mixture." *Arithmetick Vulgar and Decimal*, 128.

Saturday the 12th of March.

To Day is clear'd of very Pleasant. I attended Prayers as usual, & did some Choers, & my Chum went down in Town & said he recon'd he saw Benjn. Gage, so I went down & it was he. He had some Business with Mr. Sewall. He came up to my Chamber & drank a Glass of Wine & smok'd a Pipe & [I] went with him into the Library & show'd all the Curiosities & then he set out for Home. I wrote a Line to Br. John & sent him my Chronicles, & sent Home some dirty Things. I began to read in the Alcoren. Scammel got Fletchers Cyropedia to Day for me to keep it away from Bowers. In the Evening I attended private Meeting in Fletchers Chamber. Read in Daves. I did not like Sr. Smiths talk very well to Night. His Charity is remarkable extensive. I wrote a little.

CHARITY had a complicated place in theological discussions in eighteenth-century New England. Most New Englanders believed that the parable of the Good Samaritan directed them to be universally charitable both in sentiment and action, but they also recognized practical human limits both to their compassion and to their alms. The result was a widely accepted apologetic explanation for the practical impossibility of universal charity. If Isaac SMITH, A.B. 1767, was REMARKABLE EXTENSIVE in his discussion of charity, then Peabody must have found him insufficiently aware of the everyday constraints on benevolence and beneficence, a position identified with the New Divinity followers of Jonathan Edwards. On charity in colonial New England, see Conrad Edick Wright, *The Transformation of Charity in Postrevolutionary New England* (Boston: Northeastern University Press, 1992), 16–47.

Sunday the 13th.

To Day is cloudy & snows a little in Mane but clears of P.M. attended Prayers & went to Meeting & heard Mr. Appleton expound from the 3 of Revelations from the 7th to the 13th Verse. P.M. he preach'd from the 1 of Proverbs 22 Verse. I read a Sermon which Mr. Appleton lent me, & one of Mr. Daves's. In the Evening I went to Osgoods Chamber, & we had a Meeting there to talk upon Points.

The POINTS were the main doctrinal points of Nathaniel Appleton's sermon.

Monday the 14th.

To Day is clear & cold. I attended Prayers & reciting to Willard.

My Chum had News from Home, & had some things Brought. They came to him from Charleston.

I was not much troubled with Bowers. [S]ent to Scammel & got Cyropedia & returnd it. I Broke a Square of Glass to Day in Wetmores Chamber playing Ball. Sargent [t]old me he heard something that I say'd [a]bout his staying behind the Chappel, & he [s]eems to resent it. I cant tell who told [him al]tho' it is the truth. He did do it for fear of being talk'd to for some of his Behavior.

[A]fter Prayers I went with a Number of [o]thers & drank Tea with Peter Coffin. We had a little Short Dance amongst [o]urselves. We came up to College, & I got my Lesson at Scammels Chamber & then we had a Foderation at my Chamber on sasigis & Pye & had some of our Friends.

What was Stephen Peabody doing playing ball in William WETMORE's chamber? As tensions increased between the faculty and the undergraduates, Peabody seems to have succumbed to his more immature inclinations. PETER COFFIN, A.B. 1769, a classmate of Stephen's at Dummer Academy, was from Gloucester, where he returned for a career as a merchant after college. *Sibley's Harvard Graduates*, 17:135–36.

Tuesday the 15th of March.

To Day is clear & Cold & Russel came down with his Syder & drove it before the Meeting House so they went & tasted it, & my Chum & I took one Barrel of it & with that he dispos'd of Six & he could not sell the other two, so he left them with us to sell & went Home, but we hear ther[e] is a Man coming from Wouster with some which he will sell under, so I can hardly expect to sell it. He got it into our Cellar before he went away. Wigglesworth had a Lecture to Day, & such a Noise as there was amongst the Scholars I never heard. He desir'd those who did not desire to be instructed to withdraw, but none stir'd, but when he began again the Noise was much increas'd & so continued till Lecture was over & then they his'd him out of the Chappel. He & Danforth stop'd at the Door but said nothing. They sent for several Scholars but could get nothing out of them. What can be done I can't tell. When we went to carry our Bills he look'd Dull & seem'd to be in a great Study, & they say he is very much grieved of it. I came to my Chamber, read a little & studie'd Xnophon.

Wednesday the 16th of March.

To Day is clear & Cold. I attended Prayers & reciting in Mane, & then got leave to go out of Town. I wrote a Let[ter] to Mr. Holt in Answer to one I rec[eived] from him last Evening about Syder, & then Bulkley & I walk'd to Boston togather.

I left a Letter for Parsons to go to Cape Ann & left two Peices at the Printers, got my Watch & the main Spring was not broke, got Mr. Hemingways Sermons & several small Things, din'd at Gridleys, & left my Letter for Mr. Holt with him. He is going up next Friday.

I call'd to see my Class-Mate Jones & there was one [. . .][1] tiket there & we had a large Talk upon Election, & greater Errors I never hear'd advanced than they had. I stay'd some Time, & then I came off & Mr. Jones give me to read a Pamphlet on universal Redemption by one Smith.

I came over the Ferry & came the bigger Part of the Way to College & Colo. Phipps over took me in a Chaise & invited me to ride with him, which I gladly excepted.

Osgood, my Chum & I had a little Fodderation at our Chamber & finish'd our Stores. No News about Wigglesworth to Day.

Peabody's discussion about ELECTION, or God's choice of those who would be saved, and UNIVERSAL REDEMPTION, or the un-Calvinist belief that all sinners would be saved, reveals once again the central role of religion in his life. Moses HEMMENWAY wrote *Seven Sermons on the Obligation and Encouragement of the Unregenerate to Labour for Eternal Life* (Boston, 1767). JOHN SMITH (fl. 1675–1711) wrote *An Essay on Universal Redemption*, a reprint of which appeared in Boston in 1767. COL. DAVID PHIPPS (1724–1811), A.B. 1741, of Cambridge, was the sheriff of Middlesex County. *Sibley's Harvard Graduates*, 13:609–18; 11:53–56.

1. Illegible [one word].

Thursday the 17th.

To Day is clear & a little more moderate. I attended Prayers & reciting in Mane & then Willard went out of Town. Now we have done reciting at 11 o Clock only to Scales, which is a very pleasing Reflection. I was not very Well & so did but little. I wrote a little in Journal after having put some more Paper into it, & read my Chronicle. I went in & heard the Seniors despute forensickelly, & then went & drank Kelly with Chadwick. After dinner sang a little with Cook, drank Coffee with my Chum. [I]n the Evening had a sing at Foggs Chamber. Wm. Searl was here to Day & brings News that Colo. Moulton had lately two Barns burnt with a large Stock in them, suppos'd to be set on Fire purposely, & that there was a House lately burnt at Boxford belonging to one Androus, & also that Master Fisher is dismis'd from Rowley School & they have chose Searl. Nihil majos.

The dismissal of Nathaniel FISHER, A.B. 1763, teetered on the boundary between local news and pure gossip. Although Peabody did not offer an explanation for Rowley's action, Fisher's later career—as an Episcopal clergyman—may suggest why he was unacceptable to the Congregationalist and Whig leaders of the town. Noah COOKE (1749–1829), A.B. 1769, of Hadley, became a lawyer. WILLIAM SEARLE (b. 1730) lived in Rowley. Jonathan SEARLE (1744–1812), A.B. 1764, later the Congregationalist minister in Mason, New Hampshire, succeeded Fisher and must have been related to William Searle, although the precise connection is uncertain. Col. (later Gen.) Jonathan MOULTON of Hampton, New Hampshire, lost a "large new Barn" to a fire on March 13, 1768. He also lost nineteen head of cattle as well as some pigs. A previous fire in 1766 had likewise destroyed a barn of his. ANDROUS is unidentified but was probably a member of the Andrews family of Boxford. Amos Everett Jewett and Emily Mabel Adams Jewett, Rowley, Massachusetts, *"Mr Ezechi Rogers Plantation," 1639–1850* (Rowley, Mass.: Jewett Family of America, 1946), 132; *Sibley's Harvard Graduates*, 17:136–38, 15:387–92, 16:90–92; *Massachusetts Gazette and Boston News-Letter*, March 24, 1768.

Friday the 18th of March.

To Day is clear & cool. I attended Prayers & some of the Rogues shut Bowers's Door so he could not get out to Prayers, & he was punish'd in Mane. I studie'd in Arithmatick A.M. & P.M. Mr. Holt came down here to see about selling Syder but he could get no Market so he went Home. Just before prayers Bowers invited a Number of us to drink Tea with him & we had a genteal Dish which should be recorded to his Honor. In the Evening I was a little While at Hales Chamber & play'd upon a Fiddle there. This being the Day of the Year the Stamp Act was repeal'd Colman went about & collected Money & they bought a Quantity of Fagots & made a vast Number of Crackers & Serpants & set them on Fire on the Common in the Evening & spent the Time very merrily.

I came to my Chamber & in lighting my Candle hu[rt] one of my Eyes by a Spark so that it pain[ed] me some, but however I made my Them[e.] I heard Cabot is orderd into Prayers tomorrow morning, I suppose for not attending his Exercises better. He has been talking some Time of leaving College & going to sea.

Aside from preparing for a career in the ministry, Peabody's most important objective in college was to develop the social polish of a gentleman. Thus his comment that his classmate William BOWERS served a GENTEEL DISH of tea was a genuine statement of appreciation. The STAMP ACT, adopted by Parliament in 1765, attached tax stamps to legal documents, newspapers, almanacs, playing cards, and dice.

Saturday the 19th of March.

To Day it clouds up & looks like a Storm. I attended Prayers & coppy'd over my Theme & carry'd it up. Made me a Bill. A.M. Cabot did not come into Prayers & the President said his staying out was upon his perril, so after Breakfast he went to the Presidents & gave up his Chamber & is going immediately from College, so I suppose they can do nothing to him.

P.M. I went down in Town to my Quondam's Chamber where I began to make my analices. They had got Henry out of the Library. I bargain'd with Darling for two Dozens of Bottles for 40/. After Prayers Jewett Dow & I had a smart Talk, & Dow is exactely of Haynes's Opinion.

I attended private Meeting at Fletchers Chamber & we read Daves. Came to my own & wrote a little. It is a very cold out wind & looks likely for a heavy Storm.

The college library owned several works by Matthew HENRY, an English Presbyterian clergyman remembered for his Bible commentary, including his *Exposition on the Old and New Testament* (London, 1721). William DARLING (c. 1725–1809) was the only adult male of that surname active in Cambridge and its environs in the late 1760s. *Catalogus librorum bibliotecæ Collegij Harvardini quod est in Cantabrigiæ in Nova Anglia* (Boston, 1723), 105; *Vital Records of Cambridge*, 2:526.

Sunday the 20th.

To Day is a smart storm of snow. I attended Prayers & went to Meeting & heard Appleton expound from the 3 of Revelations from the 14th to the 17th Verse. P.M. Mr. Eliot preach'd from the 24 of Luke & the 46th Verse.

I wrote to Mason, drank Tea with Scammel & Wadsworth, & read one of Mr. Daves's Sermons & got out his Vollume. Read Fordises Elequence of the Pulpit.

Pike is come from York & came out with his Wife to Day for the first Time. His looks pleas'd me, & I had but just Opportunity to speak with him.

John Alford MASON (1750–1830), A.B. 1771, of Charlestown, became a government clerk. He sustained fatal injuries in 1830 when run over by a milk cart. James FORDYCE (1720–96), a Presbyterian minister from Scotland, wrote *The Eloquence of the Pulpit* (Aberdeen, 1752). *Sibley's Harvard Graduates*, 17:554–55.

Monday the 21 of March.

To Day is clear & Pleasant. Brister was here very early. He brought some Letters for my Chum, & is going to Roxbury with a flock of Colo. Osgoods Sheep.

I attended Prayers but we had no reciting. The President & Tutors met & have got some Proff against Dodge in at Wigglesworths Lectures, & have orderd him in to Prayers tomorrow Morning.

Pike came here with a Gentleman with him from York & stay'd till after noon & we had a good Drink of Kelly & a fine Sing. He tells me that his Father Bowman treats him very well & has said but little about his being married. Privately though he said it was disagreeable to him, but seeing it was so he wanted to say but little about it, but would do what he could for his Daughter.

He tells me he is going to cary his Wife down to his Fathers to stay several Months.

Brister came back but we had not got Letter wrote to send by him. P.M. I wrote some & drank Tea with Greene. In the Evening a Number of us went up to Bowmans & spent the Evening & had a fine drink & sing with Pike & Wife. I came Home & read a little in Chronicle.

Joshua DODGE (1752–1814), A.B. 1771, of Salem, became a merchant. He received a public admonishment for misbehaving at the lectures of Professor Wigglesworth. *Sibley's Harvard Graduates*, 17:504–5.

Tuesday the 22.

I attended Prayers & reciting in Mane. Dodge was publicly admonished & the president talk'd very severe to him & cast some Reflections on him & his Parents which the Scholars resented much. When we ware in at reciting in Mane Scales told us of a New Law which was made, & sent us to Danforth to hear what the Law was & I verely believe he was ashamed to mention it. When we came to hear it from Danforth it was this, that no Scholar should send in an Excuse for not reciting, but come to them before hand & get leive to stay out, which is so rediculous that it is really sickish, & is resented highly by the Class. The President & Tutors met & receiv'd Lee & Sweat who ware rusticated last Year into College again, Lee into our Class & Sweet in to the Freshman.

I finish'd reading my Chronicle & finish'd writing three Letters Home, & after Prayers we had a Class-meeting at Websters Chamber & agreed to take no Notice of what Danforth said to us, but send in Excuses as usual, & if any went & got leave beforehand to stay out of reciting, he should immediately be expel'd the Class. The whole Meeting was cary'd on with great Order. I studie'd in Fordice this P.M. In the Evening wrote some.

For Peabody and the other undergraduates, the tutors' decision to impose new regulations limiting the right to decline to recite was the final straw, resulting in a severe rupture in relations with the faculty. Stephen's declaration that the new rules were REALLY SICKISH reflected a view widespread among the students, whose threat to EXPEL from the class anyone who observed the policy promoted undergraduate solidarity. In his claim that Tutor Thomas DANFORTH . . . WAS ASHAMED TO MENTION the new rule, however, he was probably projecting his own conclusions onto the instructor, although Danforth later acted as an intermediary between the rest of the faculty and the undergraduates. Joshua DODGE's parents were George, a sea captain, and his wife, Lydia, of Salem. Joseph LEE (1748–85), A.B. 1769, of Marblehead, became a merchant. *Sibley's Harvard Graduates*, 17:504, 183–84.

Wednesday the 23d of March.

To Day is fair Weather. Lee & Sweet had their Recommondations & Confessions read publickly this Morning & ware receiv'd into College publickly. I attended Prayers, reciting & Desputing. Scales mention'd nothing to us about this affair, but we hear Willard did, & was hiss'd by the Sophomores. After Prayers I made up a little Difference I have had with Sargent. With Fletchers & old Jewetts help we have agree'd to bury old Storrys wholly, & I talk'd with Bower who had been a little out of Temper with me. I came to my Chamber & Peter Osgood was come down. He brought me some Shirts & Stockings & a Letter from my Sisters but no News which is remarkable. I wrote a Return to my Sisters. The Sophomore & Freshmen met to Night & ware unanimous not to come into these Measures which the Tutors have agree'd upon. True Sons of Liberty.

Thursday the 24th of March.

To Day is cold. I attended Prayers & reciting in Mane & then got leave to go out of Town but did not. Sr. Pike came here & give an Invitation to a Number of us to go up to Mr. Boman's P.M. & then I went down with him to see my Quondam where we stay'd till noon. I finished making my Annalisis there, & got Manning to mend my Shoe a little. P.M. I dres'd myself & there was a Number of us went up to Mr. Bowmans where was a Number of Ladies & some gentleman. We had a fine Dish of Tea & Liquor in plenty, & spent the afternoon & Evening in diverse Sorts of Exercises & very Agreeably. A little after nine we came from there waited upon the Ladies Home. I stop'd a[t] Stedmans a while & then came to my Chamber between ten & Eliven. I breakfasted with Osgood at his

Chamber this Morning, & then he went from here & I sent Letters by him ad Amicos.[1]

1. To [my] friends.

Friday the 25th.

To Day is clear. I attended Prayers as usual, & then I read Fordice on the Action of the [Pulpit?] & a fine Peice it is. Then I studie'd a little in Arithmatick in the Square Root. M[r.] Winthrop did not come up, so I went [to] the Library & return'd Fordice & took [out] the History of New York. Sr. Pike ca[me] down here & we went & drank Tea with Parsons & Wine with Hill, & spent the bigger Part of the Evening with Parsons whe[re] we had a Fiddle & a plenty of Liquore, & th[en] Pike came to my Chamber. He tells me h[e] is going of Tomorrow & I am to go up & see him.

I annalic'd to Night. Bright is come down & is taken into the Sophemore Class.

William SMITH (1728–93), the chief justice of New York and soon to become a Loyalist, wrote *The History of the Province of New-York* (London, 1757).

Saturday the 26th of March.

To Day is Pleasant. I attended Prayers but not reciting & Danforth punish'd me a Shilling for not giting leave, though I had Company all the Evening, & he serv'd some others so, which rais'd the Class very much. He sent the Punishments by Coolidge but he did not cary them. After Breakfast I went up to see Sr. Pike & spent the A.M. with him & his Wife & din'd there, & then took leave of them & they went of for Boston (they are going to York by Water) & I came to College & went & drank a Glass of Wine with Rogers. Bright had his Confession read this Morning. Welch was here from the School & drank Tea with my Chum. He brings nothing Strange. In the Evening I attended private Meeting at Fletchers Chamber. Read in Mr. Daves. Mr. Danforth had two Squares of Glass broke in his studie Window to Night.

The faculty records do not mention Peabody's fine. Thomas WELSH (1752–1831), A.B. 1772, of Charlestown, in the spring of 1768 still a student at Dummer Academy, became a physician. Faculty Records, 3:74–75; *Sibley's Harvard Graduates*, 18:183–88.

Sunday the 27th of March.

To Day is Pleasant. I attended Prayers as usual, & went to Meeting & heard Mr. Appleton expound A.M. from the 3d of Revelations from the 17th Verse to the End. P.M. he preach'd from the 8 of Romans 6th Verse. I read one of Mr. Hemmingways Sermons which I like middling well, & read part of a Piece I got of Mr. Jones on universal Redemption which I don't like. I drank Tea with Scammel & in the Evening we came over to old Jewetts Chamber & talk'd as usual.

Monday the 28th of March.

To Day is cloudy & P.M. it Snows. I attended Prayers & we ware all in to reciting in the Morning. At eliven we have done. P.M. we recited there was a Number sent in Excuses as usual & after we had done reciting Mr. Danforth took Occation to lay down the Reason of this Proceedings of late, & we made all the Objections we could, & finally he told us the Law must & would be enforced, & so took none of the Excuses which ware sent in, but punish'd all, & when we came out of the Door he was his'd & clap'd & there was some hazahing. I attend'd Mr. Sewalls Lecture, & went to Colmans Chamber a little while. I saw Judge Danforth go up to his Sons Chamber, & heard Mr. Danforth had sent for the old Chappel Key. It is supposed he intends to keep a Watch there [to] guard his Chamber, but he went from hi[s] Chamber in the Evening & his Windows were broke all to Pieces between seven & Eight o Clock. He came back but I can [. . .][1] but little of what he says. Mr. Willard goes on in the same Manner with the Freshmen & he has been his'd all Day by them. My Chum was not well & did not get leave to be sick, & was punish'd. We have had a great Deal of College Company to Day. I read a little in Mr. Jones's Book to Day.

Thomas COLMAN (1751–81), A.B. 1770, of Byfield, became a lawyer based in Groton but drowned at age thirty. Tutor Thomas DANFORTH was apparently the most conciliatory member of the faculty in the face of the student uprising. His attempt to justify the new regulation was in clear contrast with the attitude of other faculty members, who expected obedience without explanation. JUDGE DANFORTH was Thomas's father, Samuel (1696–1777), A.B. 1715, president of the provincial council and chief justice of the Middlesex County Court of Common Pleas. *Sibley's Harvard Graduates*, 17:380–81; 6:80–86.

1. Illegible [one word].

Tuesday the 29th of March.

To Day is cloudy & snows a little. I attended Prayers & when we came into reciting Danforth treated us just as usual but such Work with Windows I scarcely ever saw. There was about 20 Squares broke and his Sashes was tore all to Peices, & when reciting was over he punish'd those who sent in excuses & when we went out he was loudly his'd again. He sprang to the Door to make discoveries but could not. He got his Windows mended, but there was such Confusion in College there was very little Study done. P.M. Danforth sent for me. Talk'd a long Time on this affair & told me that let the Consequence be what it would, it would be enforc'd, & that notwithstanding the Scholars lay the Blame all to him, yet Mr. Scales was the first promoter of it. I told him the many Inconveniencies which would attend it & that the Scholars ware vastly set against & I believ'd never would come into it. [He] said they must, & talk'd very affectionately & try'd to flatter me, but no, I am not going [to] be flatterd into a Compliance

I recited & after we had done he did [n]ot ask for any, so we went out orderly. In the Evening Mr. Willards Windows ware broke & Mr. Scaless ware very much dash'd to Peices, & we heard the tutors are in the greatest Confusion. It is suppos'd Scales's ware broke on account of what Danforth said to me, & if what he said is True, Scales is an underhanded cowardly low live'd Rascal, as he was the first Cause of the Distourbence, & has try'd to Shurk his Head out of the Coller.

I have had so much Company as to study none. Read my Chronicle.

Wednesday the 30th of March.

To Day is clear & Pleasant. I attended Prayers & reciting. We talk of drawing up a Remonstrance & there was some of us went to Tudors Chamber, & there they did it, & I got Wentworth to coppy it, but after-wards Willard was hear'd to say it was to late for that, & some of our Class ware very much against signing a Remonstrance, & others thought what was wrote was too sevear so we let the matter drop. I went up & told Danforth that I had mentioned to the Scholars what he said to me about Complying, & they ware vastly set against it. Fletcher was told to cary some Punishments to the Butery this Morning (for there was some punish'd & Danforth his'd as usual) & they seaz'd upo[n] him & got his punishments from him which I told Danforth of, & when we ware going in[to] Wigglesworths private Lecture he call'd up Tudor & examin'd him who got them, but he could not tell, & then he examin'd about ou[r] having a Class-Meeting at Websters Chamber & he deny'd it. Say'd there was no Class me[et]ing, only a few of the Class happened to get to gather there. Then he inquir'd who was chief Speakers & Moderator & he say'd they had no Moderator & all spoke alike But I am very much affraid there will be some found out and punish'd. P.M. Danforth was his'd after reciting as they all ware but Eliot, going in to Commons, & he has punish'd none & so has escap'd. Willards Class recited in the old Chappel & while he was gone from his Chamber some Body got a false Key & unlock'd his Door & Broke his looking Glass worth about 15 Dollars, & all his Tea Things, & has done a great Deal of Mischief. Who it was it is not gus'd. Thacher & I went up & told Danforth of it & ask'd him what we could do to stop these Things, & to have matters settled, for we told him there could be no study done till there was an End put to them. He advis'd us to inform, realy, but no, we shant I believe. We ask'd him what a Remonstrance would do, & he did not incourage it very much, but insisted upon it the Law should be enforc'd.

Willards & Scaless Windows ware a little broke to Night. I had College Company the whole Day & Evening.

Thursday the 31 of March.

To Day is cloudy & looks like fowl Weather. [I] attended Prayers & reciting in Mane & Danforth talk'd again to us, & advis'd us to comply, & if we ware affraid to ask leave to stay out from reciting, to come up privately & it would never be known. We told him that if we asked we must either Lye, or be kill'd for going up by the Scholars. He made no direct Answer but dismiss'd us, & was compleatly his'd. As they ware all at breakfast the President & Tutors meet at Mr. Winthrops. Have sent for a Number & examin'd concerning our Class-Meeting but cant find out as we had any, only as there was had a small Number at Websters Chamber. They are desirous to know who ware chief speakers & say if they can be found out, they will be sevearly punish'd. Webster is threttned if he wont tell; but he has not yet, though I am very much affraid they will find out. I hear they think that I was one of the chief Acters. This Morning there was a Number punish'd & the Punishments ware sent by Willington. They catch'd him as soon as he came down. Some body came behind him &

put a Handkerchief over his Eyes & forced the Punishments from him. He was sent for & thretned with being rusticated if he did not tell who got them from him, when it was not possible he should, for he was fast Blinded. I am a little affraid of the Consequences as I acted in the Place of a Moderater at Websters Chamber. They did not meet P.M. so I wrote a little, & went to the Funeral of Judge Foxcroft. There was a great Number of People there. Last Evening Mr. Roe was here & asked me to go down to De[cn.] Whitmore's to Night to a Singing Meeting so I went down & spent the Evening & had something of a Sing with the Town People & had an Invitation to go up to Prentices next Thursday to a Singing Meeting with some other of the Scholars & went up to Plumers Chamber a little While & then came to College. Scales's Door was horridly beshit to Day when he was from his Chamber.

Francis FOXCROFT (1695–1768), A.B. 1715, of Cambridge, was a judge of the Middlesex County Court of Common Pleas. Samuel WHITTEMORE (1693–1784) was a currier and for more than forty years a deacon of the First Church in Cambridge. Samuel PLUMMER (1752–1815), A.B. 1771, of Gloucester, disappeared from Massachusetts shortly after graduation under suspicion of having murdered a slave girl whom he impregnated. *Sibley's Harvard Graduates*, 5:636–38, 17:605; Paige, *History of Cambridge*, 688.

April 1768

Friday the 1 of April 1768.

To Day is stormy some Snow & some Rain. I attended Prayers & they met again are inquiring about Willard & his Class's being fasten'd into the old Chappel, & they are like to find out Whiting Junr. & Bowdoin. There are several order'd to their Chambers & what will be the End of these Things I cant think. I had a great Deal of Company viz of Scholars. I wrote a little, & heard that my Name had been mention'd at the Presidents but for what I cant tell, but it is suppos'd they think I am one of the guilty. Mr. Danforths Door was amazingly dob'd this forenoon, by I know not who. After Commons I went into Osgoods Chamber & stay'd till two o Clock.

The Tutors ware his'd faithfully at Diner.

It clear'd of very cold at Night & an exceeding high Wind. I went up to Websters Chamber to study Volebious & just at 9 o Clock there was a cry that Massachusetts was on fire. We all run out, Professors Tutors scholars & all, & it was soon put out. It was catch'd by Bowers's Chimney taking fire.

If Thomas DANFORTH retained any residual sympathy for the students' position, his feelings must have been sorely tried when his door was AMAZINGLY DOB'D with manure. The college felt especially susceptible to FIRES because everyone could remember the one in 1764 that destroyed Harvard Hall, which housed the school's library. MASSACHUSETTS Hall (1720), now the oldest surviving Harvard building, was a dormitory. It housed approximately sixty students and two tutors. Thurston WHITING, class of 1770, of Wrentham, became the minister of the church in Newcastle, Maine, then a land agent and developer in northern New England. James BOWDOIN (1752–1811), A.B. 1771, of Boston, became a merchant, land speculator, and philanthropist. *Sibley's Harvard Graduates*, 17:452–57, 487–500.

Saturday the 2d of April.

To Day is very cold & Blustering. I attended Prayers as usual, wrote some, & had a good Deal of Company. Heard no News. In the Evening went to Bowers's Chamber & had a private Meeting there. Read in Mr. Daves. When I came to my Chamber I heard that little Whiting had reported all over College that he had been shut up in Mr. Willards Study the chief of this cold Day without Victuals Fire or Drink & the Scholars ware very much disturbed at it & talk'd of mobing Willard & four of them had been & broke his Windows & he had found out who they were. Putnam he catch'd & made him till of the rest who ware Hill Dodge & Stebbings. Tuder & Varnum came to my Chamber & desir'd I should go with them up to Willards Chamber & see something about it & I did, & the Tutors ware there. We told them the uprore & they sent for the Professors & Whiting was call'd & stood to it to Mr. Willards Head that he had been there, but they sent us out to appease the Minds of the Scholars & when we came back he told something of a different Story at first but soon resum'd his first again, & I went with him to his Chamber & he affirm'd he had been there & told so many Circumstances that he was universally believ'd. John Gill was call'd & offered to take his Oath he saw him there through the Window. I came to my Chamber & it was very late.

Scales & Willard told us that if the Scholars really believ'd Whiting was there they did not blame them for their Conduct.

At a time when relations between the faculty and the members of the student body were dysfunctional, rumors that tutor Joseph Willard had confined sophomore Thurston Whiting to compel him to reveal what he knew about the disturbances caused an explosion among the undergraduates. Nevertheless, Peabody continued to try to act as an intermediary. Ebenezer PUTNAM (1750–76), A.B. 1771, of Danvers, read medicine after college but died before completing his studies. *Sibley's Harvard Graduates*, 17:607.

Sunday the 3d of April.

To Day is fair Weather. I went to meeting & heard Mr. Appleton preach but the text I have forgot. The Scholars seem to be very much discompos'd. I drank a glass of Wine with Scammel at noon, & Tea with Sr. Smith after Prayers. It is Sacriment Day but not withstanding Mr. Wigglesworth sent for John Gill in the Morning & examin'd him from 8 oClock till ten about his seeing Whiting [in Mr.] Willards Study & before sun Down the Preside[nt,] Professors & Tutors met at Winthrops & order[ed] Hill, Dodge, Putnam & Stebbings into Pray[ers] tomorrow Morning & sent for little Whiting which put the Scholars into a terrable uprore & they would not let Whiting go. I was order'd to my Chamber, & the Scholars a great Number of them went down to Winthrops & chose a Committe to go and talk with the Tutors but they would not let them in but ordered them to their Chambers. There was an allarm that there was a guard coming up to take Whiting & the Scholars got them Clubbs & went out on the Common in order to meet them, & I went out with a Number of others & got them in & told them it was time anough when they come for us to stir, & went down in Town & found there was to be a Guard in town but that we ware not to be molested unless we ware disorderly in town. The Scholars are determin'd to meet under the Tree tomorrow Morning before Prayers & to go to the Presidents to get these Fellows Punishments put of till we can have a hearing or else all to give up our Chambers. There was some Writings drawn up at Scammels Chamber on what Terms we will come back if we leave College which Varnum did. There was some disputing with regard to our proceedings but matters ware gone so far we could not go back. I went to my Chamber but got but very little Rest. There was some writing on Willards Door to Day & one tremendous Sylogism, & a report that he did not partake of the Sacriment.

Monday the 4th of April.

To Day is cold. We met in the Morning as we agreed. The Tutors ware in agitation. Scales came & talk'd to us. We told him what we ware going to do. At the ringing of the Bell, we all went to the President & desir'd this punishment might be put of, but were answer'd very short that it should not be put of, so the President Professors & Tutors came up & went in to Prayers, but the Scholars all but a very Few stay'd out, & they proceeded & expell'd those four who ware ordered in. Immediatly after we follow'd them down to the Presidents & went in according to Seniority & gave up our Connections with College. (Though the Seniors did not because the law which was made did not affect them.) We ware in very great Confusion all Day moving out our Things, which my Chum & I did to Mr. Warlands. The Seniors ware very uneasy petitioned that we might have a hearing & had a promise that we should but they sent for two or three & examined them & told them they ware Lyers, so there was not more sent for though I went to Jones's Chamber & collected all the Evidence I could. The Corporation met & confirm'd what the Tutors had done with respect to the Law & those who ware expell'd. I talk'd with Mr. Adams to Day & Mr. Austin who came up & commanded his son to go & humble himself to the Tutors & was very high. I did a great many Choers & heard a great Deal of Talk & with a day of Confusion I never scarcely saw. The Seniors seeing our Situation met & agreed to go & ask for a Recommendation to new Haven tomorrow morning, which mark of their Generosity will forever live in my Memory, & Wests in particular. Mr. Bowman came down & talk'd with me about affairs. I lodg'd at Warlands but did not rest very well. Danforth came & took our Keys.

The decision of most of the undergraduates to resign their dormitory rooms and give up their connection with the college brought the controversy to a climax. The faculty must have found the petition of the seniors to transfer to Yale especially galling, since the new regulation did not directly affect them. The four expelled students were Jeremiah Hill, class of 1770; Joshua Dodge, A.B. 1771; Ebenezer Putnam, A.B. 1771; and Gad Stebbins, A.B. 1771. MR. AUSTIN was Samuel Austin of Boston, the father of Jonathan Williams AUSTIN. Faculty Records, 3:75; *Sibley's Harvard Graduates*, 17:116–22.

Tuesday the 5th of April.

To Day is some Cloudy & snow'd some towards the middle of the Day. We got up & got Things ready & went with Varnum & talk'd with Sr. Ward a While, & when I came to take leave of Sr. Smith, Honeywill, Tenny, Scammel, & some others, it affected me prodigiously. There was a Number of others set of togather & came up to Newalls where we went to Breakfast. I call'd & took leave at Mr. Bowmans. We came from there a little after ten & came up to Wymans & din'd & so proceeded as far as possible, parted with some of our Company at the uper end of Andover. We call'd at mr. Fryes & then part of us came to Esqr. Phillipses where we stop'd & told the whole story & he did not seem to blame us. I came from there with Osgood & lodg'd at the Capts. Told him the whole story. I was very much fategued with my Walk. Lodg'd with one Swallow from Dunstable.

Nathaniel WARD, A.B. 1765, was the college librarian. In this role he was a member of the faculty, but because he had no classroom responsibilities he could try to function as an intermediary between the teachers and the students. *Sibley's Harvard Graduates*, 16:250–51.

Wednesday the 6.

To Day is clear & cool. I got a Horse at the Capts. & came Home for my Feet was so sore I could not walk. Our People ware a little surpriz'd at seeing me but when they came to hear the story I cant tell what they thought, but I believe did not blame me for coming a way. I got my Father to take Capt. Osgoods Horse back, & just before noon John White came here from Esqr. Phillips's where he lodg'd last Night & wanted me to go Home with him. [T]he Esqr. sent a Boy to cary him so I took [a] Horse & went with him to Haverhill to [h]is Fathers where I din'd & told them the story & then went to Isaac Osgoods & told it to him & Mr. Parker & they are very high about it, & think the Court will take the matter in to their Hands. I came from there over the River. Call'd a few Minutes at Mr. Websters & then I came to Nathaniel Kimballs where I drank Tea & spent the fore Part of the Evening. I told the College Story where ever I went & it allarms People very much. I came Home & my Father is just come from Town & tells me the Seniors are come from College, which pleas'd me exceedingly. John Simmons is at Work here.

Public opinion about the controversy proved to be very important to Peabody. After first believing without evidence that most of his acquaintances sympathized with the undergraduates, he began to realize to his dismay that the majority of the people whose opinions he valued most believed that the students were in the wrong. ISAAC OSGOOD was probably Capt. Isaac Osgood (1713–82), of Andover, father of Samuel Osgood, A.B. 1771, but possibly Isaac's son Isaac (1749–74), also of Andover. Mr. Benjamin PARKER (1718–89), A.B. 1737, was the minister of the East Parish of Haverhill. NATHANIEL KIMBALL was either Nathaniel Kimball (b. 1744), of Bradford, or Nathaniel Kimball (1706–84), farmer of Boxford. Osgood, *Descendants of . . . Osgood*, 35; *Sibley's Harvard Graduates*, 10:220–22; Morrison and Sharples, *Kimball Family*, 1:66, 87, 112, 155.

Thursday the 7th of April.

To Day is pleasant. After Breakfast I set of for Cambridge. I call'd at Capt. Osgoods & there was Fogg, Parsons, Tenny & Emery, & they told me they went down to the Presidents & ask'd for a Recomendation, & he was very much affected with it & told them he could not give them one under Six Weeks, & then a large Number of them ask'd leave to go Home & tarry till this affair is settled, & got leave.

Fogg told me it was reported there that I had been a ring leader in this affair & that they would be unwilling to receive me if the rest came back & also that I said that I would bring a Mobb down there to tair them to Peaces, which looks very dark upon my side, though I remember no such thretning. I came from the[re] & Osgood is going with me & is to call me in Town. I stop'd at Esqr. Phillips's & Br. Oliver was there we stay'd a while & then went to Br. Peters's & Osgood call'd me there. Br. went wit[h] us to the uper end of Andover. We proceeded on our Journey & got to Cambridge about dark, put up our Horses at Frosts & went to College to Cummings's & what should we hear there but that Sr. Ward & French had been to Wrentham & had Whiting before a Justice & two Ministers & he took oath that all he said was a Lye that he never was in Mr. Willards study as he had reported which News struck me to the Heart. The Scholars are coming down upon it, & making humble Confessions & going into College again, & it is reported that there is a Number who can not get in upon any account & that I am one of that Number. I went to Mr. Nuttings & heard the same Story, but John Gill stan[d]s to what he said about seeing Whiting in Willards Study which looks very strange indeed. I was very much discompos'd and talk'd with all I could see about it & went to Mr. Goffs & talk'd with Mr. Dana & then I went to Warlands & attempted to get some rest. I hear there was a considerable Number who pretended to give up their Chambers who did not but deceiv'd us, & I think they are not worthy to be rank'd amongst rationals.

It is hard to know what to make of WHITING's original charge that he had been imprisoned, followed by his recantation. Presumably he would not have perjured himself lightly before a justice of the peace. Nevertheless, he must have known that if he persisted in his accusation, he would have jeopardized his standing at college. After earlier hints on March 31 and April 1 that the college faculty had concluded that Peabody was among the most active student agitators, Jeremiah FOGG's report that the faculty considered him a RINGLEADER was very disturbing news, especially when Peabody confirmed it. Stephen would spend the next three months trying to return to the college's good graces. Joseph CUMMINGS (1745–88), A.B. 1768, of Ipswich, became the minister in Rockingham, Vermont. John NUTTING (b. 1739), a carpenter in Cambridge, lived on North Avenue near the common. *Sibley's Harvard Graduates*, 17:11–12, 307–10; Paige, *History of Cambridge*, 616.

Friday the 8th of April.

After Breakfast I went to Mr. Appletons to talk with him about something he said against me to White. The old Gentleman talk'd pretty well but upon the whole blamed me considerably. I talk'd with Sewall Wigglesworth & Scales & they seem to lay a great deal to me & are all rais'd with the Behavior of the Scholars. I went & saw Ward & French & they told me the same story which I had heard before about Whiting, & it appears to me that Death is much too good for that Vilian, as any thing possibly can be. Ward seems to think that I cant get in again [by] any means. The Overseers meet to Day [&] have confirm'd all the President & Tutors [ha]ve done. There was a grand Funeral in town to Day. The Governors Son was buried who died very suddenly at the Stewards with the Fever. I was up at College some though it looks very lonesome. I was at Greene's Chamber & took a Letter from him to my Chum. There are many down to apply for a readmission. I supp'd with Sayer at Mrs. Nuttings, saw Putnam & Stebbings & Putnam swore ably at the Governors. Lodg'd at Warlands with Osgood again.

Within a few days of resigning his connection with the college, Peabody began to realize the gravity of the step he had taken. As more and more schoolmates returned to Cambridge and applied for readmission, he felt increasingly isolated. Shute Bernard, the fourth SON of GOVERNOR Thomas Bernard, died in Boston in his sixteenth year on April 5, 1768. MRS. NUTTING was Mary, wife of the carpenter John Nutting of Cambridge. *Boston Gazette*, April 11, 1768; Paige, *History of Cambridge*, 616.

Saturday the 9th of April.

To Day is clear, cool & Windy. I understand it is generally thought in Cambridge that I was at the bottom of all this Dispute & that my Caracter suffers very much, so I went & talk'd a little with Danforth Eliot & Willard a bout it & they said but a little, but ware pretty crusty & told me the President & Tutors ware going to meet & that I might have a hearing. I got Darling to move my Bottles out of my Celler to his House & got my Horse & then went & waited at the Presidents till after noon & there ware many making application so that it was late when I went before them, & I attempted to vindicate my Caracter & they ask'd me several Questions, & told me I should have a hearing if I had a mind to after the Vacation. I came out & went & din'd & fitted my Things & Osgood & I call'd Doct'r

Cobb & [set] of for Andover. I rode with Pool & Burnap who came down for some of their Things. W[e] came through Mistick up to Wymans of Woburn where we stop'd & so at Jacoes aga[in] came to Esqr. Phillips's & told them the [Story] of Whiting's Oath which astonish'd them so much. Cobb came to Doctr. Osgoods, & I came Home & told my News which is truly astonishing! I feel very much fategued with my Journey.

The depth of the faculty's anger against Peabody and a few other supposed ringleaders was now apparent. It was clear that the student strike had failed, so from this point until early July—after the close of this diary—Stephen's main objective was to win readmission to school. Samuel Sheldon POOL (1751–1835), A.B. 1770, of Reading, became a Loyalist and a jurist in Nova Scotia. *Sibley's Harvard Graduates*, 17:420–21.

Sunday the 10th of April.

To Day is Pleasant but I was so fategue'd & decompos'd in my Mind that I did not go to meeting nor did any Thing Else only sleep a little & wrote a Letter to Mr. Willard which Things I am not a little asham'd of. Nihil majus.

Br. Oliver & his Son & Asa Robinson ware here this Evening.

Public contrition in the form of an apology in chapel was required of any student returning from a suspension. Peabody's letter to tutor Joseph WILLARD was his attempt to begin the process of apologizing.

Monday the 11th.

To Day is cool & pleasant. I went up to Capt. Osgoods & Esqr. Phillips's & their Sons ware going to Cambridge to get a Readmition in to College. I sent my Letter to Willard. Just after they were gone Fogg & Emery came there & ware going to Cambridge, & Chadwick came up there also & we came from there & he came part of the Way with me. I call'd at Samuel Johnsons & stay'd till almost noon & then I came Home.

& just before Night I took my Mare & went down to Bradford to Old Mr. Websters & drank Tea & spent the Evening. I saw Sally Webster & Betty at Johnsons to Day &c.

Tuesday the 12th.

To Day is cool but clear. I wash'd my leather Breeches & [a] pare of my Fathers & did a good many choers. Our Folks all went from Home so that I spent the Evening in Br. Johns Room.

Wednesday the 13th of April.

To Day is clear & remarkably Windy. I help'd our People mend a little Fence & some round the Yard, & I mended my Things up a little my Breeches & other Things & just before Night Greene, Leonard & Fogg came here from Cambridge. They are in haste & will not stop but they tell me that Osgood & Phillips have made Confessions & are got into College again, & that Willington made Application & they examin'd him about who got the Punishments away from him & he would not tell neither could he & they have rusticated him, which is beyond Account. How they would do it I cant tell. They went from here over to Haverhill. I can think of nothing more remarkable.

Thursday the 14th.

To Day is clear & it is our general Fast. I went to meeting & heard Mr. Symmes A.M. from the 122 Psalms & ye 4 last Verses. P.M. Mr. Batchelor preach'd from the 13 of Luke the 8 & 9th Verses. Br. Oliver & I went to Lovejoys at Noon. I call'd at Capt. Osgoods in Mane & left my Camel & walk'd to meeting. Saw Samuel & my Chum & they tell me that they have got in to College again & that by some Hints they have had, my situation is pretty Difficult. I came Home & read a little in Mr. Hemingway & wrote a little in Journal. This Morning my Father came up & wak'd me & told me that his Ox that had been so long lame & so much trouble was Dead, which seems very strange as he had got so well as to rise alone. We all went out & skinn'd him in ma[ne].

In colonial New England the annual FAST DAY was the spring counterpart to Thanksgiving in the fall. Every spring, Christians meditated on their shortcomings. In the fall, they thanked God for His mercy. Samuel BATCHELLER (1707–96), A.B. 1731, was a former minister of Haverhill's Third, or West, Church. *Sibley's Harvard Graduates*, 9:11–18.

Friday the 15th of April.

To Day is pleasant but cool. Siste[r] Wood came up here in Mane & was goin[g] up to Andover & wanted me to go with her so after Breakfast I went & call'd with [her] at several Places where she had Business [to] do. I stop'd at Esqr. Phillips's & din'd & she went to Sister Peterss. I went over to Mr. Symmes's & talk'd with him about my Affair & he talks pretty discouraging, but says he will use his Influence for me & if he sees Mr. Scales he will talk with him. If not he will write. I went from there to Br. Peterss & drank Tea, & came from there with sister Wood & call'd at Frazers where I had a Sing with Isaac Osgood who was there. I came wit[h] Sister down to Uncle Fosters where I lodg'd with Jonathan. Told him all our Difficulties & we set up & talk'd upon Affairs till two o Clock, & he says if I am obligd to leave College he believes I can have Boxford School.

Peabody's oldest SISTER, Sarah (b. 1723), was the wife of John PETERS. Stephen's cousin Lt. JONATHAN Foster (1727–94) was the third child of his aunt Hannah (Peabody) and her husband, Jonathan Foster, of Boxford. *Peabody Genealogy*, 25; Pierce, *Foster Genealogy*, 148, 193.

Saturday the 16th.

To Day is cool. I went from there after Breakfast down to Sister Woods & from there to Mr. Holyokes where I din'd with him Mr. Galman [?] & Doctr Hale. Told them our affair & ask'd Mr. Holyoke's advise & he seems to advise me to go down & attempt to be readmitted but he says he would be glad to have me come & see him next Thursday which I promised to do. I came from there over to see David Jewett & he tells me there [w]ere some very particular Reasons why [he] did not give up his Connections when [the] rest of us did. I stay'd a while with [hi]m & then he walk'd with me up to Esqr. [G]oods where we went in & talk'd & he [t]hinks it is probable the general Court will [ta]ke the Matter under Consideration & make [s]ome perticular inquiry about it. I came [f]rom there & parted with Jewett. Stop'd a few minutes at Sisters & then I came Home.

As Peabody investigated the circumstances of his classmates, most of whom were now returning to school, he began to discover that some, such as DAVID JEWETT, had not actually withdrawn from college but had simply gone home until tempers cooled. Stephen now began to look for strings to pull to win himself readmission. He dined with Elizur HOLYOKE (1731–1806), A.B. 1750, minister of the First (East) Parish in Boxford and a nephew of President Edward Holyoke. Elizur's wife, Hannah, was Stephen's cousin. *Sibley's Harvard Graduates*, 12:563–65.

Sunday the 17th of April.

To Day is clear & cool. I went to meeting at Andover & heard Mr. Symmes Preach A.M. from the 1 of Cor 11 Chapt. 27 & 29 Verses. P.M. he preach'd from the Epistle of Jude 1 Verse. I din'd with Samuel Osgoods. After Service I went down to Br. Olivers where I stop'd & drank Tea, & had some talk with him & then came Home.

Monday the 18th.

To Day is clear & cool. I went & try'd to hier a Horse of Richard Hovey to ride to Byfield but could not. I came back & help'd Br. John up with some Water & then I took my Camel & set of to see Mr. Moody. I call'd at Rowley & see Fisher & Tenny & stay'd a while & then Tenny took a walk with me. I parted with him & went to Mr. Parsons's, & they tell me there Mr. Moody is gone from Home, & has been gone some Time & that he is very much incens'd at the Scholars and at me in Particular, though Mr. Parsons & his [. . .][1] are much for us & Mr. Hale has bee[n] over to see Mr. Moody & he is inrag[ed] at the Tutors for their Conduct. I din['d at] Mr. Parsons's & my Class-Mate is m[uch] against making a Confession but upo[n] the whole the general advise is to go do[wn] & try for a readmission. I went from ther[e] to Mr. Noyes's & put up my Mare & the[n] went down to see Mr. Jos. Moody where I saw Colman who had been keeping Schoo[l] to Day for Master as the Parsonss have don[e] before. I told Mr. Moody my story, & he told me he believ'd master blam'd me, but would be glad to see me, so I concluded to come down again on Saturday. I came up to Mr. Noyes's & drank Tea with Judith & some of the Scholars, & desir'd them to do an Arrand to Moses Isacson from Oliver who is not well at Home, & then I came from there Homewards. I call'd just & saw Wheeler & then proceded & came up through the lower End of Bradford but did not reach Home. I saw Mr. Webster of Salsbury & told him our College story &c. The several Stars & Moon ware the nearest together to night that I ever saw them.

Peabody looked up to Samuel MOODY, so the news that his former MASTER at Dummer Academy blamed him in particular for the disruption at Harvard must have been especially difficult to hear. RICHARD HOVEY (1733–1818) was a farmer in West Boxford. MR. PARSONS was Rev. Moses Parsons, A.B. 1736. MR. HALE was probably either Capt. Joseph Hale or his son Joseph, Jr., both cordwainers of Byfield. *Hovey Book*, 167–68; *Descendants of Thomas Hale*, 154, 267–68.

1. Torn [one word].

Tuesday the 19th of April.

To Day is pleasant & wormer. I stay'd & went to Breakfast where I was & spent the bigger Part of the forenoon & Mr. Webster give me his advise & talk'd as Sensibly about the Matter as any Man I have heard. I came from there to Mr. Williams's where I din'd & give him a detail of the Affair & he says but little about it, but advises me to go down again and try for a readmission. I came from [there] up through Boxford to Br. Olivers [w]here I saw Jas. Frye & he is more Crazy [t]han I ever saw him. I talk'd with Br. a [w]hile & then went up to Mr. Symmes's. Scales had been there, & Mr. Symmes had [tal]k'd with him a little but he was sparing [. . .][1] Speaking but what I can learn there [is] but little likelyhoods of my being accepted if [I] go down, & by the Way I am jelous Mr. Symmes is no Friend to me. He expects to see Mr. Scales again. I came over to Esqr. Phillips's & Lovejoy & Osgood came there. The Esqr. seems to give considerable Incouragement that the Court will act upon this affair when they meet. Osgood, my Chum, & I went from there to John Abbots to a Singing meeting where we met Br. John & some others & had some pretty good Singing & spent a pretty long Evening & so came from there Home. Osgood & my Chum seem to think it is a Doubt whether I get into College or no. They talk of coming to see me tomorrow. When I came Home Sister Peters was here, & Varnum & Chadwick had been here, & Varnum had left a Letter for me & determines never to attempt to go to College again & seems to urge me not to, & writes very wormly, & that the gentlemen in the Ministry are generally on our Side. I am more of the Opinion I will be rejected than ever I have been.

In appraising his prospects for readmission, Peabody began to divide his acquaintances into friends (such as MR. WEBSTER) and enemies (for instance, MR. SYMMES), part of an essentially political effort to regain his place at college.

1. Torn [one or two words].

Wednesday the 20th of April.

To Day is clear & some Wormer. I was at Home all Day. Wrote in Journal all the Time I had. Doctr. Hale from Boxford came here & stay'd the bigger Part of the Day & din'd. Sister Peters went from here Home. John Day & Wife ware in the other Room making a Visit. Nihil majus.

Thursday the 21 of April.

To Day is very pleasant & dry Weather. I wrote a little in Mane, & then I too[k] the Chaise & carry'd my Mother down [to] Boxford to Sister Woods. I then went over to Mr. Holyokes & din'd & had another talk with him & he talks of going to Cambridg[e] next Monday if I can get him a Horse. I try'd at Richard Fosters, & am to try at other Places & if I cant get him one he is to look out himself. I came from there to Rich'd Peabody's & lay in with him to hier some Money for me of the Town which Sister Wood is to pay in & he tells me he will. I try'd there for a Horse for Mr. Holyoke & at Jona. Woods & Nathans but could not get any. I came from Sister Woods a little before dark with Sister Polly & came up to Gideon Tylers where I stop'd & Br. Oliver & Wife & my Class-Mate Sargent & Chadwick ware there. Sargent tells me he has seen Varnum & that he is now at Fathers & that he has been where he has heard that Willard & Ward have spread this Report, that Varnum & I ware the Persons who lay the Plan for Whiting to tell this Lye about his being shut up in Willards Study. He says it is reported so all along the Eastward Road, & I understand he has left coppies of Whitings oath & there is something of this there, but that is not known. Sargent lodg'd with Chadwick & I came Home & lodg'd with Varnum & he give me a Detail of what he has heard in his Travils.

[If] this Report is credited there is no likelihoods of my ever being admitted into College again but it seems as though Willard had expos'd himself to the sivil Law which I am determin'd to inquire into a little.

The rumor that Peabody and James Mitchell VARNUM had plotted to spread the word that Joseph WILLARD had confined Thurston WHITING in his college room promised to be devastating if widely believed, because it would confirm suspicions that they had set out to foment trouble. Peabody weighed the possibility that Willard had slandered him, a potential accusation that required meeting four tests: (1) the statement had to be false and defamatory, (2) it had to have been made in a public setting, (3) it had to be at least negligent, and (4) it had to be actionable. Peabody's cousin RICHARD FOSTER (b. 1733) lived in Boxford, where cousin RICHARD PEABODY (1731–1820) also resided. JONATHAN WOOD (1716–81) was a farmer in Boxford. *Black's Law Dictionary*, 5th edn. (St. Paul, Minn.: West Publishing, 1979), 1244; Pierce, *Foster Genealogy*, 148, 193; *Peabody Genealogy*, 33–34; Endicott, "Peabody Family," 365; *Vital Records of Boxford*, 106, 272; *Essex County Probate Index*, 2:1010.

Friday the 22d of April.

To Day is cloudy & some Rain, Wind Est. Varnum went from here & we concluded to meet at Cambridge on next Tuesday Night to see how Things are & he is to consult Esqr. Varnum & I am to see Colo. Frye. I was out with our People a plowing a while & then I came in & wrote a little in Journal & a Letter to Benjn. Chadwick, & one for my Father to Mr. Shierman. I agreed with Mr. Holyoke yesterday to see him in Boston on Tuesday by eliven or twelve o Clock.

Just before Night I got ready to go down by Byfield & took my Mare & went as far as Mr. Kimballs where I tarry'd all Night & it was very rainey &c.

Saturday the 23d of April.

Is exceeding Stormy Wind N.E. After Breakfast I set out to Byfield. Went down to Mr. Jackmans where I stop'd & dry'd myself a little & Timothy went with me to his Grandfathers. Call'd at Mr. Parsons's, & they tell me Mr. Moody is very much inrag'd with me, & that he has heard a great many Storries & in perticular one from Webster concerning my threten-ing him which is an absolute Lye. I made no stop but went down to Mr. Moodys but he was gone to Glocester, so I in part have lost my Journey. He left word he would see me on Monday but I am not going after him any more at present. I came back to Mr. Noyeses & din'd, & then ca[lled] at Decn. Colmans & so came to M[r] Parsons's again & made a Consid-erable [. . .][1] & took his advise. It is remarkable [the] stories they have got against me, but I cant hear as they have asserted that I wa[s] at the Bottom of all the Mischief. I cam[e] from there as directly as I could to my Fathers & a very Wet Time I have had of [it].

Peabody had become a scapegoat. Many undergraduates had helped in stirring up turmoil, but once the authorities fingered Stephen and a few other potential targets, it was convenient to limit the blame to those they had singled out.

1. Torn [one word].

Sunday the 24 of April.

To Day is some Stormy. I stayd at Home read three Sermons of Mr. Hemmingways & some in the Gospel Sonnets tho' my Affairs very much disturb my Mind.

Monday the 25th.

To Day it is clear Wind N.W. I wrote some in Journal & fitted up my Things a little that I wet on Saturday & then I went up into Andover to Esqr. Phillips's & talk'd with my Chum a while & he told me by what he could understand it was not intended that I should be taken in to College again, & he also tells me he hear'd Colo. Frye said he had something against me which he heard concerning John Frye's being rusticated. We agree'd not to go to old Mr. Phillips as we had determin'd. I went from there to Br. Peterss where I din'd, & then I went up to Colo. Fryes but he was not at Home. I came to the School House & saw Lovejoy & went to Benja. Stevens's to see Colo. Frye but he was gone over the Hill Home again, so I came back & went to his House & had a long Talk with him about the Affair at College, & told him [w]hat I had heard he said about John Frye [&] he said it was false. He says take our [Co]llege Storry all togather & it is pretty Divilish. He seems to think that there might be something done in the Corts about it if all storrys are true. I came from there to Mr. Symmes's & talk'd with him a little & I very much dislike his talk & believe he will rather hurt me than help me. I came to Esqr. Phillips's again & am to call him early tomorrow Morning to go to Boston. My Chum came down with me to Lieut. Pearsons & met Br. John & some other & had a singing Meeting. We call'd to see Osgood as we came along & he has got the Mumps & could not come out. Br. John tells me Chadwick & Sargent is gone over to Haverhill to talk with Mr. Smith about going to Road-Island College if they should not get in here. I came Home with Br. John & it was some late.

By now, Stephen was carefully weighing the reaction he anticipated from each person he considered contacting. Rev. Samuel PHILLIPS, the minister of Andover's South Parish, was too stern and traditional to be a likely ally. Peabody's willingness to consider entering RHODE ISLAND COLLEGE, now Brown University, reveals how much he worried about his prospects for readmission at Harvard. Founded by Baptists only four years earlier in 1764, Rhode Island College had not yet graduated its first class. New England's Congregationalists expected their ministers to hold bachelor's degrees, so Stephen's separation from Harvard threatened his aspirations for ordination. In order to prepare for the pulpit he needed to complete a liberal education, but a degree from an infant institution, and one organized by Baptists, was a distinctly undesirable path to this end. Lt. John PEARSON lived in Andover's North Parish. Peabody assumed that Rev. Hezekiah SMITH, Haverhill's Baptist minister, was well informed about the new school's progress. *Andover Tax Assessments*, Tax for 1768.

Tuesday the 26 of April.

To Day is clear & Worm. I got up very early & fitted my Things & set of for Boston. I got to Esqr. Phillips's a little after sun rise & he set of with me & we stop'd at Fowles's & refresh'd ourselves & Horses. I call'd by the Way & left a letter for Mr. Shierman. We went from there & got into Charleston a little after 11. I put up my Camel at Capt. Adams's & went over the Ferry with the President, but he said nihil to me nor I to him. I went & found Mr. Holyoke & he told me he had not seen the President, for he was from Home Yesterday, but he says he will see him to Day & meet me at two oClock at the Town House. I parted with him & w[ent] to see my Class-Mate Tuder, & din'd with him & was genteally treated & he tells me he has attempted to get in to College but is put of for the present, bu[t] he thinks we shall all get in again. He say[s] it makes a good deal of talk in Boston. We came up to the Town-House & went to Mr. Holyoke & he told me he had seen the President & he told him that I should never be taken in to College again, for it appeared [that] I had been very active & had done it all under a Clok of Religeon (he is an old ungenerous Rascal). I parted with him & Austin came there with Tuder & we talk'd upon Matters & then went upon Bacon Hill where we stay'd some Time. We came down & I parted with them & went to Mr. Phillips's Wair-House where I saw the Esqr. & told him what I had heard but it did not seem to discourige him any but he says he shall be in Cambridge tomorrow. I came out of Town and call'd to see Frothingham & drank Tea there & had a very large Talk with the Decn. & Mr. Call & they seem to come a little more over to our Side of the Question. I came to Capt. Adams's & give him a short Detail of the Affair & took my Camel from there. Call'd & drank a Bowl of Punch with Benjn. Call & then came up to Cambridge. Went to Decn. Prentices & got my Mare kept there. I went to Mr. Warlands & lodg'd there. They tell me John Gill is Sick with the Fever & is very sad so that he is given over by the Doctr. [. . .][1] they ask'd him whether he saw Whiting as [he] at first said he did. He said he did actually [se]e him in Mr. Willards study. Richard Jaquish & one Coburn ware at Fathers last Night.

The assertion that Stephen had acted UNDER A CLOAK OF RELIGION is ambiguous. It is clearly a recognition that his strong orthodoxy was out of step with prevailing views at the college. It may mean, additionally, that the faculty felt that he was hypocritically using a facade of piety to camouflage his misconduct. John Gill's continued assertion at this late date that HE SAW WHITING in Willard's chamber is strong evidence that Whiting's original account was true. John FROTHINGHAM, A.B. 1771, was one of Peabody's former schoolmates at Dummer Academy. His father was DEACON John Frothingham, a mason. Mr. CALL must have been one of Deacon Frothingham's in-laws, a relative of his wife, Esther (Call). *Sibley's Harvard Graduates*, 17:520–21.

1. Torn [one word].

Wednesday the 27th of April.

To Day is cooler. I went up to College & talk'd with Mr. Danforth & he treated me sivelly & told me if I had a mind for a readmission he would not advise me to try now but to wate a while first till some others had got in. I went round to see some of the Scholars, & went up into Bigelows Chamber & see a Number of my Class-Mates. Mr. Dix & Goodhue ware there discoursing about our affair, & Esqr. Phillips came in & went round to some of the Gentlemen in Government & spoke to them concerning my Case & he tells me they all talk good-natured & says if I have a Mind to apply I may have a fair hearing. I went with the Esqr. to Frosts & brought some Things to Warlands he brought down for his Son, & then I parted with him & he went & lodg'd at Colo. Brattles & is going Home early tomorrow Morning. In the Evening I went over to see Mr. Honeywill & stay'd till late & sup'd with him. He urgis me very much to try for a Readmission. I hear Webster is come down. Lodg'd at Warlands with Sargent who came down to Day.

Isaac BIGLOW (1750–77), A.B. 1769, of Weston, read for the ministry and supplied pulpits but died before being called or ordained. DIX was probably Jonas Dix, the father of Jonas Dix (1749–96), A.B. 1769. *Sibley's Harvard Graduates*, 17:122–23, 139.

Thursday the 28th.

To Day is clear. I went up in the Morning to see Webster at Bordmans & he told me he never told Mr. Moody that I threatn'd him as I heard [at] Byfield. How it is I cant tell. I went to Ward & got a Coppy of Whitings Oath, & there is known Falsehoods in it. After Breakfast I went up to see Scales & he treated me like a Hog, but as he acted in Caracter I did not think so strange of it. I went up [to?] Emerys Chamber where I saw several Scholars & had a talk with Esqr. Webster & he seems to blame the Scholars but little. I saw Mr. Hutchenson & had a good Deal of Talk with him. At noon saw my Class-Mate Moore & he laments that he did not give up his Chamber. Drank some Syder with him & he say[s] if the Scholars will forgive him he will make a humble Confession to them in a publick Manner. Such a Gloom as there is upon the Minds of the Scholars I never saw. Some are sorry they have enter'd & accuse themselves with numberless Lyes in their Confession, others are swearing they wont apply under such an infamous Government & others are desiring to get in, in order to be reveng'd upon the Tutors; & it seems as though there never could be Harmony at College again under these Tutors. Senior Parsons came down & brought me a Letter from Mr. Moody & he seems to be apeas'd but advises me to go & live with Doctr. Langdon a spell & some other advice which I don't like, & I believe I shant comply with it by any Means. Mr. Parsons & Madam sent their love to me & tell me if I am rejected to come there & any thing they have I shall be welcome to. Exceeding Friendly indeed which I acknowledge with Gratitude.

[I] receiv'd two friendly Letters from Sr. Pike & one from Tenny. Pike intimates as tho Willard had given me a very bad Caracter at the Eastward. My Class-Mate Parsons has been before the Tutors & they have found out he was a Committee Man & treated him very roughly & he expects to meet with Difficulty. I went to see Mr. Apleton & he talk'd friendly & I stay'd with him some Time. I drank Tea with Governor Hutchensons Son, & in the Evening went to see Sr. Smith & Greene, & then call'd a few Minutes upon Senior Parsons & visited Sayer also, then went to my Lodgings. Tuder was up from Boston to Day.

The strike was a test of undergraduate solidarity as the consequences of resisting the college became increasingly apparent. WHITING'S OATH, an account of the disruption calculated to win the favor of the faculty members who would assess his petition for readmission, revealed that under pressure the students had begun to turn on one another. The lament of Thomas MOORE (1745–96), A.B. 1769, that he had not resigned his room seems incomprehensible, especially in view of Peabody's difficulties, until one realizes that he risked ostracism by his classmates for his failure to act with them. Moore, from Bolton, later became the minister of the First Church in Wiscasset, Maine. Aaron BORDMAN (1746–72), A.B. 1767, of Cambridge, planned a career in commerce before his early death. Samuel LANGDON (1723–97), A.B. 1740, was the minister of the First Church in Portsmouth. From 1774 to 1780 he served as the president of Harvard College. He received the D.D. from the University of Aberdeen in 1761. GOVERNOR HUTCHINSON'S SON was William Sanford Hutchinson, A.B. 1770. *Sibley's Harvard Graduates*, 17:187–88, 397–98, 399–401; 16:448; 12:172–81; 10:508–28.

Friday the 29th of April.

To Day is clear. I got up early & went & saw Frost & Crosby at Reeds & talk'd with Mr. Frost. I came from there & went up & talk'd with Willard & to my Surprize he treated me pretty well, & seem'd to hint as though he should not very much oppose my being taken into College again, but would not advise me to apply now. I went over to Decn. Prentices & got my Mare, & went to Breakfast with old Jewett & had a long Talk with him but dont like his talk very well, nor dont think that he has acted the Gentleman in this Affair, but I am uncertain how matters are with him. I left my Monitor Bills with Fletcher to give to Whiting who is chose in my room. They are turning out all the old Waiters shifting the Scholars as much as possible into other Chambers seemingly on purpose to show their Author[ity] to discompose the students. I put up the Things I am going to carry home. Went into see Gill who is a little better. I ask'd him about Whiting & he told me he certainly saw him as he said before. I saw Willington & h[e] told me the Manner of his being rusticated, & in Guilds Chamber Edwards told me the manner of his Examination before the President & Tutors that he did not know who were Heads but coming up to College & inquiring he heard that Varnum & I ware, so he went down & told the[m] & they accepted his Confession. Guild, & Coolidge can Witness to this, & it seems that a very considerable Part of their Evidence against me is such as this. Varnum got his Things ready & we set of on our Journey Home. I call'd at Mr. Bowmans & he told me a story he heard about John Gills refusing to take his Oath which looks a little strange to me.

We got to Wymans at Woburn & Esqr. Webster over took us & we din'd there. I call'd at Mr. Shiermans to do an Arrand for my Father & he tells me if we could pass Examination he is of Opinion we could enter N Haven College for all any Thing we have done here. I came from there & we stop'd at Jacoes awhile & then I parted with Esqr Webster & Varnum & came Home. Call'd at Br. Peters's & Esqr. Phillips's & the Esqr. tells me that Scales was very grand when he talk'd with him that he had been mild with the Scholars till now & found it would not do & now he determin'd to be as severe as was possible without overturning government that way, which seems to be as hard to swallow as any thing I have heard yet.

Br. Oliver has lost his youngest Child Stephen since I went away. He dy'd with Convultion Fitts though not actually in one. I heard of it in Cambridge by Sargeant. Nihil majus.

Peabody's conversation with Thomas EDWARDS (1753–1806), A.B. 1771, of Boston, provides a convincing description of how early accusations against him snowballed: HE DID NOT KNOW WHO WERE HEADS BUT COMING UP TO COLLEGE & INQUIRING HE HEARD THAT VARNUM & I WARE, SO HE WENT DOWN & TOLD THE[m] & THEY ACCEPTED HIS CONFESSION. Edwards became a lawyer. One response by the college to the uprising was to reassign roommates. Peabody was correct when he maintained that the faculty took this step ON PURPOSE TO SHOW THEIR AUTHOR[-ity] TO DISCOMPOSE THE STUDENTS. Shuffling roommates broke up the small circles of friends that were common. Amariah FROST (1750–1819), A.B. 1770, of Mendon, became a storekeeper after an unsuccessful attempt to enter the ministry. Aaron CROSBY (1745–1824), A.B. 1770, of Shrewsbury, became a missionary. REED has not been identified. He was not an undergraduate but could have been any of a number of men named Reed or Read who lived in Cambridge at the time. MR. Amariah FROST (1720–92), A.B. 1740, the father of the younger Frost, was the minister of the church in Milford. The entry refers without clear distinctions to two students surnamed WHITING: Samuel Whiting (1750–1819), A.B. 1769, of Wrentham, who became the minister of the First Church in Rockingham, Vermont, replaced Peabody as a MONITOR. Thurston Whiting was the subject of Peabody's conversation with GILL. BROTHER OLIVER'S son STEPHEN, the first of two sons by the same name, was baptized on June 1, 1766. *Sibley's Harvard Graduates*, 17:384–86, 381–83, 507–10, 10:494–96; Paige, *History of Cambridge*, 636–39; *Peabody Genealogy*, 37.

Saturday the 30th of April 1768.

To Day is some cloudy & at Night it rains. I wrote a little in Journal & began a worm Letter to my Class-Mate Scammel & then Br. Oliver came here & old Mr. Osgood. The old Gentleman, seems to be very much disorderd & says he shall certainly make way with himself & nothing that can be said seems to pacify him. A malancholy sight to behold! Br. Oliver lent me a Book of Mr. Bostons which is call'd a Crook in the Lot, which I read some in & it seems to suit my Case very exactly & is very instructive. They went from here & I went out & help'd dig Gardin a little while & then little Oliver came here & told me some of the Difficulties they had had at School & he says Mr. Moody hant[1] treated him of late as he us'd to, but he has been very Cross for what Reason he cant tell. He tells me he is going down on Monday. He went from here & I went & put up Some top rails on a Peice of Fence. Br. John has got another of Thos. Peabody's Sons to live with him. His Name is Phinehas.

Thomas BOSTON (1677–1732) wrote *The Crook in the Lot; or, The Sovereignty and Wisdom of God in the Afflictions of Men Display* (many editions). In it Boston asks why God allows man to suffer. Thomas PEABODY (1715–76) lived in Boxford but moved to Lunenburg, where his son PHINEAS (1750–1835) also moved. *Peabody Genealogy*, 34, 35, 62.

1. I.e., hasn't.

May 1768

Sunday the 1 of May.

To Day is very cold Wind N.West. It is Squally. I read some in the Crook in the Lot & then I went to meeting & heard Mr. Symmes preach A.M. from the 103 Psalm 15, 16 & 17th Verses. P.M. he preach'd from the 3d of Hebrews 1 Verse. I din'd with Sr. Lovejoy. Saw my Chum after Meeting & he told me Sargeant was come Home & he had not got into College but intends to go down some Time soon again. I came down to Br. Olivers w[here] I stay'd all Night. Read in Mr. Flavil. It is a very cold Night.

John FLAVEL (1630–91) was an English clergyman and writer.

Monday the 2d of May.

To Day is clear & cold. I got Tyler to shew my Came[l] & told our College Story to James Ingals, & then I came from there over to Methuen. Saw Doctr. Peabody & he told me he had seen Scales but I was in a hurry to go over & he say'd he would call & see me at Mr. Sar[gents.] I went up there & saw my Class-Mate & stay'd there till towards Night. Had a long talk with Mr. Sargant & Mr. Batchelor, then we went over to see Elijah Sargent. Saw Doctr. Baker & Doctr. Thom, but Doctr. Peabody did not come. I agree'd to meet Kitt at Haverhill on Thursday. I came from there with Mr. Batchelor & rode with him some Ways & then I came over at Gages. Harrick was a mending his Boat so I was oblig'd to make some stop there. I came over & took a Ride down into Bradford & came back part of the Way pretty soon with Company. Nihil majus &c.

Christopher SERGEANT (1704–90), A.B. 1725, was the Congregationalist minister in Methuen and father of Christopher (KITT) Sergeant, A.B. 1769. Elijah SARGENT was a farmer in Methuen. HARRICK may have been Henry Herrick (1748–1800), A.B. 1767, of Beverly, a schoolteacher. *Sibley's Harvard Graduates*, 7:567–69, 16:474; Pruitt, *Massachusetts Tax Valuation List*, 108–9; *Vital Records of Methuen*, 278, 123.

Tuesday the 3d.

To Day is cool & cloudy. I help'd my Father Dock a Colt & then I wrote the chief of the Day in Journal. Samuel Johnson was here A.M. The Colt Bleed so that we stop'd the Blood with some Difficulty. Just before Night I went down to Deac. Chadwicks to invite them to come up to Fathers & dine. They ware not at Home but came Home in the Evening & they are to come next Monday. Colo. James Frye came down there & we drank a Mug of Flip & I stay'd there till [so]mething late & talk'd about our College Affairs, & the Decn. tells me that they have hier'd Mr. Adams to preach with them & he is to come next Sabbath. I came from there Home & it mists a little.

Without immediate prospects for returning to class, Peabody now made himself useful through farm work when he helped his father DOCK the tail of a COLT.

Wednesday the 4th of May.

To Day is cloudy but at noon it clear'd of worm. I read a little in the crook in the lot, wrote a little in Journal, & finish'd my long Letter to my Friend Scammel, & then I mended a saddle a little, & took a walk to Mr. Barkers where my Sister Polly was at Work. Weber overtook me by the Way & we had a good Deal of talk after we got there. I stay'd there & drank Tea & was very handsomely treated. Got Home a little after nine. Uncle Robinsons Garls ware there.

It is uncertain whether MR. BARKER paid SISTER POLLY for her labor or whether she was simply being neighborly in lending the Barkers a hand. What is clear is that in towns such as Andover, a market for day labor allowed people without urgent chores to make productive use of their available time.

Thursday the 5th of May.

To Day is cloudy but no rain Wind Est. I went up to Br. Olivers in Mane & Breakfasted with him & he told me some talk which he had with

Doctr. Peabody & Peabody had seen Scales. Scales intimated that I had been an Enimy to their procedings & that I was too much of a new Light & seem'd to be much against me. Peabody advis'd little Oliver if he went to College not to be sober by any Means if he intended to get through College but to do as others did. He said he had seen Doctr. Langdon & he said he did not doubt but I could have a Degree if I went & liv'd with some able Divine & I behaved myself well if I n[ow?] went to College again & Br. advised me to see Mr. Langdon. Doctr. Peabody had been to Mr. Symmes's & Br. tells me he believes Mr. Symmes is no Friend to me which I was convinced of before. I cam[e] Home, & after Diner took my Camel & went down to Haverhill. I call'd at David Halls as I went along & as I [ca]me back. Let Mrs. Hall have a Sermon of McGregorie's to read, & she lent me one of Mr. Caldwells.

At Haverhill I went to Esqr. Sargents where I found my Class-Mates Sargent Varnum & Dow. Sargent dont think of going down very soon, & Dow has but little Expectation of staying. Mr. Eames came there & the Esqr. & he talk'd largely upon College affairs & say'd they believ'd there was blame on both sides & hinted as though they thought my situation was diffecult but would advise me to make a Trial to reenter College. We drank Punch & Tea there & then came from there just before night. They had a small lease try'd there this P.M. We took a little Walk & then parted. I went in to see Mr. Osgood & he seems to be very much at a loss about our Affairs. I stay'd & help'd him drink Punch & just at nine o Clock I came over the River. Inquired at Chadwicks & James Campbells for a Conue for Br. John to go to Newbury with. It begins to rain this Evening & is a rainy Night &c.

Peabody's difficulties had a number of causes, some undoubtedly of his own making. The report that tutor Stephen SCALES considered Stephen too much of a NEW LIGHT underscores the role that religion must have played. In the early 1740s, during the Great Awakening, Harvard leaned in the direction of the Old Lights, or opponents of revivalism. Subsequent years confirmed the college's hostility to the expression of Calvinism that Peabody favored. College authorities, who were willing to make use of the secret information on undergraduate misbehavior that Peabody provided, were quick to distance themselves from him when he seemed to be fomenting disorder. The advice of DR. SAMUEL LANGDON, A.B. 1740, urging contrition and penance was the traditional remedy for a serious student misdeed. Peabody was tracing an exchange during the early 1740s between David McGREGORE (1710–77), the Presbyterian minister of Londonderry, New Hampshire, and JOHN CALDWELL, an obscure itinerant, probably of

British origins. McGregore published several works in the early 1740s, including *The Spirits of the Present Day Tried*, 2nd edn. (Boston, 1742). Caldwell replied with *An Answer to the Appendix of the Second Edition of Mr. McGregore's Sermon on the Spirits of the Present Day Tried* (Boston, 1743).

Friday the 6 of May.

To Day it rains till afternoon. I read some in the Crook in the Lot & wrote a little in Journal, & wrote Mr. Daves's Poem on the Birth of one of his Children. Help'd our People kill a Calf. A little after 3 it clears of & I drest myself & set of down to Byfield. I call'd to see Tenny but he was gone from Home. I proceeded to Mr. Jones's where I drank Tea, & they till me Mr. Moody is very much lower'd to what he was, & they are exceeding friendly to me. My Class-Mate took a Walk with me to Mr. Noyse's where I put up my Horse & in the Evening John Noyes & Parsons & I went down to see Mr. Moody & he is not very well, & very low in Spirits. He said not a Word about my Affair at College. He let us see Whitings Oath which is a true Coppy, & a Manifesto which they have drawn up which is Just as I could expect from them. We came from there & Mr. Moody gave me an Invitation to come & Breakfast with him tomorrow. I lodg'd at Mr. Noyes's with John.

Saturday the 7th.

To Day is showery all Day. I waited upon Mr. Moody & Breakfasted with him & talk'd largely upon my College Affairs & he is extreme mild & seems as though he would befriend me all he can. He thinks it would be best for me not to apply for an admission at present. I parted with him about nine o Clock & came up to Mr. Noyes where I spent the A.M. & din'd. I hav[e] some Thoughts of going down there again [the] Night before Ordination in compliance with a strong Invitation of Judiths. I came from there & call'd at Decn. Colmans. Had the usual Talk over. Thos. is not going down at present. I call'd at Mr. Parsons's & all they advis'd me to make no Application at present. They read Pikes Letter. Tell [m]e they believe he thinks it may be taken [. . .][1] the civil Law by what he has wrote, & if they was I, it may could not get into College they would persue that so far as they would, let it please or affront who it would, but they advise me to say but little about them Things now. I came from there.

Shew my Class Mates a Letter I have wrote to Scammel, & then parted with him. I went up through Rowley. Saw Tenny & he says he believes by what he heard at the Estward that Willard has exposed himself but he could not tell me any Thing in perticular. I came from there, call'd to see Master Adams & talk'd with him upon College Affairs & stay'd till Just Night. I came up to Sister Woods made a short stop there & then came Home. Mr. Williams has been here to Day. He was married last Thursday.

Samuel WILLIAMS, A.B. 1761, married Jane Kilbourne of Rowley on May 5. *Sibley's Harvard Graduates*, 15:134–36.

1. Torn [one word].

Sunday the 8th.

To Day is clear & cool. I went to Boxford Meeting on foot & heard Mr. Adams preach A.M. from the 46 of Isaiah 8 Verse. P.M. he preach'd from the 2 of Peter 3 Chapt. 8th [?] Verse. Lik'd him in some Respects well, though not equil to what I expected, not so clear in the calvinistical Scheme. I din'd with him at John Chadwicks & stop'd there after Meeting for a few Minutes, so at the Decns., & then came Home. Read a little in the crook in the Lot.

ADAMS was filling the Boxford West Parish pulpit for a Sunday according to the arrangements Peabody learned of the previous Tuesday. Thomas Chadwick and Joseph Hovey were the church's DEACONS. Worthley, "Inventory," 113.

Monday the 9th of May.

[To] Day is Pleasant. I rode my Father's colt down to John Days & borrow'd his Horse for my Sisters to go to Ordaination. Went to Thos. Osgoods to get one but could not. I came Home & wrote some in Journal & then Sargent came here & Decn. Chadwick & Wife & Br. Oliver & Wife & Hilton & another Man with him. They all din'd here & then Sr. Holt & Osgood came here. Bring nothing new. Holt is going to Newbury & went of pretty soon. Fogg call'd here in his Way to Cambridge & told me Scales was talk'd to, very plain over their Way, & that he jear'd at me because I was a new light as he call'd me. He says his Credit is very much sunk among the chief of the Ministers over the River & that he himself is sensible of it. He would not stop to come in. Our Company stayd till Night & we had a Sing & then they all went of but Hilton & the Stranger who came with him & they lodg'd with Br. John. I had a good Deal of Talk with Br. Oliver & he thinks Mr. Symmes is my Enimy.

Mary (Porter) CHADWICK (d. 1788) was the wife of DEACON Thomas CHADWICK. Sarah (Robinson) Peabody was the WIFE of Stephen's BROTHER OLIVER. HILTON may have been Daniel Hilton of New Market, New Hampshire, a former student at Dummer Academy. *Descendants of John and Joan Chadwick*, C12; *Peabody Genealogy*, 36–37; *Officers and Students of Dummer Academy*, 14.

Tuesday the 10th of May.

To Day is pleasant. I wrote a Letter to Sr. Pike & sent it by Hilton & then I walkd down to the Cove with Br. John to bring bac[k] his Horse. He is going to Newbury in Jam[es] Campbells Canue which was on the other Side of the River. I assisted him till he got away & then I came Homeward. Whe[n I] got up to Abraham Days I met Emery & Chadwick who are lately come from College. Emery pertends to be sick & Chadwick is come to bring him Home. They brought me a Letter from Parsons & he writes discouraging about my ever giting into College again though they seem to speak incouraging. They tell me Butler has brought out Rogers & Junr. Adams for breaking Windows & Adams is put by for a year but Rogers is not come & what his punishment will be is not determin'd. I believe there are but few who will pitty Rogers. I don't surely, for he was very forward in telling all he knew, & some more. I parted with them & came & took John Days Horse & came Home, & wrote a little in Journal, & then my Sisters & I got ready for Ordination & put Days Horse into the Chaise & he was pritty firce so that I rode some in the Chase before we set of & then with Polly as far as the Widow Lacys, & Becca rode my Mare. Then they went round & I went by Decn. Chadwicks. We call'd at Uncle Fosters & I spent some Time with Jonathan & then we started from there & went down to Byfield they went directly to Mr. Noyes's & I stop'd at Mr. Parsons's but they could tell me nothing new. I came from there & my Class-Mate walk'd a little Way with me & I told him the News of Rogers, & he laughed heartily at it. I parted with him & came to Noyes's where I tarry'd all Night. Emerson was there. Nihil majus.

Zebulon BUTLER (1749–90), A.B. 1770, of Edgartown, became the minister of the church in Falmouth. Daniel ROGERS (1749–1804), A.B. 1771, of Littleton, who entered with the class of 1770, was rusticated for a year on May 20. He became a farmer in his hometown. Moses ADAMS (1749–1819), A.B. 1771, entered Harvard with the class of 1770 but was rusticated for a year for the misdeeds recounted here. He became the minister of the church in Acton. WIDOW Martha LACY lived in Andover's North Parish. BECCA may have been Peabody's younger sister Rebecca (1746–1806). *Sibley's Harvard Graduates*, 17:343–44, 609–10, 468–71; Faculty Records, 3:83; *Andover Tax Assessments*, Tax for 1768; *Peabody Genealogy*, 25.

Wednesday the 11th of May.

[To] Day is very pleasant. I stop'd there [at] Breakfast & then went along before the rest & stop'd at Jos. Hales but he was not at Home. His Wife is sick.

When they came along I went with them. Mr. Moody came along & I rode with him, & he talks very friendly to me & says he will do all he can to get me into College again. I parted with him & we all went down to Lemuel Noyes's where we drest & left our Horses, & walk'd up to Ordination. I got into the Meeting-House, & got a very good Berth with Tracy. They began & ended Servise with an Antham. Mr. Johnson made the first Prayer, Mr. Barnard preach'd, Mr. Wingate gave the Charge, Mr. Prentice the right Hand, & Mr. Fogg concluded with Prayer. So much Regularity among the People I never saw. I went to Capt. Tracys with a Number of others & we had the most genteal & Rich Entertainment I ever saw. We took a Walk to see what we could, & I did see a good Many of my Acquaintance. I saw Mr. Fogg & he talk'd with me about College & says he will break Scales's Neck if he says one Word against my giting into College, [&] seems to be exceeding Friendly. I came to Capt. Tracys & drank Tea & then I went with Wm. Ingals [to] to find my Sisters, & it rains some. [I] went almost all over Town & finally found the[m] at Lemuel Noyes's. He invited them to go hom[e] with him so we tackled the Chaise & set of though it was very dark & the Horse was lot[h] to go but we got him to go along, & it began to rain & rain'd very fast so that we ware some Wet when we got to Ingals's. Lieut. Pearsons there. My Sisters stay'd there all Night & I [. . .][1] & lodg'd with Winship at Capt. Tracys. Wm. Coffin was there & talks very worm for the Scholars.

ORDINATIONS were entertainments in colonial New England, so it is unsurprising that Peabody attended the ordination and installation of Thomas Cary

(1745–1808), A.B. 1761, as the minister of the First Church of Newburyport on May 11, 1768. Nevertheless, Stephen's networking at the function seems to reflect renewed optimism that Harvard would readmit him, making his plans for the ministry once more possible. The WIFE of Joseph HALES was either Mary (Noyes) Hale (1709–94) or her daughter-in-law Mary (Northend) Hale (1740–1830), both of Byfield. William JOHNSON (1706–72), A.B. 1727, was the minister of the Second Church in West Newbury. Paine WINGATE, Jr. (1739–1838), A.B. 1759, was the minister of the Second Parish in Hampton, New Hampshire, now Hampton Falls, in 1768. A few years later he left the ministry, eventually serving in public office, including the U.S. Senate. Thomas PRENTICE (1702–82), A.B. 1726, was the minister of the Congregational church in Charlestown. Jeremiah FOGG (1712–89), A.B. 1730, was the minister of the Congregational church in Kensington, New Hampshire. WILLIAM INGALLS (1737–98) was born in Andover but moved to Newburyport, where he became a deputy sheriff. Amos WINDSHIP (1745–1813), A.B. 1771, of Holliston, became a physician. Edward Barnard, *A Sermon Preached at the Ordination of the Rev. Mr. Thomas Cary* (Boston, 1768); *Sibley's Harvard Graduates*, 15:29–33, 8:218–19, 81–89, 14:533–48, 10:4–11, 17:673–79; *Descendants of Thomas Hale*, 154, 267–68; *Ingalls Family*, 53.

1. Torn [one word].

Thursday the 12th of May.

To Day is clear & cool, wind N.W. I took a walk with Winship in Mane. Came back & went to Breakfast & then Mr. Moody came there & had a very Worm Talk with Mr. Coffin & Capt. Tracy & they tell me Mr. Fogg & Mr. Moody had it last Night without reserve & Mr. Fogg give the Tutors their Carecters. I lit of Tenny & we went & drank Punch with Curtis & Holt & had a pleasant sing. Then I parted with them & went to Ingals's & took Days Horse & sent to Lem Noyes & got my Mare & all my Things which I left there & took my leave. I came back to Ingals's & din'd & my Sisters fitted their Things & we set of for Home. I came to Capt. Tracys & took leave of them all. Saw some others & did a little Business. Lit of Wyman & his Wife & came out of Town with them. I rode along before & call'd at Mr. Hales & talk'd with him some Time. Met his son going [to] Almsbury Ferry with his brother Noyes & sister. I came up to Uncle Sawyers & over took my Sisters there I stop'd & drank Tea & they tell me Wyman has broke his Chair & is [d]etain'd. I saw Emery & Colman go by Mr. Hales when I was there. We came from Uncle Sawyers & came up through Bradford. Call'd a minute at Uncle Kimballs, & I parted with the Garls at Uncle Williams's. Went in there to cary some things they brought up for Wyman. I made [o]ne stop with Mr. Williams, & then took [. . .][1] Rounds. Got Home a little before eliven.

CURTIS may have been Benjamin Curtis (1753–84), A.B. 1771, who practiced medicine in Boston, his hometown, before his early death. It is also possible, though, that Peabody meant Samuel Curtis, A.B. 1766, a onetime roommate of Moses HOLT (1744–72), A.B. 1767, who was teaching school in Newburyport. UNCLE SAWYER was Elisha Sawyer, the husband of Sarah Peabody's half-sister Rebecca Pike. MR. HALE and his SON were probably Joseph Hale, Sr., and Joseph Hale, Jr., of Byfield. *Sibley's Harvard Graduates*, 17:502–3, 16:352–54, 485; *Vital Records of Newbury*, 2:393; *Descendants of Thomas Hale*, 154, 267–68.

1. Illegible [one or two words].

Friday the 13th of May.

To day is worm. I rode the Colt & drove Home Mr. Days Horse, & when I came back I wrote a Letter to Parsons in Answer to what he sent me, & P.M. I went down to Haverhill in Order to see Mr. Manning the President of Rode Island College. He is down here. I saw him & talk'd with him largely upon our College Affair, & told him the whole story & he says if I have related things as they are he should have no Objection to taking any that would come of good Caracter. He told me the Plan of Study they went upon which I like pretty will, & told me if any of us determin'd to come he would have us take a Ride up & see them first. I talk'd with him at Capt. Greenliefs, & he appears to be very much of a Gentleman.

I saw Mr. Herrick as I went over & went with him to where I us'd to bord & drank Tea the[n] I came over the Ferry a little before no[on] & rode towards two Miles &c.

James MANNING (1738–91), Princeton A.B. 1762, was the first president of Rhode Island College. In 1768, the school, which probably had fewer than twenty students, was not above taking advantage of Harvard's crisis to add to its student body. CAPT. William GREENLEAF of Haverhill was a militia officer. *Princetonians*, 1:389–93; *Historical Catalogue of Brown University, 1764–1904* (Providence, R.I., 1905), 67–68, 595; Chase, *History of Haverhill*, 357, 367.

Saturday the 14th of May.

To Day is rainey. I wrote a Letter to my quondam Class-mate Sargeant & then I took a Walk up to Capt. Osgoods [to] see my good Friend Samuel where I din['d] & then he went up with me to see my as good a Friend Chum where we spent the P.M. & drank Tea had a pleasant Sing & Chat. Esqr. Phillips is very Sociable & exceeding Friendly, & thinks these College Affairs will be talk'd of in the Court. I left my Letters, & my Chum walk'd with us down to the Capts. & then left us. Osgood talks of going to Cambridge the beginning of the Week. I took leave of him, & came Home call'd at Samuel Johnsons by the Way. I have had an exceeding agreeable Visit to Day. Last Night Dow came here from College & stay'd all Night (my Chum came to accompany him down & went back). He brings nothing new from there. Says he intends to go down & get in again. He went from here about nine o Clock with Cushing who lives with Doctr. Osgood.

Peabody viewed publicity about the college crisis as his friend, since he continued to believe that the fault lay primarily with the faculty and its autocratic behavior toward the students. He must have welcomed the opinion of Samuel PHILLIPS, A.B. 1734, one of Andover's leading citizens, that the Massachusetts legislature would soon investigate the situation. Still, by calling Christopher Sergeant, A.B. 1769, his QUONDAM, or former, classmate, Peabody conceded how unpromising his circumstances were.

Sunday the 15th.

To Day is pleasant & cool. I went on foot to Meeting to Boxford & heard Mr. Adams preach A.M. from the 24th of Acts & 25th Verse. P.M. he preach'd very Well from the 72 Psalm 2 Verse. I din'd at Decn. Chadwicks & came there after servise with Mr. Adams where I stay'd some Time & eat again. Got Home a little after Sun down & read in The Crook in the Lot. Br. John went to Haverhill [. . .][1] & heard Mr. Murry preach excellently at Mr. Smith's Meeting-House.

MURRAY was presumably John Murray (1742–93), University of Edinburgh A.B. 1761, at the time the minister of the Congregational church in Boothbay, Maine, and later the minister of the Presbyterian church in Newburyport, not to be confused with the Universalist minister of the same name. Weis, *Colonial Clergy*, 148; *Princetonians*, 1:411–13.

1. Illegible [one word].

Monday the 16th of May.

To Day is worm & Pleasant. I went down early in Mane to Thos. Osgoods in Order to see Mr. Manning as he went to Boston. I breakfasted there & stay'd till near eliven oClock, & he did not come, so I went Home, & went down there again about three, & he had been there & was gone, so that I did not see him. I came Home & wrote largely in Journal. Mehetabel Day was at Work here & there was a Number of Garls came here a visiting & stay'd till some Time in the Evening & I play'd on the Fiddle to them, & then they went away & I took my Camel & took a ride a few Miles &c.

Tuesday the 17th.

To Day is very worm. I felt not right. Went to work P.M. & labored smartly carrying out Doar-Dung. Wm. Croos was here making a Plow to Day. Susannah Robinson was here A.M. In the Evening Hipsabah Kimbal came here & stay'd all Night.

Br. John & his Wife went to Newbu[ry] to Day & I began a Letter for him to [. . .][1] Br. Israel Perley, & he is to finish it [in] Newbury.

Peabody was now undertaking some of the farm's more distasteful chores, including carrying the DOOR DUNG, "a manure taken from the back yards and doors of dwellings." In addition to animal waste it often contained wood chips and sweepings. SUSANNAH ROBINSON was possibly Susannah Robinson (b. 1746) of Andover. Samuel Deane, *The New-England Farmer; or, Georgical Dictionary*, 3rd edn. (Boston, 1822), 109; *Vital Records of Andover*, 1:318.

1. Torn [one word].

Wednesday the 18th of May.

To Day is worm. I work'd a little help[ed] Br. John out with a Load or two of Dung. A.M. & read a Sermon which was printed by one Caldwell which is pretty Sensible. P.M. I mended & fix'd up some of my Things a little. Drank Tea in the other Room. In the Evening Wyman came here for a Bed Quilt for Mrs. Williams. Hipsabah Kimbal went from here & the Garls walk'd part of the Way with her, & I kept on quite up to Br. Olivers where she stay'd all Night. I went to Supper there & stay'd till about 11 o Clock & then I came home across the Farm. Nihil majus hodie.[1]

1. Nothing important today.

Thursday the 19th.

To Day is Worm. I wrote a little & read some in The Crook in the Lot, & some in A History of The Devil which Br. John borrow'd of Lieut. Foster & a very drole Peice it is as I ever saw. P.M. I went out with my Father & help'd him plant his little Field of Corn & it took us till Night. In the Evening [L]emuel Wood & John Chadwick came [h]ere & stay'd till late. Nihil majus.

Daniel Defoe wrote *A Political History of the Devil* (many editions). Lieutenant FOSTER was Peabody's cousin Jonathan Foster, who had been a lieutenant in the Seven Years' War. LEMUEL WOOD, or Woods, may have been the resident of that name in Groton (b. 1742). Pierce, *Foster Genealogy*, 148, 193; Henry Ernest Woods, "The Woods Family of Groton, Mass.," *NEHGR* 64 (1910): 147.

Friday the 20th of May.

To Day is clear & Hot. A little after Six o Clock I was surpriz'd by seeing Master Moody & my Chum come here. The old Gentleman came [t]o see me about College Affairs. Has [rec]eiv'd a Letter from Mr. Sewall, & there seems to be a little Incourigement for me to apply again. Mr. Moody is very full of Discourse. He stop'd & breakfasted & I drest myself, & my Chum & I accompany'd him down into new Rowley & then parted with him. I am to go & see him the latter End of next Week.

We went from there to Haverhill, & I parted with my Chum, & went up to Plastow to see my Class-Mate Dow. Got there a little after noon but he was gone from Home & I did not see him. I stay'd there till a little after 5, & eat, & drank Tea, & had a long Talk with Doctr. Peabody & Mrs. Night who were there. I came from there down to Mr. Merrils, made a short stop, & then came down to Haverhill & came over the Ferry. Took a ride ubi videbam[1] Daniel Hardy sed sine successu.[2] I came home & Daniel Jaquish was at Br. Johns, & we stood out in the Yard & talk'd till very late & then he went Home.

Gyles MERRILL (1739–1801), A.B. 1759, was the minister in Plaistow, New Hampshire. *Sibley's Harvard Graduates*, 14:466–68.

1. Where I saw.
2. But without success.

Saturday the 21 of May.

To Day is remarkable Hot ti[ll] just Night & then came up cool. Was writing Letters all Day to C[ollege] to my Friends there. Just at Nigh[t] I rode the Colt to John Days, & pay'd him for his Horse to Newbury Port. Th[e] Colt pitch'd me over his Head but di[d] no hurt.

Sunday the 22d.

To Day is a cloudy & cool Wind East. I went to meeting to Andover & heard Mr. Barnard of Haverhill preach A.M. from the 15th of Job. 21 Verse. P.M. he preach'd well but the Text I have forgot. I din'd with my Chum, heard him read in Jenks's Meditations. When Meeting was done it rain'd fast Wind N.E. & I came Home & was pretty Wet. I finish'd reading The Crook in the Lot. I hear'd this Morning that Scales lodg'd last Night at Hoveys, & is gone down to preach at Bradford to Day.

Benjamin JENKS wrote *MEDITATIONS with Short Prayers Annexed* (London, 1701).

Monday the 23d.

To Day is cool. I seal'd my Letters, & Uncle Robinson & Mr. Ingals came here & hinder'd me some Time. I took the Colt & went up to Andover, call'd at Doctr. Osgoods, & then went up to Esqr. Phillipss where I stay'd & [din]'d again upon Salmon. Talk'd longly [wi]th the Esqr. & my Chum & had a [p]leasant Sing. Went over to see Mr. [Sy]mmes & he says he is going to [Ca]mbridge & will talk with the Tutors [a]bout my Affair, but seems to speak against the Scholars & treated me pretty [re]servedly & I have no Charity for his [F]riendship. I came from there, & from Esqrs. See Porter & stop'd at the Doctrs. a while again & then I came Home. Took my Mare & went down to Boxford & Sister Woods where I tarry'd all Night. I stop'd with Jonathan Foster a while a going along.

Thus I have wrote the Transactions of another Year which has brought about such Embarrassments & Difficulties as I never before had Experience of. May the Fruit of Affliction be to take away my Sin, & may I daily acknowledge God in all his Ways.

Finis.

How Vain are earthly fleeting Joys,
A Labrynth of glittering Toys,
The Gayest Welth between the Gales,
Cant Satisfy immortal Souls.

Nathaniel PORTER (1745–1836), A.B. 1768, of Topsfield, became the minister of the First Church in North Conway, New Hampshire. A source for the closing verse has not been found, so it may be Peabody's own composition. *Sibley's Harvard Graduates*, 17:82–86.

APPENDIX ONE

Stephen Peabody's Family

May 24, 1767–May 23, 1768

In the course of his diary for 1767–68, Stephen Peabody mentioned dozens of relatives. This appendix reports on the journal appearances for those closest to him in his parents' generation, his own, and that of his nieces and nephews.

Paternal Line

Father

John Peabody (1695–1780), 40 appearances

Aunts and Uncles

Stephen (1685–1759); m. Hannah (Swan, d. 1764)
Mary (b. 1687), no appearances; m. Joseph Symonds, no appearances
Ephraim (1689–1740); m. Hannah (Redington), no appearances
Richard (1691–1769), moved to Pomfret, Connecticut, in 1735, no appearances; m. Ruth (Kimball), no appearances

Sources: *Peabody Genealogy,* 19–20, 23–26, 32–38; *Vital Records of Andover,* 1:343, 346, 347, 351, 2:549, 579; *Vital Records of Boxford,* 97–98, 106–7, 206–7, 267; Pierce, *Foster Genealogy,* 134, 148; Morrison and Sharples, *Kimball Family,* 84, 148–51; Edmond Frank Peters, comp., *Peters of New England: A Genealogy and Family History* (New York: Knickerbocker Press, 1903), 102–3; George A. Gordon and Silas R. Coburn, prep., *Genealogy of the Descendants of Edward Colburn/Coburn* (Lowell, Mass.: W. Colburn, 1913), 48; Franklin Abbott Dorman, *Thomas Dorman of Topsfield, Massachusetts* (Bowie, Md.: Heritage Books, 1994), 1:43, 411; Richard Safford Hale, *Genealogy of the Descendants of Thomas Hale* (Albany, 1889), 43–44; Henry S. Nourse, ed., *The Birth, Marriage and Death Register, Church Records and Epitaphs of Lancaster, Massachusetts, 1643–1850* (Lancaster, Mass., 1890), 71, 74, 76; Franklin T. Cole, *The Early Genealogy of the Cole Family in America* (Columbus, Ohio, 1887), 32, 118; *Genealogy: Solomon Keyes of Newbury and Chelmsford, Mass., and His Descendants, 1653–1880, 2nd Part* (Brattleboro, Vt., 1880), 27–28; Robert Brand Hanson, ed., *Vital Records of Needham, Massachusetts, 1711–1845* (Camden, Maine: Picton Press, 1997), 21, 164; *The Holyoke Diaries, 1709–1856* (Salem, Mass.: Essex Institute, 1911), xvi.

Hannah (1693–1769), no appearances; m. Jonathan Foster, 7 appearances
Oliver (1698–1752), m. Hannah (Baxter), no appearances
Abial (1700–1791), 2 appearances; m. Joseph Kimball, 6 appearances

SIBLINGS

Sarah (b. 1723), 7 appearances; m. (1) James Stevens (1721–55); m. (2) John Peters, 12 appearances
Oliver (1725–96), 33 appearances; m. Sarah (Robinson), 5 appearances
Mehitable (b. 1727), 18 appearances; m. Solomon Wood, no appearances
John (1730–32)
John (1732–1820), 55 appearances; m. Mary (Perley), 3 appearances
Elizabeth (b. 1735), 1 appearance; m. Moses Coburn, 1 appearance
Mary (1737–38)
Mary (1739–1809), 6 appearances; unmarried
Rebecca (1746–1806), 4 appearances; m. Alexander Montgomery in 1785

COUSINS

Stephen had approximately thirty-nine living cousins on his father's side in 1767–68. Of them, eight male cousins and one female cousin made appearances: Richard (son of Stephen), 1; Abigail Keyes (daughter of Richard), 2; Nathaniel (son of Ephraim), 10; Jonathan Foster, 3 or 4, and Richard Foster, 1 (both sons of Hannah Foster); and Joseph Kimball, 2, Richard Kimball, 5, Daniel Kimball, 1, and Francis Kimball, 5 (all sons of Abial Kimball). In addition, Stephen also mentioned Abigail Keyes's husband, Stephen, once and her son Amasa twice as well as Richard Kimball's wife, Annie, once, and Hannah (Peabody) Holyoke's husband, Reverend Elizur Holyoke, the minister of the East Parish in Boxford and a nephew of President Edward Holyoke, four times.

NIECES AND NEPHEWS

During the year of this diary, Peabody had ten nephews and seven nieces. None of the nieces but five of the nephews appear in the journal: sister Sarah's sons James Stevens (6), Jonathan Stevens (2), and Joseph Peters (1), as well as brother Oliver's sons Oliver (5) and Stephen (1), whose death is reported on April 29.

Maternal Line

MOTHER

Sarah (Head) Peabody (1702–80), 3 appearances

AUNTS AND UNCLES

Joannah Pike (b. 1711), no appearances; m. John Chaney, no appearances

Elisabeth Pike (b. 1712), no appearances; m. Benjamin Morrill, no appearances
Rebecca Pike (b. 1714), no appearances; m. Elisha Sawyer, 1 appearance

Cousins

Stephen seems to have had eight cousins on his mother's side, seven of whom were living at the time of his journal, six girls and one boy. None of them appears in the diary.

Nieces and Nephews

No nieces and nephews on Stephen's mother's side appear in his diary.

APPENDIX TWO

Harvard College Corporation, Faculty, Staff, and Students

May 24, 1767–May 23, 1768

Corporation

Edward Holyoke (1689–1769), A.B. 1705, Tutor, 1712–16, President and Fellow, 1737–69; 36 appearances (also Faculty)
Nathaniel Appleton (1693–1784), A.B. 1712, Fellow, 1717–79; 31 appearances
Thomas Hubbard (1702–73), A.B. 1721, Treasurer and Fellow, 1752–73; 1 appearance
Belcher Hancock (1709–71), A.B. 1727, Fellow, 1760–67; 7 appearances (also Faculty)
John Winthrop (1714–79), A.B. 1732, Fellow, 1765–79; 15 appearances (also Faculty)
Andrew Eliot (1718–78), A.B. 1737, Fellow, 1765–78; no appearances
Samuel Cooper (1725–83), A.B. 1743, Fellow, 1767–78; no appearances
Thomas Danforth (1744–1820), A.B. 1762, Fellow, 1767–68; 20 appearances (also Faculty)

Faculty (in order of rank and date of appointment)

Edward Holyoke (see Corporation)
John Winthrop (see Corporation)
Edward Wigglesworth (1732–94), A.B. 1749, Hollis Professor of Divinity, 1765–91; 23 appearances

Sources: *Quinquennial Catalogue of the Officers and Graduates of Harvard University, 1636–1905* (Cambridge, Mass., 1905), 9, 12, 13, 21, 26, 30, 33, 39, 95–96, 130–33; *Sibley's Harvard Graduates,* 5:265–78, 599–609, 6:490–95, 8:137–40, 720–23, 9:240–64, 10:128–61, 11:192–213, 12:507–16, 15:80–82, 107–14, 217–20, 492–93, 224–29, 16:253–65, 250–51, 440–552, 17:*passim,* 18:144–48; Corporation Records, 2:276–77; Paige, *History of Cambridge,* 576, 484, 680; Gozzaldi, *Supplement to Paige,* 30, 627, 360, 377.

Stephen Sewall (1734–1804), A.B. 1761, Librarian, 1762–63, Hancock Professor of Hebrew and Other Oriental Languages, 1764–85; 12 appearances
Belcher Hancock (see Corporation)
Thomas Danforth (see Corporation)
Joseph Willard (1738–1804), A.B. 1764, Tutor, 1766–72, President, 1781–1804; 36 appearances
Stephen Scales (1741–72), A.B. 1763, Tutor, 1767–70; 33 appearances
Andrew Eliot (1744–1805), A.B. 1762, Librarian, 1763–67, Tutor, 1767–74; 15 appearances
Jonathan Moore (1739–1814), A.B. 1761, Librarian, 1768; 1 appearance

Staff

Jonathan Hastings (1709–83), A.B. 1730, Steward, 1750–79; 8 appearances
Elizabeth Hastings (c. 1722–82), supervisor of College Commons (unofficial); no appearances
Nathaniel Ward (1746–68), A.B. 1765, Butler, 1766–68, Librarian, 1768; 6 appearances
Margaret Barret (c. 1710–94), College Sexton (part time); no appearances
Abraham Hasey (n.d.), College Carpenter (on call); no appearances
Moses Richardson (1722–75), College Carpenter (on call); 1 appearance
Jonathan Watson (b. 1732), College Carpenter (on call); no appearances
Samuel Hastings (1724–85), College Glazier (on call); 2 appearances
Aaron Hill (1730–92), College Mason (on call); 2 appearances
Isaac Bradish (1723–90), College Smith (on call); 4 possible appearances
James Munroe (1735–1804), College Smith (on call); 1 appearance
Mrs. Pierce or Pearce, Sweeper
The college also employed an uncounted number of unidentified "sweepers" (cleaning ladies) and cooks.

Students*

Class of 1767

Thomas Bernard (1750–1818), of Boston; 1 appearance
Adam Winthrop (1748–74), of Cambridge; no appearances
Edward Oxnard (1747–1803), of Boston; no appearances
Lemuel Cushing (1746–76), of Scituate; member, Association for the Suppression of Vice; 1 appearance
Samuel Hancock (1744–75), of Martha's Vineyard; member, Association for the Suppression of Vice; no appearances

* In the order of the published rank list. Adapted from *Sibley's Harvard Graduates,* 16:440–41; 17:2–3, 114–15, 332–33, 466–67, to correspond to student status in 1767–68.

Isaac Mansfield (1750–1826), of Marblehead; no appearances
Josiah Moulton (1749–96), of Hampton, N.H.; 1 appearance
John Rogers (1748–1827), of Gloucester; no appearances
Isaac Smith (1749–1829), of Boston; member, Association for the Suppression of Vice; Tutor, 1774-75; Librarian, 1787–91; 8 appearances
Daniel Johnson (1747–77), of Bridgewater; no appearances
Simon Tufts (1750–1802), of Medford; no appearances
William Mayhew (1746–85), of Martha's Vineyard; member, Association for the Suppression of Vice; Librarian, 1769–72; no appearances
Zephaniah Briggs (1742–c. 1785), of Rochester; no appearances
Elisha Thayer (1748–74), of Braintree; no appearances
Henry Herrick (1748–1800), of Beverly; 1 appearance
Edmund Freeman (1750–80), of Marblehead; no appearances
Burrill Devereaux (1747–96), of Marblehead; no appearances
John Marston Minot (1747–c. 1833), of Jamaica, W.I.; no appearances
Samuel Willard (1748–1811), of Worcester; no appearances
Increase Sumner (1746–99), of Roxbury; no appearances
Nicholas Dudley (1740–c. 1836), of Epping, N.H.; no appearances
Abraham Wood (1748–1823), of Sudbury; 2 appearances
William Moore (1745–c. 1776), of Cambridge; no appearances
William Turner (1747–1808), of Scituate; no appearances
Jeremiah Shaw (1747–1834), of Hampton, N.H.; no appearances
Simeon Chase (1745–1829), of Newbury; 1 appearance
Enos Hitchcock (1745–1803), of Brookfield; no appearances
Samuel Cheney (1745–1820), of Roxbury; 1 appearance
Asa Dunbar (1745–87), of Bridgewater; no appearances
Sylvanus Ames (1744–78), of Bridgewater; no appearances
Timothy Farrar (1747–1849), of Lincoln; no appearances
Joseph Farrar (1744–1816), of Lincoln; member, Association for the Suppression of Vice; no appearances
Nathaniel Kidder (1747–1828), of Cambridge; no appearances
Jonathan Frost (1744–71), of Cambridge (Menotomy); member, Association for the Suppression of Vice; no appearances
Asarelah Morse (1745–1803), of Falmouth; no appearances
Aaron Bordman (1746–72), of Cambridge; 1 appearance
William Gamage (1748–1821), of Cambridge; no appearances
John Porter (1748–1813), of Boxford; 22 appearances
Amos Cotting (1749–1807), of Waltham; no appearances
Moses Holt (1744–72), of Andover; member, Association for the Suppression of Vice; 13 appearances
William Kelly (1744–1813), of Hampstead, N.H.; no appearances
Nathaniel Merrill (1743–91), of Plaistow, N.H.; member, Association for the Suppression of Vice; 2 appearances

Class of 1768

Roland Cushing (1750–88), of Scituate; 3 appearances
William Paine (1750–1833), of Worcester; no appearances
Nathaniel Chandler (1750–1801), of Worcester; 1 appearance
Henry Sewall (1750–72), of Brookline; 2 appearances
Andrew Henshaw (1752–82), of Boston; 2 appearances
William Hunt (1750–1804), of Cambridge; 1 appearance
David Greene (1749–1812), of Boston; 7 appearances
Ebenezer Sayer (1751–78), of Wells, Maine; Dummer Academy; 4 appearances
Thomas Leonard (1744–71), of Norton; 2 appearances
Jonathan Hastings (1751–1831), of Cambridge; 1768 deposition (mentions SP); 1 appearance
Kenneth McKenzie (1746–98), Martin County, N.C.; member, Association for the Suppression of Vice; 1 appearance
James Diman (1750–1823), of Salem; no appearances
John Wentworth (1745–87), of Somersworth, N.H.; Dummer Academy; 12 appearances
Jeremiah Fogg (1749–1808), of Kensington, N.H.; 12 appearances
John Ballantine (1749–1832), of Westfield; no appearances
Gad Hitchcock (1749–1836), of Pembroke; no appearances
Benjamin West (1746–1817), of Martha's Vineyard; 2 appearances
Lawrence Sprague (1748–c. 1785), of Boston; no appearances
Timothy Orne (1750–89), of Salem; no appearances
Obadiah Parsons (1747–1801), of Newbury; Dummer Academy; approximately 5 appearances
Joseph Thaxter (1742–1827), of Hingham; 1768 deposition; 3 appearances
William Fessenden (1750–1805), of Cambridge; 1 appearance
Samuel Hill (1750–69), of Boston; 4 appearances
John Coffin Jones (1750–1829), of Boston; 5 appearances
Ephraim Wales (1745–1805), of Braintree; no appearances
Lemuel Hayward (1749–1821), of Braintree; no appearances
Samuel Parker (1740–1811), of Barnstable; no appearances
Isaac Knowles (1741–1818), of Eastham; 8 appearances
Jonathan Smith (1748–1829), of Hadley; 2 possible appearances
Aaron Bascom (1746–1814), of Western (renamed Warren); no appearances
David Tenny (1749–78), of Rowley; Dummer Academy; member, Association for the Suppression of Vice; 60 appearances
Joseph Cummings (1745–88), of Ipswich; 1 appearance
Timothy Upham (1748–1811), of Malden; 2 appearances
Benjamin Hichborn (1746–1817), of Boston; 2 appearances
Moses Brown (1748–1820), of Waltham; no appearances
Thomas Emery (1750–70), of Newbury; Dummer Academy; 6 appearances
Nathaniel Porter (1745–1836), of Topsfield; 1 appearance

Daniel Newcomb (1747–1818), of Norton (Mansfield); no appearances
Jonathan Gove (1746–1818), of Lincoln; 1 appearance
Ebenezer Starr (1744–98), of Dedham; no appearances
Samuel Nutting (1744–97), of Cambridge; no appearances
William Keous (1741–1814), of Dedham; member, Association for the Suppression of Vice; no appearances

CLASS OF 1769

Peter Oliver (1749–95), of Boston; Dummer Academy; no appearances
James Winthrop (1752–1821), of Cambridge; College Librarian, 1772–87; 2 appearances
John Williams (1751–1816), of Deerfield; 1768 deposition (mentions SP); 1 possible appearance
Peter Thacher (1752–1802), of Boston; 1768 deposition (mentions SP); 14 appearances
Joseph Lee (1748–85), of Marblehead; 2 appearances
Christopher Sargeant (1747–78), of Methuen; 13 appearances
Nehemiah Williams (1749–96), of Hadley; 1768 deposition (mentions SP); 1 possible appearance
Theophilus Parsons (1750–1813), of Newbury; Dummer Academy; Fellow, 1806–12; at least 11 appearances plus 23 possible
William Tudor (1750–1819), of Boston; 1768 deposition (mentions SP); 8 appearances
John Bulkley (1749–74), of Groton; 2 appearances
Nathaniel Webster (1749–1830); Dummer Academy; 2 1768 depositions (both mention SP); 22 appearances
Thomas Kast (1750–1820), of Boston; 2 1768 depositions; 7 appearances
Peter Coffin (1752–1821), of Gloucester; Dummer Academy; 1768 deposition (mentions SP); 2 appearances
Nathaniel Tracy (1751–96), of Newburyport; 1768 deposition (mentions SP); 5 appearances
Nathaniel Harrington (1750–81), of Watertown; 1768 deposition; no appearances
James Mitchell Varnum (1748–89), of Dracut; 15 appearances
Isaac Biglow (1750–77), of Weston; 1 appearance
Jonathan Williams Austin (1751–79), of Boston; 18 appearances
Daniel Jones (1750–79), of Boston; 2 appearances
John Frye (1750–?), of Andover; Dummer Academy; did not graduate; 26 appearances
Jonas Dix (1749–96), of Waltham; no appearances
George Wheaton (1751–73), of Norton; 1768 deposition; 2 appearances
Alexander Scammell (1747–81), of Mendon; member, Association for the Suppression of Vice; 1768 deposition (mentions SP); 21 appearances
William Bowers (1744–1820), of Billerica; member, Association for the Suppression of Vice; 24 appearances

Benjamin Wadsworth (1750–1826), of Milton; 2 appearances plus 3 possible
Peleg Wadsworth (1748–1829), of Duxbury; 3 appearances plus 3 possible
James Blake (1751–71), of Dorchester; 1768 deposition (mentions SP); no appearances
Ebenezer Bradish (1746–1818), of Cambridge; 4 appearances
Elias Fisher (1749–1831), of Wrentham; 5 appearances
Benjamin Guild (1749–92), of Wrentham; 1768 deposition; Tutor, 1776–80; 4 appearances
Thomas Moore (1745–96), of Bolton; 2 appearances
Jacob Jewett (1747–1812), of Rowley; Dummer Academy; "quondam" roommate; 1768 deposition (mentions SP); 38 appearances
Noah Cooke (1749–1829), of Hadley; 1768 deposition (mentions SP); 1 appearance
William Goodhue (1747–82), of Waltham; 2 appearances
Elijah Fletcher (1747–86), of Westford; member, Association for the Suppression of Vice; 1768 deposition; 11 appearances
Joseph Adams (1749–68), of Rowley; Dummer Academy; did not graduate; 14 appearances
Stephen Peabody (1741–1819), of Andover; Dummer Academy; member, Association for the Suppression of Vice
Samuel Whiting (1750–1819), of Wrentham; 1768 deposition (mentions SP); 1 appearance
Benjamin Bradshaw (1749–79), of Stoughton; member, Association for the Suppression of Vice; 1768 deposition; no appearances
Samuel Coolidge (1751–90), of Watertown; 4 appearances
David Jewett (1744–83), of Boxford; Dummer Academy; member, Association for the Suppression of Vice; 23 appearances
Palsgrave Wellington (1748–1808), of Cambridge; graduated after rustication with the class of 1770; 4 appearances
Moses Dow (1747–1811), of Plaistow, N.H.; member, Association for the Suppression of Vice; 7 appearances

Class of 1770

William Sanford Hutchinson (1752–80), of Boston; 1 appearance plus 1 possible
Gilbert Saltonstall (1752–97), of New London, Conn.; 1 appearance
William Winthrop (1753–1826), of Cambridge; no appearances
John Winthrop (1751–80), of New London, Conn.; 1768 deposition; no appearances
Daniel Rogers (1749–1804), of Littleton; 2 depositions (both mention SP); graduated with the class of 1771; 4 appearances
Paul Langdon (1752–1834), of Portsmouth, N.H.; 1 possible appearance
Ward Chipman (1754–1824), of Marblehead; 1768 deposition (mentions SP); 1 appearance
Jonathan Stearns (1751–98), of Lunenburg; 1768 deposition; 3 possible appearances

Amariah Frost (1750–1819), of Mendon; 1768 deposition; 1 appearance
John Mellen (1752–1828), of Lancaster; 1768 deposition; Tutor, 1780–83; no appearances
Aaron Hutchinson (1754–1843), of Grafton; 1768 deposition; 1 possible appearance
Jeremiah Hill (1747–1820), of Biddeford, Maine; Dummer Academy; no appearances
Jonathan Newell (1749–1830), of Needham; 1768 deposition; 4 appearances
Edward Sprague (1750–1817), of Boston; no appearances
Samuel Adams (1751–88), of Boston; 1768 deposition (mentions SP); no appearances
Winthrop Sargent (1753–1820), of Gloucester; 1768 deposition (mentions SP); graduated with the class of 1771; 4 appearances
George Cabot (1752–1823), of Salem; did not graduate; 3 appearances
Samuel Osgood (1748–1813), of Andover; Dummer Academy; 1768 deposition; 77 appearances
Joseph Hunt (1750–1812), of Concord; 1768 deposition; 1 appearance
Zebulon Butler (1749–90), of Edgartown; 1768 deposition; 1 appearance
William Wetmore (1749–1830), of Middletown, Conn.; 1768 deposition (mentions SP); 3 appearances
Joshua Dodge (1752–1814), of Salem; graduated with the class of 1771; 4 appearances
John Gill (1750–1804), of Cambridge; 1768 deposition; graduated with the class of 1771; 4 appearances
Ebenezer Putnam (1750–76), of Danvers; graduated with the class of 1771; 3 appearances
Jonathan Barns (1749–1805), of Marlborough; 1 appearance
Abner Smith (1744–1843), of Springfield; 1768 deposition; 2 possible appearances
Nathan Goddard (1747–95), of Shrewsbury; 1 appearance
Samuel Sheldon Pool (1751–1835), of Reading; 1 appearance
Thomas Colman (1751–81), of Byfield; Dummer Academy; 7 appearances
William Stearns (1749–83), of Lunenburg; 1768 deposition; 3 possible appearances
Benjamin Chadwick (1745–1819), of Boxford; Dummer Academy; 29 appearances
Isaac Stone (1748–1837), of Shrewsbury; 2 appearances
Gad Stebbins (1748–1826), of Springfield; graduated with the class of 1771; 4 appearances
Henry Bright (1744–74), of Spencer; 7 appearances
Moses Adams (1749–1819), of Hopkinton; 1768 deposition; graduated with the class of 1771; 1 appearance
David Townsend (1753–1829), of Boston; 2 appearances
Joseph Pope (1746–1826), of Pomfret, Conn.; no appearances
Hezekiah Taylor (1748–1814), of Grafton; 2 appearances
Jonathan Hicks (1752–1826), of Cambridge; no appearances
Owen Warland (1752–75), of Cambridge; no appearances

Jacob Burnap (1748–1821), of Reading; 1768 deposition; 2 appearances
Aaron Crosby (1745–1824), of Shrewsbury; 2 appearances
Thurston Whiting (1753–1829), of Wrentham; did not graduate; 11 appearances

Class of 1771

Samuel Hirst Sparhawk (1752–89), of Kittery, Maine; no appearances
James Bowdoin (1752–1811), of Boston; Fellow, 1792–99; 1 appearance
Andrew Bradford (1745–1837), of Duxbury; no appearances
Samuel Paine (1754–1807), of Worcester; 1768 deposition (mentions SP); 1 appearance
Edward Kitchen Turner (1751–c. 1785), of Salem; no appearances
William Vassell (1753–1843), of Boston; no appearances
Daniel Murray (1751–1832), of Rutland; no appearances
Samuel Ruddock (1752–73), of Boston; 1768 deposition; graduated with the class of 1772; no appearances
Joseph Emerson (1751–1822), of Topsfield; Dummer Academy; 7 appearances
John Alford Mason (1750–1831), of Charlestown; 1 appearance
David Parsons (1749–1823), of Amherst; 1768 deposition (mentions SP); no appearances
Walter Hastings (1752–82), of Cambridge; 1 appearance
Jacob Bacon (1751–1816), of Plymouth; no appearances
Samuel Phillips (1752–1802), of Andover; Dummer Academy; roommate; 1768 deposition (mentions SP); 76 appearances
Moses Hale (1749–86), of Newbury; Dummer Academy; 3 appearances
William Gay Ballantine (1751–1820), of Westfield; 1 appearance
William Vinal (1752–81), of Newport, R.I.; no appearances
David Tappan (1752–1803), of Manchester; Dummer Academy; Hollis Professor of Divinity, 1792–1803; no appearances
Samuel Plummer (1752–c. 1815), of Gloucester; Dummer Academy; 1 appearance
John Barnard Swett (1752–96), of Marblehead; 3 appearances
John White (1752–1816), of Haverhill; Dummer Academy; 4 appearances
Robert Roberts (1754–1801), of Newburyport; Dummer Academy; no appearances
John Tracy (1753–1815), of Newburyport; Dummer Academy; 1 appearance
Joseph Pearse Palmer (1750–97), of Germantown; 2 appearances
William Cheever (1752–86), of Boston; no appearances
Greenleaf Dole (1751–1829), of Rowley; 1768 deposition; 3 appearances
Zedekiah Sanger (1748–1820), of Sherborn; no appearances
Isaac Bangs (1752–1780), of Harwich; 1768 deposition (mentions SP); 1 appearance
Daniel Tyler (1750–1832), of Canterbury, Conn.; 3 appearances
Joseph Avery (1751–1824), of Dedham; no appearances
John Frothingham (1750–1826), of Charlestown; Dummer Academy; 1768 deposition (mentions SP); 1 appearance

Michael Joy (1754–1825), of Boston; 1768 deposition (mentions SP); no appearances

David Osgood (1748–1822), of Andover; 3 appearances

John Warren (1753–1815), of Roxbury; Hersey Professor of Anatomy and Surgery, 1782–1815; no appearances

Thomas Sanders (1753–95), of Gloucester; graduated with the class of 1772; no appearances

Crocker Sampson (1749–1823), of Kingston; no appearances

William Scott (1749–c. 1806), of Palmer; no appearances

Samuel Prentice (1753–1815), of Cambridge; 1 appearance

Thomas Edwards (1753–1806), of Boston; 1768 deposition (mentions SP); 1 appearance

Perez Morton (1751–1837), of Boston; 1768 deposition (mentions SP); no appearances

Jonathan Norwood (1751–82), of Lynn; 1768 deposition; no appearances

Melzar Turner Oakman (1750–96), of Marshfield; no appearances

Israel Keith (1751–1819), of Easton; no appearances

Abraham Watson (1752–c. 1804), of Cambridge; 1768 deposition (mentions SP); 3 appearances

Nathaniel Dickinson (1751–1802), of Amherst; 1768 deposition; no appearances

John Noyes (1750–1819), of Newbury; Dummer Academy; 20 appearances

Moses Everett (1750–1813), of Dedham; no appearances

Samuel Wheeler (1748–1817), of Byfield; Dummer Academy; 2 appearances

Samuel Nye (1749–1837), of Harwich; 1768 deposition; no appearances

Thomas Little (1750–71), of Shirley; 1768 deposition; no appearances

Amos Windship (1745–1813), of Springfield; 2 appearances

Benjamin Curtis (1753–84), of Roxbury; 1768 deposition (mentions SP); 1 appearance

Jonathan French (1740–1809), of Braintree; 6 appearances

David Stinson (1744–69), of Woolwich, Maine; did not graduate; no appearances

Moses Johnson (1751–73), of Rowley; Dummer Academy; 1 appearance

Jedidiah Estabrook (1741–82), of Paxton; 1 appearance

Ebenezer Allen (1748–1806), of Tisbury; 1768 deposition; 1 appearance

William Scales (1741–1807), of Georgetown; no appearances

Benjamin Hasey (1752–?), of Cambridge; 1768 deposition (mentions SP); no appearances

APPENDIX THREE

Peter Thacher's "Account of the Late Disturbances & Commotions"

Peter Thacher to Jeremy Belknap[1]

Milton, April 20th, 1768.

Dear Sir,—I this morning received your very welcome epistle, and permit me in answer thereto sincerely to congratulate you & your dear lady on her safe delivery.[2] May the God of mercy perfect his begun goodness unto her, bless & prosper the tender babe. May it live & be a great blessing to its parents. Very sensible I am, revd. sir, (permit me to say, from experience,) that the votaries of God & of virtue alone enjoy true happiness. Now, sir, if you please, I will give you an account of the late disturbances & commotions in our *Alma Mater.*

But before I begin the unwelcome tale, let me tell you that, in all this rebellion (as it is called), I myself have had no part; to this I doubt not you will give entire credit, as my tutors, the governors of the College, & my freinds in Boston are entirely satisfied with my conduct. The tutors on Monday morning told the scholars that they had entered into an agreement to excuse no scholars from reciting, unless they shoud first ask leave of them therefor. This the scholars esteemed a great greivance, & made objections to their tutors; yet they overruled them all, & punished some that were absent. Upon the scholars going out from their respective tutors' chambers, they hiss'd & clap'd, &c., & in the evening Mr. Danforth's windows were broke by some persons unknown. The tutors prosecuted the affair the next day, & in the evening Mr. Willard's & Mr. Scales' windows were broke; on Wednesday in the afternoon some persons unknown broke into Mr Willard's chamber, destro[y]ed his glass, his teacups, &c.; on Thursday in the foreno[on] the President, professors, & tutors met in order to discover something of a class meeting wh the several classes had had in order to consult upon the affair, but discovered nothing. On Friday they met again, and met with the same success.

1. Peter Thacher to Jeremy Belknap, April 20, 1768, *Collections of the Massachusetts Historical Society,* 6th ser., 4 (1891): 25–28.
2. Belknap's daughter Sarah was born on April 7, 1768.

On Saturday evening there was a report in College that Mr Willard had shut up one Whiting in his study without fire or victuals from 8 o'clock A. M. till 3 P. M., in order to make him confess something in relation to the breaking of his glass; but you should observe that ths Whitg had been detected fastening the chapel door, when Mr. Willard was there with his class reciting. This story had a natural tendency to enrage the minds of the scholars, and the same evening as 2 of the tutors were in Mr. Willard's chamber setting with him, when, behold! with a mighty noise came bursting thro' the window 4 brickbats. They immediately issued out of the chamber & caught one of the culprits, Putnam of Danvers, who discovered his confederates, Stebbins of Hadley, Hill of Saco, & Dodge of Salem. On Sabbath day there were several letters, &c., put up at Mr. Willard's door threatening him, telling him to leave the society, &c.; in the evening the President, professors, &c. met, ordered the persons who had been detected breaking Mr. W.'s windows into prayers the next morning. They sent up for Whiting, but some of the scholars returned answer that he should not come, &c.; but at length a number of the [sc]holars went down to the place where the President, &c. were convened, and told thm if thy wd. admit some scholars with him he might come before them; the reason they alledged for wc. was that he wd. otherwise be daunted & confess wt. was not true; ths. they refused to suffer. In the night there were great disorders; the gaurd of the town assembling prevented any attack upon the President or any other of the Governors of the College. In the morning the scholars went down to the President's & desired him to suspend executing any punishment upon the delinquents at present, as they had proof wc they imagined wd. in a great measure palliate, if not entirely exterminate their guilt. Ths request the President with his usual haughtiness denied. The sentence was executed, & after breakfast 104 or 5 of the scholars went down & gave up there chambers, all the 3 junior classes except 40. On Sabbath day evening I betook myself to Boston, as I foresaw if I stayed at Cambridge I should be compelled to resign my chamber, which I was very unwilling to do, as I was sensible it would be attended with very bad consequences. I forgot before to tell you that the Senior Class had no hand in this affair, as they were not obliged to conform to the regulation. Thus much journalwise, as for writing a *terræ filius* I have no inclination for it at present. I don't know what I may do when I return to college. At present I am engaged in keeping school at Milton for the schoolmaster, who has been absent ths 2 or 3 days. So, Sir, I am at least a *pro tempore* successor to yourself in tht agreable employment. As for the health of my grandfather, &c., he is very well, & has been so all winter, but my grandmother has been poorly almost all winter, but has now grown much better & seems to be upon the recovery very fast. The scholars had such very probable circumstances related to the charge agst Mr Willard, tht it will very much tend to lessen their fault (if their conduct be faulty). I should be glad if you would communicate the account I have given you to Mr Merriam & my sister, as I cannot without much time write them another journal. Be pleased to present my sincere love & respect to your amiable & beloved consort, my compliments, &c., to Miss Sally. You ask me when I shall come to Dover? Indeed I can't tell, but I intend to try hard to get there next summer vacancy. What more shall I say? Indeed I can't tell you; for shd I say I continue the same love (& permit me to say reverence) for you wh I always had, you would accuse me of impertinence in telling you the same thing so many times over. However, I will subscribe myself,

Yr sincere & affectionate freind,

Peter Thacher.

April 25th, 1768. You will excuse the dirtiness of my paper, for I carried it in my pocket from the time I began it till now, to school & back again, to get opportunity to write it.

Yrs. ut supra,

P. Thacher.

The Reverend Mr. Belknap.

Acknowledgments

This edition of the student diary of Stephen Peabody has been in the works since the late 1990s. Obligations are bound to accrue when a project takes so long. Editing the diary began shortly after William M. Fowler, Jr., became the director of the Massachusetts Historical Society (MHS). Bill recognized the value of the journal and readily supported a plan to publish the document. After he left the MHS at the end of 2005, his successor, Dennis A. Fiori, confirmed the society's continued commitment to the project. I am grateful to both Bill and Dennis for their encouragement.

Bill and Dennis are only two of the MHS's staff past and present who contributed to this edition. For their help I owe thanks to many of these colleagues. Seth Vose provided the original transcription, which volunteer Kristin Lynch helped to perfect. Former Adams Papers editor in chief Jim Taylor read a substantial fraction of the text of this book as I was working on it; his comments were invaluable. Also on the staff of the Adams Papers, Sara Sikes developed diagrams of Peabody's social connections with the collaboration of Laura Wulf after a suggestion from Sara Georgini. The society's digital team, headed by Nancy Heywood, provided the image used here of Paul Revere's 1768 view of Boston Harbor from a facsimile at the MHS. Special thanks go to Laura Wulf for scanning the image. I am grateful to Jim Connolly for his important contributions to the diagrams and index. On countless occasions I benefited from consultations with members of our reader services staff, including Elaine Heavey, Anna Clutterbuck-Cook, Dan Hinchen, and Andrea Cronin. In my own department, Research, Kate Viens's efficiency afforded me the time I needed to complete work on the journal and intern Serena Mocci organized data for many of the diagrams. Peter Drummey, the MHS's Stephen T. Riley Librarian, always astounds with the breadth of information at his fingertips, as thousands of scholars have learned over the years. I am in his debt for his help with the Peabody journal, and for almost every other project I have undertaken since I arrived at the MHS in 1985.

Farther afield, Serena Zabin of Carleton College helped me both through her comments on a draft of the introduction and through her review of my rusty schoolboy Latin. I was unable to decipher Peabody's one Greek word, but Serena figured it out. Cartographer Kate Blackmer provided necessary research as well as handsome maps. Thanks to Serena and Kate and to Linda Baumgarten of the Colonial Williamsburg Foundation, who explained knee bands to me. Jill Bouchillon of the University of Stirling provided valuable guidance on social network analysis. For taking on this project and being delightful to work with I am grateful to the staff of the University of Massachusetts Press—including Mary Dougherty, Brian Halley, Carol Betsch, Mary Bellino, Jack Harrison, and Sally Nichols. Drawing on her background as the managing editor of the Adams Papers to April 2013, Margaret Hogan brought rare expertise to editing the manuscript for the press.

I am grateful to the following institutions for allowing me to use material in their collections: American Antiquarian Society, Harvard University Archives, and Library Company of Philadelphia. The manuscript of Peabody's diary for 1767–68 is at the Massachusetts Historical Society and appears here through the society's permission. The society also provided a publication subvention for this volume.

At home, my wife, Mary, is ever understanding and supportive. And our two daughters, Abby and Betsy, to whom this volume is dedicated, make me proud.

Conrad Edick Wright
Boston, Massachusetts
February 2016

Index

Note: Page references in italics indicate images, graphs, and maps.

Conrad Edick Wright is the Ford Editor and Director of Research at the Massachusetts Historical Society, where he has been a member of the staff since 1985. He previously held positions at the Omohundro Institute of Early American History and Culture and the New-York Historical Society. Born in Boston and raised in Cambridge, Massachusetts, Wright is a 1972 graduate of Harvard College; he received his A.M. (1975) and Ph.D. (1980) from Brown University. Wright's previous publications include two University of Massachusetts Press titles: *Revolutionary Generation: Harvard Men and the Consequences of Independence* (2005) and *Massachusetts and the Civil War: The Commonwealth and National Disunion* (2015; coeditor with Matthew Mason and Katheryn P. Viens). He and his wife, Mary, have two daughters and live in Watertown, Massachusetts.